SCHAUM'S OUTLINE OF

THEORY AND PRO

of

DATA
STRUCTURES

SEYMOUR LIPSCHUTZ, Ph.D.
Professor of Mathematics
Temple University

SCHAUM'S OUTLINE SERIES

McGRAW-HILL BOOK COMPANY

New York   St. Louis   San Francisco   Auckland   Bogotá   Guatemala   Hamburg   Johannesburg
Lisbon   London   Madrid   Mexico   Montreal   New Delhi   Panama   Paris
San Juan   São Paulo   Singapore   Sydney   Tokyo   Toronto

SEYMOUR LIPSCHUTZ, who is presently on the mathematics faculty of Temple University, formerly taught at the Polytechnic Institute of Brooklyn and was a visiting professor in the Computer Science Department of Brooklyn College. He received his Ph.D. in 1960 at the Courant Institute of Mathematical Sciences of New York University. His books in the Schaum's Outline Series include *Fortran* (with Arthur Poe), *Essential Computer Mathematics* and *Linear Algebra*, among others.

Schaum's Outline of Theory and Problems of
DATA STRUCTURES

1 2.3 4 5 6 7 8 9 10 11 12 13 14 15 16 17 18 19 20 SHP SHP 8 9 8 7 6

ISBN 0-07-038001-5

Sponsoring Editor, Jeffrey McCartney
Production Manager, Nick Monti
Editing Supervisor, Marthe Grice

Library of Congress Cataloging-in-Publication Data

Lipschutz, Seymour.
  Schaum's outline of data structures.

  Includes index.
  1. Data structures (Computer science) I. Title.
II. Title: Data structures.
QA76.9.D35L57   1986   005.7'3   85-23108
ISBN 0-07-038001-5

This book is dedicated to my previous, current and future students with whom I want to share this poem:

The basic truths in all teachings of mankind are alike
and amount to one common thing:
to find your way to the thing you feel when you love dearly,
or when you create,
or when you build your home,
or when you give birth to your children,
or when you look at the stars at night.

Wilhelm Reich

Preface

The study of data structures is an essential part of virtually every under-graduate and graduate program in computer science. This text, in presenting the more essential material, may be used as a textbook for a formal course in data structures or as a supplement to almost all current standard texts.

The chapters are mainly organized in increasing degree of complexity. Chapter 1 is an introduction and overview of the material, and Chapter 2 presents the mathematical background and notation for the presentation and analysis of our algorithms. Chapter 3, on pattern matching, is independent and tangential to the text and hence may be postponed or omitted on a first reading. Chapters 4 through 8 contain the core material in any course on data structures. Specifically, Chapter 4 treats arrays and records, Chapter 5 is on linked lists, Chapter 6 covers stacks and queues and includes recursion, Chapter 7 is on binary trees and Chapter 8 is on graphs and their applications. Although sorting and searching is discussed through-out the text within the context of specific data structures (e.g., binary search with linear arrays, quicksort with stacks and queues and heapsort with binary trees), Chapter 9, the last chapter, presents additional sorting and searching algorithms such as merge-sort and hashing.

Algorithms are presented in a form which is machine and language indepen-dent. Moreover, they are written using mainly IF-THEN-ELSE and REPEAT-WHILE modules for flow of control, and using an indentation pattern for easier reading and understanding. Accordingly, each of our algorithms may be readily translated into almost any standard programming language.

Adopting a deliberately elementary approach to the subject matter with many examples and diagrams, this book should appeal to a wide audience, and is particularly suited as an effective self-study guide. Each chapter contains clear statements of definitions and principles together with illustrative and other descriptive material. This is followed by graded sets of solved and supplementary problems. The solved problems illustrate and amplify the material, and the supplementary problems furnish a complete review of the material in the chapter.

I wish to thank many friends and colleagues for invaluable suggestions and critical review of the manuscript. I also wish to express my gratitude to the staff of the McGraw-Hill Schaum's Outline Series, especially Jeffrey McCartney, for their helpful cooperation. Finally, I join many other authors in explicitly giving credit to Donald E. Knuth who wrote the first comprehensive treatment of the subject of data structures, which has certainly influenced the writing of this and many other texts on the subject.

SEYMOUR LIPSCHUTZ

Contents

Chapter *1* INTRODUCTION AND OVERVIEW.. **1**

1.1 Introduction.. 1
1.2 Basic Terminology; Elementary Data Organization....................... 1
1.3 Data Structures.. 2
1.4 Data Structure Operations.. 8
1.5 Algorithms: Complexity, Time-Space Tradeoff........................... 9

Chapter *2* PRELIMINARIES **17**

2.1 Introduction.. 17
2.2 Mathematical Notation and Functions 18
2.3 Algorithmic Notation 21
2.4 Control Structures 23
2.5 Complexity of Algorithms 27
2.6 Subalgorithms 30
2.7 Variables, Data Types 31

Chapter *3* STRING PROCESSING **41**

3.1 Introduction.. 41
3.2 Basic Terminology 41
3.3 Storing Strings 42
3.4 Character Data Type... 46
3.5 String Operations 47
3.6 Word Processing... 49
3.7 Pattern Matching Algorithms 53

Chapter *4* ARRAYS, RECORDS AND POINTERS **67**

4.1 Introduction.. 67
4.2 Linear Arrays.. 67
4.3 Representation of Linear Arrays in Memory............................... 69
4.4 Traversing Linear Arrays.. 70
4.5 Inserting and Deleting 71
4.6 Sorting; Bubble Sort... 73
4.7 Searching; Linear Search 76
4.8 Binary Search.. 78
4.9 Multidimensional Arrays 81
4.10 Pointers; Pointer Arrays.. 86
4.11 Records; Record Structures 90

CONTENTS

4.12 Representation of Records in Memory; Parallel Arrays 92
4.13 Matrices 94
4.14 Sparse Matrices 97

Chapter 5 LINKED LISTS **114**

5.1 Introduction 114
5.2 Linked Lists 115
5.3 Representation of Linked Lists in Memory 116
5.4 Traversing a Linked List 120
5.5 Searching a Linked List 121
5.6 Memory Allocation; Garbage Collection 123
5.7 Insertion into a Linked List 127
5.8 Deletion from a Linked List 134
5.9 Header Linked Lists 140
5.10 Two-Way Lists 144

Chapter 6 STACKS, QUEUES, RECURSION **164**

6.1 Introduction 164
6.2 Stacks 165
6.3 Array Representation of Stacks 166
6.4 Arithmetic Expressions; Polish Notation 168
6.5 Quicksort, an Application of Stacks 173
6.6 Recursion 176
6.7 Towers of Hanoi 180
6.8 Implementation of Recursive Procedures by Stacks 183
6.9 Queues 188
6.10 Deques 192
6.11 Priority Queues 193

Chapter 7 TREES **214**

7.1 Introduction 214
7.2 Binary Trees 214
7.3 Representing Binary Trees in Memory 217
7.4 Traversing Binary Trees 221
7.5 Traversal Algorithms Using Stacks 224
7.6 Header Nodes; Threads 229
7.7 Binary Search Trees 233
7.8 Searching and Inserting in Binary Search Trees 234
7.9 Deleting in a Binary Search Tree 238
7.10 Heap; Heapsort 243
7.11 Path Lengths; Huffman's Algorithm 249
7.12 General Trees 255

CONTENTS

Chapter 8   **GRAPHS AND THEIR APPLICATIONS**.................................... **277**

8.1 Introduction.. 277
8.2 Graph Theory Terminology... 277
8.3 Sequential Representation of Graphs; Adjacency Matrix; Path Matrix............ 280
8.4 Warshall's Algorithm; Shortest Paths 282
8.5 Linked Representation of a Graph 286
8.6 Operations on Graphs 289
8.7 Traversing a Graph.. 294
8.8 Posets; Topological Sorting 297

Chapter 9   **SORTING AND SEARCHING**... **318**

9.1 Introduction.. 318
9.2 Sorting.. 318
9.3 Insertion Sort.. 322
9.4 Selection Sort 324
9.5 Merging 325
9.6 Merge-Sort 328
9.7 Radix Sort... 330
9.8 Searching and Data Modification.................................... 332
9.9 Hashing 333

INDEX **341**

Chapter 1

Introduction and Overview

1.1 INTRODUCTION

This chapter introduces the subject of data structures and presents an overview of the content of the text. Basic terminology and concepts will be defined and relevant examples provided. An overview of data organization and certain data structures will be covered along with a discussion of the different operations which are applied to these data structures. Last, we will introduce the notion of an algorithm and its complexity, and we will discuss the time-space tradeoff that may occur in choosing a particular algorithm and data structure for a given problem.

1.2 BASIC TERMINOLOGY; ELEMENTARY DATA ORGANIZATION

Data are simply values or sets of values. A *data item* refers to a single unit of values. Data items that are divided into subitems are called *group items*; those that are not are called *elementary items*. For example, an employee's name may be divided into three subitems—first name, middle initial and last name—but the social security number would normally be treated as a single item.

Collections of data are frequently organized into a hierarchy of *fields*, *records* and *files*. In order to make these terms more precise, we introduce some additional terminology.

An *entity* is something that has certain *attributes* or properties which may be assigned values. The values themselves may be either numeric or nonnumeric. For example, the following are possible attributes and their corresponding values for an entity, an employee of a given organization:

Attributes:	Name	Age	Sex	Social Security Number
Values:	JOHN BROWN	34	M	134-24-5533

Entities with similar attributes (e.g., all the employees in an organization) form an *entity set*. Each attribute of an entity set has a *range* of values, the set of all possible values that could be assigned to the particular attribute.

The term "information" is sometimes used for data with given attributes, or, in other words, meaningful or processed data.

The way that data are organized into the hierarchy of fields, records and files reflects the relationship between attributes, entities and entity sets. That is, a *field* is a single elementary unit of information representing an attribute of an entity, a *record* is the collection of field values of a given entity and a *file* is the collection of records of the entities in a given entity set.

Each record in a file may contain many field items, but the value in a certain field may uniquely determine the record in the file. Such a field K is called a *primary key*, and the values $k_1, k_2, \ldots$ in such a field are called *keys* or *key values*.

EXAMPLE 1.1

(*a*) Suppose an automobile dealership maintains an inventory file where each record contains the following data:

$$\text{Serial Number,} \quad \text{Type,} \quad \text{Year,} \quad \text{Price,} \quad \text{Accessories}$$

The Serial Number field can serve as a primary key for the file, since each automobile has a unique serial number.

(*b*) Suppose an organization maintains a membership file where each record contains the following data:

$$\text{Name,} \quad \text{Address,} \quad \text{Telephone Number,} \quad \text{Dues Owed}$$

Although there are four data items, Name and Address may be group items. Here the Name field is a primary key. Note that the Address and Telephone Number fields may not serve as primary keys, since some members may belong to the same family and have the same address and telephone number.

Records may also be classified according to length. A file can have fixed-length records or variable-length records. In *fixed-length records*, all the records contain the same data items with the same amount of space assigned to each data item. In *variable-length records*, file records may contain different lengths. For example, student records usually have variable lengths, since different students take different numbers of courses. Usually, variable-length records have a minimum and a maximum length.

The above organization of data into fields, records and files may not be complex enough to maintain and efficiently process certain collections of data. For this reason, data are also organized into more complex types of structures. The study of such data structures, which forms the subject matter of this text, includes the following three steps:

(1) Logical or mathematical description of the structure
(2) Implementation of the structure on a computer
(3) Quantitative analysis of the structure, which includes determining the amount of memory needed to store the structure and the time required to process the structure

The next section introduces us to some of these data structures.

Remark: The second and third of the steps in the study of data structures depend on whether the data are stored (*a*) in the main (primary) memory of the computer or (*b*) in a secondary (external) storage unit. This text will mainly cover the first case. This means that, given the address of a memory location, the time required to access the content of the memory cell does not depend on the particular cell or upon the previous cell accessed. The second case, called *file management* or *data base management*, is a subject unto itself and lies beyond the scope of this text.

1.3 DATA STRUCTURES

Data may be organized in many different ways; the logical or mathematical model of a particular organization of data is called a *data structure*. The choice of a particular data model depends on two considerations. First, it must be rich enough in structure to mirror the actual relationships of the data in the real world. On the other hand, the structure should be simple enough that one can effectively process the data when necessary. This section will introduce us to some of the data structures which will be discussed in detail later in the text.

Arrays

The simplest type of data structure is a *linear* (or *one-dimensional*) *array*. By a linear array, we mean a list of a finite number n of similar data elements referenced respectively by a set of n consecutive numbers, usually $1, 2, 3, \ldots, n$. If we choose the name A for the array, then the elements of A are denoted by subscript notation

$$a_1, a_2, a_3, \ldots, a_n$$

or by the parenthesis notation

$$A(1), A(2), A(3), \ldots, A(N)$$

or by the bracket notation

$$A[1], A[2], A[3], \ldots, A[N]$$

Regardless of the notation, the number K in A[K] is called a *subscript* and A[K] is called a *subscripted variable*.

Remark: The parentheses notation and the bracket notation are frequently used when the array name consists of more than one letter or when the array name appears in an algorithm. When using this notation we will use ordinary uppercase letters for the name and subscripts as indicated above by the A and N. Otherwise, we may use the usual subscript notation of italics for the name and subscripts and lowercase letters for the subscripts as indicated above by the a and n. The former notation follows the practice of computer-oriented texts whereas the latter notation follows the practice of mathematics in print.

EXAMPLE 1.2

A linear array STUDENT consisting of the names of six students is pictured in Fig. 1-1. Here STUDENT[1] denotes John Brown, STUDENT[2] denotes Sandra Gold, and so on.

STUDENT

1	John Brown
2	Sandra Gold
3	Tom Jones
4	June Kelly
5	Mary Reed
6	Alan Smith

Fig. 1-1

Linear arrays are called one-dimensional arrays because each element in such an array is referenced by one subscript. A *two-dimensional array* is a collection of similar data elements where each element is referenced by two subscripts. (Such arrays are called *matrices* in mathematics, and *tables* in business applications.) Multidimensional arrays are defined analogously. Arrays will be covered in detail in Chap. 4.

EXAMPLE 1.3

A chain of 28 stores, each store having 4 departments, may list its weekly sales (to the nearest dollar) as in Fig. 1-2. Such data can be stored in the computer using a two-dimensional array in which the first subscript denotes the store and the second subscript the department. If SALES is the name given to the array, then

$$\text{SALES}[1, 1] = 2872, \quad \text{SALES}[1, 2] = 805, \quad \text{SALES}[1, 3] = 3211, \ldots, \quad \text{SALES}[28, 4] = 982$$

The size of this array is denoted by 28×4 (read 28 by 4), since it contains 28 *rows* (the horizontal lines of numbers) and 4 *columns* (the vertical lines of numbers).

Dept.　Store	1	2	3	4
1	2872	805	3211	1560
2	2196	1223	2525	1744
3	3257	1017	3686	1951
. . .	. . .	. . .	. . .	. . .
28	2618	931	2333	982

Fig. 1-2

Linked Lists

Linked lists will be introduced by means of an example. Suppose a brokerage firm maintains a file where each record contains a customer's name and his or her salesperson, and suppose the file contains the data appearing in Fig. 1-3. Clearly the file could be stored in the computer by such a table, i.e., by two columns of nine names. However, this may not be the most useful way to store the data, as the following discussion shows.

	Customer	Salesperson
1	Adams	Smith
2	Brown	Ray
3	Clark	Jones
4	Drew	Ray
5	Evans	Smith
6	Farmer	Jones
7	Geller	Ray
8	Hill	Smith
9	Infeld	Ray

Fig. 1-3

Another way of storing the data in Fig. 1-3 is to have a separate array for the salespeople and an entry (called a *pointer*) in the customer file which gives the location of each customer's salesperson. This is done in Fig. 1-4, where some of the pointers are pictured by an arrow from the location of the pointer to the location of the corresponding salesperson. Practically speaking, an integer used as a pointer requires less space than a name; hence this representation saves space, especially if there are hundreds of customers for each salesperson.

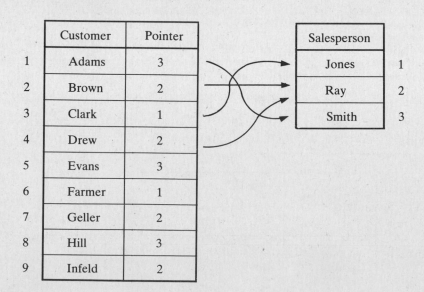

Fig. 1-4

Suppose the firm wants the list of customers for a given salesperson. Using the data representation in Fig. 1-4, the firm would have to search through the entire customer file. One way to simplify such a search is to have the arrows in Fig. 1-4 point the other way; each salesperson would now have a set of pointers giving the positions of his or her customers, as in Fig. 1-5. The main disadvantage of this representation is that each salesperson may have many pointers and the set of pointers will change as customers are added and deleted.

	Salesperson	Pointer
1	Jones	3, 6
2	Ray	2, 4, 7, 9
3	Smith	1, 5, 8

Fig. 1-5

Another very popular way to store the type of data in Fig. 1-3 is shown in Fig. 1-6. Here each salesperson has one pointer which points to his or her first customer, whose pointer in turn points to the second customer, and so on, with the salesperson's last customer indicated by a 0. This is pictured with arrows in Fig. 1-6 for the salesperson Ray. Using this representation one can easily obtain the entire list of customers for a given salesperson and, as we will see in Chap. 5, one can easily insert and delete customers.

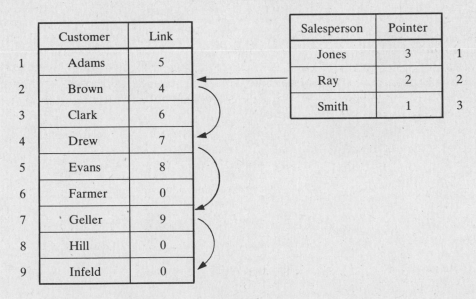

Fig. 1-6

The representation of the data in Fig. 1-6 is an example of linked lists. Although the terms "pointer" and "link" are usually used synonymously, we will try to use the term "pointer" when an element in one list points to an element in a different list, and to reserve the term "link" for the case when an element in a list points to an element in that same list.

Trees

Data frequently contain a hierarchical relationship between various elements. The data structure which reflects this relationship is called a *rooted tree graph* or, simply, a *tree*. Trees will be defined and discussed in detail in Chap. 7. Here we indicate some of their basic properties by means of two examples.

EXAMPLE 1.4   Record Structure

Although a file may be maintained by means of one or more arrays, a record, where one indicates both the group items and the elementary items, can best be described by means of a tree structure. For example, an employee personnel record may contain the following data items:

Social Security Number,   Name,   Address,   Age,   Salary,   Dependents

However, Name may be a group item with the subitems Last, First and MI (middle initial). Also, Address may be a group item with the subitems Street address and Area address, where Area itself may be a group item having subitems City, State and ZIP code number. This hierarchical structure is pictured in Fig. 1-7(*a*). Another way of picturing such a tree structure is in terms of levels, as in Fig. 1-7(*b*).

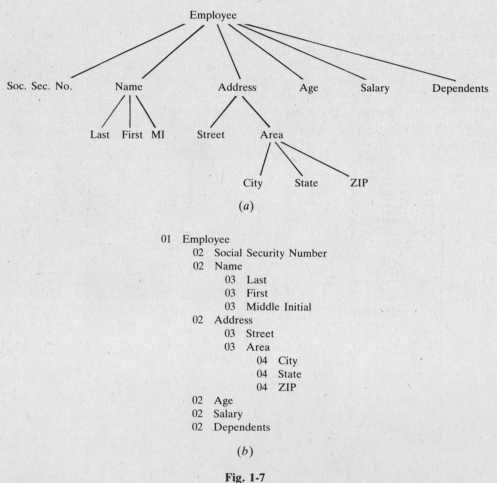

(*a*)

```
01  Employee
      02   Social Security Number
      02   Name
             03   Last
             03   First
             03   Middle Initial
      02   Address
             03   Street
             03   Area
                    04   City
                    04   State
                    04   ZIP
      02   Age
      02   Salary
      02   Dependents
```

(*b*)

Fig. 1-7

EXAMPLE 1.5   Algebraic Expressions

Consider the algebraic expression

$$(2x + y)(a - 7b)^3$$

Using a vertical arrow ($\uparrow$) for exponentiation and an asterisk ($*$) for multiplication, we can represent the expression by the tree in Fig. 1-8. Observe that the order in which the operations will be performed is reflected in the diagram: the exponentiation must take place after the subtraction, and the multiplication at the top of the tree must be executed last.

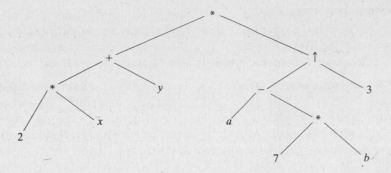

Fig. 1-8

There are data structures other than arrays, linked lists and trees which we shall study. Some of these structures are briefly described below.

(a) *Stack*. A stack, also called a last-in first-out (LIFO) system, is a linear list in which insertions and deletions can take place only at one end, called the *top*. This structure is similar in its operation to a stack of dishes on a spring system, as pictured in Fig. 1-9(a). Note that new dishes are inserted only at the top of the stack and dishes can be deleted only from the top of the stack.

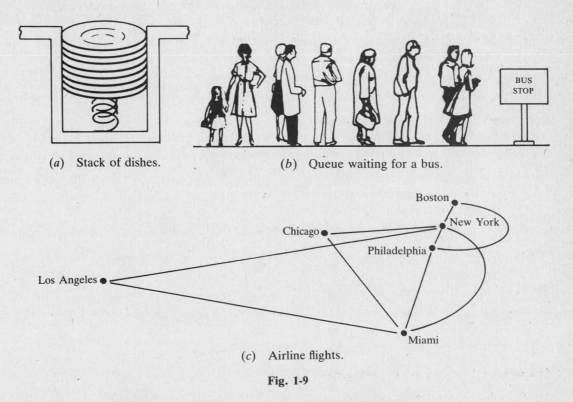

(a) Stack of dishes.   (b) Queue waiting for a bus.

(c) Airline flights.

Fig. 1-9

(b) *Queue*. A queue, also called a first-in first-out (FIFO) system, is a linear list in which deletions can take place only at one end of the list, the "front" of the list, and insertions can take place only at the other end of the list, the "rear" of the list. This structure operates in much the same way as a line of people waiting at a bus stop, as pictured in Fig. 1-9(b): the first person in line is the first person to board the bus. Another analogy is with automobiles waiting to pass through an intersection—the first car in line is the first car through.

(c) *Graph*. Data sometimes contain a relationship between pairs of elements which is not necessarily hierarchical in nature. For example, suppose an airline flies only between the cities connected by lines in Fig. 1-9(c). The data structure which reflects this type of relationship is called a *graph*. Graphs will be formally defined and studied in Chap. 8.

Remark: Many different names are used for the elements of a data structure. Some commonly used names are "data element," "data item," "item aggregate," "record," "node" and "data object." The particular name that is used depends on the type of data structure, the context in which the structure is used and the people using the name. Our preference shall be the term "data element," but we will use the term "record" when discussing files and the term "node" when discussing linked lists, trees and graphs.

1.4 DATA STRUCTURE OPERATIONS

The data appearing in our data structures are processed by means of certain operations. In fact, the particular data structure that one chooses for a given situation depends largely on the frequency with which specific operations are performed. This section introduces the reader to some of the most frequently used of these operations.

The following four operations play a major role in this text:

(1) *Traversing*: Accessing each record exactly once so that certain items in the record may be processed. (This accessing and processing is sometimes called "visiting" the record.)

(2) *Searching*: Finding the location of the record with a given key value, or finding the locations of all records which satisfy one or more conditions.

(3) *Inserting*: Adding a new record to the structure.

(4) *Deleting*: Removing a record from the structure.

Sometimes two or more of the operations may be used in a given situation; e.g., we may want to delete the record with a given key, which may mean we first need to search for the location of the record.

The following two operations, which are used in special situations, will also be considered:

(1) *Sorting*: Arranging the records in some logical order (e.g., alphabetically according to some NAME key, or in numerical order according to some NUMBER key, such as social security number or account number)

(2) *Merging*: Combining the records in two different sorted files into a single sorted file

Other operations, e.g., copying and concatenation, will be discussed later in the text.

EXAMPLE 1.6

An organization contains a membership file in which each record contains the following data for a given member:

Name,   Address,   Telephone Number,   Age,   Sex

(a) Suppose the organization wants to announce a meeting through a mailing. Then one would traverse the file to obtain Name and Address for each member.

(b) Suppose one wants to find the names of all members living in a certain area. Again one would traverse the file to obtain the data.

(c) Suppose one wants to obtain Address for a given Name. Then one would search the file for the record containing Name.

(d) Suppose a new person joins the organization. Then one would insert his or her record into the file.

(e) Suppose a member dies. Then one would delete his or her record from the file.

(*f*) Suppose a member has moved and has a new address and telephone number. Given the name of the member, one would first need to search for the record in the file. Then one would perform the "update"—i.e., change items in the record with the new data.

(*g*) Suppose one wants to find the number of members 65 or older. Again one would traverse the file, counting such members.

1.5 ALGORITHMS: COMPLEXITY, TIME-SPACE TRADEOFF

An algorithm is a well-defined list of steps for solving a particular problem. One major purpose of this text is to develop efficient algorithms for the processing of our data. The time and space it uses are two major measures of the efficiency of an algorithm. The complexity of an algorithm is the function which gives the running time and/or space in terms of the input size. (The notion of complexity will be treated in Chap. 2.)

Each of our algorithms will involve a particular data structure. Accordingly, we may not always be able to use the most efficient algorithm, since the choice of data structure depends on many things, including the type of data and the frequency with which various data operations are applied. Sometimes the choice of data structure involves a time-space tradeoff: by increasing the amount of space for storing the data, one may be able to reduce the time needed for processing the data, or vice versa. We illustrate these ideas with two examples.

Searching Algorithms

Consider a membership file, as in Example 1.6, in which each record contains, among other data, the name and telephone number of its member. Suppose we are given the name of a member and we want to find his or her telephone number. One way to do this is to linearly search through the file, i.e., to apply the following algorithm:

Linear Search: Search each record of the file, one at a time, until finding the given Name and hence the corresponding telephone number.

First of all, it is clear that the time required to execute the algorithm is proportional to the number of comparisons. Also, assuming that each name in the file is equally likely to be picked, it is intuitively clear that the average number of comparisons for a file with n records is equal to $n/2$; that is, the complexity of the linear search algorithm is given by $C(n) = n/2$.

The above algorithm would be impossible in practice if we were searching through a list consisting of thousands of names, as in a telephone book. However, if the names are sorted alphabetically, as in telephone books, then we can use an efficient algorithm called binary search. This algorithm is discussed in detail in Chap. 4, but we briefly describe its general idea below.

Binary Search: Compare the given Name with the name in the middle of the list; this tells which half of the list contains Name. Then compare Name with the name in the middle of the correct half to determine which quarter of the list contains Name. Continue the process until finding Name in the list.

One can show that the complexity of the binary search algorithm is given by

$$C(n) = \log_2 n$$

Thus, for example, one will not require more than 15 comparisons to find a given Name in a list containing 25 000 names.

Although the binary search algorithm is a very efficient algorithm, it has some major drawbacks. Specifically, the algorithm assumes that one has direct access to the middle name in the list or a sublist. This means that the list must be stored in some type of array. Unfortunately, inserting an element in an array requires elements to be moved down the list, and deleting an element from an array requires elements to be moved up the list.

The telephone company solves the above problem by printing a new directory every year while keeping a separate temporary file for new telephone customers. That is, the telephone company updates its files every year. On the other hand, a bank may want to insert a new customer in its file almost instantaneously. Accordingly, a linearly sorted list may not be the best data structure for a bank.

An Example of Time-Space Tradeoff

Suppose a file of records contains names, social security numbers and much additional information among its fields. Sorting the file alphabetically and using a binary search is a very efficient way to find the record for a given name. On the other hand, suppose we are given only the social security number of the person. Then we would have to do a linear search for the record, which is extremely time-consuming for a very large number of records. How can we solve such a problem? One way is to have another file which is sorted numerically according to social security number. This, however, would double the space required for storing the data. Another way, pictured in Fig. 1-10, is to have the main file sorted numerically by social security number and to have an auxiliary array with only two columns, the first column containing an alphabetized list of the names and the second column containing pointers which give the locations of the corresponding records in the main file. This is one way of solving the problem that is used frequently, since the additional space, containing only two columns, is minimal for the amount of extra information it provides.

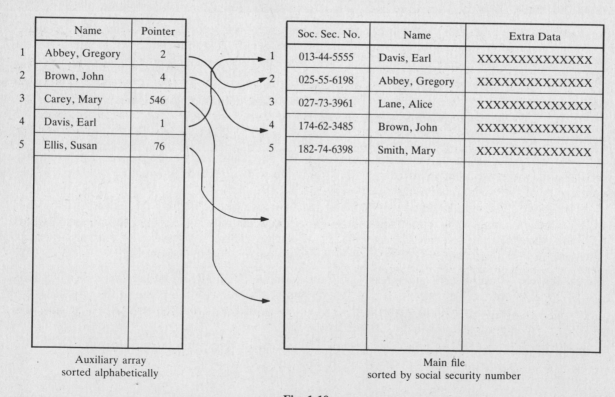

	Name	Pointer
1	Abbey, Gregory	2
2	Brown, John	4
3	Carey, Mary	546
4	Davis, Earl	1
5	Ellis, Susan	76

Auxiliary array
sorted alphabetically

	Soc. Sec. No.	Name	Extra Data
1	013-44-5555	Davis, Earl	XXXXXXXXXXXXXX
2	025-55-6198	Abbey, Gregory	XXXXXXXXXXXXXX
3	027-73-3961	Lane, Alice	XXXXXXXXXXXXXX
4	174-62-3485	Brown, John	XXXXXXXXXXXXXX
5	182-74-6398	Smith, Mary	XXXXXXXXXXXXXX

Main file
sorted by social security number

Fig. 1-10

Remark: Suppose a file is sorted numerically by social security number. As new records are inserted into the file, data must be constantly moved to new locations in order to maintain the sorted order. One simple way to minimize the movement of data is to have the social security number serve as the address of each record. Not only would there be no movement of data when records are inserted, but there would be instant access to any record. However, this method of storing data would require one billion (10^9) memory locations for only hundreds or possibly thousands of records. Clearly, this tradeoff of space for time is not worth the expense. An alternative method is to define a function H from the set K of key values—social security numbers—into the set L of addresses of memory cells. Such a function H is called a *hashing function*. Hashing functions and their properties will be covered in Chap. 9.

Solved Problems

BASIC TERMINOLOGY

1.1 A professor keeps a class list containing the following data for each student:

> Name,   Major,   Student Number,   Test Scores,   Final Grade

(a) State the entities, attributes and entity set of the list.

(b) Describe the field values, records and file.

(c) Which attributes can serve as primary keys for the list?

(a) Each student is an entity, and the collection of students is the entity set. The properties, name, major, and so on, of the students are the attributes.

(b) The field values are the values assigned to the attributes, i.e., the actual names, test scores, and so on. The field values for each student constitute a record, and the collection of all the student records is the file.

(c) Either Name or Student Number can serve as a primary key, since each uniquely determines the student's record. Normally the professor uses Name as the primary key, but the registrar may use Student Number.

1.2 A hospital maintains a patient file in which each record contains the following data:

> Name,   Admission Date,   Social Security Number,   Room,   Bed Number,   Doctor

(a) Which items can serve as primary keys?

(b) Which pair of items can serve as a primary key?

(c) Which items can be group items?

(a) Name and Social Security Number can serve as primary keys. (We assume that no two patients have the same name.)

(b) Room and Bed Number in combination also uniquely determine a given patient.

(c) Name, Admission Date and Doctor may be group items.

1.3 Which of the following data items may lead to variable-length records when included as items in the record: (a) age, (b) sex, (c) name of spouse, (d) names of children, (e) education, (f) previous employers?

Since (d) and (f) may contain a few or many items, they may lead to variable-length records. Also, (e) may contain many items, unless it asks only for the highest level obtained.

1.4   Data base systems will be only briefly covered in this text. Why?

   "Data base systems" refers to data stored in the secondary memory of the computer. The implementation and analysis of data structures in the secondary memory are very different from those in the main memory of the computer. This text is primarily concerned with data structures in main memory, not secondary memory.

DATA STRUCTURES AND OPERATIONS

1.5   Give a brief description of (*a*) traversing, (*b*) sorting and (*c*) searching.

   (*a*)   Accessing and processing each record exactly once
   (*b*)   Arranging the data in some given order
   (*c*)   Finding the location of the record with a given key or keys

1.6   Give a brief description of (*a*) inserting and (*b*) deleting.

   (*a*)   Adding a new record to the data structure, usually keeping a particular ordering
   (*b*)   Removing a particular record from the data structure

1.7   Consider the linear array NAME in Fig. 1-11, which is sorted alphabetically.

   (*a*)   Find NAME[2], NAME[4] and NAME[7].
   (*b*)   Suppose Davis is to be inserted into the array. How many names must be moved to new locations?
   (*c*)   Suppose Gupta is to be deleted from the array. How many names must be moved to new locations?

   (*a*)   Here NAME[K] is the *k*th name in the list. Hence,

$$NAME[2] = Clark, \qquad NAME[4] = Gupta, \qquad NAME[7] = Pace$$

   (*b*)   Since Davis will be assigned to NAME[3], the names Evans through Smith must be moved. Hence six names are moved.
   (*c*)   The names Jones through Smith must be moved up the array. Hence four names must be moved.

NAME

1	Adams
2	Clark
3	Evans
4	Gupta
5	Jones
6	Lane
7	Pace
8	Smith

Fig. 1-11

1.8   Consider the linear array NAME in Fig. 1-12. The values of FIRST and LINK[K] in the figure
determine a linear ordering of the names as follows. FIRST gives the location of the first name
in the list, and LINK[K] gives the location of the name following NAME[K], with 0 denoting
the end of the list. Find the linear ordering of the names.

The ordering is obtained as follows:

FIRST = 5, so the first name in the list is NAME[5], which is Brooks.

LINK[5] = 2, so the next name is NAME[2], which is Clark.

LINK[2] = 8, so the next name is NAME[8], which is Fisher.

LINK[8] = 4, so the next name is NAME[4], which is Hansen.

LINK[4] = 10, so the next name is NAME[10], which is Leary.

LINK[10] = 6, so the next name is NAME[6], which is Pitt.

LINK[6] = 1, so the next name is NAME[1], which is Rogers.

LINK[1] = 7, so the next name is NAME[7], which is Walker.

LINK[7] = 0, which indicates the end of the list.

Thus the linear ordering of the names is Brooks, Clark, Fisher, Hansen, Leary, Pitt, Rogers, Walker. Note
that this is the alphabetical ordering of the names.

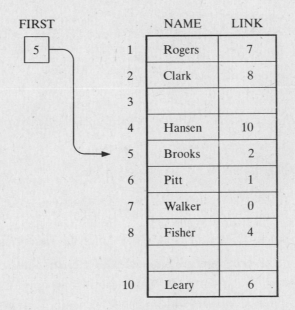

FIRST		NAME	LINK
5	1	Rogers	7
	2	Clark	8
	3		
	4	Hansen	10
	5	Brooks	2
	6	Pitt	1
	7	Walker	0
	8	Fisher	4
	10	Leary	6

Fig. 1-12

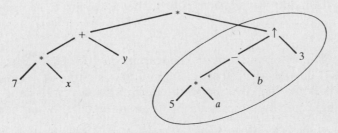

Fig. 1-13

1.9 Consider the algebraic expression $(7x + y)(5a - b)^3$. (*a*) Draw the corresponding tree diagram as in Example 1.5. (*b*) Find the scope of the exponential operation. (The scope of a node v in a tree is the subtree consisting of v and the nodes following v.)

(*a*) Use a vertical arrow (↑) for exponentiation and an asterisk (∗) for multiplication to obtain the tree in Fig. 1-13.

(*b*) The scope of the exponentiation operation ↑ is the subtree circled in the diagram. It corresponds to the expression $(5a - b)^3$.

1.10 The following is a tree structure given by means of level numbers as discussed in Example 1.4:

01 Employee   02 Name   02 Number   02 Hours   03 Regular   03 Overtime   02 Rate

Draw the corresponding tree diagram.

      The tree diagram appears in Fig. 1-14. Here each node v is the successor of the node which precedes v and has a lower level number than v.

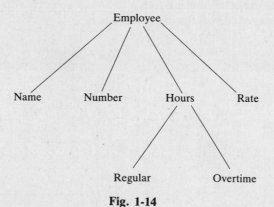

Fig. 1-14

1.11 Discuss whether a stack or a queue is the appropriate structure for determining the order in which elements are processed in each of the following situations.

(*a*) Batch computer programs are submitted to the computer center.

(*b*) Program A calls subprogram B, which calls subprogram C, and so on.

(*c*) Employees have a contract which calls for a seniority system for hiring and firing.

(*a*) Queue. Excluding priority cases, programs are executed on a first come, first served basis.

(*b*) Stack. The last subprogram is executed first, and its results are transferred to the next-to-last program, which is then executed, and so on, until the original calling program is executed.

(*c*) Stack. In a seniority system, the last to be hired is the first to be discharged.

1.12 The daily flights of an airline company appear in Fig. 1-15. CITY lists the cities, and ORIG[K] and DEST[K] denote the cities of origin and destination, respectively, of the flight NUMBER[K]. Draw the corresponding directed graph of the data. (The graph is directed because the flight numbers represent flights from one city to another but not returning.)

      The nodes of the graph are the five cities. Draw an arrow from city A to city B if there is a flight from A to B, and label the arrow with the flight number. The directed graph appears in Fig. 1-16.

	CITY
1	Atlanta
2	Boston
3	Chicago
4	Miami
5	Philadelphia

(a)

	NUMBER	ORIG	DEST
1	701	2	3
2	702	3	2
3	705	5	3
4	708	3	4
5	711	2	5
6	712	5	2
7	713	5	1
8	715	1	4
9	717	5	4
10	718	4	5

(b)

Fig. 1-15

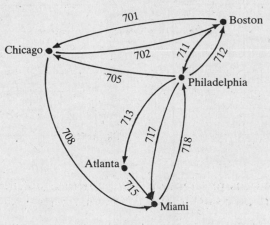

Fig. 1-16

COMPLEXITY; SPACE-TIME TRADEOFFS

1.13 Briefly describe the notions of (a) the complexity of an algorithm and (b) the space-time tradeoff of algorithms.

(a) The complexity of an algorithm is a function $f(n)$ which measures the time and/or space used by an algorithm in terms of the input size n.

(b) The space-time tradeoff refers to a choice between algorithmic solutions of a data processing problem that allows one to decrease the running time of an algorithmic solution by increasing the space to store the data and vice versa.

1.14 Suppose a data set S contains n elements.

(a) Compare the running time T_1 of the linear search algorithm with the running time T_2 of the binary search algorithm when (i) $n = 1000$ and (ii) $n = 10\,000$.

(b) Discuss searching for a given item in S when S is stored as a linked list.

(a) Recall (Sec. 1.5) that the expected running of the linear search algorithm is $f(n) = n/2$ and that the binary search algorithm is $f(n) = \log_2 n$. Accordingly, (i) for $n = 1000$, $T_1 = 500$ but $T_2 = \log_2 1000 \approx 10$; and (ii) for $n = 10\,000$, $T_1 = 5000$ but $T_2 = \log_2 10\,000 \approx 14$.

(b) The binary search algorithm assumes that one can directly access the middle element in the set S. But one cannot directly access the middle element in a linked list. Hence one may have to use a linear search algorithm when S is stored as a linked list.

1.15 Consider the data in Fig. 1-15, which gives the different flights of an airline. Discuss different ways of storing the data so as to decrease the time in executing the following:

(a) Find the origin and destination of a flight, given the flight number.

(b) Given city A and city B, find whether there is a flight from A to B, and if there is, find its flight number.

(a) Store the data of Fig. 1-15(b) in arrays ORIG and DEST where the subscript is the flight number, as pictured in Fig. 1-17(a).

(b) Store the data of Fig. 1-15(b) in a two-dimensional array FLIGHT where FLIGHT[J, K] contains the flight number of the flight from CITY[J] to CITY[K], or contains 0 when there is no such flight, as pictured in Fig. 1-17(b).

	ORIG	DEST
701	2	3
702	3	2
703	0	0
704	0	0
705	5	3
706	0	0
⋮	⋮	⋮
715	1	4
716	0	0
717	5	4
718	4	5

(a)

FLIGHT	1	2	3	4	5
1	0	0	0	715	0
2	0	0	701	0	711
3	0	702	0	708	0
4	0	0	0	0	718
5	713	712	705	717	0

(b)

Fig. 1-17

1.16 Suppose an airline serves n cities with s flights. Discuss drawbacks to the data representations used in Fig. 1-17(a) and Fig. 1-17(b).

(a) Suppose the flight numbers are spaced very far apart; i.e., suppose the ratio of the number s of flights to the number of memory locations is very small, e.g., approximately 0.05. Then the extra storage space may not be worth the expense.

(b) Suppose the ratio of the number s of flights to the number n of memory locations in the array FLIGHT is very small, i.e., that the array FLIGHT is one that contains a large number of zeros (such an array is called a sparse matrix). Then the extra storage space may not be worth the expense.

Chapter 2

Preliminaries

2.1 INTRODUCTION

The development of algorithms for the creation and processing of data structures is a major feature of this text. This chapter describes, by means of simple examples, the format that will be used to present our algorithms. The format we have selected is similar to the format used by Knuth in his well-known text *Fundamental Algorithms*. Although our format is language-free, the algorithms will be sufficiently well structured and detailed that they can be easily translated into some programming language such as Pascal, FORTRAN, PL/1 or BASIC. In fact, some of our algorithms will be translated into such languages in the problems sections.

Algorithms may be quite complex. The computer programs implementing the more complex algorithms can be more easily understood if these programs are organized into hierarchies of modules similar to the one in Fig. 2-1. In such an organization, each program contains first a main module, which gives a general description of the algorithm; this main module refers to certain submodules, which contain more detailed information than the main module; each of the submodules may refer to more detailed submodules; and so on. The organization of a program into such a hierarchy of modules normally requires the use of certain basic flow patterns and logical structures which are usually associated with the notion of structured programming. These flow patterns and logical structures will be reviewed in this chapter.

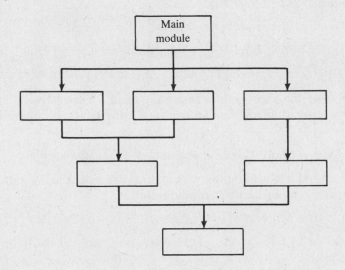

Fig. 2-1 A hierarchy of modules.

The chapter begins with a brief outline and discussion of various mathematical functions which occur in the study of algorithms and in computer science in general, and the chapter ends with a discussion of the different kinds of variables that can appear in our algorithms and programs.

The notion of the complexity of an algorithm is also covered in this chapter. This important measurement of algorithms gives us a tool to compare different algorithmic solutions to a particular problem such as searching or sorting. The concept of an algorithm and its complexity is fundamental not only to data structures but also to almost all areas of computer science.

2.2 MATHEMATICAL NOTATION AND FUNCTIONS

This section gives various mathematical functions which appear very often in the analysis of algorithms and in computer science in general, together with their notation.

Floor and Ceiling Functions

Let x be any real number. Then x lies between two integers called the floor and the ceiling of x. Specifically,

$\lfloor x \rfloor$, called the *floor* of x, denotes the greatest integer that does not exceed x.

$\lceil x \rceil$, called the *ceiling* of x, denotes the least integer that is not less than x.

If x is itself an integer, then $\lfloor x \rfloor = \lceil x \rceil$; otherwise $\lfloor x \rfloor + 1 = \lceil x \rceil$.

EXAMPLE 2.1

$$\lfloor 3.14 \rfloor = 3, \quad \lfloor \sqrt{5} \rfloor = 2, \quad \lfloor -8.5 \rfloor = -9, \quad \lfloor 7 \rfloor = 7$$
$$\lceil 3.14 \rceil = 4, \quad \lceil \sqrt{5} \rceil = 3, \quad \lceil -8.5 \rceil = -8, \quad \lceil 7 \rceil = 7$$

Remainder Function; Modular Arithmetic

Let k be any integer and let M be a positive integer. Then

$$k \pmod{M}$$

(read k *modulo* M) will denote the integer remainder when k is divided by M. More exactly, $k \pmod{M}$ is the unique integer r such that

$$k = Mq + r \quad \text{where} \quad 0 \le r < M$$

When k is positive, simply divide k by M to obtain the remainder r. Thus

$$25 \pmod 7 = 4, \quad 25 \pmod 5 = 0, \quad 35 \pmod{11} = 2, \quad 3 \pmod 8 = 3$$

Problem 2.2(b) shows a method to obtain $k \pmod{M}$ when k is negative.

The term "mod" is also used for the mathematical congruence relation, which is denoted and defined as follows:

$$a \equiv b \pmod{M} \quad \text{if and only if} \quad M \text{ divides } b - a$$

M is called the *modulus*, and $a \equiv b \pmod{M}$ is read "a is congruent to b modulo M." The following aspects of the congruence relation are frequently useful:

$$0 \equiv M \pmod{M} \quad \text{and} \quad a \pm M \equiv a \pmod{M}$$

Arithmetic modulo M refers to the arithmetic operations of addition, multiplication and subtraction where the arithmetic value is replaced by its equivalent value in the set

$$\{0, 1, 2, \ldots, M - 1\}$$

or in the set

$$\{1, 2, 3, \ldots, M\}$$

For example, in arithmetic modulo 12, sometimes called "clock" arithmetic,

$$6 + 9 \equiv 3, \quad 7 \times 5 \equiv 11, \quad 1 - 5 \equiv 8, \quad 2 + 10 \equiv 0 \equiv 12$$

(The use of 0 or M depends on the application.)

Integer and Absolute Value Functions

Let x be any real number. The *integer value* of x, written $\text{INT}(x)$, converts x into an integer by deleting (truncating) the fractional part of the number. Thus

$$\text{INT}(3.14) = 3, \qquad \text{INT}(\sqrt{5}) = 2, \qquad \text{INT}(-8.5) = -8, \qquad \text{INT}(7) = 7$$

Observe that $\text{INT}(x) = \lfloor x \rfloor$ or $\text{INT}(x) = \lceil x \rceil$ according to whether x is positive or negative.

The *absolute value* of the real number x, written $\text{ABS}(x)$ or $|x|$, is defined as the greater of x or $-x$. Hence $\text{ABS}(0) = 0$, and, for $x \neq 0$, $\text{ABS}(x) = x$ or $\text{ABS}(x) = -x$, depending on whether x is positive or negative. Thus

$$|-15| = 15, \qquad |7| = 7, \qquad |-3.33| = 3.33, \qquad |4.44| = 4.44, \qquad |-0.075| = 0.075$$

We note that $|x| = |-x|$ and, for $x \neq 0$, $|x|$ is positive.

Summation Symbol; Sums

Here we introduce the summation symbol Σ (the Greek letter sigma). Consider a sequence $a_1, a_2, a_3, \ldots$. Then the sums

$$a_1 + a_2 + \cdots + a_n \qquad \text{and} \qquad a_m + a_{m+1} + \cdots + a_n$$

will be denoted, respectively, by

$$\sum_{j=1}^{n} a_j \qquad \text{and} \qquad \sum_{j=m}^{n} a_j$$

The letter j in the above expressions is called a *dummy index* or *dummy variable*. Other letters frequently used as dummy variables are i, k, s and t.

EXAMPLE 2.2

$$\sum_{i=1}^{n} a_i b_i = a_1 b_1 + a_2 b_2 + \cdots + a_n b_n$$

$$\sum_{j=2}^{5} j^2 = 2^2 + 3^2 + 4^2 + 5^2 = 4 + 9 + 16 + 25 = 54$$

$$\sum_{j=1}^{n} j = 1 + 2 + \cdots + n$$

The last sum in Example 2.2 will appear very often. It has the value $n(n+1)/2$. That is,

$$1 + 2 + 3 + \cdots + n = \frac{n(n+1)}{2}$$

Thus, for example,

$$1 + 2 + \cdots + 50 = \frac{50(51)}{2} = 1275$$

Factorial Function

The product of the positive integers from 1 to n, inclusive, is denoted by $n!$ (read "n factorial"). That is,

$$n! = 1 \cdot 2 \cdot 3 \cdots (n-2)(n-1)n$$

It is also convenient to define $0! = 1$.

EXAMPLE 2.3

(*a*) $$2! = 1 \cdot 2 = 2; \qquad 3! = 1 \cdot 2 \cdot 3 = 6; \qquad 4! = 1 \cdot 2 \cdot 3 \cdot 4 = 24$$

(*b*) For $n > 1$, we have $n! = n \cdot (n-1)!$ Hence

$$5! = 5 \cdot 4! = 5 \cdot 24 = 120; \qquad 6! = 6 \cdot 5! = 6 \cdot 120 = 720$$

Permutations

A *permutation* of a set of n elements is an arrangement of the elements in a given order. For example, the permutations of the set consisting of the elements a, b, c are as follows:

$$abc, \quad acb, \quad bac, \quad bca, \quad cab, \quad cba$$

One can prove: *There are $n!$ permutations of a set of n elements.* Accordingly, there are $4! = 24$ permutations of a set with 4 elements, $5! = 120$ permutations of a set with 5 elements, and so on.

Exponents and Logarithms

Recall the following definitions for integer exponents (where m is a positive integer):

$$a^m = a \cdot a \cdots a \ (m \text{ times}), \qquad a^0 = 1, \qquad a^{-m} = \frac{1}{a^m}$$

Exponents are extended to include all rational numbers by defining, for any rational number m/n,

$$a^{m/n} = \sqrt[n]{a^m} = (\sqrt[n]{a})^m$$

For example,

$$2^4 = 16, \qquad 2^{-4} = \frac{1}{2^4} = \frac{1}{16}, \qquad 125^{2/3} = 5^2 = 25$$

In fact, exponents are extended to include all real numbers by defining, for any real number x,

$$a^x = \lim_{r \to x} a^r \qquad \text{where } r \text{ is a rational number}$$

Accordingly, the exponential function $f(x) = a^x$ is defined for all real numbers.

Logarithms are related to exponents as follows. Let b be a positive number. The logarithm of any positive number x to the base b, written

$$\log_b x$$

represents the exponent to which b must be raised to obtain x. That is,

$$y = \log_b x \qquad \text{and} \qquad b^y = x$$

are equivalent statements. Accordingly,

$$\log_2 8 = 3 \quad \text{since} \quad 2^3 = 8; \quad \log_{10} 100 = 2 \quad \text{since} \quad 10^2 = 100$$
$$\log_2 64 = 6 \quad \text{since} \quad 2^6 = 64; \quad \log_{10} 0.001 = -3 \quad \text{since} \quad 10^{-3} = 0.001$$

Furthermore, for any base b,

$$\log_b 1 = 0 \quad \text{since} \quad b^0 = 1$$
$$\log_b b = 1 \quad \text{since} \quad b^1 = b$$

The logarithm of a negative number and the logarithm of 0 are not defined.

One may also view the exponential and logarithmic functions

$$f(x) = b^x \qquad \text{and} \qquad g(x) = \log_b x$$

as inverse functions of each other. Accordingly, the graphs of these two functions are related. (See Prob. 2.5.)

Frequently, logarithms are expressed using approximate values. For example, using tables or calculators, one obtains

$$\log_{10} 300 = 2.4771 \qquad \text{and} \qquad \log_e 40 = 3.6889$$

as approximate answers. (Here $e = 2.718281\cdots$.)

Logarithms to the base 10 (called *common logarithms*), logarithms to the base *e* (called *natural logarithms*) and logarithms to the base 2 (called *binary logarithms*) are of special importance. Some texts write:

$$\ln x \quad\quad \text{instead of} \quad\quad \log_e x$$
$$\lg x \text{ or } \operatorname{Log} x \quad\quad \text{instead of} \quad\quad \log_2 x$$

This text on data structures is mainly concerned with binary logarithms. Accordingly,

> The term $\log x$ shall mean $\log_2 x$ unless otherwise specified.

Frequently, we will require only the floor or the ceiling of a binary logarithm. This can be obtained by looking at the powers of 2. For example,

$$\lfloor \log_2 100 \rfloor = 6 \quad\quad \text{since} \quad\quad 2^6 = 64 \quad\quad 2^7 = 128$$
$$\lceil \log_2 1000 \rceil = 9 \quad\quad \text{since} \quad\quad 2^8 = 512 \quad\quad \text{and} \quad\quad 2^9 = 1024$$

and so on.

2.3 ALGORITHMIC NOTATION

An algorithm, intuitively speaking, is a finite step-by-step list of well-defined instructions for solving a particular problem. The formal definition of an algorithm, which uses the notion of a Turing machine or its equivalent, is very sophisticated and lies beyond the scope of this text. This section describes the format that is used to present algorithms throughout the text. This algorithmic notation is best described by means of examples.

EXAMPLE 2.4

An array DATA of numerical values is in memory. We want to find the location LOC and the value MAX of the largest element of DATA. Given no other information about DATA, one way to solve the problem is as follows:

Initially begin with LOC = 1 and MAX = DATA[1]. Then compare MAX with each successive element DATA[K] of DATA. If DATA[K] exceeds MAX, then update LOC and MAX so that LOC = K and MAX = DATA[K]. The final values appearing in LOC and MAX give the location and value of the largest element of DATA.

A formal presentation of this algorithm, whose flowchart appears in Fig. 2-2, follows.

Algorithm 2.1: (Largest Element in Array) A nonempty array DATA with N numerical values is given. This algorithm finds the location LOC and the value MAX of the largest element of DATA. The variable K is used as a counter.

Step 1. [Initialize.] Set K := 1, LOC := 1 and MAX := DATA[1].
Step 2. [Increment counter.] Set K := K + 1.
Step 3. [Test counter.] If K > N, then:
        Write: LOC, MAX, and Exit.
Step 4. [Compare and update.] If MAX < DATA[K], then:
        Set LOC := K and MAX := DATA[K].
Step 5. [Repeat loop.] Go to Step 2.

The format for the formal presentation of an algorithm consists of two parts. The first part is a paragraph which tells the purpose of the algorithm, identifies the variables which occur in the algorithm and lists the input data. The second part of the algorithm consists of the list of steps that is to be executed.

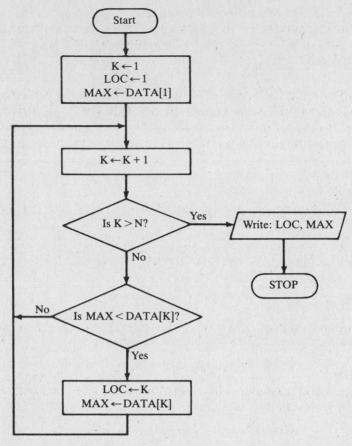

Fig. 2-2

The following summarizes certain conventions that we will use in presenting our algorithms. Some control structures will be covered in the next section.

Identifying Number

Each algorithm is assigned an identifying number as follows: Algorithm 4.3 refers to the third algorithm in Chap. 4; Algorithm P5.3 refers to the algorithm in Prob. 5.3 in Chap. 5. Note that the letter "P" indicates that the algorithm appears in a problem.

Steps, Control, Exit

The steps of the algorithm are executed one after the other, beginning with Step 1, unless indicated otherwise. Control may be transferred to Step n of the algorithm by the statement "Go to Step n." For example, Step 5 transfers control back to Step 2 in Algorithm 2.1. Generally speaking, these Go to statements may be practically eliminated by using certain control structures discussed in the next section.

If several statements appear in the same step, e.g.,

$$\text{Set } K := 1, \text{ LOC} := 1 \text{ and MAX} := \text{DATA}[1].$$

then they are executed from left to right.

The algorithm is completed when the statement

$$\text{Exit.}$$

is encountered. This statement is similar to the STOP statement used in FORTRAN and in flowcharts.

Comments

Each step may contain a comment in brackets which indicates the main purpose of the step. The comment will usually appear at the beginning or the end of the step.

Variable Names

Variable names will use capital letters, as in MAX and DATA. Single-letter names of variables used as counters or subscripts will also be capitalized in the algorithms (K and N, for example), even though lowercase may be used for these same variables (k and n) in the accompanying mathematical description and analysis. (Recall the discussion of italic and lowercase symbols in Sec. 1.3 of Chap. 1, under "Arrays.")

Assignment Statement

Our assignment statements will use the dots-equal notation $:=$ that is used in Pascal. For example,

$$Max := DATA[1]$$

assigns the value in DATA[1] to MAX. Some texts use the backward arrow $\leftarrow$ or the equal sign $=$ for this operation.

Input and Output

Data may be input and assigned to variables by means of a Read statement with the following form:

$$\text{Read: Variables names.}$$

Similarly, messages, placed in quotation marks, and data in variables may be output by means of a Write or Print statement with the following form:

$$\text{Write: Messages and/or variable names.}$$

Procedures

The term "procedure" will be used for an independent algorithmic module which solves a particular problem. The use of the word "procedure" or "module" rather than "algorithm" for a given problem is simply a matter of taste. Generally speaking, the word "algorithm" will be reserved for the solution of general problems. The term "procedure" will also be used to describe a certain type of subalgorithm which is discussed in Sec. 2.6.

2.4 CONTROL STRUCTURES

Algorithms and their equivalent computer programs are more easily understood if they mainly use self-contained modules and three types of logic, or flow of control, called

(1) Sequence logic, or sequential flow

(2) Selection logic, or conditional flow

(3) Iteration logic, or repetitive flow

These three types of logic are discussed below, and in each case we show the equivalent flowchart.

Sequence Logic (Sequential Flow)

Sequence logic has already been discussed. Unless instructions are given to the contrary, the modules are executed in the obvious sequence. The sequence may be presented explicitly, by means of numbered steps, or implicitly, by the order in which the modules are written. (See Fig. 2-3.) Most processing, even of complex problems, will generally follow this elementary flow pattern.

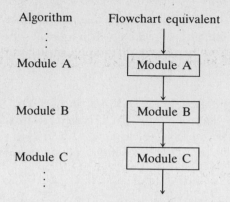

Fig. 2-3   Sequence logic.

Selection Logic (Conditional Flow)

Selection logic employs a number of conditions which lead to a selection of one out of several alternative modules. The structures which implement this logic are called conditional structures or If structures. For clarity, we will frequently indicate the end of such a structure by the statement

[End of If structure.]

or some equivalent.

These conditional structures fall into three types, which are discussed separately.

(1)   *Single alternative*. This structure has the form

If condition, then:
[Module A]
[End of If structure.]

The logic of this structure is pictured in Fig. 2-4(*a*). If the condition holds, then Module A, which may consist of one or more statements, is executed; otherwise Module A is skipped and control transfers to the next step of the algorithm.

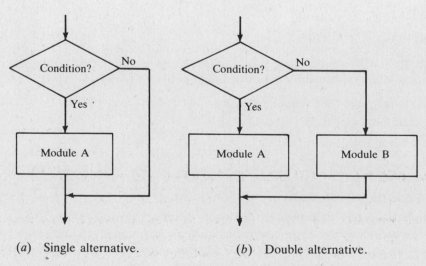

(*a*)   Single alternative.   (*b*)   Double alternative.

Fig. 2-4

(2) *Double alternative*. This structure has the form

> If condition, then:
>> [Module A]
> Else:
>> [Module B]
> [End of If structure.]

The logic of this structure is pictured in Fig. 2-4(*b*). As indicated by the flowchart, if the condition holds, then Module A is executed; otherwise Module B is executed.

(3) *Multiple alternatives*. This structure has the form:

> If condition(1), then:
>> [Module A_1]
> Else if condition(2), then:
>> [Module A_2]
>> $\vdots$
> Else if condition(M), then:
>> [Module A_M]
> Else:
>> [Module B]
> [End of If structure.]

The logic of this structure allows only one of the modules to be executed. Specifically, either the module which follows the first condition which holds is executed, or the module which follows the final Else statement is executed. In practice, there will rarely be more than three alternatives.

EXAMPLE 2.5

The solutions of the quadratic equation

$$ax^2 + bx + c = 0$$

where $a \neq 0$, are given by the quadratic formula

$$x = \frac{-b \pm \sqrt{b^2 - 4ac}}{2a}$$

The quantity $D = b^2 - 4ac$ is called the *discriminant* of the equation. If D is negative, then there are no real solutions. If $D = 0$, then there is only one (double) real solution, $x = -b/2a$. If D is positive, the formula gives the two distinct real solutions. The following algorithm finds the solutions of a quadratic equation.

Algorithm 2.2: (Quadratic Equation) This algorithm inputs the coefficients A, B, C of a quadratic equation and outputs the real solutions, if any.

  Step 1. Read: A, B, C.
  Step 2. Set $D := B^2 - 4AC$.
  Step 3. If $D > 0$, then:
    (*a*) Set $X1 := (-B + \sqrt{D})/2A$ and $X2 := (-B - \sqrt{D})/2A$.
    (*b*) Write: X1, X2.
  Else if $D = 0$, then:
    (*a*) Set $X := -B/2A$.
    (*b*) Write: 'UNIQUE SOLUTION', X.
  Else:
    Write: 'NO REAL SOLUTIONS'.
  [End of If structure.]
  Step 4. Exit.

Remark: Observe that there are three mutually exclusive conditions in Step 3 of Algorithm 2.2 that depend on whether D is positive, zero or negative. In such a situation, we may alternatively list the different cases as follows:

Step 3.   (1)   If $D > 0$, then:
....

(2)   If $D = 0$, then:
....

(3)   If $D < 0$, then:
....

This is similar to the use of the CASE statement in Pascal.

Iteration Logic (Repetitive Flow)

The third kind of logic refers to either of two types of structures involving loops. Each type begins with a Repeat statement and is followed by a module, called the *body of the loop*. For clarity, we will indicate the end of the structure by the statement

[End of loop.]

or some equivalent.

Each type of loop structure is discussed separately.

The *repeat-for loop* uses an index variable, such as K, to control the loop. The loop will usually have the form:

Repeat for $K = R$ to S by T:
[Module]
[End of loop.]

The logic of this structure is pictured in Fig. 2-5(a). Here R is called the *initial value*, S the *end value* or *test value*, and T the *increment*. Observe that the body of the loop is executed first with $K = R$, then with $K = R + T$, then with $K = R + 2T$, and so on. The cycling ends when $K > S$. The flowchart

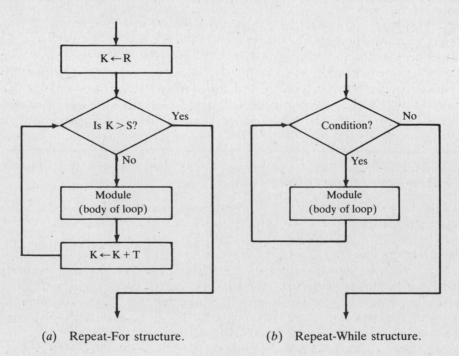

(a)   Repeat-For structure.   (b)   Repeat-While structure.

Fig. 2-5

assumes that the increment T is positive; if T is negative, so that K decreases in value, then the cycling ends when K < S.

The *repeat-while loop* uses a condition to control the loop. The loop will usually have the form

Repeat while condition:
   [Module]
[End of loop.]

The logic of this structure is pictured in Fig. 2-5(b). Observe that the cycling continues until the condition is false. We emphasize that there must be a statement before the structure that initializes the condition controlling the loop, and in order that the looping may eventually cease, there must be a statement in the body of the loop that changes the condition.

EXAMPLE 2.6

Algorithm 2.1 is rewritten using a repeat-while loop rather than a Go to statement:

Algorithm 2.3: (Largest Element in Array) Given a nonempty array DATA with N numerical values, this algorithm finds the location LOC and the value MAX of the largest element of DATA.

1. [Initialize.] Set K := 1, LOC := 1 and MAX := DATA[1].
2. Repeat Steps 3 and 4 while K ≤ N:
3.   If MAX < DATA[K], then:
        Set LOC := K and MAX := DATA[K].
    [End of If structure.]
4.   Set K := K + 1.
    [End of Step 2 loop.]
5. Write: LOC, MAX.
6. Exit.

Algorithm 2.3 indicates some other properties of our algorithms. Usually we will omit the word "Step." We will try to use repeat structures instead of Go to statements. The repeat statement may explicitly indicate the steps that form the body of the loop. The "End of loop" statement may explicitly indicate the step where the loop begins. The modules contained in our logic structures will normally be indented for easier reading. This conforms to the usual format in structured programming.

Any other new notation or convention either will be self-explanatory or will be explained when it occurs.

2.5 COMPLEXITY OF ALGORITHMS

The analysis of algorithms is a major task in computer science. In order to compare algorithms, we must have some criteria to measure the efficiency of our algorithms. This section discusses this important topic.

Suppose M is an algorithm, and suppose n is the size of the input data. The time and space used by the algorithm M are the two main measures for the efficiency of M. The time is measured by counting the number of key operations—in sorting and searching algorithms, for example, the number of comparisons. That is because key operations are so defined that the time for the other operations is much less than or at most proportional to the time for the key operations. The space is measured by counting the maximum of memory needed by the algorithm.

The *complexity* of an algorithm M is the function $f(n)$ which gives the running time and/or storage space requirement of the algorithm in terms of the size n of the input data. Frequently, the storage space required by an algorithm is simply a multiple of the data size n. Accordingly, unless otherwise stated or implied, the term "complexity" shall refer to the running time of the algorithm.

The following example illustrates that the function $f(n)$, which gives the running time of an algorithm, depends not only on the size n of the input data but also on the particular data.

EXAMPLE 2.7

Suppose we are given an English short story TEXT, and suppose we want to search through TEXT for the first occurrence of a given 3-letter word W. If W is the 3-letter word "the," then it is likely that W occurs near the beginning of TEXT, so $f(n)$ will be small. On the other hand, if W is the 3-letter word "zoo," then W may not appear in TEXT at all, so $f(n)$ will be large.

The above discussion leads us to the question of finding the complexity function $f(n)$ for certain cases. The two cases one usually investigates in complexity theory are as follows:

(1)   *Worst case*: the maximum value of $f(n)$ for any possible input

(2)   *Average case*: the expected value of $f(n)$

Sometimes we also consider the minimum possible value of $f(n)$, called the *best case*.

The analysis of the average case assumes a certain probabilistic distribution for the input data; one such assumption might be that all possible permutations of an input data set are equally likely. The average case also uses the following concept in probability theory. Suppose the numbers $n_1, n_2, \ldots, n_k$ occur with respective probabilities $p_1, p_2, \ldots, p_k$. Then the *expectation* or *average value* E is given by

$$E = n_1 p_1 + n_2 p_2 + \cdots + n_k p_k$$

These ideas are illustrated in the following example.

EXAMPLE 2.8   Linear Search

Suppose a linear array DATA contains n elements, and suppose a specific ITEM of information is given. We want either to find the location LOC of ITEM in the array DATA, or to send some message, such as LOC = 0, to indicate that ITEM does not appear in DATA. The linear search algorithm solves this problem by comparing ITEM, one by one, with each element in DATA. That is, we compare ITEM with DATA[1], then DATA[2], and so on, until we find LOC such that ITEM = DATA[LOC]. A formal presentation of this algorithm follows.

Algorithm 2.4:   (Linear Search) A linear array DATA with N elements and a specific ITEM of information are given. This algorithm finds the location LOC of ITEM in the array DATA or sets LOC = 0.

1.   [Initialize] Set K := 1 and LOC := 0.
2.   Repeat Steps 3 and 4 while LOC = 0 and K ≤ N.
3.   If ITEM = DATA[K], then: Set LOC := K.
4.   Set K := K + 1. [Increments counter.]
     [End of Step 2 loop.]
5.   [Successful?]
     If LOC = 0, then:
         Write: ITEM is not in the array DATA.
     Else:
         Write: LOC is the location of ITEM.
     [End of If structure.]
6.   Exit.

The complexity of the search algorithm is given by the number C of comparisons between ITEM and DATA[K]. We seek $C(n)$ for the worst case and the average case.

Worst Case

Clearly the worst case occurs when ITEM is the last element in the array DATA or is not there at all. In either situation, we have

$$C(n) = n$$

Accordingly, $C(n) = n$ is the worst-case complexity of the linear search algorithm.

Average Case

Here we assume that ITEM does appear in DATA, and that it is equally likely to occur at any position in the array. Accordingly, the number of comparisons can be any of the numbers $1, 2, 3, \ldots, n$, and each number occurs with probability $p = 1/n$. Then

$$C(n) = 1 \cdot \frac{1}{n} + 2 \cdot \frac{1}{n} + \cdots + n \cdot \frac{1}{n}$$

$$= (1 + 2 + \cdots + n) \cdot \frac{1}{n}$$

$$= \frac{n(n+1)}{2} \cdot \frac{1}{n} = \frac{n+1}{2}$$

This agrees with our intuitive feeling that the average number of comparisons needed to find the location of ITEM is approximately equal to half the number of elements in the DATA list.

Remark: The complexity of the average case of an algorithm is usually much more complicated to analyze than that of the worst case. Moreover, the probabilistic distribution that one assumes for the average case may not actually apply to real situations. Accordingly, unless otherwise stated or implied, the complexity of an algorithm shall mean the function which gives the running time of the worst case in terms of the input size. This is not too strong an assumption, since the complexity of the average case for many algorithms is proportional to the worst case.

Rate of Growth; Big *O* Notation

Suppose M is an algorithm, and suppose n is the size of the input data. Clearly the complexity $f(n)$ of M increases as n increases. It is usually the rate of increase of $f(n)$ that we want to examine. This is usually done by comparing $f(n)$ with some standard function, such as

$$\log_2 n, \qquad n, \qquad n \log_2 n, \qquad n^2, \qquad n^3, \qquad 2^n$$

The rates of growth for these standard functions are indicated in Fig. 2-6, which gives their approximate values for certain values of n. Observe that the functions are listed in the order of their rates of growth: the logarithmic function $\log_2 n$ grows most slowly, the exponential function 2^n grows most rapidly, and the polynomial functions n^c grow according to the exponent c. One way to compare the function $f(n)$ with these standard functions is to use the functional O notation defined as follows:

n \ $g(n)$	$\log n$	n	$n \log n$	n^2	n^3	2^n
5	3	5	15	25	125	32
10	4	10	40	100	10^3	10^3
100	7	100	700	10^4	10^6	10^{30}
1000	10	10^3	10^4	10^6	10^9	10^{300}

Fig. 2-6   Rate of growth of standard functions.

Suppose $f(n)$ and $g(n)$ are functions defined on the positive integers with the property that $f(n)$ is bounded by some multiple of $g(n)$ for almost all n. That is, suppose there exist a positive integer n_0 and a positive number M such that, for all $n > n_0$, we have

$$|f(n)| \le M|g(n)|$$

Then we may write

$$f(n) = O(g(n))$$

which is read "$f(n)$ is of order $g(n)$." For any polynomial $P(n)$ of degree m, we show in Prob. 2.10 that $P(n) = O(n^m)$; e.g.,

$$8n^3 - 576n^2 + 832n - 248 = O(n^3)$$

We can also write

$$f(n) = h(n) + O(g(n)) \qquad \text{when} \qquad f(n) - h(n) = O(g(n))$$

(This is called the "big O" notation since $f(n) = o(g(n))$ has an entirely different meaning.)

To indicate the convenience of this notation, we give the complexity of certain well-known searching and sorting algorithms:

(*a*)   Linear search: $O(n)$

(*b*)   Binary search: $O(\log n)$

(*c*)   Bubble sort: $O(n^2)$

(*d*)   Merge-sort: $O(n \log n)$

These results are discussed in Chap. 9, on sorting and searching.

2.6 SUBALGORITHMS

A *subalgorithm* is a complete and independently defined algorithmic module which is used (or *invoked* or *called*) by some main algorithm or by some other subalgorithm. A subalgorithm receives values, called *arguments*, from an originating (calling) algorithm; performs computations; and then sends back the result to the calling algorithm. The subalgorithm is defined independently so that it may be called by many different algorithms or called at different times in the same algorithm. The relationship between an algorithm and a subalgorithm is similar to the relationship between a main program and a subprogram in a programming language.

The main difference between the format of a subalgorithm and that of an algorithm is that the subalgorithm will usually have a heading of the form

$$\text{NAME}(\text{PAR}_1, \text{PAR}_2, \ldots, \text{PAR}_K)$$

Here NAME refers to the name of the subalgorithm which is used when the subalgorithm is called, and $\text{PAR}_1, \text{PAR}_2, \ldots, \text{PAR}_K$ refer to parameters which are used to transmit data between the subalgorithm and the calling algorithm.

Another difference is that the subalgorithm will have a Return statement rather than an Exit statement; this emphasizes that control is transferred back to the calling program when the execution of the subalgorithm is completed.

Subalgorithms fall into two basic categories: *function* subalgorithms and *procedure* subalgorithms. The similarities and differences between these two types of subalgorithms will be examined below by means of examples. One major difference between the subalgorithms is that the function subalgorithm returns only a single value to the calling algorithm, whereas the procedure subalgorithm may send back more than one value.

EXAMPLE 2.9

The following function subalgorithm MEAN finds the average AVE of three numbers A, B and C.

Function 2.5:   MEAN(A, B, C)

        1.   Set $AVE := (A + B + C)/3$.
        2.   Return(AVE).

Note that MEAN is the name of the subalgorithm and A, B and C are the parameters. The Return statement includes, in parentheses, the variable AVE, whose value is returned to the calling program.

The subalgorithm MEAN is invoked by an algorithm in the same way as a function subprogram is invoked by a calling program. For example, suppose an algorithm contains the statement

$$\text{Set TEST} := \text{MEAN}(T_1, T_2, T_3)$$

where T_1, T_2 and T_3 are test scores. The argument values T_1, T_2 and T_3 are transferred to the parameters A, B, C in the subalgorithm, the subalgorithm MEAN is executed, and then the value of AVE is returned to the program and replaces $\text{MEAN}(T_1, T_2, T_3)$ in the statement. Hence the average of T_1, T_2 and T_3 is assigned to TEST.

EXAMPLE 2.10

The following procedure SWITCH interchanges the values of AAA and BBB.

Procedure 2.6:   SWITCH(AAA, BBB)

        1.   Set $TEMP := AAA$, $AAA := BBB$ and $BBB := TEMP$.
        2.   Return.

The procedure is invoked by means of a Call statement. For example, the Call statement

$$\text{Call SWITCH(BEG, AUX)}$$

has the net effect of interchanging the values of BEG and AUX. Specifically, when the procedure SWITCH is invoked, the argument of BEG and AUX are transferred to the parameters AAA and BBB, respectively; the procedure is executed, which interchanges the values of AAA and BBB; and then the new values of AAA and BBB are transferred back to BEG and AUX, respectively.

Remark: Any function subalgorithm can be easily translated into an equivalent procedure by simply adjoining an extra parameter which is used to return the computed value to the calling algorithm. For example, Function 2.5 may be translated into a procedure

$$\text{MEAN(A, B, C, AVE)}$$

where the parameter AVE is assigned the average of A, B, C. Then the statement

$$\text{Call MEAN}(T_1, T_2, T_3, \text{TEST})$$

also has the effect of assigning the average of T_1, T_2 and T_3 to TEST. Generally speaking, we will use procedures rather than function subalgorithms.

2.7   VARIABLES, DATA TYPES

Each variable in any of our algorithms or programs has a data type which determines the code that is used for storing its value. Four such data types follow:

(1)   *Character*. Here data are coded using some character code such as EBCDIC or ASCII. The 8-bit EBCDIC code of some characters appears in Fig. 2-7. A single character is normally stored in a byte.

Char.	Zone	Numeric	Hex	Char.	Zone	Numeric	Hex	Char.	Zone	Numeric	Hex
				S	1110	0010	E2	blank	0100	0000	40
A	1100	0001	C1	T		0011	E3	.		1011	4B
B		0010	C2	U		0100	E4	<		1100	4C
C		0011	C3	V		0101	E5	(		1101	4D
D		0100	C4	W		0110	E6	+	0100	1110	4E
E		0101	C5	X		0111	E7	&	0101	0000	50
F		0110	C6	Y		1000	E8	$		1011	5B
G		0111	C7	Z	1110	1001	E9	*		1100	5C
H		1000	C8					)		1101	5D
I	1100	1001	C9	0	1111	0000	F0	;	0101	1110	5E
J	1101	0001	D1	1		0001	F1	–	0110	0000	60
K		0010	D2	2		0010	F2	/		0001	61
L		0011	D3	3		0011	F3	,		1011	6B
M		0100	D4	4		0100	F4	%		1100	6C
N		0101	D5	5		0101	F5	>		1110	6E
O		0110	D6	6		0110	F6	?	0110	1111	6F
P		0111	D7	7		0111	F7	:	0111	1010	7A
Q		1000	D8	8		1000	F8	#		1011	7B
R	1101	1001	D9	9	1111	1001	F9	@		1100	7C
								=	0111	1110	7E

Fig. 2-7   Part of the EBCDIC code.

(2)   *Real* (or *floating point*). Here numerical data are coded using the exponential form of the data.

(3)   *Integer* (or *fixed point*). Here positive integers are coded using binary representation, and negative integers by some binary variation such as 2's complement.

(4)   *Logical*. Here the variable can have only the value true or false; hence it may be coded using only one bit, 1 for true and 0 for false. (Sometimes the bytes 1111 1111 and 0000 0000 may be used for true and false, respectively.)

The data types of variables in our algorithms will not be explicitly stated as with computer programs but will usually be implied by the context.

EXAMPLE 2.11

Suppose a 32-bit memory location X contains the following sequence of bits:

$$0110\ 1100 \qquad 1100\ 0111 \qquad 1101\ 0110 \qquad 0110\ 1100$$

There is no way to know the content of the cell unless the data type of X is known.

(*a*)   Suppose X is declared to be of character type and EBCDIC is used. Then the four characters %GO% are stored in X.

(*b*)   Suppose X is declared to be of some other type, such as integer or real. Then an integer or real number is stored in X.

Local and Global Variables

The organization of a computer program into a main program and various subprograms has led to the notion of local and global variables. Normally, each program module contains its own list of variables, called *local variables*, which can be accessed only by the given program module. Also, subprogram modules may contain parameters, variables which transfer data between a subprogram and its calling program.

EXAMPLE 2.12

Consider the procedure SWITCH(AAA, BBB) in Example 2.10. The variables AAA and BBB are parameters; they are used to transfer data between the procedure and a calling algorithm. On the other hand, the variable TEMP in the procedure is a local variable. It "lives" only in the procedure; i.e., its value can be accessed and changed only during the execution of the procedure. In fact, the name TEMP may be used for a variable in any other module and the use of the name will not interfere with the execution of the procedure SWITCH.

Language designers realized that it would be convenient to have certain variables which can be accessed by some or even all the program modules in a computer program. Variables that can be accessed by all program modules are called *global* variables, and variables that can be accessed by some program modules are called *nonlocal* variables. Each programming language has its own syntax for declaring such variables. For example, FORTRAN uses a COMMON statement to declare global variables, and Pascal uses scope rules to declare global and nonlocal variables.

Accordingly, there are two basic ways for modules to communicate with each other:

(1) *Directly*, by means of well-defined parameters

(2) *Indirectly*, by means of nonlocal and global variables

The indirect change of the value of a variable in one module by another module is called a *side effect*. Readers should be very careful when using nonlocal and global variables, since errors caused by side effects may be difficult to detect.

Solved Problems

MATHEMATICAL NOTATION AND FUNCTIONS

2.1   Find (a) $\lfloor 7.5 \rfloor$, $\lfloor -7.5 \rfloor$, $\lfloor -18 \rfloor$, $\lfloor \sqrt{30} \rfloor$, $\lfloor \sqrt[3]{30} \rfloor$, $\lfloor \pi \rfloor$; and (b) $\lceil 7.5 \rceil$, $\lceil -7.5 \rceil$, $\lceil -18 \rceil$, $\lceil \sqrt{30} \rceil$, $\lceil \sqrt[3]{30} \rceil$, $\lceil \pi \rceil$.

(a)   By definition, $\lfloor x \rfloor$ denotes the greatest integer that does not exceed x, called the floor of x. Hence,

$$\lfloor 7.5 \rfloor = 7 \qquad \lfloor -7.5 \rfloor = -8 \qquad \lfloor -18 \rfloor = -18$$
$$\lfloor \sqrt{30} \rfloor = 5 \qquad \lfloor \sqrt[3]{30} \rfloor = 3 \qquad \lfloor \pi \rfloor = 3$$

(b)   By definition, $\lceil x \rceil$ denotes the least integer that is not less than x, called the ceiling of x. Hence,

$$\lceil 7.5 \rceil = 8 \qquad \lceil -7.5 \rceil = -7 \qquad \lceil -18 \rceil = -18$$
$$\lceil \sqrt{30} \rceil = 6 \qquad \lceil \sqrt[3]{30} \rceil = 4 \qquad \lceil \pi \rceil = 4$$

2.2   (a)   Find 26 (mod 7), 34 (mod 8), 2345 (mod 6), 495 (mod 11).

(b)   Find -26 (mod 7), -2345 (mod 6), -371 (mod 8), -39 (mod 3).

(c)   Using arithmetic modulo 15, evaluate $9 + 13$, $7 + 11$, $4 - 9$, $2 - 10$.

(a)   Since k is positive, simply divide k by the modulus M to obtain the remainder r. Then $r = k \pmod{M}$. Thus

$$5 = 26 \pmod{7} \qquad 2 = 34 \pmod{8} \qquad 5 = 2345 \pmod{6} \qquad 0 = 495 \pmod{11}$$

(b) When k is negative, divide $|k|$ by the modulus to obtain the remainder r'. Then $k \equiv -r'$ (mod M). Hence k (mod M) $= M - r'$ when $r' \neq 0$. Thus

$$-26 \text{ (mod 7)} = 7 - 5 = 2 \qquad -371 \text{ (mod 8)} = 8 - 3 = 5$$
$$-2345 \text{ (mod 6)} = 6 - 5 = 1 \qquad -39 \text{ (mod 3)} = 0$$

(c) Use $a \pm M \equiv a$ (mod M):

$$9 + 13 = 22 \equiv 22 - 15 = 7 \qquad 7 + 11 = 18 \equiv 18 - 15 = 3$$
$$4 - 9 = -5 \equiv -5 + 15 = 10 \qquad 2 - 10 = -8 \equiv -8 + 15 = 7$$

2.3 List all the permutations of the numbers 1, 2, 3, 4.

Note first that there are $4! = 24$ such permutations:

1234	1243	1324	1342	1423	1432
2134	2143	2314	2341	2413	2431
3124	3142	3214	3241	3412	3421
4123	4132	4213	4231	4312	4321

Observe that the first row contains the six permutations beginning with 1, the second row those beginning with 2, and so on.

2.4 Find: (a) 2^{-5}, $8^{2/3}$, $25^{-3/2}$; (b) $\log_2 32$, $\log_{10} 1000$, $\log_2 (1/16)$; (c) $\lfloor \log_2 1000 \rfloor$, $\lfloor \log_2 0.01 \rfloor$.

(a) $2^{-5} = 1/2^5 = 1/32$; $8^{2/3} = (\sqrt[3]{8})^2 = 2^2 = 4$; $25^{-3/2} = 1/25^{3/2} = 1/5^3 = 1/125$.

(b) $\log_2 32 = 5$ since $2^5 = 32$; $\log_{10} 1000 = 3$ since $10^3 = 1000$; $\log_2(1/16) = -4$ since $2^{-4} = 1/2^4 = 1/16$.

(c) $\lfloor \log_2 1000 \rfloor = 9$ since $2^9 = 512$ but $2^{10} = 1024$;
$\lfloor \log_2 0.01 \rfloor = -7$ since $2^{-7} = 1/128 < 0.01 < 2^{-6} = 1/64$.

2.5 Plot the graphs of the exponential function $f(x) = 2^x$, the logarithmic function $g(x) = \log_2 x$ and the linear function $h(x) = x$ on the same coordinate axis. (a) Describe a geometric property of the graphs $f(x)$ and $g(x)$. (b) For any positive number c, how are $f(c)$, $g(c)$ and $h(c)$ related?

Figure 2-8 pictures the three functions.

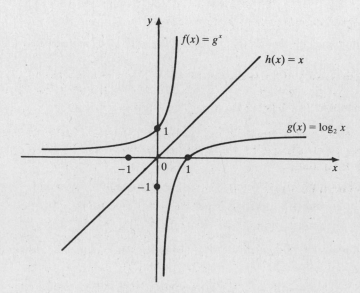

Fig. 2-8

(a) Since $f(x) = 2^x$ and $g(x) = \log_2 x$ are inverse functions, they are symmetric with respect to the line $y = x$.

(b) For any positive number c, we have

$$g(c) < h(c) < f(c)$$

In fact, as c increases in value, the vertical distances between the functions,

$$h(c) - g(c) \qquad \text{and} \qquad f(c) - h(c),$$

increase in value. Moreover, the logarithmic function $g(x)$ grows very slowly compared with the linear function $h(x)$, and the exponential function $f(x)$ grows very quickly compared with $h(x)$.

ALGORITHMS, COMPLEXITY

2.6 Consider Algorithm 2.3, which finds the location LOC and the value MAX of the largest element in an array DATA with n elements. Consider the complexity function $C(n)$, which measures the number of times LOC and MAX are updated in Step 3. (The number of comparisons is independent of the order of the elements in DATA.)

(a) Describe and find $C(n)$ for the worst case.

(b) Describe and find $C(n)$ for the best case.

(c) Find $C(n)$ for the average case when $n = 3$, assuming all arrangements of the elements in DATA are equally likely.

(a) The worst case occurs when the elements of DATA are in increasing order, where each comparison of MAX with DATA[K] forces LOC and MAX to be updated. In this case, $C(n) = n - 1$.

(b) The best case occurs when the largest element appears first and so when the comparison of MAX with DATA[K] never forces LOC and MAX to be updated. Accordingly, in this case, $C(n) = 0$.

(c) Let 1, 2 and 3 denote, respectively, the largest, second largest and smallest elements of DATA. There are six possible ways the elements can appear in DATA, which correspond to the $3! = 6$ permutations of 1, 2, 3. For each permutation p, let n_p denote the number of times LOC and MAX are updated when the algorithm is executed with input p. The six permutations p and the corresponding values n_p follow:

Permutation p:	123	132	213	231	312	321
Value of n_p:	0	0	1	1	1	2

Assuming all permutations p are equally likely,

$$C(3) = \frac{0 + 0 + 1 + 1 + 1 + 2}{6} = \frac{5}{6}$$

(The evaluation of the average value of $C(n)$ for arbitrary n lies beyond the scope of this text. One purpose of this problem is to illustrate the difficulty that may occur in finding the complexity of the average case of an algorithm.)

2.7 Suppose Module A requires M units of time to be executed, where M is a constant. Find the complexity $C(n)$ of each algorithm, where n is the size of the input data and b is a positive integer greater than 1.

(a) **Algorithm P2.7A:** 1. Repeat for I = 1 to N:
2.   Repeat for J = 1 to N:
3.   Repeat for K = 1 to N:
4.   Module A.
          [End of Step 3 loop.]
        [End of Step 2 loop.]
      [End of Step 1 loop.]
5. Exit.

(b)   **Algorithm P2.7B:**   1.   Set $J := 1$.
                            2.   Repeat Steps 3 and 4 while $J \leq N$:
                            3.   Module A.
                            4.   Set $J := B \times J$.
                            [End of Step 2 loop.]
                            5.   Exit.

Observe that the algorithms use N for n and B for b.)

(a)   Here $$C(n) = \sum_{i=1}^{n} \sum_{i=1}^{n} \sum_{k=1}^{n} M$$

The number of times M occurs in the sum is equal to the number of triplets (i, j, k), where i, j, k are integers from 1 to n inclusive. There are n^3 such triplets. Hence

$$C(n) = Mn^3 = O(n^3)$$

(b)   Observe that the values of the loop index J are the powers of b:

$$1, b, b^2, b^3, b^4, \ldots$$

Therefore, Module A will be repeated exactly T times, where T is the first exponent such that

$$b^T > n$$

Hence, $$T = \lfloor \log_b n \rfloor + 1$$

Accordingly, $$C(n) = MT = O(\log_b n)$$

2.8   (a)   Write a procedure FIND(DATA, N, LOC1, LOC2) which finds the location LOC1 of the largest element and the location LOC2 of the second largest element in an array DATA with $n > 1$ elements.

(b)   Why not let FIND also find the values of the largest and second largest elements?

(a)   The elements of DATA are examined one by one. During the execution of the procedure, FIRST and SECOND will denote, respectively, the values of the largest and second largest elements that have already been examined. Each new element DATA[K] is tested as follows. If

$$\text{SECOND} \leq \text{FIRST} < \text{DATA[K]}$$

then FIRST becomes the new SECOND element and DATA[K] becomes the new FIRST element. On the other hand, if

$$\text{SECOND} < \text{DATA[K]} \leq \text{FIRST}$$

then DATA[K] becomes the new SECOND element. Initially, set FIRST := DATA[1] and SECOND := DATA[2], and check whether or not they are in the right order. A formal presentation of the procedure follows:

Procedure P2.8:   FIND(DATA, N, LOC1, LOC2)

1.   Set FIRST := DATA[1], SECOND := DATA[2], LOC1 := 1, LOC2 := 2.
2.   [Are FIRST and SECOND initially correct?]
     If FIRST < SECOND, then:
         (a)   Interchange FIRST and SECOND,
         (b)   Set LOC1 := 2 and LOC2 := 1.
     [End of If structure.]
3.   Repeat for K = 3 to N:
         If FIRST < DATA[K], then:
             (a)   Set SECOND := FIRST and FIRST := DATA[K].
             (b)   Set LOC2 := LOC1 and LOC1 := K.
         Else if SECOND < DATA[K], then:
             Set SECOND := DATA[K] and LOC2 := K.
         [End of If structure.]
     [End of loop.]
4.   Return.

(b) Using additional parameters FIRST and SECOND would be redundant, since LOC1 and LOC2 automatically tell the calling program that DATA[LOC1] and DATA[LOC2] are, respectively, the values of the largest and second largest elements of DATA.

2.9 An integer $n > 1$ is called a *prime* number if its only positive divisors are 1 and n; otherwise, n is called a *composite* number. For example, the following are the prime numbers less than 20:

$$2, 3, 5, 7, 11, 13, 17, 19$$

If $n > 1$ is not prime, i.e., if n is composite, then n must have a divisor $k \neq 1$ such that $k \leq \sqrt{n}$ or, in other words, $k^2 \leq n$.

Suppose we want to find all the prime numbers less than a given number m, such as 30. This can be done by the "sieve method," which consists of the following steps. First list the 30 numbers:

$$1, 2, 3, 4, 5, 6, 7, 8, 9, 10, 11, 12, 13, 14, 15$$
$$16, 17, 18, 19, 20, 21, 22, 23, 24, 25, 26, 27, 28, 29, 30$$

Cross out 1 and the multiples of 2 from the list as follows:

$$\not{1}, 2, 3, \not{4}, 5, \not{6}, 7, \not{8}, 9, \not{10}, 11, \not{12}, 13, \not{14}, 15$$
$$\not{16}, 17, \not{18}, 19, \not{20}, 21, \not{22}, 23, \not{24}, 25, \not{26}, 27, \not{28}, 29, \not{30}$$

Since 3 is the first number following 2 that has not been eliminated, cross out the multiples of 3 from the list as follows:

$$\not{1}, 2, 3, \not{4}, 5, \not{6}, 7, \not{8}, \not{9}, \not{10}, 11, \not{12}, 13, \not{14}, \not{15}$$
$$\not{16}, 17, \not{18}, 19, \not{20}, \not{21}, \not{22}, 23, \not{24}, 25, \not{26}, \not{27}, \not{28}, 29, \not{30}$$

Since 5 is the first number following 3 that has not been eliminated, cross out the multiples of 5 from the list as follows:

$$\not{1}, 2, 3, \not{4}, 5, \not{6}, 7, \not{8}, \not{9}, \not{10}, 11, \not{12}, 13, \not{14}, \not{15}$$
$$\not{16}, 17, \not{18}, 19, \not{20}, \not{21}, \not{22}, 23, \not{24}, \not{25}, \not{26}, \not{27}, \not{28}, 29, \not{30}$$

Now 7 is the first number following 5 that has not been eliminated, but $7^2 > 30$. This means the algorithm is finished and the numbers left in the list are the primes less than 30:

$$2, 3, 5, 7, 11, 13, 17, 19, 23, 29$$

Translate the sieve method into an algorithm to find all prime numbers less than a given number n.

First define an array A such that

$$A[1] = 1, \quad A[2] = 2, \quad A[3] = 3, \quad A[4] = 4, \ldots, A[N-1] = N-1, \quad A[N] = N$$

We cross out an integer L from the list by assigning A[L] = 1. The following procedure CROSSOUT tests whether A[K] = 1, and if not, it sets

$$A[2K] = 1, \quad A[3K] = 1, \quad A[4K] = 1, \ldots$$

That is, it eliminates the multiples of K from the list

Procedure P2.9A: CROSSOUT(A, N, K)

```
    1.  If A[K] = 1, then: Return.
    2.  Repeat for L = 2K to N by K:
            Set A[L] := 1.
        [End of loop.]
    3.  Return.
```

The sieve method can now be simply written:

Algorithm P2.9B: This algorithm prints the prime numbers less than N.

    1. [Initialize array A.] Repeat for K = 1 to N:
          Set A[K] := K.
    2. [Eliminate multiples of K.] Repeat for K = 2 to $\sqrt{N}$.
          Call CROSSOUT(A, N, K).
    3. [Print the primes.] Repeat for K = 2 to N:
          If A[K] $\neq$ 1, then: Write: A[K].
    4. Exit.

2.10 Suppose $P(n) = a_0 + a_1 n + a_2 n^2 + \cdots + a_m n^m$; that is, suppose degree $P(n) = m$. Prove that $P(n) = O(n^m)$.

Let $b_0 = |a_0|$, $b_1 = |a_1|$, ..., $b_m = |a_m|$. Then, for $n \geq 1$,

$$P(n) \leq b_0 + b_1 n + b_2 n^2 + \cdots + b_m n^m = \left(\frac{b_0}{n^m} + \frac{b_1}{n^{m-1}} + \cdots + b_m \right) n^m$$
$$\leq (b_0 + b_1 + \cdots + b_m) n^m = M n^m$$

where $M = |a_0| + |a_1| + \cdots + |a_m|$. Hence $P(n) = O(n^m)$.
For example, $5x^3 + 3x = O(x^3)$ and $x^5 - 4\,000\,000 x^2 = O(x^5)$.

VARIABLES, DATA TYPES

2.11 Describe briefly the difference between local variables, parameters and global variables.

Local variables are variables which can be accessed only within a particular program or subprogram. Parameters are variables which are used to transfer data between a subprogram and its calling program. Global variables are variables which can be accessed by all of the program modules in a computer program. Each programming language which allows global variables has its own syntax for declaring them.

2.12 Suppose NUM denotes the number of records in a file. Describe the advantages in defining NUM to be a global variable. Describe the disadvantages in using global variables in general.

Many of the procedures will process all the records in the file using some type of loop. Since NUM will be the same for all these procedures, it would be advantageous to have NUM declared a global variable. Generally speaking, global and nonlocal variables may lead to errors caused by side effects, which may be difficult to detect.

2.13 Suppose a 32-bit memory location AAA contains the following sequence of bits:

        0100 1101   1100 0001   1110 1001   0101 1101

Determine the data stored in AAA.

There is no way of knowing the data stored in AAA unless one knows the data type of AAA. If AAA is a character variable and the EBCDIC code is used for storing data, then (AZ) is stored in AAA. If AAA is an integer variable, then the integer with the above binary representation is stored in AAA.

2.14 Mathematically speaking, integers may also be viewed as real numbers. Give some reasons for having two different data types.

The arithmetic for integers, which are stored using some type of binary representation, is much simpler than the arithmetic for real numbers, which are stored using some type of exponential form. Also, certain round-off errors occurring in real arithmetic do not occur in integer arithmetic.

Supplementary Problems

MATHEMATICAL NOTATION AND FUNCTIONS

2.15 Find (a) $\lfloor 3.4 \rfloor$, $\lfloor -3.4 \rfloor$, $\lfloor -7 \rfloor$, $\lfloor \sqrt{75} \rfloor$, $\lfloor \sqrt[3]{75} \rfloor$, $\lfloor e \rfloor$; (b) $\lceil 3.4 \rceil$, $\lceil -3.4 \rceil$, $\lceil -7 \rceil$, $\lceil \sqrt{75} \rceil$, $\lceil \sqrt[3]{75} \rceil$, $\lceil e \rceil$.

2.16 (a) Find 48 (mod 5), 48 (mod 7), 1397 (mod 11), 2468 (mod 9).

  (b) Find -48 (mod 5), -152 (mod 7), -358 (mod 11), -1326 (mod 13).

  (c) Using arithmetic modulo 13, evaluate

$$9 + 10, \qquad 8 + 12, \qquad 3 + 4, \qquad 3 - 4, \qquad 2 - 7, \qquad 5 - 8$$

2.17 Find (a) $|3 + 8|$, $|3 - 8|$, $|-3 + 8|$, $|-3 - 8|$; (b) 7!, 8!, 14!/12!, 15!/16!

2.18 Find (a) 3^{-4}, $4^{7/2}$, $27^{-2/3}$; (b) $\log_2 64$, $\log_{10} 0.001$, $\log_2 (1/8)$; (c) $\lfloor \lg 1\,000\,000 \rfloor$, $\lfloor \lg 0.001 \rfloor$.

ALGORITHMS, COMPLEXITY

2.19 Consider the complexity function $C(n)$ which measures the number of times LOC is updated in Step 3 of Algorithm 2.3. Find $C(n)$ for the average case when $n = 4$, assuming all arrangements of the given four elements are equally likely. (Compare with Prob. 2.6.)

2.20 Consider Procedure P2.8, which finds the location LOC1 of the largest element and the location LOC2 of the second largest element in an array DATA with $n > 1$ elements. Let $C(n)$ denote the number of comparisons during the execution of the procedure.

  (a) Find $C(n)$ for the best case.

  (b) Find $C(n)$ for the worst case.

  (c) Find $C(n)$ for the average case for $n = 4$, assuming all arrangements of the given elements in DATA are equally likely.

2.21 Repeat Prob. 2.20, except now let $C(n)$ denote the number of times the values of FIRST and SECOND (or LOC1 and LOC2) must be updated.

2.22 Suppose the running time of a Module A is a constant M. Find the order of magnitude of the complexity function $C(n)$ which measures the execution time of each of the following algorithms, where n is the size of the input data (denoted by N in the algorithms).

  (a) **Procedure P2.22A:** 1. Repeat for I = 1 to N:
  2.   Repeat for J = 1 to I:
  3.   Repeat for K = 1 to J:
  4.   Module A.
                  [End of Step 3 loop.]
              [End of Step 2 loop.]
          [End of Step 1 loop.]
  5. Exit.

  (b) **Procedure P2.22B:** 1. Set J := N.
  2. Repeat Steps 3 and 4 while J > 1.
  3.   Module A.
  4.   Set J := J/2.
          [End of Step 2 loop.]
  5. Return.

Programming Problems

2.23   Write a function subprogram DIV(J, K), where J and K are positive integers such that DIV(J, K) = 1 if J divides K but otherwise DIV(J, K) = 0. (For example, DIV(3, 15) = 1 but DIV(3, 16) = 0.)

2.24   Write a program using DIV(J, K) which reads a positive integer N > 10 and determines whether or not N is a prime number. (*Hint*: N is prime if (i) DIV(2, N) = 0 (i.e., N is odd) and (ii) DIV(K, N) = 0 for all odd integers K where $1 < K^2 \leq N$.)

2.25   Translate Procedure P2.8 into a computer program; i.e., write a program which finds the location LOC1 of the largest element and the location LOC2 of the second largest element in an array DATA with N > 1 elements. Test the program using 70, 30, 25, 80, 60, 50, 30, 75, 25, and 60.

2.26   Translate the sieve method for finding prime numbers, described in Prob. 2.9, into a program to find the prime numbers less than N. Test the program using (*a*) N = 1000 and (*b*) N = 10 000.

2.27   Let C denote the number of times LOC is updated using Algorithm 2.3 to find the largest element in an array A with N elements.

(*a*)   Write a subprogram COUNT(A, N, C) which finds C.

(*b*)   Write a Procedure P2.27 which (i) reads N random numbers between 0 and 1 into an array A and (ii) uses COUNT(A, N, C) to find the value of C.

(*c*)   Write a program which repeats Procedure P2.27 1000 times and finds the average of the 1000 C's.
   (i)   Test the program for N = 3 and compare the result with the value obtained in Prob. 2.6.
   (ii)   Test the program for N = 4 and compare the result with the value in Prob. 2.19.

Chapter 3

String Processing

3.1 INTRODUCTION

Historically, computers were first used for processing numerical data. Today, computers are frequently used for processing nonnumerical data, called *character data*. This chapter discusses how such data are stored and processed by the computer.

One of the primary applications of computers today is in the field of word processing. Such processing usually involves some type of pattern matching, as in checking to see if a particular word S appears in a given text T. We discuss this pattern matching problem in detail and, moreover, present two different pattern matching algorithms. The complexity of these algorithms is also investigated.

Computer terminology usually uses the term "string" for a sequence of characters rather than the term "word," since "word" has another meaning in computer science. For this reason, many texts sometimes use the expression "string processing," "string manipulation" or "text editing" instead of the expression "word processing."

The material in this chapter is essentially tangential and independent of the rest of the text. Accordingly, the reader or instructor may choose to omit this chapter on a first reading or cover this chapter at a later time.

3.2 BASIC TERMINOLOGY

Each programming language contains a *character set* that is used to communicate with the computer. This set usually includes the following:

Alphabet: A B C D E F G H I J K L M N O P Q R S T U V W X Y Z

Digits: 0 1 2 3 4 5 6 7 8 9

Special characters: + − / * ( ) , . $ = ' □

The set of special characters, which includes the blank space, frequently denoted by □, varies somewhat from one language to another.

A finite sequence S of zero or more characters is called a *string*. The number of characters in a string is called its *length*. The string with zero characters is called the *empty string* or the *null string*. Specific strings will be denoted by enclosing their characters in single quotation marks. The quotation marks will also serve as string delimiters. Hence

$$\text{'THE END'} \qquad \text{'TO BE OR NOT TO BE'} \qquad \text{' '}, \qquad \text{'□□'}$$

are strings with lengths 7, 18, 0 and 2, respectively. We emphasize that the blank space is a character and hence contributes to the length of the string. Sometimes the quotation marks may be omitted when the context indicates that the expression is a string.

Let S_1 and S_2 be strings. The string consisting of the characters of S_1 followed by the characters of S_2 is called the *concatenation* of S_1 and S_2; it will be denoted by $S_1 /\!/ S_2$. For example,

$$\text{'THE'} /\!/ \text{'END'} = \text{'THEEND'} \qquad \text{but} \qquad \text{'THE'} /\!/ \text{'□'} /\!/ \text{'END} = \text{'THE END'}$$

Clearly the length of $S_1 /\!/ S_2$ is equal to the sum of the lengths of the strings S_1 and S_2.

A string Y is called a *substring* of a string S if there exist strings X and Z such that

$$S = X /\!/ Y /\!/ Z$$

If X is an empty string, then Y is called an *initial substring* of S, and if Z is an empty string then Y is called a *terminal substring* of S. For example,

41

'BE OR NOT'   is a substring of   'TO BE OR NOT TO BE'
'THE'   is an initial substring of   'THE END'

Clearly, if Y is a substring of S, then the length of Y cannot exceed the length of S.

Remark: Characters are stored in the computer using either a 6-bit, a 7-bit or an 8-bit code. The unit equal to the number of bits needed to represent a character is called a *byte*. However, unless otherwise stated or implied, a byte usually means 8 bits. A computer which can access an individual byte is called a *byte-addressable machine*.

3.3 STORING STRINGS

Generally speaking, strings are stored in three types of structures: (1) fixed-length structures, (2) variable-length structures with fixed maximums and (3) linked structures. We discuss each type of structure separately, giving its advantages and disadvantages.

Record-Oriented, Fixed-Length Storage

In fixed-length storage each line of print is viewed as a record, where all records have the same length, i.e., where each record accommodates the same number of characters. Since data are frequently input on terminals with 80-column images or using 80-column cards, we will assume our records have length 80 unless otherwise stated or implied.

EXAMPLE 3.1

Suppose the input consists of the FORTRAN program in Fig. 3-1. Using a record-oriented, fixed-length storage medium, the input data will appear in memory as pictured in Fig. 3-2, where we assume that 200 is the address of the first character of the program.

The main advantages of the above way of storing strings are:

(1) The ease of accessing data from any given record

(2) The ease of updating data in any given record (as long as the length of the new data does not exceed the record length)

The main disadvantages are:

(1) Time is wasted reading an entire record if most of the storage consists of inessential blank spaces.

(2) Certain records may require more space than available.

(3) When the correction consists of more or fewer characters than the original text, changing a misspelled word requires the entire record to be changed.

```
C     PROGRAM PRINTING TWO INTEGERS IN INCREASING ORDER
      READ *, J, K
      IF(J.LE.K) THEN
          PRINT *, J, K
      ELSE
          PRINT *, K, J
      ENDIF
      STOP
      END
```

Fig. 3-1 Input data.

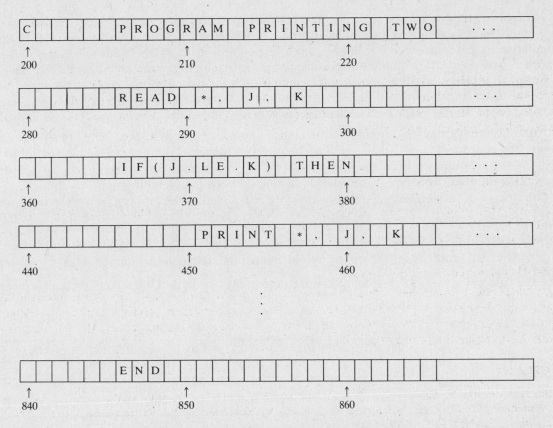

Fig. 3-2 Records stored sequentially in the computer.

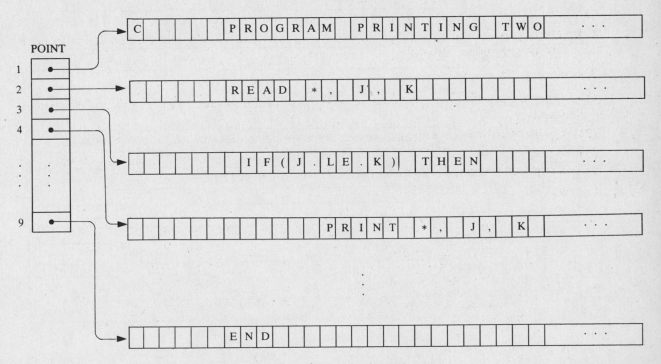

Fig. 3-3 Records stored using pointers.

Remark: Suppose we wanted to insert a new record in Example 3.1. This would require that all succeeding records be moved to new memory locations. However, this disadvantage can be easily remedied as indicated in Fig. 3-3. That is, one can use a linear array POINT which gives the address of each successive record, so that the records need not be stored in consecutive locations in memory. Accordingly, inserting a knew record will require only an updating of the array POINT.

Variable-Length Storage with Fixed Maximum

Although strings may be stored in fixed-length memory locations as above, there are advantages in knowing the actual length of each string. For example, one then does not have to read the entire record when the string occupies only the beginning part of the memory location. Also, certain string operations (discussed in Sec. 3.4) depend on having such variable-length strings.

The storage of variable-length strings in memory cells with fixed lengths can be done in two general ways:

(1)   One can use a marker, such as two dollar signs ($$), to signal the end of the string.

(2)   One can list the length of the string—as an additional item in the pointer array, for example.

Using the data in Fig. 3-1, the first method is pictured in Fig. 3-4(*a*) and the second method is pictured in Fig. 3-4(*b*).

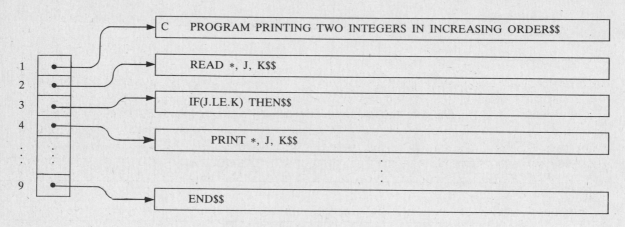

(*a*)   Records with sentinels.

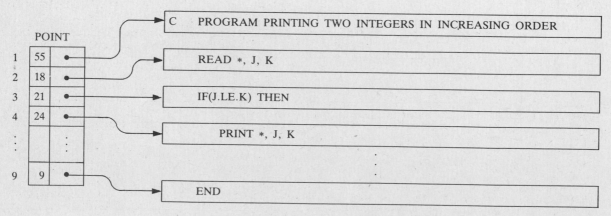

(*b*)   Records whose lengths are listed.

Fig. 3-4

Remark: One might be tempted to store strings one after another by using some separation marker, such as the two dollar signs ($$) in Fig. 3-5(*a*), or by using a pointer array giving the location of the strings, as in Fig. 3-5(*b*). These ways of storing strings will obviously save space and are sometimes used in secondary memory when records are relatively permanent and require little change. However, such methods of storage are usually inefficient when the strings and their lengths are frequently being changed.

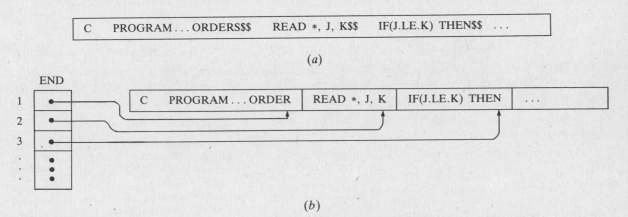

(*a*)

(*b*)

Fig. 3-5 Records stored one after another.

Linked Storage

Computers are being used very frequently today for word processing, i.e., for inputting, processing and outputting printed matter. Therefore, the computer must be able to correct and modify the printed matter, which usually means deleting, changing and inserting words, phrases, sentences and even paragraphs in the text. However, the fixed-length memory cells discussed above do not easily lend themselves to these operations. Accordingly, for most extensive word processing applications, strings are stored by means of linked lists. Such linked lists, and the way data are inserted and deleted in them, are discussed in detail in Chap. 5. Here we simply look at the way strings appear in these data structures.

By a (one-way) linked list, we mean a linearly ordered sequence of memory cells, called *nodes*, where each node contains an item, called a *link*, which points to the next node in the list (i.e., which contains the address of the next node). Figure 3-6 is a schematic diagram of such a linked list.

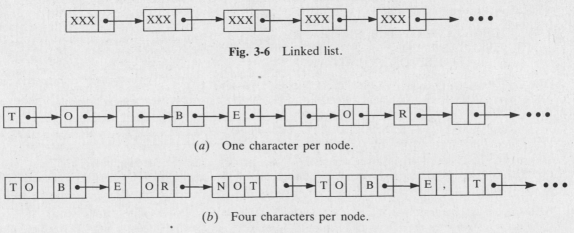

Fig. 3-6 Linked list.

(*a*) One character per node.

(*b*) Four characters per node.

Fig. 3-7

Strings may be stored in linked lists as follows. Each memory cell is assigned one character or a fixed number of characters, and a link contained in the cell gives the address of the cell containing the next character or group of characters in the string. For example, consider this famous quotation:

To be or not to be, that is the question.

Figure 3-7(a) shows how the string would appear in memory with one character per node, and Fig. 3-7(b) shows how it would appear with four characters per node.

3.4 CHARACTER DATA TYPE

This section gives an overview of the way various programming languages handle the *character* data type. As noted in the preceding chapter (in Sec. 2.7), each data type has its own formula for decoding a sequence of bits in memory.

Constants

Many programming languages denote string constants by placing the string in either single or double quotation marks. For example,

'THE END'   and   'TO BE OR NOT TO BE'

are string constants of lengths 7 and 18 characters respectively. Our algorithms will also define character constants in this way.

Variables

Each programming language has its own rules for forming character variables. However, such variables fall into one of three categories: static, semistatic and dynamic. By a *static* character variable, we mean a variable whose length is defined before the program is executed and cannot change throughout the program. By a *semistatic* character variable, we mean a variable whose length may vary during the execution of the program as long as the length does not exceed a maximum value determined by the program before the program is executed. By a *dynamic* character variable, we mean a variable whose length can change during the execution of the program. These three categories correspond, respectively, to the ways the strings are stored in the memory of the computer as discussed in the preceding section.

EXAMPLE 3.2

(a) Many versions of FORTRAN use static CHARACTER variables. For example, consider the following FORTRAN program segment:

```
CHARACTER ST1*10, ST2*14
ST1 = 'THE END'
ST2 = 'TO BE OR NOT TO BE'
```

The first statement declares ST1 and ST2 to be CHARACTER variables with lengths 10 and 14, respectively. After both assignment statements are executed, ST1 and ST2 will appear in memory as follows:

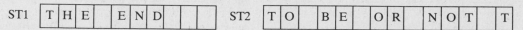

That is, a string is stored left-justified in memory. Either blank spaces are added on the right of the string, or the string is truncated on the right, depending on whether the length of the string is less than or exceeds the length of the memory location.

(b) BASIC defines character variables as those variables whose name ends with a dollar sign. Generally speaking, the variables are semistatic ones whose lengths cannot exceed a fixed bound. For example, the BASIC program segment

A$ = ''THE BEGINNING''
B$ = ''THE END''

defines A$ and B$ to be character variables. When the segment is executed, the lengths of A$ and B$ will be 13 and 7, respectively.

Also, BASIC uses double quotation marks to denote string constants.

(c) SNOBOL uses dynamic character variables. For example, the SNOBOL program segment

WORD = 'COMPUTER'
TEXT = 'IN THE BEGINNING'

defines WORD and TEXT as character variables. When the segment is executed, the lengths of WORD and TEXT will be 8 and 16, respectively. However, the lengths may change later in the program.

(d) PL/1 uses both static and semistatic CHARACTER variables. For example, the PL/1 statement

DECLARE NAME CHARACTER(20),
        WORD CHARACTER(15) VARYING;

designates NAME as a static CHARACTER variable of length 20 and designates WORD as a semistatic CHARACTER variable whose length may vary but may not exceed 15.

(e) In Pascal, a character variable (abbreviated CHAR) can represent only a single character, and hence a string is represented by a linear array of characters. For example,

VAR WORD: ARRAY[1 .. 20] OF CHAR

declares WORD to be a string of 20 characters. Furthermore, WORD[1] is the first character of the string, WORD[2] the second character and so on. In particular, CHAR arrays have fixed lengths and hence are static variables.

3.5 STRING OPERATIONS

Although a string may be viewed simply as a sequence or linear array of characters, there is a fundamental difference in use between strings and other types of arrays. Specifically, groups of consecutive elements in a string (such as words, phrases and sentences), called *substrings*, may be units unto themselves. Furthermore, the basic units of access in a string are usually these substrings, not individual characters.

Consider, for example, the string

'TO BE OR NOT TO BE'

We may view the string as the 18-character sequence T, O, □, B, . . . , E. However, the substrings TO, BE, OR, . . . have their own meaning.

On the other hand, consider an 18-element linear array of 18 integers,

4, 8, 6, 15, 9, 5, 4, 13, 8, 5, 11, 9, 9, 13, 7, 10, 6, 11

The basic unit of access in such an array is usually an individual element. Groups of consecutive elements normally do not have any special meaning.

For the above reason, various string operations have been developed which are not normally used with other kinds of arrays. This section discusses these string-oriented operations. The next section shows how these operations are used in word processing. (Unless otherwise stated or implied, we assume our character-type variables are dynamic and have a variable length determined by the context in which the variable is used.)

Substring

Accessing a substring from a given string requires three pieces of information: (1) the name of the string or the string itself, (2) the position of the first character of the substring in the given string and

(3) the length of the substring or the position of the last character of the substring. We call this operation SUBSTRING. Specifically, we write

$$\text{SUBSTRING(string, initial, length)}$$

to denote the substring of a string S beginning in a position K and having a length L.

EXAMPLE 3.3

(*a*)   Using the above function we have:

$$\text{SUBSTRING('TO BE OR NOT TO BE', 4, 7)} = \text{'BE OR N'}$$
$$\text{SUBSTRING('THE END', 4, 4)} = \text{'□END'}$$

(*b*)   Our function SUBSTRING(S, 4, 7) is denoted in some programming languages as follows:

PL/1:	SUBSTR(S, 4, 7)
FORTRAN 77:	S(4:10)
UCSD Pascal:	COPY(S, 4, 7)
BASIC:	MID$(S, 4, 7)

Indexing

Indexing, also called *pattern matching*, refers to finding the position where a string pattern P first appears in a given string text T. We call this operation INDEX and write

$$\text{INDEX(text, pattern)}$$

If the pattern P does not appear in the text T, then INDEX is assigned the value 0. The arguments "text" and "pattern" can be either string constants or string variables.

EXAMPLE 3.4

(*a*)   Suppose T contains the text

$$\text{'HIS FATHER IS THE PROFESSOR'}$$

Then,

$$\text{INDEX(T, 'THE')}, \quad \text{INDEX(T, 'THEN')} \quad \text{and} \quad \text{INDEX(T, '□THE□')}$$

have the values 7, 0 and 14, respectively.

(*b*)   The function INDEX(text, pattern) is denoted in some of the programming languages as follows:

PL/1:	INDEX(text, pattern)
UCSD Pascal:	POS(pattern, text)

Observe the reverse order of the arguments in UCSD Pascal.

Concatenation

Let S_1 and S_2 be strings. Recall (Sec. 3.2) that the *concatenation* of S_1 and S_2, which we denote by $S_1 /\!/ S_2$, is the string consisting of the characters of S_1 followed by the characters of S_2.

EXAMPLE 3.5

(*a*)   Suppose $S_1 = \text{'MARK'}$ and $S_2 = \text{'TWAIN'}$. Then:

$$S_1 /\!/ S_2 = \text{'MARKTWAIN'} \quad \text{but} \quad S_1 /\!/ \text{'□'} /\!/ S_2 = \text{'MARK TWAIN'}$$

(b)   Concatenation is denoted in some programming languages as follows:

PL/1:	$S_1 \| S_2$
FORTRAN 77:	$S_1 /\!/ S_2$
BASIC:	$S_1 + S_2$
SNOBOL:	$S_1 \, S_2$ (juxtaposition with a blank space between S_1 and S_2)

Length

The number of characters in a string is called its length. We will write

$$\text{LENGTH(string)}$$

for the length of a given string. Thus

$$\text{LENGTH(}\,'\text{COMPUTER}\,') = 8 \qquad \text{LENGTH(}\,'\square'\,) = 0 \qquad \text{LENGTH(}\,''\,) = 0$$

Some of the programming languages denote this function as follows:

PL/1:	LENGTH(string)
BASIC:	LEN(string)
UCSD Pascal:	LENGTH(string)
SNOBOL:	SIZE(string)

FORTRAN and standard Pascal, which use fixed-length string variables, do not have any built-in LENGTH functions for strings. However, such variables may be viewed as having variable length if one ignores all trailing blanks. Accordingly, one could write a subprogram LENGTH in these languages so that

$$\text{LENGTH(}\,'\text{MARC}\ \ '\,) = 4$$

In fact, SNOBOL has a built-in string function TRIM which omits trailing blanks:

$$\text{TRIM(}\,'\text{ERIK}\ \ '\,) = \,'\text{ERIK}\,'$$

This TRIM function is occasionally used in our algorithms.

3.6   WORD PROCESSING

In earlier times, character data processed by the computer consisted mainly of data items, such as names and addresses. Today the computer also processes printed matter, such as letters, articles and reports. It is in this latter context that we use the term "word processing."

Given some printed text, the operations usually associated with word processing are the following:

(a)   *Replacement*. Replacing one string in the text by another.

(b)   *Insertion*. Inserting a string in the middle of the text.

(c)   *Deletion*. Deleting a string from the text.

The above operations can be executed by using the string operations discussed in the preceding section. This we show below when we discuss each operation separately. Many of these operations are built into or can easily be defined in each of the programming languages that we have cited.

Insertion

Suppose in a given text T we want to insert a string S so that S begins in position K. We denote this operation by

$$\text{INSERT(text, position, string)}$$

For example,

$$\text{INSERT}('\text{ABCDEFG}', 3, '\text{XYZ}') = '\text{ABXYZCDEFG}'$$
$$\text{INSERT}('\text{ABCDEFG}', 6, '\text{XYZ}') = '\text{ABCDEXYZFG}'$$

This INSERT function can be implemented by using the string operations defined in the previous section as follows:

$$\text{INSERT}(T, K, S) = \text{SUBSTRING}(T, 1, K - 1) /\!/ S /\!/ \text{SUBSTRING}(T, K, \text{LENGTH}(T) - K + 1)$$

That is, the initial substring of T before the position K, which has length $K - 1$, is concatenated with the string S, and the result is concatenated with the remaining part of T, which begins in position K and has length $\text{LENGTH}(T) - (K - 1) = \text{LENGTH}(T) - K + 1$. (We are assuming implicitly that T is a dynamic variable and that the size of T will not become too large.)

Deletion

Suppose in a given text T we want to delete the substring which begins in position K and has length L. We denote this operation by

$$\text{DELETE}(\text{text, position, length})$$

For example,

$$\text{DELETE}('\text{ABCDEFG}', 4, 2) = '\text{ABCFG}'$$
$$\text{DELETE}('\text{ABCDEFG}', 2, 4) = '\text{AFG}'$$

We assume that nothing is deleted if position $K = 0$. Thus

$$\text{DELETE}('\text{ABCDEFG}', 0, 2) = '\text{ABCDEFG}'$$

The importance of this "zero case" is seen later.

The DELETE function can be implemented using the string operations given in the preceding section as follows:

$$\text{DELETE}(T, K, L) =$$
$$\text{SUBSTRING}(T, 1, K - 1) /\!/ \text{SUBSTRING}(T, K + L, \text{LENGTH}(T) - K - L + 1)$$

That is, the initial substring of T before position K is concatenated with the terminal substring of T beginning in position $K + L$. The length of the initial substring is $K - 1$, and the length of the terminal substring is:

$$\text{LENGTH}(T) - (K + L - 1) = \text{LENGTH}(T) - K - L + 1$$

We also assume that $\text{DELETE}(T, K, L) = T$ when $K = 0$.

Now suppose text T and pattern P are given and we want to delete from T the first occurrence of the pattern P. This can be accomplished by using the above DELETE function as follows:

$$\text{DELETE}(T, \text{INDEX}(T, P), \text{LENGTH}(P))$$

That is, in the text T, we first compute $\text{INDEX}(T, P)$, the position where P first occurs in T, and then we compute $\text{LENGTH}(P)$, the number of characters in P. Recall that when $\text{INDEX}(T, P) = 0$ (i.e., when P does not occur in T) the text T is not changed.

EXAMPLE 3.6

(a) Suppose $T = '\text{ABCDEFG}'$ and $P = '\text{CD}'$. Then $\text{INDEX}(T, P) = 3$ and $\text{LENGTH}(P) = 2$. Hence

$$\text{DELETE}('\text{ABCDEFG}', 3, 2) = '\text{ABEFG}'$$

(b) Suppose T = 'ABCDEFG' and P = 'DC'. Then INDEX(T, P) = 0 and LENGTH(P) = 2. Hence, by the "zero case,"

$$\text{DELETE('ABCDEFG', 0, 2) = 'ABCDEFG'}$$

as expected.

Suppose after reading into the computer a text T and a pattern P, we want to delete every occurrence of the pattern P in the text T. This can be accomplished by repeatedly applying

$$\text{DELETE(T, INDEX(T, P), LENGTH(P))}$$

until INDEX(T, P) = 0 (i.e., until P does not appear in T). An algorithm which accomplishes this follows.

Algorithm 3.1: A text T and a pattern P are in memory. This algorithm deletes every occurrence of P in T.
1. [Find index of P.] Set K := INDEX(T, P).
2. Repeat while K ≠ 0:
    (a) [Delete P from T.]
         Set T := DELETE(T, INDEX(T, P), LENGTH(P))
    (b) [Update index.] Set K := INDEX(T, P).
    [End of loop.]
3. Write: T.
4. Exit.

We emphasize that after each deletion, the length of T decreases and hence the algorithm must stop. However, the number of times the loop is executed may exceed the number of times P appears in the original text T, as illustrated in the following example.

EXAMPLE 3.7

(a) Suppose Algorithm 3.1 is run with the data

$$T = XABYABZ, \qquad P = AB$$

Then the loop in the algorithm will be executed twice. During the first execution, the first occurrence of AB in T is deleted, with the result that T = XYABZ. During the second execution, the remaining occurrence of AB in T is deleted, so that T = XYZ. Accordingly, XYZ is the output.

(b) Suppose Algorithm 3.1 is run with the data

$$T = XAAABBBY, \qquad P = AB$$

Observe that the pattern AB occurs only once in T but the loop in the algorithm will be executed three times. Specifically, after AB is deleted the first time from T we have T = XAABBY, and hence AB appears again in T. After AB is deleted a second time from T, we see that T = XABY and AB still occurs in T. Finally, after AB is deleted a third time from T, we have T = XY and AB does not appear in T, and thus INDEX(T, P) = 0. Hence XY is the output.

The above example shows that when a text T is changed by a deletion, patterns may occur that did not appear originally.

Replacement

Suppose in a given text T we want to replace the first occurrence of a pattern P_1 by a pattern P_2. We will denote this operation by

$$\text{REPLACE(text, pattern}_1\text{, pattern}_2\text{)}$$

For example

$$\text{REPLACE}('\text{XABYABZ}', '\text{AB}', '\text{C}') = '\text{XCYABZ}'$$
$$\text{REPLACE}('\text{XABYABZ}', '\text{BA}', '\text{C}') = '\text{XABYABZ}'$$

In the second case, the pattern BA does not occur, and hence there is no change.

We note that this REPLACE function can be expressed as a deletion followed by an insertion if we use the preceding DELETE and INSERT functions. Specifically, the REPLACE function can be executed by using the following three steps:

$$K := \text{INDEX}(T, P_1)$$
$$T := \text{DELETE}(T, K, \text{LENGTH}(P_1))$$
$$\text{INSERT}(T, K, P_2)$$

The first two steps delete P_1 from T, and the third step inserts P_2 in the position K from which P_1 was deleted.

Suppose a text T and patterns P and Q are in the memory of a computer. Suppose we want to replace every occurrence of the pattern P in T by the pattern Q. This might be accomplished by repeatedly applying

$$\text{REPLACE}(T, P, Q)$$

until INDEX(T, P) = 0 (i.e., until P does not appear in T). An algorithm which does this follows.

Algorithm 3.2: A text T and patterns P and Q are in memory. This algorithm replaces every occurrence of P in T by Q.
1. [Find index of P.] Set K := INDEX(T, P).
2. Repeat while K ≠ 0:
   - (a) [Replace P by Q.] Set T := REPLACE(T, P, Q).
   - (b) [Update index.] Set K := INDEX(T, P).
   [End of loop.]
3. Write: T.
4. Exit.

Warning: Although this algorithm looks very much like Algorithm 3.1, there is no guarantee that this algorithm will terminate. This fact is illustrated in Example 3.8(*b*). On the other hand, suppose the length of Q is smaller than the length of P. Then the length of T after each replacement decreases. This guarantees that in this special case where Q is smaller than P the algorithm must terminate.

EXAMPLE 3.8

(*a*) Suppose Algorithm 3.2 is run with the data

$$T = \text{XABYABZ}, \qquad P = \text{AB}, \qquad Q = \text{C}$$

Then the loop in the algorithm will be executed twice. During the first execution, the first occurrence of AB in T is replaced by C to yield T = XCYABZ. During the second execution, the remaining AB in T is replaced by C to yield T = XCYCZ. Hence XCYCZ is the output.

(*b*) Suppose Algorithm 3.2 is run with the data

$$T = \text{XAY}, \qquad P = \text{A}, \qquad Q = \text{AB}$$

Then the algorithm will never terminate. The reason for this is that P will always occur in the text T, no matter how many times the loop is executed. Specifically,

$T = XABY$ at the end of the first execution of the loop

$T = XAB^2Y$ at the end of the second execution of the loop

. . . .

$T = XAB^nY$ at the end of the nth execution of the loop

(The infinite loop arises here since P is a substring of Q.)

3.7 PATTERN MATCHING ALGORITHMS

Pattern matching is the problem of deciding whether or not a given string pattern P appears in a string text T. We assume that the length of P does not exceed the length of T. This section discusses two pattern matching algorithms. We also discuss the complexity of the algorithms so we can compare their efficiencies.

Remark: During the discussion of pattern matching algorithms, characters are sometimes denoted by lowercase letters (a, b, c, . . .) and exponents may be used to denote repetition; e.g.,

$$a^2b^3ab^2 \text{ for } aabbbabb \quad \text{and} \quad (cd)^3 \text{ for } cdcdcd$$

In addition, the empty string may be denoted by Λ, the Greek letter lambda, and the concatenation of strings X and Y may be denoted by $X \cdot Y$ or, simply, XY.

First Pattern Matching Algorithm

The first pattern matching algorithm is the obvious one in which we compare a given pattern P with each of the substrings of T, moving from left to right, until we get a match. In detail, let

$$W_K = \text{SUBSTRING}(T, K, \text{LENGTH}(P))$$

That is, let W_K denote the substring of T having the same length as P and beginning with the Kth character of T. First we compare P, character by character, with the first substring, W_1. If all the characters are the same, then $P = W_1$ and so P appears in T and $\text{INDEX}(T, P) = 1$. On the other hand, suppose we find that some character of P is not the same as the corresponding character of W_1. Then $P \neq W_1$ and we can immediately move on to the next substring, W_2. That is, we next compare P with W_2. If $P \neq W_2$, then we compare P with W_3, and so on. The process stops (*a*) when we find a match of P with some substring W_K and so P appears in T and $\text{INDEX}(T, P) = K$, or (*b*) when we exhaust all the W_K's with no match and hence P does not appear in T. The maximum value MAX of the subscript K is equal to $\text{LENGTH}(T) - \text{LENGTH}(P) + 1$.

Let us assume, as an illustration, that P is a 4-character string and that T is a 20-character string, and that P and T appear in memory as linear arrays with one character per element. That is,

$$P = P[1]P[2]P[3]P[4] \quad \text{and} \quad T = T[1]T[2]T[3] \cdots T[19]T[20]$$

Then P is compared with each of the following 4-character substrings of T:

$$W_1 = T[1]T[2]T[3]T[4], \quad W_2 = T[2]T[3]T[4]T[5], \quad \ldots, \quad W_{17} = T[17]T[18]T[19]T[20]$$

Note that there are $\text{MAX} = 20 - 4 + 1 = 17$ such substrings of T.

A formal presentation of our algorithm, where P is an r-character string and T is an s-character string, is shown in Algorithm 3.3.

Observe that Algorithm 3.3 contains two loops, one inside the other. The outer loop runs through each successive R-character substring

$$W_K = T[K]T[K + 1] \cdots T[K + R - 1]$$

of T. The inner loop compares P with W_K, character by character. If any character does not match, then control transfers to Step 5, which increases K and then leads to the next substring of T. If all the R

Algorithm 3.3:   (Pattern Matching) P and T are strings with lengths R and S, respectively, and
are stored as arrays with one character per element. This algorithm finds the
INDEX of P in T.
1.   [Initialize.] Set $K := 1$ and $MAX := S - R + 1$.
2.   Repeat Steps 3 to 5 while $K \leq MAX$:
3.   Repeat for $L = 1$ to R: [Tests each character of P.]
               If $P[L] \neq T[K + L - 1]$, then: Go to Step 5.
             [End of inner loop.]
4.   [Success.] Set $INDEX = K$, and Exit.
5.   Set $K := K + 1$.
           [End of Step 2 outer loop.]
6.   [Failure.] Set $INDEX = 0$.
7.   Exit.

---

characters of P do match those of some W_K, then P appears in T and K is the INDEX of P in T. On the
other hand, if the outer loop completes all of its cycles, then P does not appear in T and so $INDEX = 0$.

The complexity of this pattern matching algorithm is measured by the number C of comparisons
between characters in the pattern P and characters of the text T. In order to find C, we let N_k denote
the number of comparisons that take place in the inner loop when P is compared with W_K. Then

$$C = N_1 + N_2 + \cdots + N_L$$

where L is the position L in T where P first appears or $L = MAX$ if P does not appear in T. The next
example computes C for some specific P and T where $LENGTH(P) = 4$ and $LENGTH(T) = 20$ and so
$MAX = 20 - 4 + 1 = 17$.

EXAMPLE 3.9

(a) Suppose P = *aaba* and T = *cdcd* $\cdots$ *cd* = $(cd)^{10}$. Clearly P does not occur in T. Also, for each of the 17 cycles,
$N_k = 1$, since the first character of P does not match W_K. Hence

$$C = 1 + 1 + 1 + \cdots + 1 = 17$$

(b) Suppose P = *aaba* and T = *ababaaba*. . . . Observe that P is a substring of T. In fact, P = W_5 and so $N_5 = 4$.
Also, comparing P with W_1 = *abab*, we see that $N_1 = 2$, since the first letters do match; but comparing P with
W_2 = *baba*, we see that $N_2 = 1$, since the first letters do not match. Similarly, $N_3 = 2$ and $N_4 = 1$.
Accordingly,

$$C = 2 + 1 + 2 + 1 + 4 = 10$$

(c) Suppose P = *aaab* and T = *aa* $\cdots$ *a* = a^{20}. Here P does not appear in T. Also, every W_K = *aaaa*; hence every
$N_k = 4$, since the first three letters of P do match. Accordingly,

$$C = 4 + 4 + \cdots + 4 = 17 \cdot 4 = 68$$

In general, when P is an r-character string and T is an s-character string, the data size for the
algorithm is

$$n = r + s$$

The worst case occurs when every character of P except the last matches every substring W_K, as in
Example 3.9(c). In this case, $C(n) = r(s - r + 1)$. For fixed n, we have $s = n - r$, so that

$$C(n) = r(n - 2r + 1)$$

The maximum value of $C(n)$ occurs when $r = (n + 1)/4$. (See Prob. 3.19.) Accordingly, substituting
this value for r in the formula for $C(n)$ yields

$$C(n) = \frac{(n+1)^2}{8} = O(n^2)$$

The complexity of the average case in any actual situation depends on certain probabilities which are usually unknown. When the characters of P and T are randomly selected from some finite alphabet, the complexity of the average case is still not easy to analyze, but the complexity of the average case is still a factor of the worst case. Accordingly, we shall state the following: *The complexity of this pattern matching algorithm is equal to* $O(n^2)$. In other words, the time required to execute this algorithm is proportional to n^2. (Compare this result with the one on page 57.)

Second Pattern Matching Algorithm

The second pattern matching algorithm uses a table which is derived from a particular pattern P but is independent of the text T. For definiteness, suppose

$$P = aaba$$

First we give the reason for the table entries and how they are used. Suppose $T = T_1 T_2 T_3 \ldots$, where T_I denotes the *i*th character of T; and suppose the first two characters of T match those of P; i.e., suppose $T = aa. \ldots$ Then T has one of the following three forms:

(i) $T = aab \ldots$,   (ii) $T = aaa \ldots$,   (iii) $T = aax$

where x is any character different from a or b. Suppose we read T_3 and find that $T_3 = b$. Then we next read T_4 to see if $T_4 = a$, which will give a match of P with W_1. On the other hand, suppose $T_3 = a$. Then we know that $P \neq W_1$; but we also know that $W_2 = aa. \ldots$, i.e., that the first two characters of the substring W_2 match those of P. Hence we next read T_4 to see if $T_4 = b$. Last, suppose $T_3 = x$. Then we know that $P \neq W_1$, but we also know that $P \neq W_2$ and $P \neq W_3$, since x does not appear in P. Hence we next read T_4 to see if $T_4 = a$, i.e., to see if the first character of W_4 matches the first character of P.

There are two important points to the above procedure. First, when we read T_3 we need only compare T_3 with those characters which appear in P. If none of these match, then we are in the last case, of a character x which does not appear in P. Second, after reading and checking T_3, we next read T_4; we do not have to go back again in the text T.

Figure 3-8(*a*) contains the table that is used in our second pattern matching algorithm for the pattern P = *aaba*. (In both the table and the accompanying graph, the pattern P and its substrings Q

	a	b	x
Q_0	Q_1	Q_0	Q_0
Q_1	Q_2	Q_0	Q_0
Q_2	Q_2	Q_3	Q_0
Q_3	P	Q_0	Q_0

(*a*) Pattern matching table.

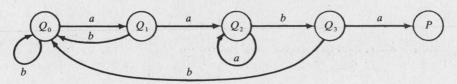

(*b*) Pattern matching graph.

Fig. 3-8

will be represented by italic capital letters.) The table is obtained as follows. First of all, we let Q_i denote the initial substring of P of length i; hence

$$Q_0 = \Lambda, \qquad Q_1 = a, \qquad Q_2 = a^2, \qquad Q_3 = a^2b, \qquad Q_4 = a^2ba = P$$

(Here $Q_0 = \Lambda$ is the empty string.) The rows of the table are labeled by these initial substrings of P, excluding P itself. The columns of the table are labeled a, b and x, where x represents any character that doesn't appear in the pattern P. Let f be the function determined by the table; i.e., let

$$f(Q_i, t)$$

denote the entry in the table in row Q_i and column t (where t is any character). This entry $f(Q_i, t)$ is defined to be the largest Q that appears as a terminal substring in the string Q_it, the concatenation of Q_i and t. For example,

a^2 is the largest Q that is a terminal substring of $Q_2a = a^3$, so $f(Q_2, a) = Q_2$

Λ is the largest Q that is a terminal substring of $Q_1b = ab$, so $f(Q_1, b) = Q_0$

a is the largest Q that is a terminal substring of $Q_0a = a$, so $f(Q_0, a) = Q_1$

Λ is the largest Q that is a terminal substring of $Q_3x = a^2bx$, so $f(Q_3, x) = Q_0$

and so on. Although $Q_1 = a$ is a terminal substring of $Q_2a = a^3$, we have $f(Q_2, a) = Q_2$ because Q_2 is also a terminal substring of $Q_2a = a^3$ and Q_2 is larger than Q_1. We note that $f(Q_i, x) = Q_0$ for any Q, since x does not appear in the pattern P. Accordingly, the column corresponding to x is usually omitted from the table.

Our table can also be pictured by the labeled directed graph in Fig. 3-8(b). The graph is obtained as follows. First, there is a node in the graph corresponding to each initial substring Q_i of P. The Q's are called the *states* of the system, and Q_0 is called the *initial* state. Second, there is an arrow (a directed edge) in the graph corresponding to each entry in the table. Specifically, if

$$f(Q_i, t) = Q_j$$

then there is an arrow labeled by the character t from Q_i to Q_j. For example, $f(Q_2, b) = Q_3$, so there is an arrow labeled b from Q_2 to Q_3. For notational convenience, we have omitted all arrows labeled x, which must lead to the initial state Q_0.

We are now ready to give the second pattern matching algorithm for the pattern P = *aaba*. (Note that in the following discussion capital letters will be used for all single-letter variable names that appear in the algorithm.) Let $T = T_1T_2T_3 \cdots T_N$ denote the n-character-string text which is searched for the pattern P. Beginning with the initial state Q_0 and using the text T, we will obtain a sequence of states $S_1, S_2, S_3, \ldots$ as follows. We let $S_1 = Q_0$ and we read the first character T_1. From either the table or the graph in Fig. 3-8, the pair (S_1, T_1) yields a second state S_2; that is, $F(S_1, T_1) = S_2$. We read the next character T_2. The pair (S_2, T_2) yields a state S_3, and so on. There are two possibilities:

(1)   Some state $S_K = P$, the desired pattern. In this case, P does appear in T and its index is K − LENGTH(P).

(2)   No state $S_1, S_2, \ldots, S_{N+1}$ is equal to P. In this case, P does not appear in T.

We illustrate the algorithm with two different texts using the pattern P = *aaba*.

EXAMPLE 3.10

(a)   Suppose T = *aabcaba*. Beginning with Q_0, we use the characters of T and the graph (or table) in Fig. 3-8 to obtain the following sequence of states:

$$Q_0 \xrightarrow{Ca} Q_1 \xrightarrow{Ca} Q_2 \xrightarrow{Cb} Q_3 \xrightarrow{Cc} Q_0 \xrightarrow{Ca} Q_1 \xrightarrow{Cb} Q_0 \xrightarrow{Ca} Q_1$$

We do not obtain the state P, so P does not appear in T.

(b)   Suppose T = *abcaabaca*. Then we obtain the following sequence of states:

$$Q_0 \xrightarrow{Ca} Q_1 \xrightarrow{Cb} Q_0 \xrightarrow{Cc} Q_0 \xrightarrow{Ca} Q_1 \xrightarrow{Ca} Q_2 \xrightarrow{Cb} Q_3 \xrightarrow{Ca} P$$

Here we obtain the pattern P as the state S_8. Hence P does appear in T and its index is $8 - \text{LENGTH}(P) = 4$.

The formal statement of our second pattern matching algorithm follows:

Algorithm 3.4: (Pattern Matching). The pattern matching table $F(Q_1, T)$ of a pattern P is in memory, and the input is an N-character string $T = T_1 T_2 \cdots T_N$. This algorithm finds the INDEX of P in T.

1. [Initialize.] Set $K := 1$ and $S_1 = Q_0$.
2. Repeat Steps 3 to 5 while $S_K \neq P$ and $K \leq N$.
3.   Read T_K.
4.   Set $S_{K+1} := F(S_K, T_K)$. [Finds next state.]
5.   Set $K := K + 1$. [Updates counter.]
   [End of Step 2 loop.]
6. [Successful?]
      If $S_K = P$, then:
           INDEX $= K - \text{LENGTH}(P)$.
      Else:
           INDEX $= 0$.
      [End of If structure.]
7. Exit.

The running time of the above algorithm is proportional to the number of times the Step 2 loop is executed. The worst case occurs when all of the text T is read, i.e., when the loop is executed $n = \text{LENGTH}(T)$ times. Accordingly, we can state the following: *The complexity of this pattern matching algorithm is equal to $O(n)$.*

Remark: A combinatorial problem is said to be *solvable in polynomial time* if there is an algorithmic solution with complexity equal to $O(n^m)$ for some m, and it is said to be *solvable in linear time* if there is an algorithmic solution with complexity equal to $O(n)$, where n is the size of the data. Thus the second of the two pattern matching algorithms described in this section is solvable in linear time. (The first pattern matching algorithm was solvable in polynomial time.)

Solved Problems

TERMINOLOGY; STORAGE OF STRINGS

3.1 Let W be the string ABCD. (*a*) Find the length of W. (*b*) List all substrings of W. (*c*) List all the initial substrings of W.

(*a*) The number of characters in W is its length, so 4 is the length of W.

(*b*) Any subsequence of characters of W is a substring of W. There are 11 such substrings:

Substrings:	ABCD,	ABC, BCD,	AB, BC, CD,	A, B, C, D,	Λ
Lengths:	4	3	2	1	0

(Here Λ denotes the empty string.)

(*c*) The initial substrings are ABCD, ABC, AB, A, Λ; that is, both the empty string and those substrings that begin with A.

3.2   Assuming a programming language uses at least 48 characters—26 letters, 10 digits and a minimum of 12 special characters—give the minimum number and the usual number of bits to represent a character in the memory of the computer.

Since $2^5 < 48 < 2^6$, one requires at least a 6-bit code to represent 48 characters. Usually a computer uses a 7-bit code, such as ASCII, or an 8-bit code, such as EBCDIC, to represent characters. This allows many more special characters to be represented and processed by the computer.

3.3   Describe briefly the three types of structures used for storing strings.

(*a*)   Fixed-length-storage structures. Here strings are stored in memory cells that are all of the same length, usually space for 80 characters.

(*b*)   Variable-length storage with fixed maximums. Here strings are also stored in memory cells all of the same length; however, one also knows the actual length of the string in the cell.

(*c*)   Linked-list storage. Here each cell is divided into two parts; the first part stores a single character (or a fixed small number of characters), and the second part contains the address of the cell containing the next character.

3.4   Find the string stored in Fig. 3-9, assuming the link value 0 signals the end of the list.

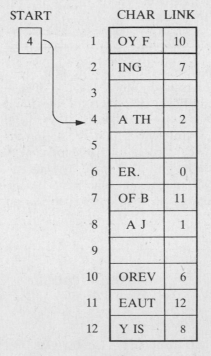

Fig. 3-9

Here the string is stored in a linked-list structure with 4 characters per node. The value of START gives the location of the first node in the list:

$$4 \quad \boxed{\text{A TH} \quad 2}$$

The link value in this node gives the location of the next node in the list:

$$2 \quad \boxed{\text{ING} \quad 7}$$

Continuing in this manner, we obtain the following sequence of nodes:

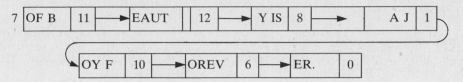

Thus the string is:

A THING OF BEAUTY IS A JOY FOREVER.

3.5 Give some (*a*) advantages and (*b*) disadvantages of using linked storage for storing strings.

    (*a*) One can easily insert, delete, concatenate and rearrange substrings when using linked storage.

    (*b*) Additional space is used for storing the links. Also, one cannot directly access a character in the middle of the list.

3.6 Describe briefly the meaning of (*a*) static, (*b*) semistatic and (*c*) dynamic character variables.

    (*a*) The length of the variable is defined before the program is executed and cannot change during the execution of the program.

    (*b*) The length of the variable may vary during the execution of the program, but the length cannot exceed a maximum value defined before the program is executed.

    (*c*) The length of the variable may vary during the execution of the program.

3.7 Suppose MEMBER is a character variable with fixed length 20. Assume a string is stored left-justified in a memory cell with blank spaces padded on the right or with the right-most characters truncated. Describe MEMBER (*a*) if 'JOHN PAUL JONES' is assigned to MEMBER and (*b*) if 'ROBERT ANDREW WASHINGTON' is assigned to MEMBER.

    The data will appear in MEMBER as follows:

    (*a*) MEMBER | J | O | H | N | | P | A | U | L | | J | O | N | E | S | | | | | |

    (*b*) MEMBER | R | O | B | E | R | T | | A | N | D | R | E | W | | W | A | S | H | I | N |

STRING OPERATIONS

In Probs. 3.8 to 3.11 and 3.13, let S and T be character variables such that

    S = 'JOHN PAUL JONES'
    T = 'A THING OF BEAUTY IS A JOY FOREVER.'

3.8 Recall that we use LENGTH(string) for the length of a string.

    (*a*) How is this function denoted in (i) PL/1, (ii) BASIC, (iii) UCSD Pascal, (iv) SNOBOL and (v) FORTRAN?

    (*b*) Find LENGTH(S) and LENGTH(T).

    (*a*) (i) LENGTH(string). (ii) LEN(string). (iii) LENGTH(string). (iv) SIZE(string). (v) FORTRAN has no length function for strings, since the language uses only fixed-length variables.

(b)   Assuming there is only one blank space character between words,

$$\text{LENGTH(S)} = 15 \quad \text{and} \quad \text{LENGTH(T)} = 35$$

3.9   Recall that we use SUBSTRING(string, position, length) to denote the substring of *string* beginning in a given *position* and having a given *length*. Determine (a) SUBSTRINGS(S, 4, 8) and (b) SUBSTRING(T, 10, 5).

    (a)   Beginning with the fourth character and recording 8 characters, we obtain

$$\text{SUBSTRING(S, 4, 8)} = \text{'N}\square\text{PAUL}\square\text{J'}$$

    (b)   Similarly, $\text{SUBSTRING(T, 10, 5)} = \text{'F}\square\text{BEAU'}$

3.10   Recall that we use INDEX(text, pattern) to denote the position where a pattern first appears in a text. This function is assigned the value 0 if the pattern does not appear in the text. Determine (a) INDEX(S, 'JO'), (b) INDEX(S, 'JOY'), (c) INDEX(S, '$\square$JO'), (d) INDEX(T, 'A'), (e) INDEX(T, '$\square$A$\square$') and (f) INDEX(T, 'THE').

    (a)   INDEX(S, 'JO') = 1,   (b)   INDEX(S, 'JOY') = 0,   (c)   INDEX(S, '$\square$JO') = 10,   (d) INDEX(T, 'A') = 1, (e) INDEX(T, '$\square$A$\square$') = 21 and (f) INDEX(T, 'THE') = 0. (Recall that $\square$ is used to denote a blank space.)

3.11   Recall that we use $S_1 /\!/ S_2$ to denote the concatenation of strings S_1 and S_2.

    (a)   How is this function denoted in (i) PL/1, (ii) FORTRAN, (iii) BASIC, (iv) SNOBOL and (v) UCSD Pascal?

    (b)   Find (i) 'THE' $/\!/$ 'END' and (ii) 'THE' $/\!/$ '$\square$' $/\!/$ 'END'.

    (c)   Find (i) SUBSTRING(S, 11, 5) $/\!/$ ',$\square$' $/\!/$ SUBSTRING(S, 1, 9) and
              (ii) SUBSTRING(T, 28, 3) $/\!/$ 'GIVEN'.

    (a)   (i) $S_1 \| S_2$, (ii) $S_1 /\!/ S_2$, (iii) $S_1 + S_2$, (iv) $S_1 \ S_2$ (juxtaposition with a blank space between S_1 and S_2) and (v) CONCAT(S_1, S_2).

    (b) $S_1 /\!/ S_2$ refers to the string consisting of the characters of S_1 followed by the characters of S_2. Hence, (i) THEEND and (ii) THE END.

    (c)   (i) JONES, JOHN PAUL and (ii) FORGIVEN.

3.12   Recall that we use INSERT(text, position, string) to denote inserting a *string* S in a given *text* T beginning in *position* K.

    (a)   Find (i) INSERT('AAAAA', 1, 'BBB'), (ii) INSERT('AAAAA', 3, 'BBB') and (iii) INSERT('AAAAA', 6, 'BBB').

    (b)   Suppose T is the text 'THE STUDENT IS ILL.' Use INSERT to change T so that it reads: (i) The student is very ill. (ii) The student is ill today. (iii) The student is very ill today.

    (a)   (i) BBBAAAAA, (ii) AABBBAAA and (iii) AAAAABBB.

    (b)   Be careful to include blank spaces when necessary. (i) INSERT(T, 15, '$\square$VERY'). (ii) INSERT(T, 19, '$\square$TODAY'). (iii) INSERT(INSERT(T, 19, '$\square$TODAY'), 15, '$\square$VERY') or INSERT(INSERT(T, 15, '$\square$VERY'), 24, '$\square$TODAY'.).

3.13   Find

    (a)   DELETE('AAABBB', 2, 2) and DELETE('JOHN PAUL JONES', 6, 5)

    (b)   REPLACE('AAABBB', 'AA', 'BB') and
              REPLACE('JOHN PAUL JONES', 'PAUL', 'DAVID')

(*a*) DELETE(T, K, L) deletes from a text T the substring which begins in position K and has length L. Hence the answers are

ABBB   and   JOHN JONES

(*b*) REPLACE(T, P_1, P_2) replaces in a text T the first occurrence of the pattern P_1 by the pattern P_2. Hence the answers are

BBABBB   and   JOHN DAVID JONES

WORD PROCESSING

In Probs. 3.14 to 3.17, S is a short story stored in a linear array LINE with *n* elements such that each LINE[K] is a static character variable storing 80 characters and representing a line of the story. Also, LINE[1], the first line, contains only the title of the story, and LINE[N], the last line, contains only the name of the author. Furthermore, each paragraph begins with 5 blank spaces, and there is no other indention except possibly the title in LINE[1] or the name of the author in LINE[N].

3.14 Write a procedure which counts the number NUM of paragraphs in the short story S.

Beginning with LINE[2] and ending with LINE[N − 1], count the number of lines beginning with 5 blank spaces. The procedure follows.

Procedure P3.14:   PAR(LINE, N, NUM)

1. Set NUM := 0 and BLANK := '□□□□□'.
2. [Initialize counter.] Set K := 2.
3. Repeat Steps 4 and 5 while K ≤ N − 1.
4.   [Compare first 5 characters of each line with BLANK.]
          If SUBSTRING(LINE[K], 1, 5) = BLANK, then:
              Set NUM := NUM + 1.
          [End of If structure.]
5.   Set K := K + 1. [Increments counter.]
      [End of Step 3 loop.]
6. Return.

3.15 Write a procedure which counts the number NUM of times the word "the" appears in the short story S. (We do not count "the" in "mother," and we assume no sentence ends with the word "the.")

Note that the word "the" can appear as THE□ at the beginning of a line, as □THE at the end of a line, or as □THE□ elsewhere in a line. Hence we must check these three cases for each line. The procedure follows.

Procedure P3.15:   COUNT(LINE, N, NUM)

1. Set WORD := 'THE' and NUM := 0.
2. [Prepare for the three cases.]
    Set BEG := WORD // '□', END := '□' // WORD and
    MID := '□' // WORD // '□'.
3. Repeat Steps 4 through 6 for K = 1 to N:
4.   [First case.] If SUBSTRING(LINE[K], 1, 4) = BEG, then:
              Set NUM := NUM + 1.
5.   [Second case.] If SUBSTRING(LINE[K], 77, 4) = END, then:
              Set NUM := NUM + 1.
6.   [General case.] Repeat for J = 2 to 76.
              If SUBSTRING(LINE[K], J, 5) = MID, then:
                  Set NUM := NUM + 1.
              [End of If structure.]
          [End of Step 6 loop.]
      [End of Step 3 loop.]
7. Return.

3.16 Discuss the changes that must be made in Procedure P3.15 if one wants to count the number of occurrences of an aribitrary word W with length R.

There are three basic types of changes.

(*a*) Clearly, 'THE' must be changed to W in Step 1.

(*b*) Since the length of W is *r* and not 3, appropriate changes must be made in Steps 3 to 6.

(*c*) One must also consider the possibility that W will be followed by some punctuation, e.g.,

$$W,   \qquad W;   \qquad W.   \qquad W?$$

Hence more than the three cases must be treated.

3.17 Outline an algorithm which will interchange the *k*th and *l*th paragraphs in the short story S.

The algorithm reduces to two procedures:

Procedure A. Find the values of arrays BEG and END where

$$\text{LINE[BEG[K]]}   \qquad \text{and} \qquad   \text{LINE[END[K]]}$$

contain, respectively, the first and last lines of paragraph K of the story S.

Procedure B. Using the values of BEG[K] and END[K] and the values of BEG[L] and END[L], interchange the block of lines of paragraph K with the block of lines of paragraph L.

PATTERN MATCHING

3.18 For each of the following patterns P and texts T, find the number C of comparisons to find the INDEX of P in T using the "slow" algorithm, Algorithm 3.3:

(*a*) $P = abc$, $T = (ab)^5 = abababab$

(*c*) $P = aaa$, $T = (aabb)^3 = aabbaabbaabb$

(*b*) $P = abc$, $T = (ab)^{2n}$

(*d*) $P = aaa$, $T = abaabbaaabbbaaaabbbb$

Recall that $C = N_1 + N_2 + \cdots + N_l$ where N_k denotes the number of comparisons that take place in the inner loop when P is compared with W_K.

(*a*) Note first that there are

$$\text{LENGTH(T)} - \text{LENGTH(P)} + 1 = 10 - 3 + 1 = 8$$

substrings W_K. We have

$$C = 2 + 1 + 2 + 1 + 2 + 1 + 2 + 1 = 4(3) = 12$$

and INDEX(T, P) = 0, since P does not appear in T.

(*b*) There are $2n - 3 + 1 = 2(n - 1)$ subwords W_K. We have

$$C = 2 + 1 + 2 + 1 + \cdots + 2 + 1 = (n + 1)(3) = 3n + 3$$

and INDEX(T, P) = 0.

(*c*) There are $12 - 3 + 1 = 10$ subwords W_K. We have

$$C = 3 + 2 + 1 + 1 + 3 + 2 + 1 + 1 + 3 + 2 = 19$$

and INDEX(T, P) = 0.

(*d*) We have

$$C = 2 + 1 + 3 + 2 + 1 + 1 + 3 = 13$$

and INDEX(T, P) = 7.

3.19   Suppose P is an *r*-character string and T is an *s*-character string, and suppose $C(n)$ denotes the number of comparisons when Algorithm 3.3 is applied to P and T. (Here $n = r + s$.)

(*a*)   Find the complexity $C(n)$ for the best case.

(*b*)   Prove that the maximum value of $C(n)$ occurs when $r = (n + 1)/4$.

(*a*)   The best case occurs when P is an initial substring of T, or, in other words, when INDEX(T, P) = 1. In this case $C(n) = r$. (We assume $r \leq s$.)

(*b*)   By the discussion in Sec. 3.7,

$$C = C(n) = r(n - 2r + 1) = nr - 2r^2 + r$$

Here *n* is fixed, so $C = C(n)$ may be viewed as a function of *r*. Calculus tells us that the maximum value of *C* occurs when $C' = dC/dr = 0$ (here C' is the derivative of *C* with respect to *r*). Using calculus, we obtain:

$$C' = n - 4r + 1$$

Setting $C' = 0$ and solving for *r* gives us the required result.

3.20   Consider the pattern $P = aaabb$. Construct the table and the corresponding labeled directed graph used in the "fast," or second pattern matching, algorithm.

First list the initial segments of *P*:

$$Q_0 = \Lambda, \qquad Q_1 = a, \qquad Q_2 = a^2, \qquad Q_3 = a^3, \qquad Q_4 = a^3b, \qquad Q_5 = a^3b^2$$

For each character *t*, the entry $f(Q_i, t)$ in the table is the largest *Q* which appears as a terminal substring in the string $Q_i t$. We compute:

$$f(\Lambda, a) = a, \qquad f(a, a) = a^2, \qquad f(a^2, a) = a^3, \qquad f(a^3, a) = a^3, \qquad f(a^3b, a) = a$$
$$f(\Lambda, b) = \Lambda, \qquad f(a, b) = \Lambda, \qquad f(a^2, b) = \Lambda, \qquad f(a^3, b) = a^3b, \qquad f(a^3b, b) = P$$

Hence the required table appears in Fig. 3-10(*a*). The corresponding graph appears in Fig. 3-10(*b*), where there is a node corresponding to each *Q* and an arrow from Q_i to Q_j labeled by the character *t* for each entry $f(Q_i, t) = Q_j$ in the table.

	a	b
Q_0	Q_1	Q_0
Q_1	Q_2	Q_0
Q_2	Q_3	Q_0
Q_3	Q_3	Q_4
Q_4	Q_1	P

(*a*)

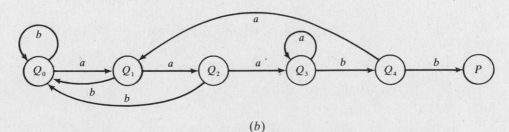

(*b*)

Fig. 3-10

3.21 Find the table and corresponding graph for the second pattern matching algorithm where the pattern is $P = ababab$.

The initial substrings of P are:

$$Q_0 = \Lambda, \qquad Q_1 = a, \qquad Q_2 = ab, \qquad Q_3 = aba, \qquad Q_4 = abab, \qquad Q_5 = ababa, \qquad Q_6 = ababab = P$$

The function f giving the entries in the table follows:

$f(\Lambda, a) = a$	$f(\Lambda, b) = \Lambda$
$f(a, a) = a$	$f(a, b) = ab$
$f(ab, a) = aba$	$f(ab, b) = \Lambda$
$f(aba, a) = a$	$f(aba, b) = abab$
$f(abab, a) = ababa$	$f(abab, b) = \Lambda$
$f(ababa, a) = a$	$f(ababa, b) = P$

The table appears in Fig. 3-11(a) and the corresponding graph appears in Fig. 3-11(b).

	a	b
Q_0	Q_1	Q_0
Q_1	Q_1	Q_2
Q_2	Q_3	Q_0
Q_3	Q_1	Q_4
Q_4	Q_5	Q_0
Q_5	Q_1	P

(a)

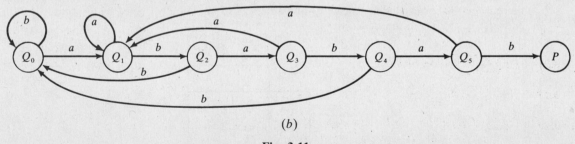

(b)

Fig. 3-11

Supplementary Problems

STRINGS

3.22 Find the string stored in Fig. 3-12.

3.23 Consider the string $W = $ 'XYZST'. List (a) all substrings of W and (b) all initial substrings of W.

3.24 Suppose W is a string of length n. Find the number of (a) substrings of W and (b) initial substrings of W.

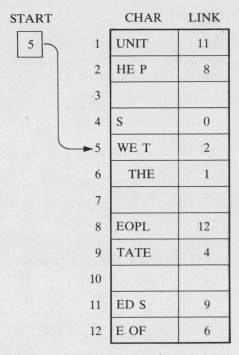

Fig. 3-12

3.25 Suppose STATE is a character variable with fixed length 12. Describe the contents of STATE after the assignment (a) STATE := 'NEW YORK', (b) STATE := 'SOUTH CAROLINA' and (c) STATE := 'PENNSYLVANIA'.

STRING OPERATIONS

In Probs. 3.26 to 3.31, let S and T be character variables such that

$$S = \text{'WE THE PEOPLE'} \quad \text{and} \quad T = \text{'OF THE UNITED STATES'}$$

3.26 Find the length of S and T.

3.27 Find (a) SUBSTRING(S, 4, 8) and (b) SUBSTRING(T, 10, 5).

3.28 Find (a) INDEX(S, 'P'), (b) INDEX(S, 'E'), (c) INDEX(S, 'THE'), (d) INDEX(T, 'THE'), (e) INDEX(T, 'THEN') and (f) INDEX(T, 'TE').

3.29 Using $S_1 \parallel S_2$ to stand for the concatenation of S_1 and S_2, find (a) 'NO' ∥ 'EXIT', (b) 'NO' ∥ '□' ∥ 'EXIT' and (c) SUBSTRING(S, 4, 10) ∥ '□ARE□' ∥ SUBSTRING(T, 8, 6).

3.30 Find (a) DELETE('AAABBB', 3, 3), (b) DELETE('AAABBB', 1, 4), (c) DELETE(S, 1, 3) and (d) DELETE(T, 1, 7).

3.31 Find (a) REPLACE('ABABAB', 'B', 'BAB'), (b) REPLACE(S, 'WE', 'ALL') and (c) REPLACE(T, 'THE', 'THESE').

3.32 Find (a) INSERT('AAA', 2, 'BBB'), (b) INSERT('ABCDE', 3, 'XYZ') and (c) INSERT('THE BOY', 5, 'BIG□').

3.33 Suppose U is the text 'MARC STUDIES MATHEMATICS.' Use INSERT to change U so that it reads: (a) MARC STUDIES ONLY MATHEMATICS. (b) MARC STUDIES MATHEMATICS AND PHYSICS. (c) MARC STUDIES APPLIED MATHEMATICS.

PATTERN MATCHING

3.34   Consider the pattern $P = abc$. Using the "slow" pattern matching algorithm, Algorithm 3.3, find the number C comparisons to find the INDEX of P in each of the following texts T:
(a) a^{10}, (b) $(aba)^{10}$, (c) $(cbab)^{10}$, (d) d^{10} and (e) d^n where $n > 3$.

3.35   Consider the pattern $P = a^5b$. Repeat Prob. 3.34 with each of the following texts T:
(a) a^{20}, (b) a^n where $n > 6$, (c) d^{20} and (d) d^n where $n > 6$.

3.36   Consider the pattern $P = a^3ba$. Construct the table and the corresponding labeled directed graph used in the "fast" pattern matching algorithm.

3.37   Repeat Prob. 3.36 for the pattern $P = aba^2b$.

Programming Problems

In Probs. 3.38 to 3.40, assume the preface of this text is stored in a linear array LINE such that LINE[K] is a static character variable storing 80 characters and represents a line of the preface. Assume that each paragraph begins with 5 blank spaces and there is no other indention. Also, assume there is a variable NUM which gives the number of lines in the preface.

3.38   Write a program which defines a linear array PAR such that PAR[K] contains the location of the Kth paragraph, and which also defines a variable NPAR which contains the number of paragraphs.

3.39   Write a program which reads a given WORD and then counts the number C of times WORD occurs in LINE. Test the program using (a) WORD = 'THE' and (b) WORD = 'HENCE'.

3.40   Write a program which interchanges the Jth and Kth paragraphs. Test the program using J = 2 and K = 4.

In Probs. 3.41 to 3.46, assume the preface of this text is stored in a single character variable TEXT. Assume 5 blank spaces indicates a new paragraph.

3.41   Write a program which constructs a linear array PAR such that PAR[K] contains the location of the Kth paragraph in TEXT, and which finds the value of a variable NPAR which contains the number of paragraphs. (Compare with Prob. 3.38.)

3.42   Write a program which reads a given WORD and then counts the number C of times WORD occurs in TEXT. Test the program using (a) WORD = 'THE' and (b) WORD = 'HENCE'. (Compare with Prob. 3.39.)

3.43   Write a program which interchanges the Jth and Kth paragraphs in TEXT. Test the program using J = 2 and K = 4. (Compare with Prob. 3.40.)

3.44   Write a program which reads words WORD1 and WORD2 and then replaces each occurrence of WORD1 in TEXT by WORD2. Test the program using WORD1 = 'HENCE' and WORD2 = 'THUS'.

3.45   Write a subprogram INST(TEXT, NEW, K) which inserts a string NEW into TEXT beginning at TEXT[K].

3.46   Write a subprogram PRINT(TEXT, K) which prints the character string TEXT in lines with at most K characters. No word should be divided in the middle and appear on two lines, so some lines may contain trailing blank spaces. Each paragraph should begin with its own line and be indented using 5 blank spaces. Test the program using (a) K = 80, (b) K = 70 and (c) K = 60.

Chapter 4

Arrays, Records and Pointers

4.1 INTRODUCTION

Data structures are classified as either linear or nonlinear. A data structure is said to be linear if its elements form a sequence, or, in other words, a linear list. There are two basic ways of representing such linear structures in memory. One way is to have the linear relationship between the elements represented by means of sequential memory locations. These linear structures are called *arrays* and form the main subject matter of this chapter. The other way is to have the linear relationship between the elements represented by means of pointers or links. These linear structures are called *linked lists*; they form the main content of Chap. 5. Nonlinear structures such as trees and graphs are treated in later chapters.

The operations one normally performs on any linear structure, whether it be an array or a linked list, include the following:

(a) *Traversal.* Processing each element in the list.

(b) *Search.* Finding the location of the element with a given value or the record with a given key.

(c) *Insertion.* Adding a new element to the list.

(d) *Deletion.* Removing an element from the list.

(e) *Sorting.* Arranging the elements in some type of order.

(f) *Merging.* Combining two lists into a single list.

The particular linear structure that one chooses for a given situation depends on the relative frequency with which one performs these different operations on the structure.

This chapter discusses a very common linear structure called an array. Since arrays are usually easy to traverse, search and sort, they are frequently used to store relatively permanent collections of data. On the other hand, if the size of the structure and the data in the structure are constantly changing, then the array may not be as useful a structure as the linked list, discussed in Chap. 5.

4.2 LINEAR ARRAYS

A *linear array* is a list of a finite number n of *homogeneous* data elements (i.e., data elements of the same type) such that:

(a) The elements of the array are referenced respectively by an *index set* consisting of n consecutive numbers.

(b) The elements of the array are stored respectively in successive memory locations.

The number n of elements is called the *length* or *size* of the array. If not explicitly stated, we will assume the index set consists of the integers $1, 2, \ldots, n$. In general, the length or the number of data elements of the array can be obtained from the index set by the formula

$$\text{Length} = \text{UB} - \text{LB} + 1 \tag{4.1}$$

where UB is the largest index, called the *upper bound*, and LB is the smallest index, called the *lower bound*, of the array. Note that length = UB when LB = 1.

The elements of an array A may be denoted by the subscript notation

$$A_1, A_2, A_3, \ldots, A_n$$

or by the parentheses notation (used in FORTRAN, PL/1 and BASIC)

$$A(1), A(2), \ldots, A(N)$$

or by the bracket notation (used in Pascal)

$$A[1], A[2], A[3], \ldots, A[N]$$

We will usually use the subscript notation or the bracket notation. Regardless of the notation, the number K in A[K] is called a *subscript* or an *index* and A[K] is called a *subscripted variable*. Note that subscripts allow any element of A to be referenced by its relative position in A.

EXAMPLE 4.1

(*a*) Let DATA be a 6-element linear array of integers such that

DATA[1] = 247   DATA[2] = 56   DATA[3] = 429   DATA[4] = 135   DATA[5] = 87   DATA[6] = 156

Sometimes we will denote such an array by simply writing

DATA: 247, 56, 429, 135, 87, 156

The array DATA is frequently pictured as in Fig. 4-1(*a*) or Fig. 4-1(*b*).

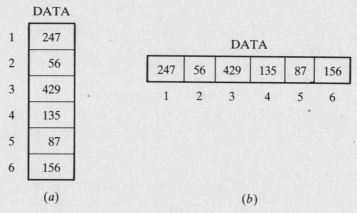

Fig. 4-1

(*b*) An automobile company uses an array AUTO to record the number of automobiles sold each year from 1932 through 1984. Rather than beginning the index set with 1, it is more useful to begin the index set with 1932 so that

AUTO[K] = number of automobiles sold in the year K

Then LB = 1932 is the lower bound and UB = 1984 is the upper bound of AUTO. By Eq. (4.1),

Length = UB − LB + 1 = 1984 − 1930 + 1 = 55

That is, AUTO contains 55 elements and its index set consists of all integers from 1932 through 1984.

Each programming language has its own rules for declaring arrays. Each such declaration must give, implicitly or explicitly, three items of information: (1) the name of the array, (2) the data type of the array and (3) the index set of the array.

EXAMPLE 4.2

(*a*) Suppose DATA is a 6-element linear array containing real values. Various programmng languages declare such an array as follows:

FORTRAN: REAL DATA(6)
PL/1:   DECLARE DATA(6) FLOAT;
Pascal: VAR DATA: ARRAY[1 . . 6] OF REAL

We will declare such an array, when necessary, by writing DATA(6). (The context will usually indicate the data type, so it will not be explicitly declared.)

(*b*)   Consider the integer array AUTO with lower bound LB = 1932 and upper bound UB = 1984. Various programming languages declare such an array as follows:

FORTRAN 77   INTEGER AUTO(1932:1984)
PL/1:   DECLARE AUTO(1932:1984) FIXED;
Pascal   VAR AUTO: ARRAY[1932 . . 1984] of INTEGER

We will declare such an array by writing AUTO(1932:1984).

Some programming languages (e.g., FORTRAN and Pascal) allocate memory space for arrays *statically*, i.e., during program compilation; hence the size of the array is fixed during program execution. On the other hand, some programming languages allow one to read an integer *n* and then declare an array with *n* elements; such programming languages are said to allocate memory *dynamically*.

4.3   REPRESENTATION OF LINEAR ARRAYS IN MEMORY

Let LA be a linear array in the memory of the computer. Recall that the memory of the computer is simply a sequence of addressed locations as pictured in Fig. 4-2. Let us use the notation

$$LOC(LA[K]) = \text{address of the element LA[K] of the array LA}$$

As previously noted, the elements of LA are stored in successive memory cells. Accordingly, the computer does not need to keep track of the address of every element of LA, but needs to keep track only of the address of the first element of LA, denoted by

$$Base(LA)$$

and called the *base address* of LA. Using this address *Base*(LA), the computer calculates the address of any element of LA by the following formula:

$$LOC(LA[K]) = Base(LA) + w(K - \text{lower bound}) \tag{4.2}$$

where *w* is the number of words per memory cell for the array LA. Observe that the time to calculate LOC(LA[K]) is essentially the same for any value of K. Furthermore, given any subscript K, one can locate and access the content of LA[K] without scanning any other element of LA.

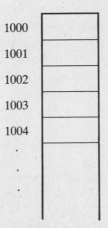

Fig. 4-2   Computer memory.

EXAMPLE 4.3

Consider the array AUTO in Example 4.1(b), which records the number of automobiles sold each year from 1932 through 1984. Suppose AUTO appears in memory as pictured in Fig. 4-3. That is, $Base$(AUTO) = 200, and $w = 4$ words per memory cell for AUTO. Then

$$\text{LOC(AUTO[1932])} = 200, \quad \text{LOC(AUTO[1933])} = 204, \quad \text{LOC(AUTO[1934])} = 208, \ldots$$

The address of the array element for the year K = 1965 can be obtained by using Eq. (4.2):

$$\text{LOC(AUTO[1965])} = Base(\text{AUTO}) + w(1965 - \text{lower bound}) = 200 + 4(1965 - 1932) = 332$$

Again we emphasize that the contents of this element can be obtained without scanning any other element in array AUTO.

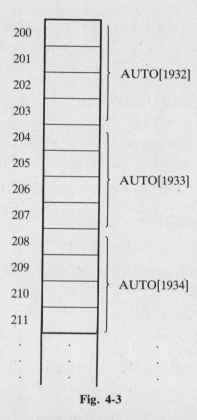

Fig. 4-3

Remark: A collection A of data elements is said to be *indexed* if any element of A, which we shall call A_K, can be located and processed in a time that is independent of K. The above discussion indicates that linear arrays can be indexed. This is very a important property of linear arrays. In fact, linked lists, which are covered in the next chapter, do not have this property.

4.4 TRAVERSING LINEAR ARRAYS

Let A be a collection of data elements stored in the memory of the computer. Suppose we want to print the contents of each element of A or suppose we want to count the number of elements of A with a given property. This can be accomplished by *traversing* A, that is, by accessing and processing (frequently called *visiting*) each element of A exactly once.

The following algorithm traverses a linear array LA. The simplicity of the algorithm comes from the fact that LA is a linear structure. Other linear structures, such as linked lists, can also be easily traversed. On the other hand, the traversal of nonlinear structures, such as trees and graphs, is considerably more complicated.

Algorithm 4.1:   (Traversing a Linear Array) Here LA is a linear array with lower bound LB and upper bound UB. This algorithm traverses LA applying an operation PROCESS to each element of LA.

1. [Initialize counter.] Set K := LB.
2. Repeat Steps 3 and 4 while K ≤ UB.
3.   [Visit element.] Apply PROCESS to LA[K].
4.   [Increase counter.] Set K := K + 1.
   [End of Step 2 loop.]
5. Exit.

We also state an alternative form of the algorithm which uses a repeat-for loop instead of the repeat-while loop.

Algorithm 4.1′:   (Traversing a Linear Array) This algorithm traverses a linear array LA with lower bound LB and upper bound UB.

1. Repeat for K = LB to UB:
       Apply PROCESS to LA[K].
   [End of loop.]
2. Exit.

Caution: The operation PROCESS in the traversal algorithm may use certain variables which must be initialized before PROCESS is applied to any of the elements in the array. Accordingly, the algorithm may need to be preceded by such an initialization step.

EXAMPLE 4.4

Consider the array AUTO in Example 4.1(*b*), which records the number of automobiles sold each year from 1932 through 1984. Each of the following modules, which carry out the given operation, involves traversing AUTO.

(*a*)   Find the number NUM of years during which more than 300 automobiles were sold.
1. [Initialization step.] Set NUM := 0.
2. Repeat for K = 1932 to 1984:
       If AUTO[K] > 300, then: Set NUM := NUM + 1.
   [End of loop.]
3. Return.

(*b*)   Print each year and the number of automobiles sold in that year.
1. Repeat for K = 1932 to 1984:
       Write: K, AUTO[K].
   [End of loop.]
2. Return.

(Observe that (*a*) requires an initialization step for the variable NUM before traversing the array AUTO.)

4.5   INSERTING AND DELETING

Let A be a collection of data elements in the memory of the computer. "Inserting" refers to the operation of adding another element to the collection A, and "deleting" refers to the operation of removing one of the elements from A. This section discusses inserting and deleting when A is a linear array.

Inserting an element at the "end" of a linear array can be easily done provided the memory space allocated for the array is large enough to accommodate the additional element. On the other hand, suppose we need to insert an element in the middle of the array. Then, on the average, half of the elements must be moved downward to new locations to accommodate the new element and keep the order of the other elements.

Similarly, deleting an element at the "end" of an array presents no difficulties, but deleting an element somewhere in the middle of the array would require that each subsequent element be moved one location upward in order to "fill up" the array.

Remark: Since linear arrays are usually pictured extending downward, as in Fig. 4-1, the term "downward" refers to locations with larger subscripts, and the term "upward" refers to locations with smaller subscripts.

EXAMPLE 4.5

Suppose TEST has been declared to be a 5-element array but data have been recorded only for TEST[1], TEST[2] and TEST[3]. If X is the value of the next test, then one simply assigns

$$TEST[4] := X$$

to add X to the list. Similarly, if Y is the value of the subsequent test, then we simply assign

$$TEST[5] := Y$$

to add Y to the list. Now, however, we cannot add any new test scores to the list.

EXAMPLE 4.6

Suppose NAME is an 8-element linear array, and suppose five names are in the array, as in Fig. 4-4(a). Observe that the names are listed alphabetically, and suppose we want to keep the array names alphabetical at all times. Suppose Ford is added to the array. Then Johnson, Smith and Wagner must each be moved downward one location, as in Fig. 4-4(b). Next suppose Taylor is added to the array; then Wagner must be moved, as in Fig. 4-4(c). Last, suppose Davis is removed from the array. Then the five names Ford, Johnson, Smith, Taylor and Wagner must each be moved upward one location, as in Fig. 4-4(d). Clearly such movement of data would be very expensive if thousands of names were in the array.

	NAME			NAME			NAME			NAME
1	Brown		1	Brown		1	Brown		1	Brown
2	Davis		2	Davis		2	Davis		2	Ford
3	Johnson		3	Ford		3	Ford		3	Johnson
4	Smith		4	Johnson		4	Johnson		4	Smith
5	Wagner		5	Smith		5	Smith		5	Taylor
6			6	Wagner		6	Taylor		6	Wagner
7			7			7	Wagner		7	
8			8			8			8	
	(a)			(b)			(c)			(d)

Fig. 4-4

The following algorithm inserts a data element ITEM into the Kth position in a linear array LA with N elements. The first four steps create space in LA by moving downward one location each element from the Kth position on. We emphasize that these elements are moved in reverse order—i.e., first LA[N], then LA[N − 1], . . . , and last LA[K]; otherwise data might be erased. (See Prob. 4.3.) In more detail, we first set J := N and then, using J as a counter, decrease J each time the loop is executed until J reaches K. The next step, Step 5, inserts ITEM into the array in the space just created. Before the exit from the algorithm, the number N of elements in LA is increased by 1 to account for the new element.

Algorithm 4.2:　(Inserting into a Linear Array) INSERT(LA, N, K, ITEM)
　　　　　　　　Here LA is a linear array with N elements and K is a positive integer such that
　　　　　　　　$K \leq N$. This algorithm inserts an element ITEM into the Kth position in LA.

　　　　1.　[Initialize counter.] Set $J := N$.
　　　　2.　Repeat Steps 3 and 4 while $J \geq K$.
　　　　3.　　　[Move Jth element downward.] Set $LA[J+1] := LA[J]$.
　　　　4.　　　[Decrease counter.] Set $J := J - 1$.
　　　　　　[End of Step 2 loop.]
　　　　5.　[Insert element.] Set $LA[K] := ITEM$.
　　　　6.　[Reset N.] Set $N := N + 1$.
　　　　7.　Exit.

The following algorithm deletes the Kth element from a linear array LA and assigns it to a variable ITEM.

Algorithm 4.3:　(Deleting from a Linear Array) DELETE(LA, N, K, ITEM)
　　　　　　　　Here LA is a linear array with N elements and K is a positive integer such that
　　　　　　　　$K \leq N$. This algorithm deletes the Kth element from LA.

　　　　1.　Set $ITEM := LA[K]$.
　　　　2.　Repeat for $J = K$ to $N - 1$:
　　　　　　　[Move J + 1st element upward.] Set $LA[J] := LA[J+1]$.
　　　　　　[End of loop.]
　　　　3.　[Reset the number N of elements in LA.] Set $N := N - 1$.
　　　　4.　Exit.

Remark:　We emphasize that if many deletions and insertions are to be made in a collection of data elements, then a linear array may not be the most efficient way of storing the data.

4.6　SORTING; BUBBLE SORT

Let A be a list of *n* numbers. *Sorting* A refers to the operation of rearranging the elements of A so they are in increasing order, i.e., so that

$$A[1] < A[2] < A[3] < \cdots < A[N]$$

For example, suppose A originally is the list

$$8, 4, 19, 2, 7, 13, 5, 16$$

After sorting, A is the list

$$2, 4, 5, 7, 8, 13, 16, 19$$

Sorting may seem to be a trivial task. Actually, sorting efficiently may be quite complicated. In fact, there are many, many different sorting algorithms; some of these algorithms are discussed in Chap. 9. Here we present and discuss a very simple sorting algorithm known as the *bubble sort*.

Remark:　The above definition of sorting refers to arranging numerical data in increasing order; this restriction is only for notational convenience. Clearly, sorting may also mean arranging numerical data in decreasing order or arranging nonnumerical data in alphabetical order. Actually, A is frequently a file of records, and sorting A refers to rearranging the records of A so that the values of a given key are ordered.

Bubble Sort

Suppose the list of numbers A[1], A[2], . . . , A[N] is in memory. The bubble sort algorithm works as follows:

Step 1. Compare A[1] and A[2] and arrange them in the desired order, so that A[1] < A[2]. Then compare A[2] and A[3] and arrange them so that A[2] < A[3]. Then compare A[3] and A[4] and arrange them so that A[3] < A[4]. Continue until we compare A[N − 1] with A[N] and arrange them so that A[N − 1] < A[N].

Observe that Step 1 involves $n - 1$ comparisons. (During Step 1, the largest element is "bubbled up" to the nth position or "sinks" to the nth position.) When Step 1 is completed, A[N] will contain the largest element.

Step 2. Repeat Step 1 with one less comparison; that is, now we stop after we compare and possibly rearrange A[N − 2] and A[N − 1]. (Step 2 involves N − 2 comparisons and, when Step 2 is completed, the second largest element will occupy A[N − 1].)

Step 3. Repeat Step 1 with two fewer comparisons; that is, we stop after we compare and possibly rearrange A[N − 3] and A[N − 2].

. ...

. ...

Step N − 1. Compare A[1] with A[2] and arrange them so that A[1] < A[2].

After $n - 1$ steps, the list will be sorted in increasing order.

The process of sequentially traversing through all or part of a list is frequently called a "pass," so each of the above steps is called a pass. Accordingly, the bubble sort algorithm requires $n - 1$ passes, where n is the number of input items.

EXAMPLE 4.7

Suppose the following numbers are stored in an array A:

32, 51, 27, 85, 66, 23, 13, 57

We apply the bubble sort to the array A. We discuss each pass separately.

Pass 1. We have the following comparisons:

(*a*) Compare A_1 and A_2. Since 32 < 51, the list is not altered.

(*b*) Compare A_2 and A_3. Since 51 > 27, interchange 51 and 27 as follows:

32, (27,) (51,) 85, 66, 23, 13, 57

(*c*) Compare A_3 and A_4. Since 51 < 85, the list is not altered.

(*d*) Compare A_4 and A_5. Since 85 > 66, interchange 85 and 86 as follows:

32, 27, 51, (66,) (85,) 23, 13, 57

(*e*) Compare A_5 and A_6. Since 85 > 23, interchange 85 and 23 as follows:

32, 27, 51, 66, (23,) (85,) 13, 57

(*f*) Compare A_6 and A_7. Since 85 > 13, interchange 85 and 13 to yield:

32, 27, 51, 66, 23, (13,) (85,) 57

(*g*) Compare A_7 and A_8. Since 85 > 57, interchange 85 and 57 to yield:

32, 27, 51, 66, 23, 13, (57,) (85)

At the end of this first pass, the largest number, 85, has moved to the last position. However, the rest of the numbers are not sorted, even though some of them have changed their positions.

For the remainder of the passes, we show only the interchanges.

Pass 2.   (27,) (33,)   51,   66,   23,   13,   57,   85

          27,   33,   51,   (23,) (66,)   13,   57,   85

          27,   33,   51,   23,   (13,) (66,)   57,   85

          27,   33,   51,   23,   13,   (57,) (66,)   85

At the end of Pass 2, the second largest number, 66, has moved its way down to the next-to-last position.

Pass 3.   27,   33,   (23,) (51,)   13,   57,   66,   85

          27,   33,   23,   (13,) (51,)   57,   66,   85

Pass 4.   27,   (23,) (33,)   13,   51,   57,   66,   85

          27,   23,   (13,) (33,)   51,   57,   66,   85

Pass 5.   (23,) (27,)   13,   33,   51,   57,   66,   85

          23,   (13,) (27,)   33,   51,   57,   66,   85

Pass 6.   (13,) (23,)   27,   33,   51,   57,   66,   85

Pass 6 actually has two comparisons, A_1 with A_2 and A_2 and A_3. The second comparison does not involve an interchange.

Pass 7.   Finally, A_1 is compared with A_2. Since $13 < 23$, no interchange takes place.

Since the list has 8 elements, it is sorted after the seventh pass. (Observe that in this example, the list was actually sorted after the sixth pass. This condition is discussed at the end of the section.)

We now formally state the bubble sort algorithm.

Algorithm 4.4:   (Bubble Sort) BUBBLE(DATA, N)
Here DATA is an array with N elements. This algorithm sorts the elements in DATA.
1.   Repeat Steps 2 and 3 for K = 1 to N − 1.
2.   Set PTR := 1. [Initializes pass pointer PTR.]
3.   Repeat while PTR ≤ N − K: [Executes pass.]
             (a)   If DATA[PTR] > DATA[PTR + 1], then:
                       Interchange DATA[PTR] and DATA[PTR + 1].
                   [End of If structure.]
             (b)   Set PTR := PTR + 1.
         [End of inner loop.]
     [End of Step 1 outer loop.]
4.   Exit.

Observe that there is an inner loop which is controlled by the variable PTR, and the loop is contained in an outer loop which is controlled by an index K. Also observe that PTR is used as a subscript but K is not used as a subscript, but rather as a counter.

Complexity of the Bubble Sort Algorithm

Traditionally, the time for a sorting algorithm is measured in terms of the number of comparisons. The number $f(n)$ of comparisons in the bubble sort is easily computed. Specifically, there are $n - 1$ comparisons during the first pass, which places the largest element in the last position; there are $n - 2$ comparisons in the second step, which places the second largest element in the next-to-last position; and so on. Thus

$$f(n) = (n-1) + (n-2) + \cdots + 2 + 1 = \frac{n(n-1)}{2} = \frac{n^2}{2} + O(n) = O(n^2)$$

In other words, the time required to execute the bubble sort algorithm is proportional to n^2, where n is the number of input items.

Remark: Some programmers use a bubble sort algorithm that contains a 1-bit variable FLAG (or a *logical* variable FLAG) to signal when no interchange takes place during a pass. If FLAG = 0 after any pass, then the list is already sorted and there is no need to continue. This may cut down on the number of passes. However, when using such a flag, one must initialize, change and test the variable FLAG during each pass. Hence the use of the flag is efficient only when the list originally is "almost" in sorted order.

4.7 SEARCHING; LINEAR SEARCH

Let DATA be a collection of data elements in memory, and suppose a specific ITEM of information is given. *Searching* refers to the operation of finding the location LOC of ITEM in DATA, or printing some message that ITEM does not appear there. The search is said to be *successful* if ITEM does appear in DATA and *unsuccessful* otherwise.

Frequently, one may want to add the element ITEM to DATA after an unsuccessful search for ITEM in DATA. One then uses a *search and insertion* algorithm, rather than simply a *search* algorithm; such search and insertion algorithms are discussed in the problem sections.

There are many different searching algorithms. The algorithm that one chooses generally depends on the way the information in DATA is organized. Searching is discussed in detail in Chap. 9. This section discusses a simple algorithm called *linear search*, and the next section discusses the well-known algorithm called *binary search*.

The complexity of searching algorithms is measured in terms of the number $f(n)$ of comparisons required to find ITEM in DATA where DATA contains n elements. We shall show that linear search is a linear time algorithm, but that binary search is a much more efficient algorithm, proportional in time to $\log_2 n$. On the other hand, we also discuss the drawback of relying only on the binary search algorithm.

Linear Search

Suppose DATA is a linear array with n elements. Given no other information about DATA, the most intuitive way to search for a given ITEM in DATA is to compare ITEM with each element of DATA one by one. That is, first we test whether DATA[1] = ITEM, and then we test whether DATA[2] = ITEM, and so on. This method, which traverses DATA sequentially to locate ITEM, is called *linear search* or *sequential search*.

To simplify the matter, we first assign ITEM to DATA[N + 1], the position following the last element of DATA. Then the outcome

$$LOC = N + 1$$

where LOC denotes the location where ITEM first occurs in DATA, signifies the search is unsuccessful. The purpose of this initial assignment is to avoid repeatedly testing whether or not we have reached the end of the array DATA. This way, the search must eventually "succeed."

A formal presentation of linear search is shown in Algorithm 4.5.

Observe that Step 1 guarantees that the loop in Step 3 must terminate. Without Step 1 (see Algorithm 2.4), the Repeat statement in Step 3 must be replaced by the following statement, which involves two comparisons, not one:

Repeat while LOC ≤ N and DATA[LOC] ≠ ITEM:

On the other hand, in order to use Step 1, one must guarantee that there is an unused memory location

---

Algorithm 4.5: (Linear Search) LINEAR(DATA, N, ITEM, LOC)
Here DATA is a linear array with N elements, and ITEM is a given item of information. This algorithm finds the location LOC of ITEM in DATA, or sets LOC := 0 if the search is unsuccessful.

1. [Insert ITEM at the end of DATA.] Set DATA[N + 1] := ITEM.
2. [Initialize counter.] Set LOC := 1.
3. [Search for ITEM.]
   Repeat while DATA[LOC] ≠ ITEM:
       Set LOC := LOC + 1.
   [End of loop.]
4. [Successful?] If LOC = N + 1, then: Set LOC := 0.
5. Exit.

---

at the end of the array DATA; otherwise, one must use the linear search algorithm discussed in Algorithm 2.4.

EXAMPLE 4.8

Consider the array NAME in Fig. 4-5(a), where n = 6.

(a) Suppose we want to know whether Paula appears in the array and, if so, where. Our algorithm temporarily places Paula at the end of the array, as pictured in Fig. 4-5(b), by setting NAME[7] = Paula. Then the algorithm searches the array from top to bottom. Since Paula first appears in NAME[N + 1], Paula is not in the original array.

(b) Suppose we want to know whether Susan appears in the array and, if so, where. Our algorithm temporarily places Susan at the end of the array, as pictured in Fig. 4-5(c), by setting NAME[7] = Susan. Then the algorithm searches the array from top to bottom. Since Susan first appears in NAME[4] (where 4 ≤ n), we know that Susan is in the original array.

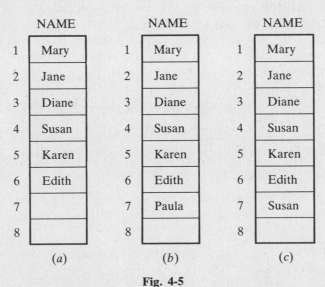

Fig. 4-5

Complexity of the Linear Search Algorithm

As noted above, the complexity of our search algorithm is measured by the number $f(n)$ of comparisons required to find ITEM in DATA where DATA contains n elements. Two important cases to consider are the average case and the worst case.

Clearly, the worst case occurs when one must search through the entire array DATA, i.e., when ITEM does not appear in DATA. In this case, the algorithm requires

$$f(n) = n + 1$$

comparisons. Thus, in the worst case, the running time is proportional to n.

The running time of the average case uses the probabilistic notion of expectation. (See Sec. 2.5.) Suppose p_k is the probability that ITEM appears in DATA[K], and suppose q is the probability that ITEM does not appear in DATA. (Then $p_1 + p_2 + \cdots + p_n + q = 1$.) Since the algorithm uses k comparisons when ITEM appears in DATA[K], the average number of comparisons is given by

$$f(n) = 1 \cdot p_1 + 2 \cdot p_2 + \cdots + n \cdot p_n + (n + 1) \cdot q$$

In particular, suppose q is very small and ITEM appears with equal probability in each element of DATA. Then $q \approx 0$ and each $p_i = 1/n$. Accordingly,

$$f(n) = 1 \cdot \frac{1}{n} + 2 \cdot \frac{1}{n} + \cdots + n \cdot \frac{1}{n} + (n + 1) \cdot 0 = (1 + 2 + \cdots + n) \cdot \frac{1}{n}$$

$$= \frac{n(n + 1)}{2} \cdot \frac{1}{n} = \frac{n + 1}{2}$$

That is, in this special case, the average number of comparisons required to find the location of ITEM is approximately equal to half the number of elements in the array.

4.8 BINARY SEARCH

Suppose DATA is an array which is sorted in increasing numerical order or, equivalently, alphabetically. Then there is an extremely efficient searching algorithm, called *binary search*, which can be used to find the location LOC of a given ITEM of information in DATA. Before formally discussing the algorithm, we indicate the general idea of this algorithm by means of an idealized version of a familiar everyday example.

Suppose one wants to find the location of some name in a telephone directory (or some word in a dictionary). Obviously, one does not perform a linear search. Rather, one opens the directory in the middle to determine which half contains the name being sought. Then one opens that half in the middle to determine which quarter of the directory contains the name. Then one opens that quarter in the middle to determine which eighth of the directory contains the name. And so on. Eventually, one finds the location of the name, since one is reducing (very quickly) the number of possible locations for it in the directory.

The binary search algorithm applied to our array DATA works as follows. During each stage of our algorithm, our search for ITEM is reduced to a *segment* of elements of DATA:

$$\text{DATA[BEG], DATA[BEG + 1], DATA[BEG + 2], \dots, DATA[END]}$$

Note that the variables BEG and END denote, respectively, the beginning and end locations of the segment under consideration. The algorithm compares ITEM with the middle element DATA[MID] of the segment, where MID is obtained by

$$\text{MID} = \text{INT}((\text{BEG} + \text{END})/2)$$

(We use INT(A) for the integer value of A.) If DATA[MID] = ITEM, then the search is successful and we set LOC := MID. Otherwise a new segment of DATA is obtained as follows:

(a) If ITEM < DATA[MID], then ITEM can appear only in the left half of the segment:

$$\text{DATA[BEG], DATA[BEG + 1], \dots, DATA[MID − 1]}$$

So we reset END := MID − 1 and begin searching again.

(b)   If ITEM > DATA[MID], then ITEM can appear only in the right half of the segment:

$$\text{DATA[MID + 1], DATA[MID + 2], } \ldots \text{, DATA[END]}$$

So we reset BEG := MID + 1 and begin searching again.

Initially, we begin with the entire array DATA; i.e., we begin with BEG = 1 and END = n, or, more generally, with BEG = LB and END = UB.

If ITEM is not in DATA, then eventually we obtain

$$\text{END} < \text{BEG}$$

This condition signals that the search is unsuccessful, and in such a case we assign LOC := NULL. Here NULL is a value that lies outside the set of indices of DATA. (In most cases, we can choose NULL = 0.)

We state the binary search algorithm formally.

Algorithm 4.6:   (Binary Search) BINARY(DATA, LB, UB, ITEM, LOC)
Here DATA is a sorted array with lower bound LB and upper bound UB, and ITEM is a given item of information. The variables BEG, END and MID denote, respectively, the beginning, end and middle locations of a segment of elements of DATA. This algorithm finds the location LOC of ITEM in DATA or sets LOC = NULL.

1.   [Initialize segment variables.]
     Set BEG := LB, END := UB and MID = INT((BEG + END)/2).
2.   Repeat Steps 3 and 4 while BEG ≤ END and DATA[MID] ≠ ITEM.
3.   If ITEM < DATA[MID], then:
             Set END := MID − 1.
         Else:
             Set BEG := MID + 1.
         [End of If structure.]
4.   Set MID := INT((BEG + END)/2).
     [End of Step 2 loop.]
5.   If DATA[MID] = ITEM, then:
         Set LOC := MID.
     Else:
         Set LOC := NULL.
     [End of If structure.]
6.   Exit.

Remark: Whenever ITEM does not appear in DATA, the algorithm eventually arrives at the stage that BEG = END = MID. Then the next step yields END < BEG, and control transfers to Step 5 of the algorithm. This occurs in part (b) of the next example.

EXAMPLE 4.9

Let DATA be the following sorted 13-element array:

DATA: 11,   22,   30,   33,   40,   44,   55,   60,   66,   77,   80,   88,   99

We apply the binary search to DATA for different values of ITEM.

(a)   Suppose ITEM = 40. The search for ITEM in the array DATA is pictured in Fig. 4-6, where the values of DATA[BEG] and DATA[END] in each stage of the algorithm are indicated by circles and the value of

DATA[MID] by a square. Specifically, BEG, END and MID will have the following successive values:
(1) Initially, BEG = 1 and END = 13. Hence

$$MID = INT[(1 + 13)/2] = 7 \quad \text{and so} \quad DATA[MID] = 55$$

(2) Since $40 < 55$, END has its value changed by END = MID − 1 = 6. Hence

$$MID = INT[(1 + 6)/2] = 3 \quad \text{and so} \quad DATA[MID] = 30$$

(3) Since $40 > 30$, BEG has its value changed by BEG = MID + 1 = 4. Hence

$$MID = INT[(4 + 6)/2] = 5 \quad \text{and so} \quad DATA[MID] = 40$$

We have found ITEM in location LOC = MID = 5.

(1) ⑪ 22, 30, 33, 40, 44, [55,] 60, 66, 77, 80, 88, ㊾

(2) ⑪ 22, [30,] 33, 40, ㊷ 55, 60, 66, 77, 80, 88, 99

(3) 11, 22, 30, ㉝ [40,] ㊷ 55, 60, 66, 77, 80, 88, 99 [Successful]

Fig. 4-6 Binary search for ITEM = 40.

(b) Suppose ITEM = 85. The binary search for ITEM is pictured in Fig. 4-7. Here BEG, END and MID will have the following successive values:

(1) Again initially, BEG = 1, END = 13, MID = 7 and DATA[MID] = 55.
(2) Since $85 > 55$, BEG has its value changed by BEG = MID + 1 = 8. Hence

$$MID = INT[(8 + 13)/2] = 10 \quad \text{and so} \quad DATA[MID] = 77$$

(3) Since $85 > 77$, BEG has its value changed by BEG = MID + 1 = 11. Hence

$$MID = INT[(11 + 13)/2] = 12 \quad \text{and so} \quad DATA[MID] = 88$$

(4) Since $85 < 88$, END has its value changed by END = MID − 1 = 11. Hence

$$MID = INT[(11 + 11)/2] = 11 \quad \text{and so} \quad DATA[MID] = 80$$

(Observe that now BEG = END = MID = 11.)

Since $85 > 80$, BEG has its value changed by BEG = MID + 1 = 12. But now BEG > END. Hence ITEM does not belong to DATA.

(1) ⑪ 22, 30, 33, 40, 44, [55,] 60, 66, 77, 80, 88, ㊾

(2) 11, 22, 30, 33, 40, 44, 55, ㊿ 66, [77,] 80, 88, ㊾

(3) 11, 22, 30, 33, 40, 44, 55, 60, 66, 77, ㊀ [88,] ㊾

(4) 11, 22, 30, 33, 40, 44, 55, 60, 66, 77, ㊀ 88, 99 [Unsuccessful]

Fig. 4-7 Binary search for ITEM = 85.

Complexity of the Binary Search Algorithm

The complexity is measured by the number $f(n)$ of comparisons to locate ITEM in DATA where DATA contains n elements. Observe that each comparison reduces the sample size in half. Hence we require at most $f(n)$ comparisons to locate ITEM where

$$2^{f(n)} > n \quad \text{or equivalently} \quad f(n) = \lfloor \log_2 n \rfloor + 1$$

That is, the running time for the worst case is approximately equal to $\log_2 n$. One can also show that the running time for the average case is approximately equal to the running time for the worst case.

EXAMPLE 4.10

Suppose DATA contains 1 000 000 elements. Observe that

$$2^{10} = 1024 > 1000 \qquad \text{and hence} \qquad 2^{20} > 1000^2 = 1\,000\,000$$

Accordingly, using the binary search algorithm, one requires only about 20 comparisons to find the location of an item in a data array with 1 000 000 elements.

Limitations of the Binary Search Algorithm

Since the binary search algorithm is very efficient (e.g., it requires only about 20 comparisons with an initial list of 1 000 000 elements), why would one want to use any other search algorithm? Observe that the algorithm requires two conditions: (1) the list must be sorted and (2) one must have direct access to the middle element in any sublist. This means that one must essentially use a sorted array to hold the data. But keeping data in a sorted array is normally very expensive when there are many insertions and deletions. Accordingly, in such situations, one may use a different data structure, such as a linked list or a binary search tree, to store the data.

4.9 MULTIDIMENSIONAL ARRAYS

The linear arrays discussed so far are also called *one-dimensional arrays*, since each element in the array is referenced by a single subscript. Most programming languages allow two-dimensional and three-dimensional arrays, i.e., arrays where elements are referenced, respectively, by two and three subscripts. In fact, some programming languages allow the number of dimensions for an array to be as high as 7. This section discusses these multidimensional arrays.

Two-Dimensional Arrays

A two-dimensional $m \times n$ array A is a collection of $m \cdot n$ data elements such that each element is specified by a pair of integers (such as J, K), called *subscripts*, with the property that

$$1 \le J \le m \qquad \text{and} \qquad 1 \le K \le n$$

The element of A with first subscript j and second subscript k will be denoted by

$$A_{J,K} \qquad \text{or} \qquad A[J, K]$$

Two-dimensional arrays are called *matrices* in mathematics and *tables* in business applications; hence two-dimensional arrays are sometimes called *matrix arrays*.

There is a standard way of drawing a two-dimensional $m \times n$ array A where the elements of A form a rectangular array with m rows and n columns and where the element A[J, K] appears in row J and column K. (A *row* is a horizontal list of elements, and a *column* is a vertical list of elements.) Figure 4-8 shows the case where A has 3 rows and 4 columns. We emphasize that each row contains those elements with the same first subscript, and each column contains those elements with the same second subscript.

```
                              Columns
                    1          2          3          4
            1  ⎡ A[1, 1]    A[1, 2]    A[1, 3]    A[1, 4] ⎤
   Rows     2  ⎢ A[2, 1]    A[2, 2]    A[2, 3]    A[2, 4] ⎥
            3  ⎣ A[3, 1]    A[3, 2]    A[3, 3]    A[3, 4] ⎦
```

Fig. 4-8 Two-dimensional 3×4 array A.

EXAMPLE 4.11

Suppose each student in a class of 25 students is given 4 tests. Assuming the students are numbered from 1 to 25, the test scores can be assigned to a 25 × 4 matrix array SCORE as pictured in Fig. 4-9. Thus SCORE[K, L] contains the Kth student's score on the Lth test. In particular, the second row of the array,

SCORE[2, 1],   SCORE[2, 2],   SCORE[2, 3],   SCORE[2, 4]

contains the four test scores of the second student.

Student	Test 1	Test 2	Test 3	Test 4
1	84	73	88	81
2	95	100	88	96
3	72	66	77	72
·	·	·	·	·
·	·	·	·	·
25	78	82	70	85

Fig. 4-9 Array SCORE.

Suppose A is a two-dimensional $m \times n$ array. The first dimension of A contains the *index set* $1, \ldots, m$, with *lower bound* 1 and *upper bound* m; and the second dimension of A contains the *index set* $1, 2, \ldots, n$, with *lower bound* 1 and *upper bound* n. The *length* of a dimension is the number of integers in its index set. The pair of lengths $m \times n$ (read "m by n") is called the *size* of the array.

Some programming languages allow one to define multidimensional arrays in which the lower bounds are not 1. (Such arrays are sometimes called *nonregular*.) However, the index set for each dimension still consists of the consecutive integers from the lower bound to the upper bound of the dimension. The length of a given dimension (i.e., the number of integers in its index set) can be obtained from the formula

$$\text{Length} = \text{upper bound} - \text{lower bound} + 1 \tag{4.3}$$

(Note that this formula is the same as Eq. (4.1), which was used for linear arrays.) Generally speaking, unless otherwise stated, we will always assume that our arrays are *regular*, that is, that the lower bound of any dimension of an array is equal to 1.

Each programming language has its own rules for declaring multidimensional arrays. (As is the case with linear arrays, all element in such arrays must be of the same data type.) Suppose, for example, that DATA is a two-dimensional 4×8 array with elements of the *real* type. FORTRAN, PL/1 and Pascal would declare such an array as follows:

FORTRAN: REAL DATA(4, 8)
PL/1:   DECLARE DATA(4, 8) FLOAT;
Pascal: VAR DATA: ARRAY[1 . . 4, 1 . . 8] OF REAL;

Observe that Pascal includes the lower bounds even though they are 1.

Remark: Programming languages which are able to declare nonregular arrays usually use a colon to separate the lower bound from the upper bound in each dimension, while using a comma to separate the dimensions. For example, in FORTRAN,

INTEGER NUMB(2:5, −3:1)

declares NUMB to be a two-dimensional array of the integer type. Here the index sets of the dimensions consist, respectively, of the integers

2, 3, 4, 5   and   −3, −2, −1, 0, 1

By Eq. (4.3), the length of the first dimension is equal to $5 - 2 + 1 = 4$, and the length of the second dimension is equal to $1 - (-3) + 1 = 5$. Thus NUMB contains $4 \cdot 5 = 20$ elements.

Representation of Two-Dimensional Arrays in Memory

Let A be a two-dimensional $m \times n$ array. Although A is pictured as a rectangular array of elements with m rows and n columns, the array will be represented in memory by a block of $m \cdot n$ sequential memory locations. Specifically, the programming language will store the array A either (1) column by column, is what is called *column-major order*, or (2) row by row, in *row-major order*. Figure 4-10 shows these two ways when A is a two-dimensional 3×4 array. We emphasize that the particular representation used depends upon the programming language, not the user.

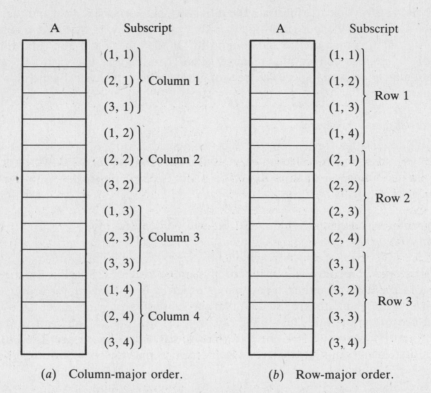

(a) Column-major order.   (b) Row-major order.

Fig. 4-10

Recall that, for a linear array LA, the computer does not keep track of the address LOC(LA[K]) of every element LA[K] of LA, but does keep track of *Base*(LA), the address of the first element of LA. The computer uses the formula

$$LOC(LA[K]) = Base(LA) + w(K - 1)$$

to find the address of LA[K] in time independent of K. (Here w is the number of words per memory cell for the array LA, and 1 is the lower bound of the index set of LA.)

A similar situation also holds for any two-dimensional $m \times n$ array A. That is, the computer keeps track of *Base*(A)—the address of the first element A[1, 1] of A—and computes the address LOC(A[J, K]) of A[J, K] using the formula

(Column-major order) $LOC(A[J, K]) = Base(A) + w[M(K - 1) + (J - 1)]$ (4.4)

or the formula

(Row-major order) $LOC(A[J, K]) = Base(A) + w[N(J - 1) + (K - 1)]$ (4.5)

Again, w denotes the number of words per memory location for the array A. Note that the formulas are linear in J and K, and that one can find the address LOC(A[J, K]) in time independent of J and K.

EXAMPLE 4.12

Consider the 25×4 matrix array SCORE in Example 4.11. Suppose $Base$(SCORE) = 200 and there are $w = 4$ words per memory cell. Furthermore, suppose the programming language stores two-dimensional arrays using row-major order. Then the address of SCORE[12, 3], the third test of the twelfth student, follows:

$$\text{LOC(SCORE[12, 3])} = 200 + 4[4(12 - 1) + (3 - 1)] = 200 + 4[46] = 384$$

Observe that we have simply used Eq. (4.5).

Multidimensional arrays clearly illustrate the difference between the logical and the physical views of data. Figure 4-8 shows how one logically views a 3×4 matrix array A, that is, as a rectangular array of data where A[J, K] appears in row J and column K. On the other hand, the data will be physically stored in memory by a linear collection of memory cells. This situation will occur throughout the text; e.g., certain data may be viewed logically as trees or graphs although physically the data will be stored linearly in memory cells.

General Multidimensional Arrays

General multidimensional arrays are defined analogously. More specifically, an n-dimensional $m_1 \times m_2 \times \cdots \times m_n$ array B is a collection of $m_1 \cdot m_2 \cdots m_n$ data elements in which each element is specified by a list of n integers—such as $K_1, K_2, \ldots, K_n$—called *subscripts*, with the property that

$$1 \le K_1 \le m_1, \qquad 1 \le K_2 \le m_2, \qquad \ldots, \qquad 1 \le K_n \le m_n$$

The element of B with subscripts $K_1, K_2, \ldots, K_n$ will be denoted by

$$B_{K_1, K_2, \ldots K_n} \qquad \text{or} \qquad B[K_1, K_2, \ldots, K_N]$$

The array will be stored in memory in a sequence of memory locations. Specifically, the programming language will store the array B either in row-major order or in column-major order. By *row-major order*, we mean that the elements are listed so that the subscripts vary like an automobile odometer, i.e., so that the last subscript varies first (most rapidly), the next-to-last subscript varies second (less rapidly), and so on. By *column-major order*, we mean that the elements are listed so that the first subscript varies first (most rapidly), the second subscript second (less rapidly), and so on.

EXAMPLE 4.13

Suppose B is a three-dimensional $2 \times 4 \times 3$ array. Then B contains $2 \cdot 4 \cdot 3 = 24$ elements. These 24 elements of B are usually pictured as in Fig. 4-11; i.e., they appear in three layers, called *pages*, where each page consists of the 2×4 rectangular array of elements with the same third subscript. (Thus the three subscripts of an element in a three-dimensional array are called, respectively, the *row*, *column* and *page* of the element.) The two ways of storing B in memory appear in Fig. 4-12. Observe that the arrows in Fig. 4-11 indicate the column-major order of the elements.

The definition of general multidimensional arrays also permits lower bounds other than 1. Let C be such an n-dimensional array. As before, the index set for each dimension of C consists of the consecutive integers from the lower bound to the upper bound of the dimension. The length L_i of dimension i of C is the number of elements in the index set, and L_i can be calculated, as before, from

$$L_i = \text{upper bound} - \text{lower bound} + 1 \tag{4.6}$$

For a given subscript K_i, the effective index E_i of L_i is the number of indices preceding K_i in the index set, and E_i can be calculated from

$$E_i = K_i - \text{lower bound} \tag{4.7}$$

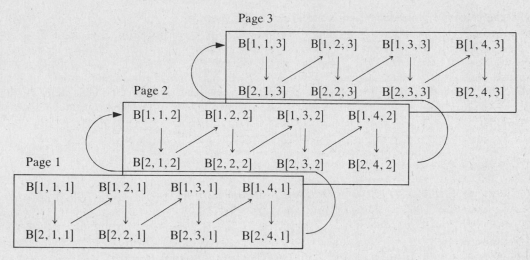

Fig. 4-11

	B	Subscripts		B	Subscripts
		$(1, 1, 1)$			$(1, 1, 1)$
		$(2, 1, 1)$			$(1, 1, 2)$
		$(1, 2, 1)$			$(1, 1, 3)$
		$(2, 2, 1)$			$(1, 2, 1)$
		$(1, 3, 1)$			$(1, 2, 2)$
		$\vdots$			$\vdots$
		$(1, 4, 3)$			$(2, 4, 2)$
		$(2, 4, 3)$			$(2, 4, 3)$

(*a*) Column-major order.   (*b*) Row-major order.

Fig. 4-12

Then the address $LOC(C[K_1, K_2, \ldots, K_N]$ of an arbitrary element of C can be obtained from the formula

$$Base(C) + w[(((\cdots(E_N L_{N-1} + E_{N-1})L_{N-2}) + \cdots + E_3)L_2 + E_2)L_1 + E_1] \qquad (4.8)$$

or from the formula

$$Base(C) + w[(\cdots((E_1 L_2 + E_2)L_3 + E_3)L_4 + \cdots + E_{N-1})L_N + E_N] \qquad (4.9)$$

according to whether C is stored in column-major or row-major order. Once again, $Base(C)$ denotes the address of the first element of C, and w denotes the number of words per memory location.

EXAMPLE 4.14

Suppose a three-dimensional array MAZE is declared using

$$MAZE(2{:}8, \ -4{:}1, \ 6{:}10)$$

Then the lengths of the three dimensions of MAZE are, respectively,

$$L_1 = 8 - 2 + 1 = 7, \qquad L_2 = 1 - (-4) + 1 = 6, \qquad L_3 = 10 - 6 + 1 = 5$$

Accordingly, MAZE contains $L_1 \cdot L_2 \cdot L_3 = 7 \cdot 6 \cdot 5 = 210$ elements.

Suppose the programming language stores MAZE in memory in row-major order, and suppose $Base(\text{MAZE}) = 200$ and there are $w = 4$ words per memory cell. The address of an element of MAZE—for example, MAZE[5, -1, 8]—is obtained as follows. The effective indices of the subscripts are, respectively,

$$E_1 = 5 - 2 = 3, \qquad E_2 = -1 - (-4) = 3, \qquad E_3 = 8 - 6 = 2$$

Using Eq. (4.9) for row-major order, we have:

$$E_1 L_2 = 3 \cdot 6 = 18$$
$$E_1 L_2 + E_2 = 18 + 3 = 21$$
$$(E_1 L_2 + E_2)L_3 = 21 \cdot 5 = 105$$
$$(E_1 L_2 + E_3)L_3 + E_3 = 105 + 2 = 107$$

Therefore,

$$\text{LOC}(\text{MAZE}[5, -1, 8]) = 200 + 4(107) = 200 + 428 = 628$$

4.10 POINTERS; POINTER ARRAYS

Let DATA be any array. A variable P is called a *pointer* if P "points" to an element in DATA, i.e., if P contains the address of an element in DATA. Analogously, an array PTR is called a *pointer array* if each element of PTR is a pointer. Pointers and pointer arrays are used to facilitate the processing of the information in DATA. This section discusses this useful tool in the context of a specific example.

Consider an organization which divides its membership list into four groups, where each group contains an alphabetized list of those members living in a certain area. Suppose Fig. 4-13 shows such a listing. Observe that there are 21 people and the groups contain 4, 9, 2 and 6 people, respectively.

Group 1	Group 2	Group 3	Group 4
Evans	Conrad	Davis	Baker
Harris	Felt	Segal	Cooper
Lewis	Glass		Ford
Shaw	Hill		Gray
	King		Jones
	Penn		Reed
	Silver		
	Troy		
	Wagner		

Fig. 4-13

Suppose the membership list is to be stored in memory keeping track of the different groups. One way to do this is to use a two-dimensional $4 \times n$ array where each row contains a group, or to use a two-dimensional $n \times 4$ array where each column contains a group. Although this data structure does allow us to access each individual group, much space will be wasted when the groups vary greatly in size. Specifically, the data in Fig. 4-13 will require at least a 36-element 4×9 or 9×4 array to store the 21 names, which is almost twice the space that is necessary. Figure 4-14 shows the representation of the 4×9 array; the asterisks denote data elements and the zeros denote unused storage locations. (Arrays whose rows—or columns—begin with different numbers of data elements and end with unused storage locations are said to be *jagged*.)

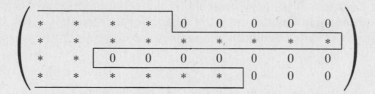

Fig. 4-14 Jagged array.

Another way the membership list can be stored in memory is pictured in Fig. 4-15(*a*). That is, the list is placed in a linear array, one group after another. Clearly, this method is space-efficient. Also, the entire list can easily be processed—one can easily print all the names on the list, for example. On the other hand, there is no way to access any particular group; e.g., there is no way to find and print only the names in the third group.

A modified version of the above method is pictured in Fig. 4-15(*b*). That is, the names are listed in a linear array, group by group, except now some sentinel or marker, such as the three dollar signs used

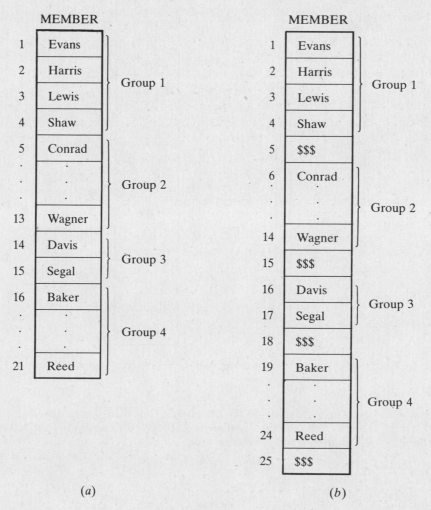

Fig. 4-15

here, will indicate the end of a group. This method uses only a few extra memory cells—one for each group—but now one can access any particular group. For example, a programmer can now find and print those names in the third group by locating those names which appear after the second sentinel and before the third sentinel. The main drawback of this representation is that the list still must be traversed from the beginning in order to recognize the third group. In other words, the different groups are not indexed with this representation.

Pointer Arrays

The two space-efficient data structures in Fig. 4-15 can be easily modified so that the individual groups can be indexed. This is accomplished by using a pointer array (here, GROUP) which contains the locations of the different groups or, more specifically, the locations of the first elements in the different groups. Figure 4-16 shows how Fig. 4-15(a) is modified. Observe that GROUP[L] and GROUP[L + 1] − 1 contain, respectively, the first and last elements in group L. (Observe that GROUP[5] points to the sentinel of the list and that GROUP[5] − 1 gives us the location of the last element in Group 4.)

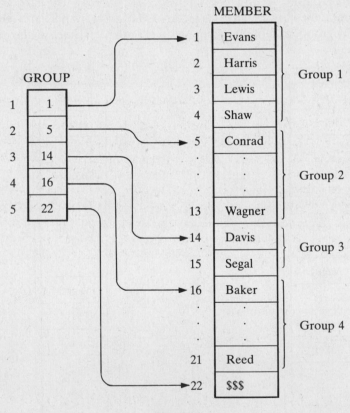

Fig. 4-16

EXAMPLE 4.15

Suppose one wants to print only the names in the Lth group in Fig. 4-16, where the value of L is part of the input. Since GROUP[L] and GROUP[L + 1] − 1 contain, respectively, the locations of the first and last name in the Lth group, the following module accomplishes our task:

1. Set FIRST := GROUP[L] and LAST := GROUP[L + 1] − 1.
2. Repeat for K = FIRST to LAST:
        Write: MEMBER[K].
    [End of loop.]
3. Return.

The simplicity of the module comes from the fact that the pointer array GROUP indexes the Lth group. The variables FIRST and LAST are used mainly for notational convenience.

A slight variation of the data structure in Fig. 4-16 is pictured in Fig. 4-17, where unused memory cells are indicated by the shading. Observe that now there are some empty cells between the groups. Accordingly, a new element may be inserted in a group without necessarily moving the elements in any

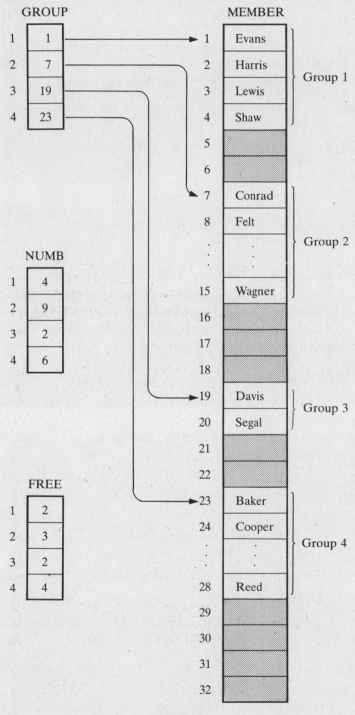

Fig. 4-17

other group. Using this data structure, one requires an array NUMB which gives the number of elements in each group. Observe that GROUP[K + 1] − GROUP[K] is the total amount of space available for Group K; hence

$$FREE[K] = GROUP[K + 1] - GROUP[K] - NUMB[K]$$

is the number of empty cells following GROUP K. Sometimes it is convenient to explicitly define the extra array FREE.

EXAMPLE 4.16

Suppose, again, one wants to print only the names in the Lth group, where L is part of the input, but now the groups are stored as in Fig. 4-17. Observe that

$$GROUP[L] \quad and \quad GROUP[L] + NUMB[L] - 1$$

contain, respectively, the locations of the first and last names in the Lth group. Thus the following module accomplishes our task:

1. Set FIRST := GROUP[L] and LAST := GROUP[L] + NUMB[L] − 1.
2. Repeat for K = FIRST to LAST:
       Write: MEMBER[K].
   [End of loop.]
3. Return.

The variables FIRST and LAST are mainly used for notational convenience.

4.11 RECORDS; RECORD STRUCTURES

Collections of data are frequently organized into a hierarchy of field, records and files. Specifically, a *record* is a collection of related data items, each of which is called a *field* or *attribute*, and a *file* is a collection of similar records. Each data item itself may be a group item composed of subitems; those items which are indecomposable are called *elementary items* or *atoms* or *scalars*. The names given to the various data items are called *identifiers*.

Although a record is a collection of data items, it differs from a linear array in the following ways:

(*a*) A record may be a collection of *nonhomogeneous* data; i.e., the data items in a record may have different data types.

(*b*) The data items in a record are indexed by attribute names, so there may not be a natural ordering of its elements.

Under the relationship of group item to subitem, the data items in a record form a hierarchical structure which can be described by means of "level" numbers, as illustrated in Examples 4.17 and 4.18.

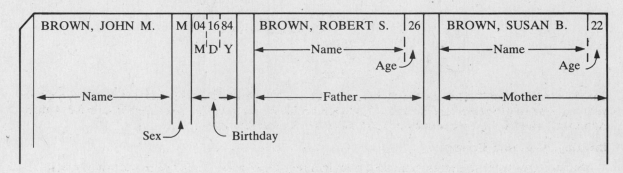

Fig. 4-18

EXAMPLE 4.17

Suppose a hospital keeps a record on each newborn baby which contains the following data items: Name, Sex, Birthday, Father, Mother. Suppose further that Birthday is a group item with subitems Month, Day and Year, and Father and Mother are group items, each with subitems Name and Age. Figure 4-18 shows how such a record could appear.

The structure of the above record is usually described as follows. (Note that Name appears three times and Age appears twice in the structure.)

```
1   Newborn
    2   Name
    2   Sex
    2   Birthday
        3   Month
        3   Day
        3   Year
    2   Father
        3   Name
        3   Age
    2   Mother
        3   Name
        3   Age
```

The number to the left of each identifier is called a level number. Observe that each group item is followed by its subitems, and the level of the subitems is 1 more than the level of the group item. Furthermore, an item is a group item if and only if it is immediately followed by an item with a greater level number.

Some of the identifiers in a record structure may also refer to arrays of elements. In fact, suppose the first line of the above structure is replaced by

$$1 \quad \text{Newborn(20)}$$

This will indicate a file of 20 records, and the usual subscript notation will be used to distinguish between different records in the file. That is, we will write

$$\text{Newborn}_1, \quad \text{Newborn}_2, \quad \text{Newborn}_3, \ldots$$

or

$$\text{Newborn[1]}, \quad \text{Newborn[2]}, \quad \text{Newborn[3]}, \ldots$$

to denote different records in the file.

EXAMPLE 4.18

A class of student records may be organized as follows:

```
1   Student(20)
    2   Name
        3   Last
        3   First
        3   MI (Middle Initial)
    2   Test(3)
    2   Final
    2   Grade
```

The identifier Student(20) indicates that there are 20 students. The identifier Test (3) indicates that there are three tests per student. Observe that there are 8 elementary items per Student, since Test is counted 3 times. Altogether, there are 160 elementary items in the entire Student structure.

Indexing Items in a Record

Suppose we want to access some data item in a record. In some cases, we cannot simply write the data name of the item since the same name may appear in different places in the record. For example,

Age appears in two places in the record in Example 4.17. Accordingly, in order to specify a particular item, we may have to *qualify* the name by using appropriate group item names in the structure. This *qualification* is indicated by using decimal points (periods) to separate group items from subitems.

EXAMPLE 4.19

(*a*) Consider the record structure Newborn in Example 4.17. Sex and year need no qualification, since each refers to a unique item in the structure. On the other hand, suppose we want to refer to the age of the father. This can be done by writing

$$\text{Newborn.Father.Age} \quad \text{or simply} \quad \text{Father.Age}$$

The first reference is said to be fully qualified. Sometimes one adds qualifying identifiers for clarity.

(*b*) Suppose the first line in the record structure in Example 4.17 is replaced by

$$1 \text{ Newborn}(20)$$

That is, Newborn is defined to be a file with 20 records. Then every item automatically becomes a 20-element array. Some languages allow the sex of the sixth newborn to be referenced by writing

$$\text{Newborn.Sex}[6] \quad \text{or simply} \quad \text{Sex}[6]$$

Analogously, the age of the father of the sixth newborn may be referenced by writing

$$\text{Newborn.Father.Age}[6] \quad \text{or simply} \quad \text{Father.Age}[6]$$

(*c*) Consider the record structure Student in Example 4.18. Since Student is declared to be a file with 20 students, all items automatically become 20-element arrays. Furthermore, Test becomes a two-dimensional array. In particular, the second test of the sixth student may be referenced by writing

$$\text{Student.Test}[6, 2] \quad \text{or simply} \quad \text{Test}[6, 2]$$

The order of the subscripts corresponds to the order of the qualifying identifiers. For example,

$$\text{Test}[3, 1]$$

does not refer to the third test of the first student, but to the first test of the third student.

Remark: Texts sometimes use functional notation instead of the dot notation to denote qualifying identifiers. For example, one writes

$$\text{Age(Father(Newborn))} \quad \text{instead of} \quad \text{Newborn.Father.Age}$$

and

$$\text{First(Name(Student}[8])) \quad \text{instead of} \quad \text{Student.Name.First}[8]$$

Observe that the order of the qualifying identifiers in the functional notation is the reverse of the order in the dot notation.

4.12 REPRESENTATION OF RECORDS IN MEMORY; PARALLEL ARRAYS

Since records may contain nonhomogeneous data, the elements of a record cannot be stored in an array. Some programming languages, such as PL/1, Pascal and COBOL, do have record structures built into the language.

EXAMPLE 4.20

Consider the record structure Newborn in Example 4.17. One can store such a record in PL/1 by the following declaration, which defines a data aggregate called a *structure*:

```
DECLARE  1  NEWBORN,
            2  NAME CHAR(20),
            2  SEX CHAR(1),
            2  BIRTHDAY,
                3  MONTH FIXED,
                3  DAY FIXED,
                3  YEAR FIXED,
            2  FATHER,
                3  NAME CHAR(20),
                3  AGE FIXED,
            2  MOTHER
                3  NAME CHAR(20),
                3  AGE FIXED;
```

Observe that the variables SEX and YEAR are unique; hence references to them need not be qualified. On the other hand, AGE is not unique. Accordingly, one should use

FATHER.AGE or MOTHER.AGE

depending on whether one wants to reference the father's age or the mother's age.

Suppose a programming language does not have available the hierarchical structures that are available in PL/1, Pascal and COBOL. Assuming the record contains nonhomogeneous data, the record may have to be stored in individual variables, one for each of its elementary data items. On the other hand, suppose one wants to store an entire file of records. Note that all data elements belonging to the same identifier do have the same type. Such a file may be stored in memory as a collection of *parallel arrays*; that is, where elements in the different arrays with the same subscript belong to the same record. This is illustrated in the next two examples.

EXAMPLE 4.21

Suppose a membership list contains the name, age, sex and telephone number of each member. One can store the file in four parallel arrays, NAME, AGE, SEX and PHONE, as pictured in Fig. 4-19; that is, for a given subscript K, the elements NAME[K], AGE[K], SEX[K] and PHONE[K] belong to the same record.

	NAME	AGE	SEX	PHONE
1	John Brown	28	Male	234-5186
2	Paul Cohen	33	Male	456-7272
3	Mary Davis	24	Female	777-1212
4	Linda Evans	27	Female	876-4478
5	Mark Green	31	Male	255-7654
⋮				

Fig. 4-19

EXAMPLE 4.22

Consider again the Newborn record in Example 4.17. One can store a file of such records in nine linear arrays, such as

NAME, SEX, MONTH, DAY, YEAR, FATHERNAME, FATHERAGE, MOTHERNAME, MOTHERAGE

one array for each elementary data item. Here we must use different variable names for the name and age of the father and mother, which was not necessary in the previous example. Again, we assume that the arrays are parallel, i.e., that for a fixed subscript K, the elements

$$\text{NAME[K], SEX[K], MONTH[K], ..., MOTHERAGE[K]}$$

belong to the same record.

Records with Variable Lengths

Suppose an elementary school keeps a record for each student which contains the following data: Name, Telephone Number, Father, Mother, Siblings. Here Father, Mother and Siblings contain, respectively, the names of the student's father, mother, and brothers or sisters attending the same school. Three such records may be as follows:

Adams, John;	345-6677;	Richard;	Mary;	Jane, William, Donald
Bailey, Susan;	222-1234;	Steven;	Sheila;	XXXX
Clark, Bruce;	567-3344;	XXXX;	Barbara;	David, Lisa

Here XXXX means that the parent has died or is not living with the student, or that the student has no sibling at the school.

The above is an example of a variable-length record, since the data element Siblings can contain zero or more names. One way of storing the file in arrays is pictured in Fig. 4-20, where there are linear arrays NAME, PHONE, FATHER and MOTHER taking care of the first four data items in the records, and arrays NUMB and PTR giving, respectively, the number and location of siblings in an array SIBLING.

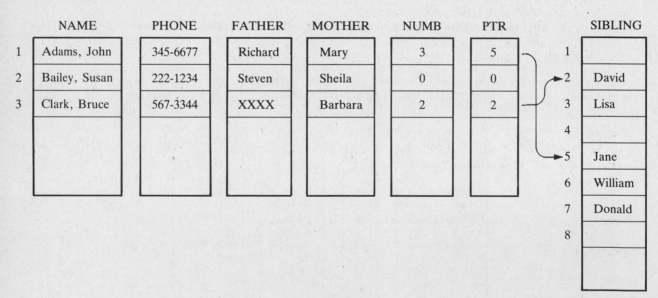

Fig. 4-20

4.13 MATRICES

"Vectors" and "matrices" are mathematical terms which refer to collections of numbers which are analogous, respectively, to linear and two-dimensional arrays. That is,

(a)   An n-element *vector* V is a list of n numbers usually given in the form

$$V = (V_1, V_2, \ldots, V_n)$$

(b) An $m \times n$ *matrix* A is an array of $m \cdot n$ numbers arranged in m rows and n columns as follows:

$$A = \begin{pmatrix} A_{11} & A_{12} & \cdots & A_{1n} \\ A_{21} & A_{22} & \cdots & A_{2n} \\ \cdots\cdots\cdots\cdots\cdots\cdots \\ A_{m1} & A_{m2} & \cdots & A_{mn} \end{pmatrix}$$

In the context of vectors and matrices, the term *scalar* is used for individual numbers.

A matrix with one row (column) may be viewed as a vector and, similarly, a vector may be viewed as a matrix with only one row (column).

A matrix with the same number n of rows and columns is called a *square matrix* or an *n-square matrix*. The *diagonal* or *main diagonal* of an n-square matrix A consists of the elements $A_{11}, A_{22}, \ldots, A_{nn}$.

The next section will review certain algebraic operations associated with vectors and matrices. Then the following section discusses efficient ways of storing certain types of matrices, called sparse matrices.

Algebra of Matrices

Suppose A and B are $m \times n$ matrices. The *sum* of A and B, written $A + B$, is the $m \times n$ matrix obtained by adding corresponding elements from A and B; and the *product* of a scalar k and the matrix A, written $k \cdot A$, is the $m \times n$ matrix obtained by multiplying each element of A by k. (Analogous operations are defined for n-element vectors.)

Matrix multiplication is best described by first defining the scalar product of two vectors. Suppose U and V are n-element vectors. Then the *scalar product* of U and V, written $U \cdot V$, is the scalar obtained by multiplying the elements of U by the corresponding elements of V, and then adding:

$$U \cdot V = U_1V_1 + U_2V_2 + \cdots + U_nV_n = \sum_{k=1}^{n} U_kV_k$$

We emphasize that $U \cdot V$ is a scalar, not a vector.

Now suppose A is an $m \times p$ and suppose B is a $p \times n$ matrix. The *product* of A and B, written AB, is the $m \times n$ matrix C whose ijth element C_{ij} is given by

$$C_{ij} = A_{i1}B_{1j} + A_{i2}B_{2j} + \cdots + A_{ip}B_{pj} = \sum_{k=1}^{p} A_{ik}B_{kj}$$

That is, C_{ij} is equal to the scalar product of row i of A and column j of B.

EXAMPLE 4.23

(a) Suppose

$$A = \begin{pmatrix} 1 & -2 & 3 \\ 0 & 4 & 5 \end{pmatrix} \quad \text{and} \quad B = \begin{pmatrix} 3 & 0 & -6 \\ 2 & -3 & 1 \end{pmatrix}$$

Then:

$$A + B = \begin{pmatrix} 1+3 & -2+0 & 3+(-6) \\ 0+2 & 4+(-3) & 5+1 \end{pmatrix} = \begin{pmatrix} 4 & -2 & -3 \\ 2 & 1 & 6 \end{pmatrix}$$

$$3A = \begin{pmatrix} 3\cdot1 & 3\cdot(-2) & 3\cdot3 \\ 3\cdot0 & 3\cdot4 & 3\cdot5 \end{pmatrix} = \begin{pmatrix} 3 & -6 & 9 \\ 0 & 12 & 15 \end{pmatrix}$$

(b) Suppose $U = (1, -3, 4, 5)$, $V = (2, -3, -6, 0)$ and $W = (3, -5, 2, -1)$. Then:

$$U \cdot V = 1\cdot2 + (-3)\cdot(-3) + 4\cdot(-6) + 5\cdot0 = 2 + 9 - 24 + 0 = -13$$
$$U \cdot W = 1\cdot3 + (-3)\cdot(-5) + 4\cdot2 + 5\cdot(-1) = 3 + 15 + 8 - 5 = 21$$

(c) Suppose

$$A = \begin{pmatrix} 1 & 3 \\ 2 & 4 \end{pmatrix} \quad \text{and} \quad B = \begin{pmatrix} 2 & 0 & -4 \\ 3 & 2 & 6 \end{pmatrix}$$

The product matrix AB is defined and is a 2×3 matrix. The elements in the first row of AB are obtained, respectively, by multiplying the first row of A by each of the columns of B:

$$\begin{pmatrix} 1 & 3 \\ 2 & 4 \end{pmatrix}\begin{pmatrix} 2 & 0 & -4 \\ 3 & 2 & 6 \end{pmatrix} = \begin{pmatrix} 1\cdot2+3\cdot3 & 1\cdot0+3\cdot2 & 1\cdot(-4)+3\cdot6 \end{pmatrix} = \begin{pmatrix} 11 & 6 & 14 \end{pmatrix}$$

Similarly, the elements in the second row of AB are obtained, respectively, by multiplying the second row of A by each of the columns of B:

$$\begin{pmatrix} 1 & 3 \\ 2 & 4 \end{pmatrix}\begin{pmatrix} 2 & 0 & -4 \\ 3 & 2 & 6 \end{pmatrix} = \begin{pmatrix} 11 & 6 & 14 \\ 2\cdot2+4\cdot3 & 2\cdot0+4\cdot2 & 2\cdot(-4)+4\cdot6 \end{pmatrix} = \begin{pmatrix} 11 & 6 & 14 \\ 16 & 8 & 16 \end{pmatrix}$$

That is,

$$AB = \begin{pmatrix} 11 & 6 & 14 \\ 16 & 8 & 16 \end{pmatrix}$$

The following algorithm finds the product AB of matrices A and B, which are stored as two-dimensional arrays. (Algorithms for matrix addition and matrix scalar multiplication, which are very similar to algorithms for vector addition and scalar multiplication, are left as exercises for the reader.)

Algorithm 4.7: (Matrix Multiplication) MATMUL(A, B, C, M, P, N)
Let A be an M × P matrix array, and let B be a P × N matrix array. This algorithm stores the product of A and B in an M × N matrix array C.

1. Repeat Steps 2 to 4 for I = 1 to M:
2.   Repeat Steps 3 and 4 for J = 1 to N:
3.   Set C[I, J] := 0. [Initializes C[I, J].]
4.   Repeat for K = 1 to P:
              C[I, J] := C[I, J] + A[I, K] * B[K, J]
          [End of inner loop.]
        [End of Step 2 middle loop.]
      [End of Step 1 outer loop.]
5. Exit.

The complexity of a matrix multiplication algorithm is measured by counting the number C of multiplications. The reason that additions are not counted in such algorithms is that computer multiplication takes much more time than computer addition. The complexity of the above Algorithm 4.7 is equal to

$$C = m \cdot n \cdot p$$

This comes from the fact that Step 4, which contains the only multiplication is executed $m \cdot n \cdot p$ times. Extensive research has been done on finding algorithms for matrix multiplication which minimize the number of multiplications. The next example gives an important and surprising result in this area.

EXAMPLE 4.24

Suppose A and B are 2×2 matrices. We have:

$$A = \begin{pmatrix} a & b \\ c & d \end{pmatrix}, \quad B = \begin{pmatrix} e & f \\ g & h \end{pmatrix} \quad \text{and} \quad AB = \begin{pmatrix} ae+bg & af+bh \\ ce+dg & cf+dh \end{pmatrix}$$

In Algorithm 4.7, the product matrix AB is obtained using $C = 2 \cdot 2 \cdot 2 = 8$ multiplications. On the other hand, AB can also be obtained from the following, which uses only 7 multiplications:

$$AB = \begin{pmatrix} (1+4-5+7) & (3+5) \\ (2+4) & (1+3-2+6) \end{pmatrix}$$

(1)　$(a+d)(e+h)$

(2)　$(c+d)e$

(3)　$a(f-h)$

(4)　$d(g-e)$

(5)　$(a+b)h$

(6)　$(c-a)(e+f)$

(7)　$(b-d)(g+h)$

Certain versions of the programming language BASIC have matrix operations built into the language. Specifically, the following are valid BASIC statements where A and B are two-dimensional arrays that have appropriate dimensions and K is a scalar:

$$MAT\ C = A + B$$

$$MAT\ D = (K) * A$$

$$MAT\ E = A * B$$

Each statement begins with the keyword MAT, which indicates that matrix operations will be performed. Thus C will be the matrix sum of A and B, D will be the scalar product of the matrix A by the scalar K, and E will be the matrix product of A and B.

4.14 SPARSE MATRICES

Matrices with a relatively high proportion of zero entries are called *sparse matrices*. Two general types of n-square sparse matrices, which occur in various applications, are pictured in Fig. 4-21. (It is sometimes customary to omit blocks of zeros in a matrix as in Fig. 4-21.) The first matrix, where all entries above the main diagonal are zero or, equivalently, where nonzero entries can only occur on or below the main diagonal, is called a (*lower*) *triangular matrix*. The second matrix, where nonzero entries can only occur on the diagonal or on elements immediately above or below the diagonal, is called a *tridiagonal matrix*.

$$\begin{pmatrix} 4 & & & & \\ 3 & -5 & & & \\ 1 & 0 & 6 & & \\ -7 & 8 & -1 & 3 & \\ 5 & -2 & 0 & 2 & -8 \end{pmatrix}$$

(*a*) Triangular matrix.

$$\begin{pmatrix} 5 & -3 & & & & & \\ 1 & 4 & 3 & & & & \\ & 9 & -3 & 6 & & & \\ & & 2 & 4 & -7 & & \\ & & & 3 & -1 & 0 & \\ & & & & 6 & -5 & 8 \\ & & & & & 3 & -1 \end{pmatrix}$$

(*b*) Tridiagonal matrix.

Fig. 4-21

The natural method of representing matrices in memory as two-dimensional arrays may not be suitable for sparse matrices. That is, one may save space by storing only those entries which may be nonzero. This is illustrated for triangular matrices in the following example. Other cases will be discussed in the solved problems.

EXAMPLE 4.25

Suppose we want to place in memory the triangular array A in Fig. 4-22. Clearly it would be wasteful to store those entries above the main diagonal of A, since we know they are all zero; hence we store only the other entries of A in a linear array B as indicated by the arrows. That is, we let

$$B[1] = a_{11}, \qquad B[2] = a_{21}, \qquad B[3] = a_{22}, \qquad B[3] = a_{31}, \qquad \cdots$$

Observe first that B will contain only

$$1 + 2 + 3 + 4 + \cdots + n = \frac{1}{2} n(n+1)$$

elements, which is about half as many elements as a two-dimensional $n \times n$ array. Since we will require the value of a_{JK} in our programs, we will want the formula that gives us the integer L in terms of J and K where

$$B[L] = a_{JK}$$

Observe that L represents the number of elements in the list up to and including a_{JK}. Now there are

$$1 + 2 + 3 + \cdots + (J - 1) = \frac{J(J-1)}{2}$$

elements in the rows above a_{JK}, and there are K elements in row J up to and including a_{JK}. Accordingly,

$$L = \frac{J(J-1)}{2} + K$$

yields the index that accesses the value a_{JK} from the linear array B.

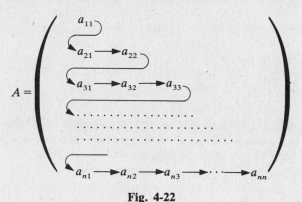

Fig. 4-22

Solved Problems

LINEAR ARRAYS

4.1   Consider the linear arrays AAA(5:50), BBB(−5:10) and CCC(18).

(a)   Find the number of elements in each array.

(b)   Suppose $Base$(AAA) = 300 and w = 4 words per memory cell for AAA. Find the address of AAA[15], AAA[35] and AAA[55].

(a)   The number of elements is equal to the length; hence use the formula

$$\text{Length} = \text{UB} - \text{LB} + 1$$

Accordingly, $\text{Length}(\text{AAA}) = 50 - 5 + 1 = 46$

$$\text{Length}(\text{BBB}) = 10 - (-5) + 1 = 16$$
$$\text{Length}(\text{CCC}) = 18 - 1 + 1 = 18$$

Note that Length(CCC) = UB, since LB = 1.

(b) Use the formula

Hence:

$$LOC(AAA[K]) = Base(AAA) + w(K - LB)$$
$$LOC(AAA[15]) = 300 + 4(15 - 5) = 340$$
$$LOC(AAA[35]) = 300 + 4(35 - 5) = 420$$

AAA[55] is not an element of AAA, since 55 exceeds UB = 50.

4.2 Suppose a company keeps a linear array YEAR(1920:1970) such that YEAR[K] contains the number of employees born in year K. Write a module for each of the following tasks:

(a) To print each of the years in which no employee was born.

(b) To find the number NNN of years in which no employee was born.

(c) To find the number N50 of employees who will be at least 50 years old at the end of the year. (Assume 1984 is the current year.)

(d) To find the number NL of employees who will be at least L years old at the end of the year. (Assume 1984 is the current year.)

Each module traverses the array.

(a) 1. Repeat for K = 1920 to 1970:
           If YEAR[K] = 0, then: Write: K.
        [End of loop.]
     2. Return.

(b) 1. Set NNN := 0.
     2. Repeat for K = 1920 to 1970:
           If YEAR[K] = 0, then: Set NNN := NNN + 1.
        [End of loop.]
     3. Return.

(c) We want the number of employees born in 1934 or earlier.

     1. Set N50 := 0.
     2. Repeat for K = 1920 to 1934:
           Set N50 := N50 + YEAR[K].
        [End of loop.]
     3. Return.

(d) We want the number of employees born in year 1984 − L or earlier.

     1. Set NL := 0 and LLL := 1984 − L.
     2. Repeat for K = 1920 to LLL:
           Set NL := NL + YEAR[K].
        [End of loop.]
     3. Return.

4.3 Suppose a 10-element array A contains the values $a_1, a_2, \ldots, a_{10}$. Find the values in A after each loop.

(a) Repeat for K = 1 to 9:
        Set A[K + 1] := A[K].
     [End of loop.]

(b) Repeat for K = 9 to 1 by −1:
        Set A[K + 1] := A[9].
     [End of loop.]

Note that the index K runs from 1 to 9 in part (a) but in reverse order from 9 back to 1 in part (b).

(a) First A[2] := A[1] sets A[2] = a_1, the value of A[1].
     Then A[3] := A[2] sets A[3] = a_1, the current value of A[2].
     Then A[4] := A[3] sets A[4] = a_1, the current value of A[3]. And so on.
     Thus every element of A will have the value x_1, the original value of A[1].

(b) First A[10] := A[9] sets A[10] = a_9.
     Then A[9] := A[8] sets A[9] = a_8.
     Then A[8] := A[7] sets A[8] = a_7. And so on.
     Thus every value in A will move to the next location. At the end of the loop, we still have A[1] = x_1.

Remark: This example illustrates the reason that, in the insertion algorithm, Algorithm 4.4, the elements are moved downward in reverse order, as in loop (b) above.

4.4   Consider the alphabetized linear array NAME in Fig. 4-23.

NAME

1	Allen
2	Clark
3	Dickens
4	Edwards
5	Goodman
6	Hobbs
7	Irwin
8	Klein
9	Lewis
10	Morgan
11	Richards
12	Scott
13	Tucker
14	Walton

Fig. 4-23

(a) Find the number of elements that must be moved if Brown, Johnson and Peters are inserted into NAME at three different times.

(b) How many elements are moved if the three names are inserted at the same time?

(c) How does the telephone company handle insertions in a telephone directory?

(a) Inserting Brown requires 13 elements to be moved, inserting Johnson requires 7 elements to be moved and inserting Peters requires 4 elements to be moved. Hence 24 elements are moved.

(b) If the elements are inserted at the same time, then 13 elements need be moved, each only once (with the obvious algorithm).

(c) The telephone company keeps a running list of new numbers and then updates the telephone directory once a year.

SEARCHING, SORTING

4.5   Consider the alphabetized linear array NAME in Fig. 4-23.

   (a)   Using the linear search algorithm, Algorithm 4.5, how many comparisons C are used to locate Hobbs, Morgan and Fisher?

   (b)   Indicate how the algorithm may be changed for such a sorted array to make an unsuccessful search more efficient. How does this affect part (a)?

   (a) C(Hobbs) = 6, since Hobbs is compared with each name, beginning with Allen, until Hobbs is found in NAME[6].
        C(Morgan) = 10, since Morgan appears in NAME[10].
        C(Fisher) = 15, since Fisher is initially placed in NAME[15] and then Fisher is compared with every name until it is found in NAME[15]. Hence the search is unsuccessful.

   (b)   Observe that NAME is alphabetized. Accordingly, the linear search can stop after a given name XXX is compared with a name YYY such that XXX < YYY (i.e., such that, alphabetically, XXX comes before YYY). With this algorithm, C(Fisher) = 5, since the search can stop after Fisher is compared with Goodman in NAME[5].

4.6   Suppose the binary search algorithm, Algorithm 4.6, is applied to the array NAME in Fig. 4-23 to find the location of Goodman. Find the ends BEG and END and the middle MID for the test segment in each step of the algorithm.

   Recall that MID = INT((BEG + END)/2), where INT means integer value.
   Step 1.   Here BEG = 1 [Allen] and END = 14 [Walton], so MID = 7 [Irwin].
   Step 2.   Since Goodman < Irwin, reset END = 6. Hence MID = 3 [Dickens].
   Step 3.   Since Goodman > Dickens, reset BEG = 4. Hence MID = 5 [Goodman].
   We have found the location LOC = 5 of Goodman in the array. Observe that there were C = 3 comparisons.

4.7   Modify the binary search algorithm, Algorithm 4.6, so that it becomes a search and insertion algorithm.

   There is no change in the first four steps of the algorithm. The algorithm transfers control to Step 5 only when ITEM does not appear in DATA. In such a case, ITEM is inserted before or after DATA[MID] according to whether ITEM < DATA[MID] or ITEM > DATA[MID]. The algorithm follows.

   Algorithm P4.7:   (Binary Search and Insertion) DATA is a sorted array with N elements, and ITEM is a given item of information. This algorithm finds the location LOC of ITEM in DATA or inserts ITEM in its proper place in DATA.
   Steps 1 through 4. Same as in Algorithm 4.6.
   5.   If ITEM < DATA[MID], then:
              Set LOC := MID.
        Else:
              Set LOC := MID + 1.
        [End of If structure.]
   6.   Insert ITEM into DATA[LOC] using Algorithm 4.2.
   7.   Exit.

4.8   Suppose A is a sorted array with 200 elements, and suppose a given element x appears with the same probability in any place in A. Find the worst-case running time $f(n)$ and the average-case running time $g(n)$ to find x in A using the binary search algorithm.

   For any value of k, let n_k denote the number of those elements in A that will require k comparisons to be located in A. Then:

k:	1	2	3	4	5	6	7	8
n_k:	1	2	4	8	16	32	64	73

The 73 comes from the fact that $1 + 2 + 4 + \cdots + 64 = 127$ so there are only $200 - 127 = 73$ elements left. The worst-case running time $f(n) = 8$. The average-case running time $g(n)$ is obtained as follows:

$$g(n) = \frac{1}{n} \sum_{k=1}^{8} k \cdot n_k$$

$$= \frac{1 \cdot 1 + 2 \cdot 2 + 3 \cdot 4 + 4 \cdot 8 + 5 \cdot 16 + 6 \cdot 32 + 7 \cdot 64 + 8 \cdot 73}{200}$$

$$= \frac{1353}{200} = 6.765$$

Observe that, for the binary search, the average-case and worst-case running times are approximately equal.

4.9 Using the bubble sort algorithm, Algorithm 4.4, find the number C of comparisons and the number D of interchanges which alphabetize the $n = 6$ letters in PEOPLE.

The sequences of pairs of letters which are compared in each of the $n - 1 = 5$ passes follow: a square indicates that the pair of letters is compared and interchanged, and a circle indicates that the pair of letters is compared but not interchanged.

Pass 1.   P̲E̲ O P L E,   E P̲O̲ P L E,   E O (P P) L E

          E O P̲P̲ L E,   E O P L̲P̲ E   E O P L E P

Pass 2.   (E O) P L E P,   E (O P) L E P,   E O P̲L̲ E P

          E O L̲P̲ E P,   E O L E P P

Pass 3.   (E O) L E P P,   E O̲L̲ E P P,   E L O̲E̲ P P

          E L E O P P

Pass 4.   (E L) E O P P,   E L̲E̲ O P P,   E E L O P P

Pass 5.   (E E) L O P P,   E E L O P P

Since $n = 6$, the number of comparisons will be $C = 5 + 4 + 3 + 2 + 1 = 15$. The number D of interchanges depends also on the data, as well as on the number n of elements. In this case $D = 9$.

4.10 Prove the following identity, which is used in the analysis of various sorting and searching algorithms:

$$1 + 2 + 3 + \cdots + n = \frac{n(n + 1)}{2}$$

Writing the sum S forward and backward, we obtain:

$$S = 1 + 2 + 3 + \cdots + (n - 1) + n$$
$$S = n + (n - 1) + (n - 2) + \cdots + 2 + 1$$

We find the sum of the two values of S by adding pairs as follows:

$$2S = (n + 1) + (n + 1) + (n + 1) + \cdots + (n + 1) + (n + 1)$$

There are n such sums, so $2S = n(n + 1)$. Dividing by 2 gives us our result.

MULTIDIMENSIONAL ARRAYS; MATRICES

4.11 Suppose multidimensional arrays A and B are declared using

$$A(-2:2, 2:22) \quad \text{and} \quad B(1:8, -5:5, -10:5)$$

(a) Find the length of each dimension and the number of elements in A and B.

(b) Consider the element B[3, 3, 3] in B. Find the effective indices E_1, E_2, E_3 and the address of the element, assuming $Base(B) = 400$ and there are $w = 4$ words per memory location.

(a) The length of a dimension is obtained by:

$$\text{Length} = \text{upper bound} - \text{lower bound} + 1$$

Hence the lengths L_i of the dimensions of A are:

$$L_1 = 2 - (-2) + 1 = 5 \quad \text{and} \quad L_2 = 22 - 2 + 1 = 21$$

Accordingly, A has $5 \cdot 21 = 105$ elements. The lengths L_i of the dimensions of B are:

$$L_1 = 8 - 1 + 1 = 8 \qquad L_2 = 5 - (-5) + 1 = 11 \qquad L_3 = 5 - (-10) + 1 = 16$$

Therefore, B has $8 \cdot 11 \cdot 16 = 1408$ elements.

(b) The effective index E_i is obtained from $E_i = k_i - LB$, where k_i is the given index and LB is the lower bound. Hence

$$E_1 = 3 - 1 = 2 \qquad E_2 = 3 - (-5) = 8 \qquad E_3 = 3 - (-10) = 13$$

The address depends on whether the programming language stores B in row-major order or column-major order. Assuming B is stored in column-major order, we use Eq. (4.8):

$$E_3 L_2 = 13 \cdot 11 = 143 \qquad E_3 L_2 + E_2 = 143 + 8 = 151$$
$$(E_3 L_2 + E_2) L_1 = 151 \cdot 8 = 1208 \qquad (E_3 L_2 + E_2) L_1 + E_1 = 1208 + 2 = 1210$$

Therefore, $LOC(B[3, 3, 3]) = 400 + 4(1210) = 400 + 4840 = 5240$

4.12 Let A be an $n \times n$ square matrix array. Write a module which

(a) Finds the number NUM of nonzero elements in A

(b) Finds the SUM of the elements above the diagonal, i.e., elements A[I, J] where $I < J$

(c) Finds the product PROD of the diagonal elements $(a_{11}, a_{22}, \ldots, a_{nn})$

(a) 1. Set NUM := 0.
   2. Repeat for I = 1 to N:
   3.   Repeat for J = 1 to N:
               If $A[I, J] \neq 0$, then: Set NUM := NUM + 1.
           [End of inner loop.]
       [End of outer loop.]
   4. Return.

(b) 1. Set SUM := 0.
   2. Repeat for J = 2 to N:
   3.   Repeat for I = 1 to J − 1:
               Set SUM := SUM + A[I, J].
           [End of inner Step 3 loop.]
   4. Return.

(c) 1. Set PROD := 1. [This is analogous to setting SUM = 0.]
   2. Repeat for K = 1 to N:
           Set PROD := PROD ∗ A[K, K].
       [End of loop.]
   3. Return.

4.13 Consider an n-square tridiagonal array A as shown in Fig. 4-24. Note that A has n elements on the diagonal and $n-1$ elements above and $n-1$ elements below the diagonal. Hence A contains at most $3n-2$ nonzero elements. Suppose we want to store A in a linear array B as indicated by the arrows in Fig. 4-24; i.e.,

$$B[1] = a_{11}, \quad B[2] = a_{12}, \quad B[3] = a_{21}, \quad B[4] = a_{22}, \quad \ldots$$

Find the formula that will give us L in terms of J and K such that

$$B[L] = A[J, K]$$

(so that one can access the value of A[J, K] from the array B).

Note that there are $3(J-2)+2$ elements above A[J, K] and $K-J+1$ elements to the left of A[J, K]. Hence

$$L = [3(J-2)+2] + [K-J+1] + 1 = 2J + K - 2$$

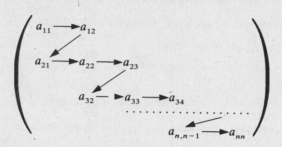

Fig. 4-24 Tridiagonal array.

4.14 An n-square matrix array A is said to be *symmetric* if A[J, K] = A[K, J] for all J and K.

(*a*) Which of the following matrices are symmetric?

$$\begin{pmatrix} 2 & -3 & 5 \\ -3 & -2 & 4 \\ 5 & 6 & 8 \end{pmatrix} \quad \begin{pmatrix} 1 & 1 & 1 & 1 \\ 1 & 1 & 1 & 1 \\ 1 & 1 & 1 & 1 \end{pmatrix} \quad \begin{pmatrix} 1 & 3 & -7 \\ 3 & 6 & -1 \\ -7 & -1 & 2 \end{pmatrix}$$

(*b*) Describe an efficient way of storing a symmetric matrix A in memory.

(*c*) Suppose A and B are two n-square symmetric matrices. Describe an efficient way of storing A and B in memory.

(*a*) The first matrix is not symmetric, since $a_{23} = 4$ but $a_{32} = 6$. The second matrix is not a square matrix so it cannot be symmetric, by definition. The third matrix is symmetric.

(*b*) Since A[J, K] = A[K, J], we need only store those elements of A which lie on or below the diagonal. This can be done in the same way as that for triangular matrices described in Example 4.25.

(*c*) First note that, for a symmetric matrix, we need store only either those elements on or below the diagonal or those on or above the diagonal. Therefore, A and B can be stored in an $n \times (n+1)$ array C as pictured in Fig. 4-25, where C[J, K] = A[J, K] when J ≥ K but C[J, K] = B[J, K-1] when J < K.

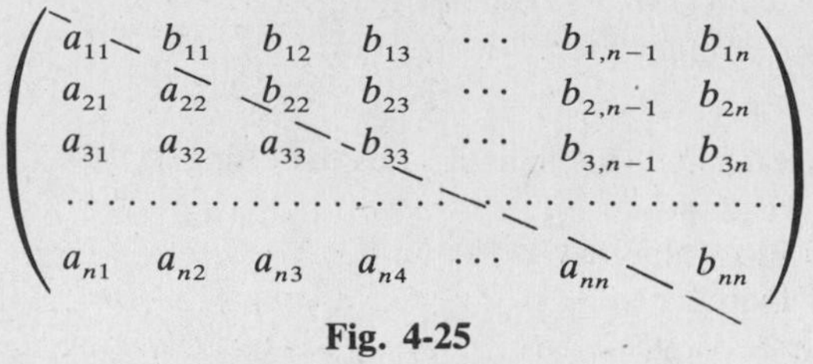

$$\begin{pmatrix} a_{11} & b_{11} & b_{12} & b_{13} & \cdots & b_{1,n-1} & b_{1n} \\ a_{21} & a_{22} & b_{22} & b_{23} & \cdots & b_{2,n-1} & b_{2n} \\ a_{31} & a_{32} & a_{33} & b_{33} & \cdots & b_{3,n-1} & b_{3n} \\ \cdots & \cdots & \cdots & \cdots & \cdots & \cdots & \cdots \\ a_{n1} & a_{n2} & a_{n3} & a_{n4} & \cdots & a_{nn} & b_{nn} \end{pmatrix}$$

Fig. 4-25

POINTER ARRAYS; RECORD STRUCTURES

4.15 Three lawyers, Davis, Levine and Nelson, share the same office. Each lawyer has his own clients. Figure 4-26 shows three ways of organizing the data.

(a) Here there is an alphabetized array CLIENT and an array LAWYER such that LAWYER[K] is the lawyer for CLIENT[K].

(b) Here there are three separate arrays, DAVIS, LEVINE and NELSON, each array containing the list of the lawyer's clients.

(c) Here there is a LAWYER array, and arrays NUMB and PTR giving, respectively, the number and location of each lawyer's alphabetized list of clients in an array CLIENT.

Which data structure is most useful? Why?

(a)

	CLIENT		LAWYER
1	Adams		Nelson
2	Brown		Davis
3	Cohen		Davis
4	Dixon		Levine
5	Eisen		Davis
6	Fischer		Levine
7	Gibson		Nelson
8	Harris		Nelson
.	.		.
.	.		.
.	.		.

(b)

	DAVIS		LEVINE		NELSON
1	Brown	1	Dixon	1	Adams
2	Cohen	2	Fischer	2	Gibson
3	Eisen	.	.	3	Harris
.	.	.	.	.	.
.	.	.	.	.	.
.	.				

(c)

	LAWYER	NUMB	PTR			CLIENT
1	Davis	94	1		1	Brown
2	Levine	72	125		2	Cohen
3	Nelson	86	275		.	.
					125	Dixon
					126	Fischer
					.	.
					275	Adams
					276	Gibson
					.	.

Fig. 4-26

The most useful data structure depends on how the office is organized and how the clients are processed.

Suppose there are only one secretary and one telephone number, and suppose there is a single monthly billing of the clients. Also, suppose clients frequently change from one lawyer to another. Then Fig. 4-26(a) would probably be the most useful data structure.

Suppose the lawyers operate completely independently: each lawyer has his own secretary and his own telephone number and bills his clients differently. Then Fig. 4-26(*b*) would likely be the most useful data structure.

Suppose the office processes all the clients frequently and each lawyer has to process his own clients frequently. Then Fig. 4-26(*c*) would likely be the most useful data structure.

4.16 The following is a list of entries, with level numbers, in a student's record:

1 Student 2 Number 2 Name 3 Last 3 First 3 MI (Middle Initial) 2 Sex
       2 Birthday 3 Day 3 Month 3 Year 2 SAT 3 Math 3 Verbal

(*a*) Draw the corresponding hierarchical structure.

(*b*) Which of the items are elementary items?

(*a*) Although the items are listed linearly, the level numbers describe the hierarchical relationship between the items. The corresponding hierarchical structure follows:

```
1  Student
      2  Number
      2  Name
            3  Last
            3  First
            3  MI
      2  Sex
      2  Birthday
            3  Day
            3  Month
            3  Year
      2  SAT
            3  Math
            3  Verbal
```

(*b*) The elementary items are the data items which do not contain subitems: Number, Last, First, MI, Sex, Day, Month, Year, Math and Verbal. Observe that an item is elementary only if it is not followed by an item with a higher level number.

4.17 A professor keeps the following data for each student in a class of 20 students:

Name (Last, First, MI), Three Tests, Final, Grade

Here Grade is a 2-character entry, for example, B+ or C or A−. Describe a PL/1 structure to store the data.

An element in a record structure may be an array itself. Instead of storing the three tests separately, we store them in an array. Such a structure follows:

```
DECLARE    1  STUDENT(20),
               2  NAME,
                    3  LAST   CHARACTER(10),
                    3  FIRST  CHARACTER(10),
                    3  MI     CHARACTER(1),
               2  TEST(3)  FIXED,
               2  FINAL    FIXED,
               2  GRADE    CHARACTER(2);
```

4.18 A college uses the following structure for a graduating class:

$$1 \quad \text{Student(200)}$$

    2 Name
        3 Last
        3 First
        3 Middle Initial
    2 Major
    2 SAT
        3 Verbal
        3 Math
    2 GPA(4)
    2 CUM

Here, GPA[K] refers to the grade point average during the *k*th year and CUM refers to the cumulative grade point average.

(*a*) How many elementary items are there in the file?

(*b*) How does one access (i) the major of the eighth student and (ii) the sophomore GPA of the forty-fifth student?

(*c*) Find each output:
   (i)   Write: Name[15]
   (ii) Write: CUM
   (iii) Write: GPA[2].
   (iv) Write: GPA[1, 3].

(*a*) Since GPA is counted 4 times per student, there are 11 elementary items per student, so there are altogether 2200 elementary items.

(*b*) (i) Student.Major[8] or simply MAJOR[8]. (ii) GPA[45, 2].

(*c*) (i)   Here Name[15] refers to the name of the fifteenth student. But Name is a group item. Hence LAST[15], First[15] and MI[15] are printed.

   (ii) Here CUM refers to all the CUM values. That is,

$$\text{CUM[1]}, \qquad \text{CUM[2]}, \qquad \text{CUM[3]}, \qquad \ldots, \qquad \text{CUM[200]}$$

   are printed.

   (iii) GPA[2] refers to the GPA array of the second student. Hence,

$$\text{GPA[2, 1]}, \qquad \text{GPA[2, 2]}, \qquad \text{GPA[2, 3]}, \qquad \text{GPA[2, 4]}$$

   are printed.

   (iv) GPA[1, 3] is a single item, the GPA during the junior year of the first student. That is, only GPA[1, 3] is printed.

4.19 An automobile dealership keeps track of the serial number and price of each of its automobiles in arrays AUTO and PRICE, respectively. In addition, it uses the data structure in Fig. 4-27, which combines a record structure with pointer variables. The new Chevys, new Buicks, new Oldsmobiles, and used cars are listed together in AUTO. The variables NUMB and PTR under USED give, respectively, the number and location of the list of used automobiles.

(*a*) How does one index the location of the list of new Buicks in AUTO?

(*b*) Write a procedure to print serial numbers of all new Buicks under $10 000.

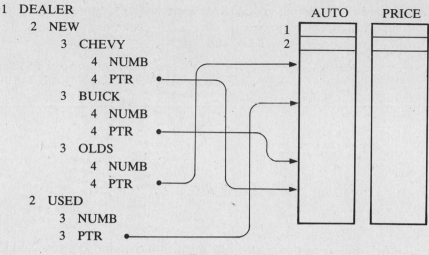

Fig. 4-27

(a) Since PTR appears more than once in the record structure, one must use BUICK.PTR to reference the location of the list of new Buicks in AUTO.

(b) One must traverse the list of new Buicks but print out only those Buicks whose price is less than $10 000. The procedure follows:

Procedure P4.19: The data are stored in the structure in Fig. 4-27. This procedure outputs those new Buicks whose price is less than $10 000.

    1. Set FIRST := BUICK.PTR. [Location of first element in Buick list.]
    2. Set LAST := FIRST + BUICK.NUMB − 1. [Location of last element in list.]
    3. Repeat for K = FIRST to LAST.
        If PRICE[K] < 10 000, then:
            Write: AUTO[K], PRICE[K].
        [End of If structure.]
        [End of loop.]
    4. Exit.

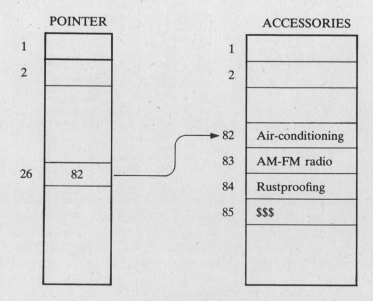

Fig. 4-28

4.20   Suppose in Prob. 4.19 the dealership had also wanted to keep track of the accessories of each automobile, such as air-conditioning, radio, and rustproofing. Since this involves variable-length data, how might this be done?

> This can be accomplished as in Fig. 4-28. That is, besides AUTO and PRICE, there is an array POINTER such that POINTER[K] gives the location in an array ACCESSORIES of the list of accessories (with sentinel '$$$') of AUTO[K].

Supplementary Problems

ARRAYS

4.21   Consider the linear arrays XXX(−10:10), YYY(1935:1985), ZZZ(35). (*a*) Find the number of elements in each array. (*b*) Suppose *Base*(YYY) = 400 and *w* = 4 words per memory cell for YYY. Find the address of YYY[1942], YYY[1977] and YYY[1988].

4.22   Consider the following multidimensional arrays:

$$X(-5:5, 3:33) \qquad Y(3:10, 1:15, 10:20)$$

(*a*)   Find the length of each dimension and the number of elements in X and Y.

(*b*)   Suppose *Base*(Y) = 400 and there are *w* = 4 words per memory location. Find the effective indices E_1, E_2, E_3 and the address of Y[5, 10, 15] assuming (i) Y is stored in row-major order and (ii) Y is stored in column-major order.

4.23   An array A contains 25 positive integers. Write a module which

(*a*)   Finds all pairs of elements whose sum is 25

(*b*)   Finds the number EVNUM of elements of A which are even, and the number ODNUM of elements of A which are odd

4.24   Suppose A is a linear array with *n* numeric values. Write a procedure

MEAN(A, N, AVE)

which finds the average AVE of the values in A. The *arithmetic mean* or *average* $\bar{x}$ of the values $x_1, x_2, \ldots, x_n$ is defined by

$$\bar{x} = \frac{x_1 + x_2 + \cdots + x_n}{n}$$

4.25   Each student in a class of 30 students takes 6 tests in which scores range between 0 and 100. Suppose the test scores are stored in a 30×6 array TEST. Write a module which

(*a*)   Finds the average grade for each test

(*b*)   Finds the final grade for each student where the final grade is the average of the student's five highest test scores

(*c*)   Finds the number NUM of students who have failed, i.e., whose final grade is less than 60

(*d*)   Finds the average of the final grades

POINTER ARRAYS; RECORD STRUCTURES

4.26   Consider the data in Fig. 4-26(*c*). (*a*) Write a procedure which prints the list of clients belonging to LAWYER[K]. (*b*) Assuming CLIENT has space for 400 elements, define an array FREE such that FREE[K] contains the number of empty cells following the list of clients belonging to LAWYER[K].

4.27   The following is a list of entries, with level numbers, in a file of employee records:

> 1   Employee(200),   2   SSN(Social Security Number),   2   Name,
> 3   Last,   3   First,   3   MI (Middle Initial),   2   Address,   3   Street,
> 3   Area,   4   City,   4   State,   4   ZIP,   2   Age,   2   Salary,   2   Dependents

(a)   Draw the corresponding hierarchical structure.

(b)   Which of the items are elementary items?

(c)   Describe a record structure—for example, a PL/1 structure or a Pascal record—to store the data.

4.28   Consider the data structure in Fig. 4-27. Write a procedure to carry out each of the following:

(a)   Finding the number of new Oldsmobiles selling for under $10 000.

(b)   Finding the number of new automobiles selling for under $10 000.

(c)   Finding the number of automobiles selling for under $10 000.

(d)   Listing all automobiles selling for under $10 000.

(*Note*: Parts (c) and (d) require only the arrays AUTO and PRICE together with the number of automobiles.)

4.29   A class of student records is organized as follows:

> 1   Student(35),   2   Name,   3   Last,   3   First,   3   MI (Middle Initial),   2   Major
> 2   Test(4),   2   Final,   2   Grade

(a)   How many elementary items are there?

(b)   Describe a record structure—for example, a PL/1 structure or a Pascal record, to store the data.

(c)   Describe the output of each of the following Write statements: (i) Write: Final[15], (ii) Write: Name[15] and (iii) Write: Test[4].

4.30   Consider the data structure in Prob. 4.18. Write a procedure which

(a)   Finds the average of the sophomore GPA scores

(b)   Finds the number of biology majors

(c)   Finds the number of CUM scores exceeding K

Programming Problems

ARRAYS

Assume that the data in Table 4-1 are stored in linear arrays SSN, LAST, GIVEN, CUM and YEAR (with space for 25 students) and that a variable NUM is defined which contains the actual number of students.

4.31   Write a program for each of the following:

(a)   Listing all students whose CUM is K or higher. (Test the program using K = 3.00.)

(b)   Listing all students in year L. (Test the program using L = 2, or sophomore.)

4.32   Translate the linear search algorithm into a subprogram LINEAR(ARRAY, LB, UB, ITEM, LOC) which either finds the location LOC where ITEM appears in ARRAY or returns LOC = 0.

4.33   Translate the binary search and insertion algorithm into a subprogram BINARY(ARRAY, LB, UB, ITEM, LOC) which finds either the location LOC where ITEM appears in ARRAY or the location LOC where ITEM should be inserted into ARRAY.

Table 4-1

Social Security Number	Last Name	Given Name	CUM	Year
211-58-1329	Adams	Bruce	2.55	2
169-38-4248	Bailey	Irene L.	3.25	4
166-48-5842	Cheng	Kim	3.40	1
187-52-4076	Davis	John C.	2.85	2
126-63-6382	Edwards	Steven	1.75	3
135-58-9565	Fox	Kenneth	2.80	2
172-48-1849	Green	Gerald S.	2.35	2
192-60-3157	Hopkins	Gary	2.70	2
160-60-1826	Klein	Deborah M.	3.05	1
166-52-4147	Lee	John	2.60	3
186-58-0430	Murphy	William	2.30	2
187-58-1123	Newman	Ronald P.	3.90	4
174-58-0732	Osborn	Paul	2.05	3
183-52-3865	Parker	David	1.55	2
135-48-1397	Rogers	Mary J.	1.85	1
182-52-6712	Schwab	Joanna	2.95	2
184-48-8539	Thompson	David E.	3.15	3
187-48-2377	White	Adam	2.50	2

4.34   Write a program which reads the social security number SOC of a student and uses LINEAR to find and print the student's record. Test the program using (a) 174-58-0732, (b) 172-55-5554 and (c) 126-63-6382.

4.35   Write a program which reads the (last) NAME of a student and uses BINARY to find and print the student's record. Test the program using (a) Rogers, (b) Johnson and (c) Bailey.

4.36   Write a program which reads the record of a student

SSNST,   LASTST,   GVNST,   CUMST,   YEARST

and uses BINARY to insert the record into the list. Test the program using:

(a)   168-48-2255, Quinn, Michael, 2.15, 3

(b)   177-58-0772, Jones, Amy, 2.75, 2

4.37   Write a program which reads the (last) NAME of a student and uses BINARY to delete the student's record from the list. Test the program using (a) Parker and (b) Fox.

4.38   Write a program for each of the following:

(a)   Using the array SSN to define arrays NUMBER and PTR such that NUMBER is a sorted array of the elements in SSN and PTR[K] contains the location of NUMBER[K] in SSN.

(b)   Reading the social security number SOC of a student and using BINAR and the array NUMBER to find and print the student's record. Test the program using (i) 174-58-0732, (ii) 172-55-5554 and (iii) 126-63-6382. (Compare with Prob. 4.34.)

POINTER ARRAYS

Assume the data in Table 4-2 are stored in a single linear array CLASS (with space for 50 names). Also assume that there are 2 empty cells between the sections, and that there are linear arrays NUMB, PTR and FREE defined so that NUMB[K] contains the number of elements in Section K, PTR[K] gives the location in CLASS of the first name in Section K, and FREE[K] gives the number of empty cells in CLASS following Section K.

Table 4-2

Section 1	Section 2	Section 3	Section 4
Brown	Abrams	Allen	Burns
Davis	Collins	Conroy	Cohen
Jones	Forman	Damario	Evans
Samuels	Hughes	Harris	Gilbert
	Klein	Rich	Harlan
	Lee	Sweeney	Lopez
	Moore		Meth
	Quinn		Ryan
	Rosen		Williams
	Scott		
	Taylor		
	Weaver		

4.39 Write a program which reads an integer K and prints the names in Section K. Test the program using (a) K = 2 and (b) K = 3.

4.40 Write a program which reads the NAME of a student and finds and prints the location and section number of the student. Test the program using (a) Harris, (b) Rivers and (c) Lopez.

4.41 Write a program which prints the names in columns as they appear in Table 4-2.

4.42 Write a program which reads the NAME and section number SECN of a student and inserts the student into CLASS. Test the program using (a) Eden, 3; (b) Novak, 4; (c) Parker, 2; (d) Vaughn, 3; and (e) Bennett, 3. (The program should handle OVERFLOW.)

4.43 Write a program which reads the NAME of a student and deletes the student from CLASS. Test the program using (a) Klein, (b) Daniels, (c) Meth and (d) Harris.

MISCELLANEOUS

4.44 Suppose A and B are n-element vector arrays in memory and X and Y are scalars. Write a program to find (a) $XA + YB$ and (b) $A \cdot B$. Test the program using A = (16, −6, 7), B = (4, 2, −3), X = 2 and Y = −5.

4.45 Translate the matrix multiplication algorithm, Algorithm 4.7, into a subprogram

$$\text{MATMUL}(A, B, C, M, P, N)$$

which finds the product C of an $m \times p$ matrix A and a $p \times n$ matrix B. Test the program using

$$A = \begin{pmatrix} 4 & -3 & 5 \\ 6 & 1 & -2 \end{pmatrix} \qquad B = \begin{pmatrix} 2 & 3 & -7 & -3 \\ 5 & -1 & 6 & 2 \\ 0 & 3 & -2 & 1 \end{pmatrix}$$

4.46   Consider the polynomial

$$f(x) = a_1 x^n + a_2 x^{n-1} + \cdots + a_n x + a_{n+1}$$

Evaluating the polynomial in the obvious way would require

$$n + (n-1) + \cdots + 1 = \frac{n(n+1)}{2}$$

multiplications and n additions. However, one can rewrite the polynomial by successively factoring out x as follows:

$$f(x) = ((\cdots((a_1 x + a_2)x + a_3)x + \cdots)x + a_n)x + a_{n+1}$$

This uses only n multiplications and n additions. This second way of evaluating a polynomial is called Horner's method.

(a)   Rewrite the polynomial $f(x) = 5x^4 - 6x^3 + 7x^2 + 8x - 9$ as it would be evaluated using Horner's method.

(b)   Suppose the coefficients of a polynomial are in memory in a linear array $A(N + 1)$. (That is, $A[1]$ is the coefficient of x^n, $A[2]$ is the coefficient of $x^{n-1}, \ldots$, and $A[N + 1]$ is the constant.) Write a procedure HORNER(A, N + 1, X, Y) which finds the value $Y = F(X)$ for a given value X using Horner's method.

Test the program using $X = 2$ and $f(x)$ from part (a).

Chapter 5

Linked Lists

5.1 INTRODUCTION

The everyday usage of the term "list" refers to a linear collection of data items. Figure 5-1(*a*) shows a shopping list; it contains a first element, a second element, . . . , and a last element. Frequently, we want to add items to or delete items from a list. Figure 5-1(*b*) shows the shopping list after three items have been added at the end of the list and two others have been deleted (by being crossed out).

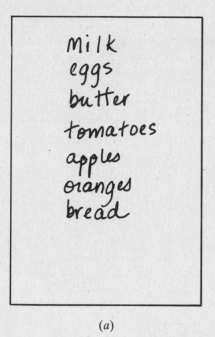
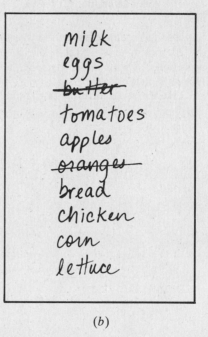

(*a*)   (*b*)

Fig. 5-1

Data processing frequently involves storing and processing data organized into lists. One way to store such data is by means of arrays, discussed in Chap. 4. Recall that the linear relationship between the data elements of an array is reflected by the physical relationship of the data in memory, not by any information contained in the data elements themselves. This makes it easy to compute the address of an element in an array. On the other hand, arrays have certain disadvantages—e.g., it is relatively expensive to insert and delete elements in an array. Also, since an array usually occupies a block of memory space, one cannot simply double or triple the size of an array when additional space is required. (For this reason, arrays are called *dense lists* and are said to be *static* data structures.)

Another way of storing a list in memory is to have each element in the list contain a field, called a *link* or *pointer*, which contains the address of the next element in the list. Thus successive elements in the list need not occupy adjacent space in memory. This will make it easier to insert and delete elements in the list. Accordingly, if one were mainly interested in searching through data for inserting and deleting, as in word processing, one would not store the data in an array but rather in a list using pointers. This latter type of data structure is called a *linked list* and is the main subject matter of this chapter. We also discuss circular lists and two-way lists—which are natural generalizations of linked lists—and their advantages and disadvantages.

114

5.2 LINKED LISTS

A *linked list*, or *one-way list*, is a linear collection of data elements, called *nodes*, where the linear order is given by means of *pointers*. That is, each node is divided into two parts: the first part contains the information of the element, and the second part, called the *link field* or *nextpointer field*, contains the address of the next node in the list. ·

Figure 5-2 is a schematic diagram of a linked list with 6 nodes, Each node is pictured with two parts. The left part represents the information part of the node, which may contain an entire record of data items (e.g., NAME, ADDRESS, . . .). The right part represents the nextpointer field of the node, and there is an arrow drawn from it to the next node in the list. This follows the usual practice of drawing an arrow from a field to a node when the address of the node appears in the given field. The pointer of the last node contains a special value, called the *null* pointer, which is any invalid address.

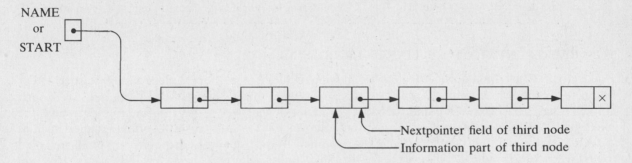

Fig. 5-2 Linked list with 6 nodes.

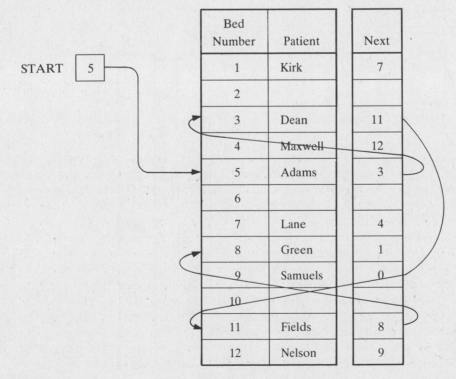

Bed Number	Patient	Next
1	Kirk	7
2		
3	Dean	11
4	Maxwell	12
5	Adams	3
6		
7	Lane	4
8	Green	1
9	Samuels	0
10		
11	Fields	8
12	Nelson	9

START 5

Fig. 5-3

(In actual practice, 0 or a negative number is used for the null pointer.) The null pointer, denoted by ×
in the diagram, signals the end of the list. The linked list also contains a *list pointer variable*—called
START or NAME—which contains the address of the first node in the list; hence there is an arrow
drawn from START to the first node. Clearly, we need only this address in START to trace through
the list. A special case is the list that has no nodes. Such a list is called the *null list* or *empty list* and is
denoted by the null pointer in the variable START.

EXAMPLE 5.1

A hospital ward contains 12 beds, of which 9 are occupied as shown in Fig. 5-3. Suppose we want an
alphabetical listing of the patients. This listing may be given by the pointer field, called Next in the figure. We use
the variable START to point to the first patient. Hence START contains 5, since the first patient, Adams,
occupies bed 5. Also, Adams's pointer is equal to 3, since Dean, the next patient, occupies bed 3; Dean's pointer is
11, since Fields, the next patient, occupies bed 11; and so on. The entry for the last patient (Samuels) contains the
null pointer, denoted by 0. (Some arrows have been drawn to indicate the listing of the first few patients.)

5.3 REPRESENTATION OF LINKED LISTS IN MEMORY

Let LIST be a linked list. Then LIST will be maintained in memory, unless otherwise specified or
implied, as follows. First of all, LIST requires two linear arrays—we will call them here INFO and
LINK—such that INFO[K] and LINK[K] contain, respectively, the information part and the
nextpointer field of a node of LIST. As noted above, LIST also requires a variable name—such as
START—which contains the location of the beginning of the list, and a nextpointer sentinel—denoted
by NULL—which indicates the end of the list. Since the subscripts of the arrays INFO and LINK will
usually be positive, we will choose NULL = 0, unless otherwise stated.

The following examples of linked lists indicate that the nodes of a list need not occupy adjacent
elements in the arrays INFO and LINK, and that more than one list may be maintained in the same
linear arrays INFO and LINK. However, each list must have its own pointer variable giving the
location of its first node.

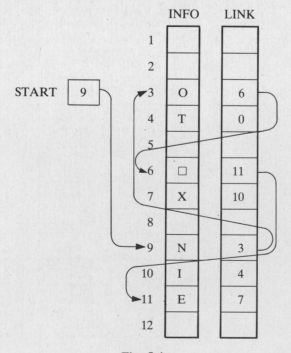

Fig. 5-4

EXAMPLE 5.2

Figure 5-4 pictures a linked list in memory where each node of the list contains a single character. We can obtain the actual list of characters, or, in other words, the string, as follows:

START = 9, so INFO[9] = N is the first character.

LINK[9] = 3, so INFO[3] = O is the second character.

LINK[3] = 6, so INFO[6] = □ (blank) is the third character.

LINK[6] = 11, so INFO[11] = E is the fourth character.

LINK[11] = 7, so INFO[7] = X is the fifth character.

LINK[7] = 10, so INFO[10] = I is the sixth character.

LINK[10] = 4, so INFO[4] = T is the seventh character.

LINK[4] = 0, the NULL value, so the list has ended.

In other words, NO EXIT is the character string.

EXAMPLE 5.3

Figure 5-5 pictures how two lists of test scores, here ALG and GEOM, may be maintained in memory where the nodes of both lists are stored in the same linear arrays TEST and LINK. Observe that the names of the lists are also used as the list pointer variables. Here ALG contains 11, the location of its first node, and GEOM contains 5, the location of its first node. Following the pointers, we see that ALG consists of the test scores

88, 74, 93, 82

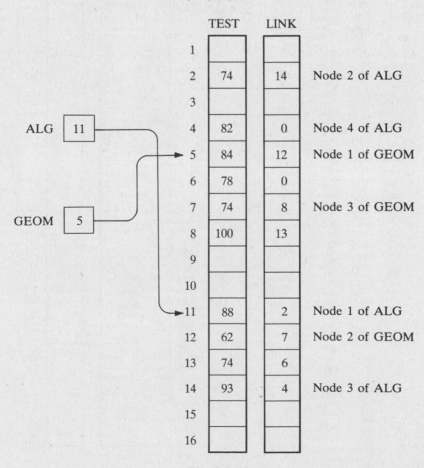

Fig. 5-5

and GEOM consists of the test scores

$$84, 62, 74, 100, 74, 78$$

(The nodes of ALG and some of the nodes of GEOM are explicitly labeled in the diagram.)

EXAMPLE 5.4

Suppose a brokerage firm has four brokers and each broker has his own list of customers. Such data may be organized as in Fig. 5-6. That is, all four lists of customers appear in the same array CUSTOMER, and an array LINK contains the nextpointer fields of the nodes of the lists. There is also an array BROKER which contains the list of brokers, and a pointer array POINT such that POINT[K] points to the beginning of the list of customers of BROKER[K].

Accordingly, Bond's list of customers, as indicated by the arrows, consists of

Grant, Scott, Vito, Katz

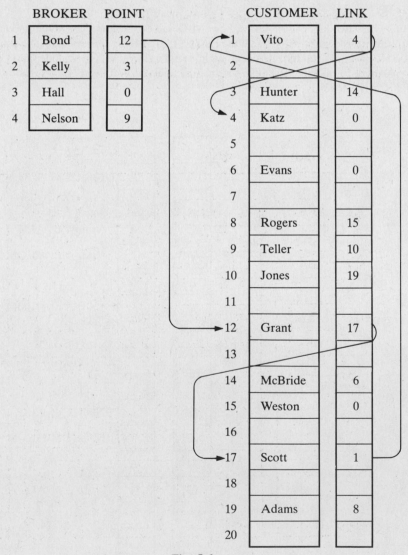

Fig. 5-6

Similarly, Kelly's list consists of

Hunter, McBride, Evans

and Nelson's list consists of

Teller, Jones, Adams, Rogers, Weston

Hall's list is the null list, since the null pointer 0 appears in POINT[3].

Generally speaking, the information part of a node may be a record with more than one data item. In such a case, the data must be stored in some type of record structure or in a collection of parallel arrays, such as that illustrated in the following example.

EXAMPLE 5.5

Suppose the personnel file of a small company contains the following data on its nine employees:

Name, Social Security Number, Sex, Monthly Salary

Normally, four parallel arrays, say NAME, SSN, SEX, SALARY, are required to store the data as discussed in Sec. 4.12. Figure 5-7 shows how the data may be stored as a sorted (alphabetically) linked list using only an additional array LINK for the nextpointer field of the list and the variable START to point to the first record in the list. Observe that 0 is used as the null pointer.

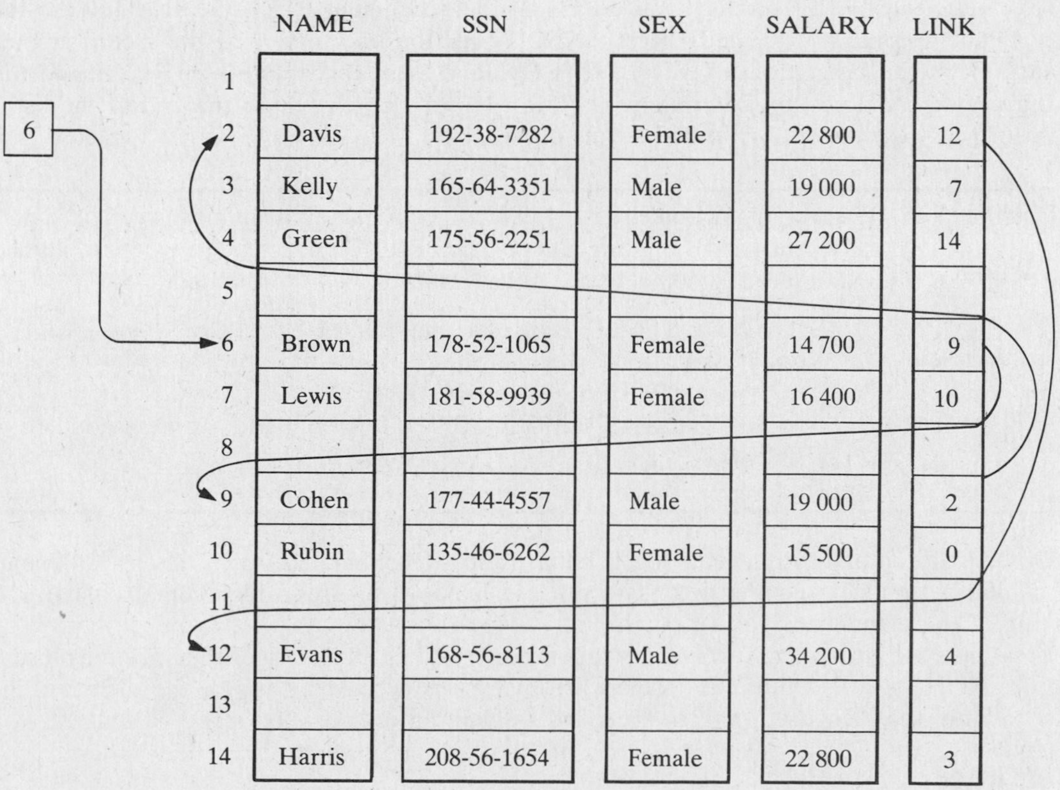

	NAME	SSN	SEX	SALARY	LINK
1					
2	Davis	192-38-7282	Female	22 800	12
3	Kelly	165-64-3351	Male	19 000	7
4	Green	175-56-2251	Male	27 200	14
5					
6	Brown	178-52-1065	Female	14 700	9
7	Lewis	181-58-9939	Female	16 400	10
8					
9	Cohen	177-44-4557	Male	19 000	2
10	Rubin	135-46-6262	Female	15 500	0
11					
12	Evans	168-56-8113	Male	34 200	4
13					
14	Harris	208-56-1654	Female	22 800	3

START = 6

Fig. 5-7

5.4 TRAVERSING A LINKED LIST

Let LIST be a linked list in memory stored in linear arrays INFO and LINK with START pointing to the first element and NULL indicating the end of LIST. Suppose we want to traverse LIST in order to process each node exactly once. This section presents an algorithm that does so and then uses the algorithm in some applications.

Our traversing algorithm uses a pointer variable PTR which points to the node that is currently being processed. Accordingly, LINK[PTR] points to the next node to be processed. Thus the assignment

$$PTR := LINK[PTR]$$

moves the pointer to the next node in the list, as pictured in Fig. 5-8.

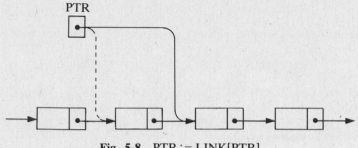

Fig. 5-8   PTR := LINK[PTR].

The details of the algorithm are as follows. Initialize PTR or START. Then process INFO[PTR], the information at the first node. Update PTR by the assignment PTR := LINK[PTR], so that PTR points to the second node. Then process INFO[PTR], the information at the second node. Again update PTR by the assignment PTR := LINK[PTR], and then process INFO[PTR], the information at the third node. And so on. Continue until PTR = NULL, which signals the end of the list.

A formal presentation of the algorithm follows.

Algorithm 5.1:   (Traversing a Linked List) Let LIST be a linked list in memory. This algorithm traverses LIST, applying an operation PROCESS to each element of LIST. The variable PTR points to the node currently being processed.

1.   Set PTR := START. [Initializes pointer PTR.]
2.   Repeat Steps 3 and 4 while PTR ≠ NULL.
3.   Apply PROCESS to INFO[PTR].
4.   Set PTR := LINK[PTR]. [PTR now points to the next node.]
     [End of Step 2 loop.]
5.   Exit.

Observe the similarity between Algorithm 5.1 and Algorithm 4.1, which traverses a linear array. The similarity comes from the fact that both are linear structures which contain a natural linear ordering of the elements.

Caution: As with linear arrays, the operation PROCESS in Algorithm 5.1 may use certain variables which must be initialized before PROCESS is applied to any of the elements in LIST. Consequently, the algorithm may be preceded by such an initialization step.

EXAMPLE 5.6

The following procedure prints the information at each node of a linked list. Since the procedure must traverse the list, it will be very similar to Algorithm 5.1.

Procedure:　PRINT(INFO, LINK, START)

　　　　　　　This procedure prints the information at each node of the list.

　　　　1.　Set PTR := START.
　　　　2.　Repeat Steps 3 and 4 while PTR ≠ NULL:
　　　　3.　　　Write: INFO[PTR].
　　　　4.　　　Set PTR := LINK[PTR]. [Updates pointer.]
　　　　　　[End of Step 2 loop.]
　　　　5.　Return.

In other words, the procedure may be obtained by simply substituting the statement

$$\text{Write:} \quad \text{INFO[PTR]}$$

for the processing step in Algorithm 5.1.

EXAMPLE 5.7

The following procedure finds the number NUM of elements in a linked list.

Procedure:　COUNT(INFO, LINK, START, NUM)

　　　　1.　Set NUM := 0. [Initializes counter.]
　　　　2.　Set PTR := START. [Initializes pointer.]
　　　　3.　Repeat Steps 4 and 5 while PTR ≠ NULL.
　　　　4.　　　Set NUM := NUM + 1. [Increases NUM by 1.]
　　　　5.　　　Set PTR := LINK[PTR]. [Updates pointer.]
　　　　　　[End of Step 3 loop.]
　　　　6.　Return.

Observe that the procedure traverses the linked list in order to count the number of elements; hence the procedure is very similar to the above traversing algorithm, Algorithm 5.1. Here, however, we require an initialization step for the variable NUM before traversing the list. In other words, the procedure could have been written as follows:

Procedure:　COUNT(INFO, LINK, START, NUM)

　　　　1.　Set NUM := 0. [Initializes counter.]
　　　　2.　Call Algorithm 5.1, replacing the processing step by:
　　　　　　　Set NUM := NUM + 1.
　　　　3.　Return.

Most list processing procedures have this form. (See Prob. 5.3.)

5.5　SEARCHING A LINKED LIST

Let LIST be a linked list in memory, stored as in Secs. 5.3 and 5.4. Suppose a specific ITEM of information is given. This section discusses two searching algorithms for finding the location LOC of the node where ITEM first appears in LIST. The first algorithm does not assume that the data in LIST are sorted, whereas the second algorithm does assume that LIST is sorted.

If ITEM is actually a key value and we are searching through a file for the record containing ITEM, then ITEM can appear only once in LIST.

LIST Is Unsorted

Suppose the data in LIST are not necessarily sorted. Then one searches for ITEM in LIST by traversing through the list using a pointer variable PTR and comparing ITEM with the contents INFO[PTR] of each node, one by one, of LIST. Before we update the pointer PTR by

$$\text{PTR} := \text{LINK[PTR]}$$

we require two tests. First we have to check to see whether we have reached the end of the list; i.e., first we check to see whether

$$PTR = NULL$$

If not, then we check to see whether

$$INFO[PTR] = ITEM$$

The two tests cannot be performed at the same time, since INFO[PTR] is not defined when PTR = NULL. Accordingly, we use the first test to control the execution of a loop, and we let the second test take place inside the loop. The algorithm follows.

Algorithm 5.2   SEARCH(INFO, LINK, START, ITEM, LOC)
LIST is a linked list in memory. This algorithm finds the location LOC of the node where ITEM first appears in LIST, or sets LOC = NULL.

1. Set PTR := START.
2. Repeat Step 3 while PTR ≠ NULL:
3.   If ITEM = INFO[PTR], then:
            Set LOC := PTR, and Exit.
       Else:
            Set PTR := LINK[PTR]. [PTR now points to the next node.]
       [End of If structure.]
   [End of Step 2 loop.]
4. [Search is unsuccessful.] Set LOC := NULL.
5. Exit.

The complexity of this algorithm is the same as that of the linear search algorithm for linear arrays discussed in Sec. 4.7. That is, the worst-case running time is proportional to the number n of elements in LIST, and the average-case running time is approximately proportional to $n/2$ (with the condition that ITEM appears once in LIST but with equal probability in any node of LIST).

EXAMPLE 5.8

Consider the personnel file in Fig. 5-7. The following module reads the social security number NNN of an employee and then gives the employee a 5 percent increase in salary.

1. Read: NNN.
2. Call SEARCH(SSN, LINK, START, NNN, LOC).
3. If LOC ≠ NULL, then:
        Set SALARY[LOC] := SALARY[LOC] + 0.05 * SALARY[LOC],
   Else:
        Write: NNN is not in file.
   [End of If structure.]
4. Return.

(The module takes care of the case in which there is an error in inputting the social security number.)

LIST Is Sorted

Suppose the data in LIST are sorted. Again we search for ITEM in LIST by traversing the list using a pointer variable PTR and comparing ITEM with the contents INFO[PTR] of each node, one by one, of LIST. Now, however, we can stop once ITEM exceeds INFO[PTR]. The algorithm follows on page 123.

The complexity of this algorithm is still the same as that of other linear search algorithms; that is, the worst-case running time is proportional to the number n of elements in LIST, and the average-case running time is approximately proportional to $n/2$.

Algorithm 5.3:　SRCHSL(INFO, LINK, START, ITEM, LOC)
　　　　　　　　　　LIST is a sorted list in memory. This algorithm finds the location LOC of the
　　　　　　　　　　node where ITEM first appears in LIST, or sets LOC = NULL.

　　　　1.　Set PTR := START.
　　　　2.　Repeat Step 3 while PTR ≠ NULL:
　　　　3.　　　　If ITEM < INFO[PTR], then:
　　　　　　　　　　　Set PTR := LINK[PTR]. [PTR now points to next node.]
　　　　　　　　Else if ITEM = INFO[PTR], then:
　　　　　　　　　　　Set LOC := PTR, and Exit. [Search is successful.]
　　　　　　　　Else:
　　　　　　　　　　　Set LOC := NULL, and Exit. [ITEM now exceeds INFO[PTR].]
　　　　　　　　[End of If structure.]
　　　　　　　[End of Step 2 loop.]
　　　　4.　Set LOC := NULL.
　　　　5.　Exit.

Recall that with a sorted linear array we can apply a binary search whose running time is proportional to $\log_2 n$. On the other hand, a *binary search algorithm cannot be applied to a sorted linked list, since there is no way of indexing the middle element in the list.* This property is one of the main drawbacks in using a linked list as a data structure.

EXAMPLE 5.9

Consider, again, the personnel file in Fig. 5-7. The following module reads the name EMP of an employee and then gives the employee a 5 percent increase in salary. (Compare with Example 5.8.)

　　　1.　Read: EMPNAME.
　　　2.　Call SRCHSL(NAME, LINK, START, EMPNAME, LOC).
　　　3.　If LOC ≠ NULL, then:
　　　　　　Set SALARY[LOC] := SALARY[LOC] + 0.05 * SALARY[LOC].
　　　　　Else:
　　　　　　　Write: EMPNAME is not in list.
　　　　　[End of If structure.]
　　　4.　Return.

Observe that now we can use the second search algorithm, Algorithm 5.3, since the list is sorted alphabetically.

5.6 MEMORY ALLOCATION; GARBAGE COLLECTION

The maintenance of linked lists in memory assumes the possibility of inserting new nodes into the lists and hence requires some mechanism which provides unused memory space for the new nodes. Analogously, some mechanism is required whereby the memory space of deleted nodes becomes available for future use. These matters are discussed in this section, while the general discussion of the inserting and deleting of nodes is postponed until later sections.

Together with the linked lists in memory, a special list is maintained which consists of unused memory cells. This list, which has its own pointer, is called the *list of available space* or the *free-storage list* or the *free pool*.

Suppose our linked lists are implemented by parallel arrays as described in the preceding sections, and suppose insertions and deletions are to be performed on our linked lists. Then the unused memory cells in the arrays will also be linked together to form a linked list using AVAIL as its list pointer variable. (Hence this free-storage list will also be called the AVAIL list.) Such a data structure will frequently be denoted by writing

$$\text{LIST(INFO, LINK, START, AVAIL)}$$

EXAMPLE 5.10

Suppose the list of patients in Example 5.1 is stored in the linear arrays BED and LINK (so that the patient in bed K is assigned to BED[K]). Then the available space in the linear array BED may be linked as in Fig. 5-9. Observe that BED[10] is the first available bed, BED[2] is the next available bed, and BED[6] is the last available bed. Hence BED[6] has the null pointer in its nextpointer field; that is, LINK[6] = 0.

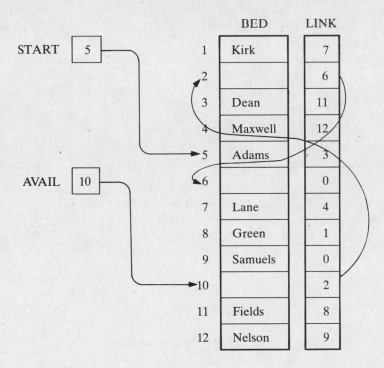

Fig. 5-9

EXAMPLE 5.11

(a) The available space in the linear array TEST in Fig. 5-5 may be linked as in Fig. 5-10. Observe that each of the lists ALG and GEOM may use the AVAIL list. Note that AVAIL = 9, so TEST[9] is the first free node in the AVAIL list. Since LINK[AVAIL] = LINK[9] = 10, TEST[10] is the second free node in the AVAIL list. And so on.

(b) Consider the personnel file in Fig. 5-7. The available space in the linear array NAME may be linked as in Fig. 5-11. Observe that the free-storage list in NAME consists of NAME[8], NAME[11], NAME[13], NAME[5] and NAME[1]. Moreover, observe that the values in LINK simultaneously list the free-storage space for the linear arrays SSN, SEX and SALARY.

(c) The available space in the array CUSTOMER in Fig. 5-6 may be linked as in Fig. 5-12. We emphasize that each of the four lists may use the AVAIL list for a new customer.

EXAMPLE 5.12

Suppose LIST(INFO, LINK, START, AVAIL) has memory space for $n = 10$ nodes. Furthermore, suppose LIST is initially empty. Figure 5-13 shows the values of LINK so that the AVAIL list consists of the sequence

$$INFO[1], \quad INFO[2], \quad \ldots, \quad INFO[10]$$

that is, so that the AVAIL list consists of the elements of INFO in the usual order. Observe that START = NULL, since the list is empty.

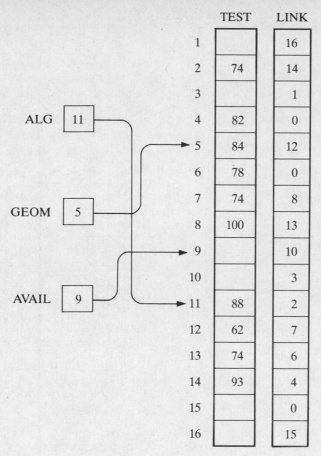

Fig. 5-10

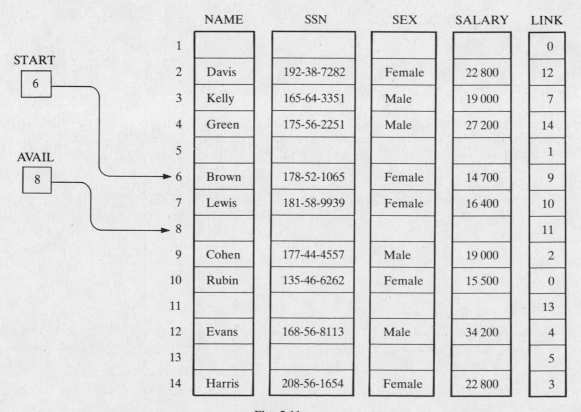

Fig. 5-11

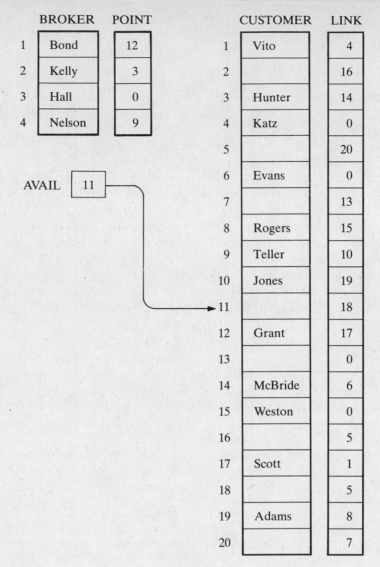

Fig. 5-12

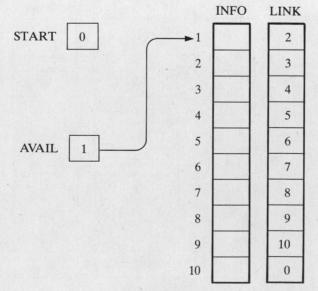

Fig. 5-13

Garbage Collection

Suppose some memory space becomes reusable because a node is deleted from a list or an entire list is deleted from a program. Clearly, we want the space to be available for future use. One way to bring this about is to immediately reinsert the space into the free-storage list. This is what we will do when we implement linked lists by means of linear arrays. However, this method may be too time-consuming for the operating system of a computer, which may choose an alternative method, as follows.

The operating system of a computer may periodically collect all the deleted space onto the free-storage list. Any technique which does this collection is called *garbage collection*. Garbage collection usually takes place in two steps. First the computer runs through all lists, tagging those cells which are currently in use, and then the computer runs through the memory, collecting all untagged space onto the free-storage list. The garbage collection may take place when there is only some minimum amount of space or no space at all left in the free-storage list, or when the CPU is idle and has time to do the collection. Generally speaking, the garbage collection is invisible to the programmer. Any further discussion about this topic of garbage collection lies beyond the scope of this text.

Overflow and Underflow

Sometimes new data are to be inserted into a data structure but there is no available space, i.e., the free-storage list is empty. This situation is usually called *overflow*. The programmer may handle overflow by printing the message OVERFLOW. In such a case, the programmer may then modify the program by adding space to the underlying arrays. Observe that overflow will occur with our linked lists when AVAIL = NULL and there is an insertion.

Analogously, the term *underflow* refers to the situation where one wants to delete data from a data structure that is empty. The programmer may handle underflow by printing the message UNDERFLOW. Observe that underflow will occur with our linked lists when START = NULL and there is a deletion.

5.7 INSERTION INTO A LINKED LIST

Let LIST be a linked list with successive nodes A and B, as pictured in Fig. 5-14(a). Suppose a node N is to be inserted into the list between nodes A and B. The schematic diagram of such an

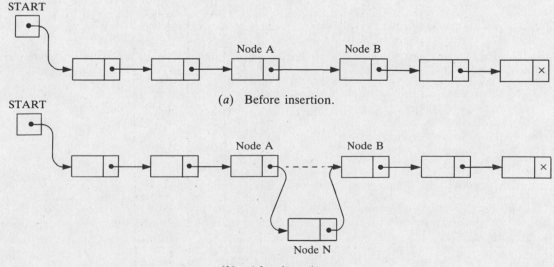

(a) Before insertion.

(b) After insertion.

Fig. 5-14

insertion appears in Fig. 5-14(*b*). That is, node A now points to the new node N, and node N points to node B, to which A previously pointed.

Suppose our linked list is maintained in memory in the form

LIST(INFO, LINK, START, AVAIL)

Figure 5-14 does not take into account that the memory space for the new node N will come from the AVAIL list. Specifically, for easier processing, the first node in the AVAIL list will be used for the new node N. Thus a more exact schematic diagram of such an insertion is that in Fig. 5-15. Observe that three pointer fields are changed as follows:

(1)   The nextpointer field of node A now points to the new node N, to which AVAIL previously pointed.

(2)   AVAIL now points to the second node in the free pool, to which node N previously pointed.

(3)   The nextpointer field of node N now points to node B, to which node A previously pointed.

There are also two special cases. If the new node N is the first node in the list, then START will point to N; and if the new node N is the last node in the list, then N will contain the null pointer.

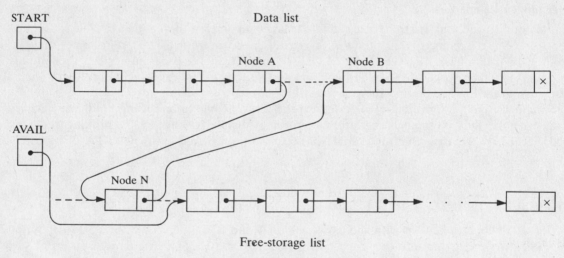

Fig. 5-15

EXAMPLE 5.13

(*a*)   Consider Fig. 5-9, the alphabetical list of patients in a ward. Suppose a patient Hughes is admitted to the ward. Observe that

　　(i)   Hughes is put in bed 10, the first available bed.

　　(ii)   Hughes should be inserted into the list between Green and Kirk.

The three changes in the pointer fields follow.

　　　　1.   LINK[8] = 10. [Now Green points to Hughes.]
　　　　2.   LINK[10] = 1. [Now Hughes points to Kirk.]
　　　　3.   AVAIL = 2. [Now AVAIL points to the next available bed.]

(*b*)   Consider Fig. 5-12, the list of brokers and their customers. Since the customer lists are not sorted, we will assume that each new customer is added to the beginning of its list. Suppose Gordan is a new customer of Kelly. Observe that

　　(i)   Gordan is assigned to CUSTOMER[11], the first available node.

　　(ii)   Gordan is inserted before Hunter, the previous first customer of Kelly.

The three changes in the pointer fields follow:

    1. POINT[2] = 11. [Now the list begins with Gordan.]
    2. LINK[11] = 3. [Now Gordan points to Hunter.]
    3. AVAIL = 18. [Now AVAIL points to the next available node.]

(c) Suppose the data elements A, B, C, D, E and F are inserted one after the other into the empty list in Fig.
5-13. Again we assume that each new node is inserted at the beginning of the list. Accordingly, after the six
insertions, F will point to E, which points to D, which points to C, which points to B, which points to A; and
A will contain the null pointer. Also, AVAIL = 7, the first available node after the six insertions, and
START = 6, the location of the first node, F. Figure 5-16 shows the new list (where $n = 10$.)

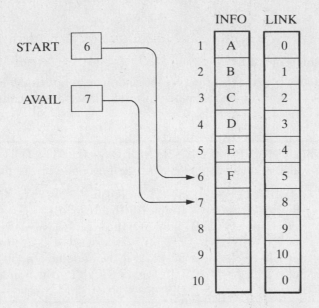

Fig. 5-16

Insertion Algorithms

Algorithms which insert nodes into linked lists come up in various situations. We discuss three of
them here. The first one inserts a node at the beginning of the list, the second one inserts a node after
the node with a given location, and the third one inserts a node into a sorted list. All our algorithms
assume that the linked list is in memory in the form LIST(INFO, LINK, START, AVAIL) and that the
variable ITEM contains the new information to be added to the list.

Since our insertion algorithms will use a node in the AVAIL list, all of the algorithms will include
the following steps:

(a) Checking to see if space is available in the AVAIL list. If not, that is, if AVAIL = NULL, then
    the algorithm will print the message OVERFLOW.

(b) Removing the first node from the AVAIL list. Using the variable NEW to keep track of the
    location of the new node, this step can be implemented by the pair of assignments (in this
    order)

$$\text{NEW} := \text{AVAIL}, \qquad \text{AVAIL} := \text{LINK[AVAIL]}$$

(c) Copying new information into the new node. In other words,

$$\text{INFO[NEW]} := \text{ITEM}$$

The schematic diagram of the latter two steps is pictured in Fig. 5-17.

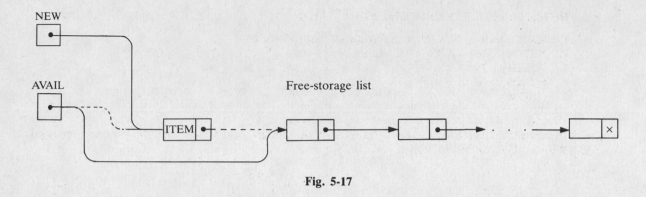

Fig. 5-17

Inserting at the Beginning of a List

Suppose our linked list is not necessarily sorted and there is no reason to insert a new node in any special place in the list. Then the easiest place to insert the node is at the begining of the list. An algorithm that does so follows.

Algorithm 5.4: INSFIRST(INFO, LINK, START, AVAIL, ITEM)
This algorithm inserts ITEM as the first node in the list.

1. [OVERFLOW?] If AVAIL = NULL, then: Write: OVERFLOW, and Exit.
2. [Remove first node from AVAIL list.]
   Set NEW := AVAIL and AVAIL := LINK[AVAIL].
3. Set INFO[NEW] := ITEM. [Copies new data into new node.]
4. Set LINK[NEW] := START. [New node now points to original first node.]
5. Set START := NEW. [Changes START so it points to the new node.]
6. Exit.

Steps 1 to 3 have already been discussed, and the schematic diagram of Steps 2 and 3 appears in Fig. 5-17. The schematic diagram of Steps 4 and 5 appears in Fig. 5-18.

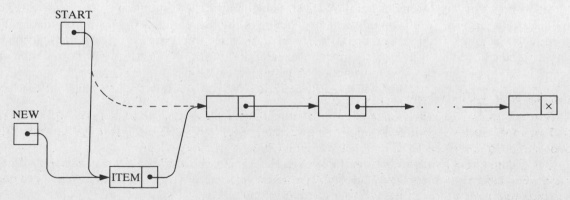

Fig. 5-18   Insertion at the beginning of a list.

EXAMPLE 5.14

Consider the lists of tests in Fig. 5-10. Suppose the test score 75 is to be added to the beginning of the geometry list. We simulate Algorithm 5.4. Observe that ITEM = 75, INFO = TEST and START = GEOM.

INSFIRST(TEST, LINK, GEOM, AVAIL, ITEM)

1. Since AVAIL ≠ NULL, control is transferred to Step 2.
2. NEW = 9, then AVAIL = LINK[9] = 10.
3. TEST[9] = 75.
4. LINK[9] = 5.
5. GEOM = 9.
6. Exit.

Figure 5-19 shows the data structure after 75 is added to the geometry list. Observe that only three pointers are changed, AVAIL, GEOM and LINK[9].

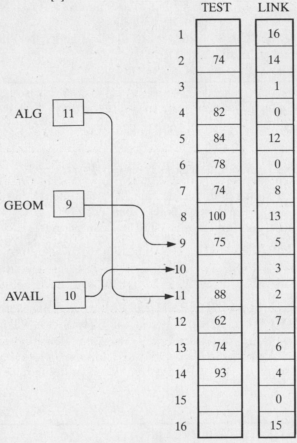

Fig. 5-19

Inserting after a Given Node

Suppose we are given the value of LOC where either LOC is the location of a node A in a linked LIST or LOC = NULL. The following is an algorithm which inserts ITEM into LIST so that ITEM follows node A or, when LOC = NULL, so that ITEM is the first node.

Let N denote the new node (whose location is NEW). If LOC = NULL, then N is inserted as the first node in LIST as in Algorithm 5.4. Otherwise, as pictured in Fig. 5-15, we let node N point to node B (which originally followed node A) by the assignment

$$LINK[NEW] := LINK[LOC]$$

and we let node A point to the new node N by the assignment

$$LINK[LOC] := NEW$$

A formal statement of the algorithm follows.

Algorithm 5.5:   INSLOC(INFO, LINK, START, AVAIL, LOC, ITEM)
This algorithm inserts ITEM so that ITEM follows the node with location LOC
or inserts ITEM as the first node when LOC = NULL.

1. [OVERFLOW?] If AVAIL = NULL, then: Write: OVERFLOW, and Exit.
2. [Remove first node from AVAIL list.]
   Set NEW := AVAIL and AVAIL := LINK[AVAIL].
3. Set INFO[NEW] := ITEM. [Copies new data into new node.]
4. If LOC = NULL, then: [Insert as first node.]
       Set LINK[NEW] := START and START := NEW.
   Else: [Insert after node with location LOC.]
       Set LINK[NEW] := LINK[LOC] and LINK[LOC] := NEW.
   [End of If structure.]
5. Exit.

Inserting into a Sorted Linked List

Suppose ITEM is to be inserted into a sorted linked LIST. Then ITEM must be inserted between nodes A and B so that

$$INFO(A) < ITEM \leq INFO(B)$$

The following is a procedure which finds the location LOC of node A, that is, which finds the location LOC of the last node in LIST whose value is less than ITEM.

Traverse the list, using a pointer variable PTR and comparing ITEM with INFO[PTR] at each node. While traversing, keep track of the location of the preceding node by using a pointer variable SAVE, as pictured in Fig. 5-20. Thus SAVE and PTR are updated by the assignments

$$SAVE := PTR \quad \text{and} \quad PTR := LINK[PTR]$$

The traversing continues as long as INFO[PTR] > ITEM, or in other words, the traversing stops as soon as ITEM ≤ INFO[PTR]. Then PTR points to node B, so SAVE will contain the location of the node A.

The formal statement of our procedure follows. The cases where the list is empty or where ITEM < INFO[START], so LOC = NULL, are treated separately, since they do not involve the variable SAVE.

Procedure 5.6:   FINDA(INFO, LINK, START, ITEM, LOC)
This procedure finds the location LOC of the last node in a sorted list such that
INFO[LOC] < ITEM, or sets LOC = NULL.

1. [List empty?] If START = NULL, then: Set LOC := NULL, and Return.
2. [Special case?] If ITEM < INFO[START], then: Set LOC := NULL, and
   Return.
3. Set SAVE := START and PTR := LINK[START]. [Initializes pointers.]
4. Repeat Steps 5 and 6 while PTR ≠ NULL.
5.   If ITEM < INFO[PTR], then:
           Set LOC := SAVE, and Return.
       [End of If structure.]
6.   Set SAVE := PTR and PTR := LINK[PTR]. [Updates pointers.]
   [End of Step 4 loop.]
7. Set LOC := SAVE.
8. Return.

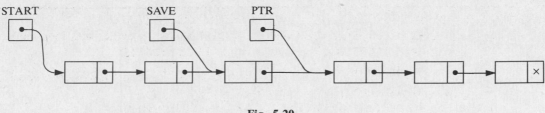

Fig. 5-20

Now we have all the components to present an algorithm which inserts ITEM into a linked list. The simplicity of the algorithm comes from using the previous two procedures.

Algorithm 5.7:   INSSRT(INFO, LINK, START, AVAIL, ITEM)
This algorithm inserts ITEM into a sorted linked list.

1.   [Use Procedure 5.6 to find the location of the node preceding ITEM.]
     Call FINDA(INFO, LINK, START, ITEM, LOC).
2.   [Use Algorithm 5.5 to insert ITEM after the node with location LOC.]
     Call INSLOC(INFO, LINK, START, AVAIL, LOC, ITEM).
3.   Exit.

EXAMPLE 5.15

Consider the alphabetized list of patients in Fig. 5-9. Suppose Jones is to be added to the list of patients. We simulate Algorithm 5.7, or more specifically, we simulate Procedure 5.6 and then Algorithm 5.5. Observe that ITEM = Jones and INFO = BED.

(a)   FINDA(BED, LINK, START, ITEM, LOC)
1.   Since START ≠ NULL, control is transferred to Step 2.
2.   Since BED[5] = Adams < Jones, control is transferred to Step 3.
3.   SAVE = 5 and PTR = LINK[5] = 3.
4.   Steps 5 and 6 are repeated as follows:
     (a)   BED[3] = Dean < Jones, so SAVE = 3 and PTR = LINK[3] = 11.
     (b)   BED[11] = Fields < Jones, so SAVE = 11 and PTR = LINK[11] = 8.
     (c)   BED[8] = Green < Jones, so SAVE = 8 and PTR = LINK[8] = 1.
     (d)   Since BED[1] = Kirk > Jones, we have:
               LOC = SAVE = 8 and Return.

(b)   INSLOC(BED, LINK, START, AVAIL, LOC, ITEM) [Here LOC = 8.]
1.   Since AVAIL ≠ NULL, control is transferred to Step 2.
2.   NEW = 10 and AVAIL = LINK[10] = 2.
3.   BED[10] = Jones.
4.   Since LOC ≠ NULL we have:
               LINK[10] = LINK[8] = 1 and LINK[8] = NEW = 10.
5.   Exit.

Figure 5-21 shows the data structure after Jones is added to the patient list. We emphasize that only three pointers have been changed, AVAIL, LINK[10] and LINK[8].

Copying

Suppose we want to copy all or part of a given list, or suppose we want to form a new list that is the concatenation of two given lists. This can be done by defining a null list and then adding the appropriate elements to the list, one by one, by various insertion algorithms. A null list is defined by simply choosing a variable name or pointer for the list, such as NAME, and then setting NAME := NULL. These algorithms are covered in the problem sections.

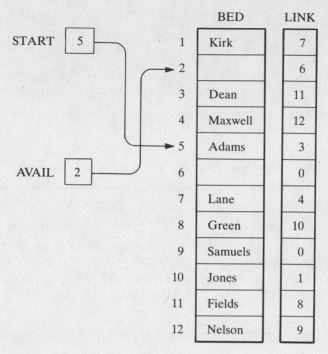

Fig. 5-21

5.8 DELETION FROM A LINKED LIST

Let LIST be a linked list with a node N between nodes A and B, as pictured in Fig. 5-22(a). Suppose node N is to be deleted from the linked list. The schematic diagram of such a deletion appears in Fig. 5-22(b). The deletion occurs as soon as the nextpointer field of node A is changed so that it points to node B. (Accordingly, when performing deletions, one must keep track of the address of the node which immediately precedes the node that is to be deleted.)

Suppose our linked list is maintained in memory in the form

LIST(INFO, LINK, START, AVAIL)

Figure 5-22 does not take into account the fact that, when a node N is deleted from our list, we will

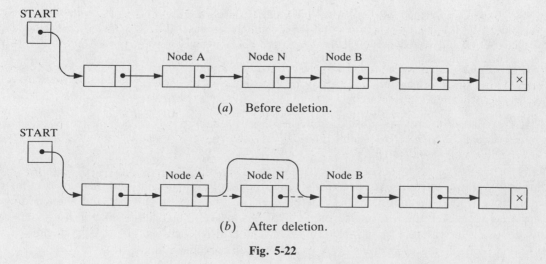

(a)   Before deletion.

(b)   After deletion.

Fig. 5-22

immediately return its memory space to the AVAIL list. Specifically, for easier processing, it will be returned to the beginning of the AVAIL list. Thus a more exact schematic diagram of such a deletion is the one in Fig. 5-23. Observe that three pointer fields are changed as follows:

(1) The nextpointer field of node A now points to node B, where node N previously pointed.

(2) The nextpointer field of N now points to the original first node in the free pool, where AVAIL previously pointed.

(3) AVAIL now points to the deleted node N.

There are also two special cases. If the deleted node N is the first node in the list, then START will point to node B; and if the deleted node N is the last node in the list, then node A will contain the NULL pointer.

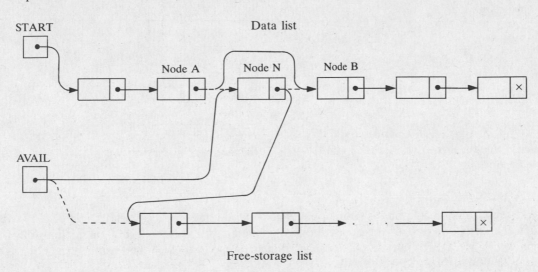

Fig. 5-23

EXAMPLE 5.16

(a) Consider Fig. 5-21, the list of patients in the hospital ward. Suppose Green is discharged, so that BED[8] is now empty. Then, in order to maintain the linked list, the following three changes in the pointer fields must be executed:

$$\text{LINK}[11] = 10 \qquad \text{LINK}[8] = 2 \qquad \text{AVAIL} = 8$$

By the first change, Fields, who originally preceded Green, now points to Jones, who originally followed Green. The second and third changes add the new empty bed to the AVAIL list. We emphasize that, before making the deletion, we had to find the node BED[11], which originally pointed to the deleted node BED[8].

(b) Consider Fig. 5-12, the list of brokers and their customers. Suppose Teller, the first customer of Nelson, is deleted from the list of customers. Then, in order to maintain the linked lists, the following three changes in the pointer fields must be executed:

$$\text{POINT}[4] = 10 \qquad \text{LINK}[9] = 11 \qquad \text{AVAIL} = 9$$

By the first change, Nelson now points to his original second customer, Jones. The second and third changes add the new empty node to the AVAIL list.

(c) Suppose the data elements E, B and C are deleted, one after the other, from the list in Fig. 5-16. The new list is pictured in Fig. 5-24. Observe that now the first three available nodes are:

INFO[3], which originally contained C

INFO[2], which originally contained B

INFO[5], which originally contained E

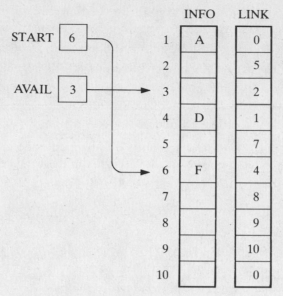

Fig. 5-24

Observe that the order of the nodes in the AVAIL list is the reverse of the order in which the nodes have been deleted from the list.

Deletion Algorithms

Algorithms which delete nodes from linked lists come up in various situations. We discuss two of them here. The first one deletes the node following a given node, and the second one deletes the node with a given ITEM of information. All our algorithms assume that the linked list is in memory in the form LIST(INFO, LINK, START, AVAIL).

All of our deletion algorithms will return the memory space of the deleted node N to the beginning of the AVAIL list. Accordingly, all of our algorithms will include the following pair of assignments, where LOC is the location of the deleted node N:

$$\text{LINK[LOC]} := \text{AVAIL} \quad \text{and then} \quad \text{AVAIL} := \text{LOC}$$

These two operations are pictured in Fig. 5-25.

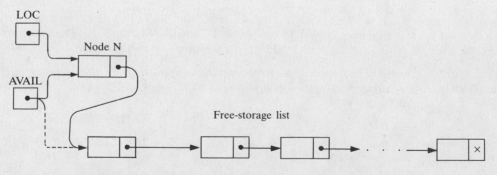

Fig. 5-25   LINK[LOC] := AVAIL and AVAIL := LOC.

Some of our algorithms may want to delete either the first node or the last node from the list. An algorithm that does so must check to see if there is a node in the list. If not, i.e., if START = NULL, then the algorithm will print the message UNDERFLOW.

Deleting the Node Following a Given Node

Let LIST be a linked list in memory. Suppose we are given the location LOC of a node N in LIST. Furthermore, suppose we are given the location LOCP of the node preceding N or, when N is the first node, we are given LOCP = NULL. The following algorithm deletes N from the list.

Algorithm 5.8:   DEL(INFO, LINK, START, AVAIL, LOC, LOCP)
This algorithm deletes the node N with location LOC. LOCP is the location of the node which precedes N or, when N is the first node, LOCP = NULL.
1. If LOCP = NULL, then:
    Set START := LINK[START]. [Deletes first node.]
 Else:
    Set LINK[LOCP] := LINK[LOC]. [Deletes node N.]
 [End of If structure.]
2. [Return deleted node to the AVAIL list.]
 Set LINK[LOC] := AVAIL and AVAIL := LOC.
3. Exit.

Figure 5-26 is the schematic diagram of the assignment

$$START := LINK[START]$$

which effectively deletes the first node from the list. This covers the case when N is the first node.

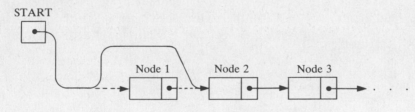

Fig. 5-26   START := LINK[START].

Figure 5-27 is the schematic diagram of the assignment

$$LINK[LOCP] := LINK[LOC]$$

which effectively deletes the node N when N is not the first node.

The simplicity of the algorithm comes from the fact that we are already given the location LOCP of the node which precedes node N. In many applications, we must first find LOCP.

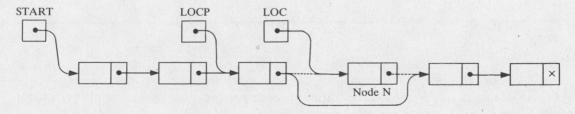

Fig. 5-27   LINK[LOCP] := LINK[LOC].

Deleting the Node with a Given ITEM of Information

Let LIST be a linked list in memory. Suppose we are given an ITEM of information and we want to delete from the LIST the first node N which contains ITEM. (If ITEM is a key value, then only one node can contain ITEM.) Recall that before we can delete N from the list, we need to know the location of the node preceding N. Accordingly, first we give a procedure which finds the location LOC of the node N containing ITEM and the location LOCP of the node preceding node N. If N is the first node, we set LOCP = NULL, and if ITEM does not appear in LIST, we set LOC = NULL. (This procedure is similar to Procedure 5.6.)

Traverse the list, using a pointer variable PTR and comparing ITEM with INFO[PTR] at each node. While traversing, keep track of the location of the preceding node by using a pointer variable SAVE, as pictured in Fig. 5-20. Thus SAVE and PTR are updated by the assignments

$$\text{SAVE} := \text{PTR} \quad \text{and} \quad \text{PTR} := \text{LINK[PTR]}$$

The traversing continues as long as INFO[PTR] $\neq$ ITEM, or in other words, the traversing stops as soon as ITEM = INFO[PTR]. Then PTR contains the location LOC of node N and SAVE contains the location LOCP of the node preceding N.

The formal statement of our procedure follows. The cases where the list is empty or where INFO[START] = ITEM (i.e., where node N is the first node) are treated separately, since they do not involve the variable SAVE.

Procedure 5.9: FINDB(INFO, LINK, START, ITEM, LOC, LOCP)

This procedure finds the location LOC of the first node N which contains ITEM and the location LOCP of the node preceding N. If ITEM does not appear in the list, then the procedure sets LOC = NULL; and if ITEM appears in the first node, then it sets LOCP = NULL.

1. [List empty?] If START = NULL, then:
   Set LOC := NULL and LOCP := NULL, and Return.
   [End of If structure.]
2. [ITEM in first node?] If INFO[START] = ITEM, then:
   Set LOC := START and LOCP = NULL, and Return.
   [End of If structure.]
3. Set SAVE := START and PTR := LINK[START]. [Initializes pointers.]
4. Repeat Steps 5 and 6 while PTR $\neq$ NULL.
5.   If INFO[PTR] = ITEM, then:
   Set LOC := PTR and LOCP := SAVE, and Return.
   [End of If structure.]
6.   Set SAVE := PTR and PTR := LINK[PTR]. [Updates pointers.]
   [End of Step 4 loop.]
7. Set LOC := NULL. [Search unsuccessful.]
8. Return.

Now we can easily present an algorithm to delete the first node N from a linked list which contains a given ITEM of information. The simplicity of the algorithm comes from the fact that the task of finding the location of N and the location of its preceding node has already been done in Procedure 5.9.

> **Algorithm 5.10:** DELETE(INFO, LINK, START, AVAIL, ITEM)
> This algorithm deletes from a linked list the first node N which contains the given ITEM of information.
>
> 1. [Use Procedure 5.9 to find the location of N and its preceding node.]
>   Call FINDB(INFO, LINK, START, ITEM, LOC, LOCP)
> 2. If LOC = NULL, then: Write: ITEM not in list, and Exit.
> 3. [Delete node.]
>   If LOCP = NULL, then:
>   Set START := LINK[START]. [Deletes first node.]
>   Else:
>   Set LINK[LOCP] := LINK[LOC].
>   [End of If structure.]
> 4. [Return deleted node to the AVAIL list.]
>   Set LINK[LOC] := AVAIL and AVAIL := LOC.
> 5. Exit.

Remark: The reader may have noticed that Steps 3 and 4 in Algorithm 5.10 already appear in Algorithm 5.8. In other words, we could replace the steps by the following Call statement:

Call DEL(INFO, LINK, START, AVAIL, LOC, LOCP)

This would conform to the usual programming style of modularity.

EXAMPLE 5.17

Consider the list of patients in Fig. 5-21. Suppose the patient Green is discharged. We simulate Procedure 5.9 to find the location LOC of Green and the location LOCP of the patient preceding Green. Then we simulate Algorithm 5.10 to delete Green from the list. Here ITEM = Green, INFO = BED, START = 5 and AVAIL = 2.

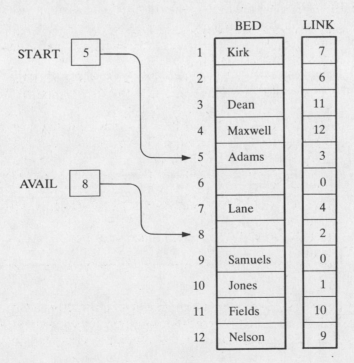

Fig. 5-28

(a) FINDB(BED, LINK, START, ITEM, LOC, LOCP)
1. Since START ≠ NULL, control is transferred to Step 2.
2. Since BED[5] = Adams ≠ Green, control is transferred to Step 3.
3. SAVE = 5 and PTR = LINK[5] = 3.
4. Steps 5 and 6 are repeated as follows:
    (a) BED[3] = Dean ≠ Green, so SAVE = 3 and PTR = LINK[3] = 11.
    (b) BED[11] = Fields ≠ Green, so SAVE = 11 and PTR = LINK[11] = 8.
    (c) BED[8] = Green, so we have:
        LOC = PTR = 8 and LOCP = SAVE = 11, and Return.

(b) DELLOC(BED, LINK, START, AVAIL, ITEM)
1. Call FINDB(BED, LINK, START, ITEM, LOC, LOCP). [Hence LOC = 8 and LOCP = 11.]
2. Since LOC ≠ NULL, control is transferred to Step 3.
3. Since LOCP ≠ NULL, we have:
        LINK[11] = LINK[8] = 10.
4. LINK[8] = 2 and AVAIL = 8.
5. Exit.

Figure 5-28 shows the data structure after Green is removed from the patient list. We emphasize that only three pointers have been changed, LINK[11], LINK[8] and AVAIL.

5.9 HEADER LINKED LISTS

A *header* linked list is a linked list which always contains a special node, called the *header node*, at the beginning of the list. The following are two kinds of widely used header lists:

(1) A *grounded header list* is a header list where the last node contains the null pointer. (The term "grounded" comes from the fact that many texts use the electrical ground symbol to indicate the null pointer.)

(2) A *circular header list* is a header list where the last node points back to the header node.

Figure 5-29 contains schematic diagrams of these header lists. Unless otherwise stated or implied, our header lists will always be circular. Accordingly, in such a case, the header node also acts as a sentinel indicating the end of the list.

Observe that the list pointer START always points to the header node. Accordingly, LINK[START] = NULL indicates that a grounded header list is empty, and LINK[START] = START indicates that a circular header list is empty.

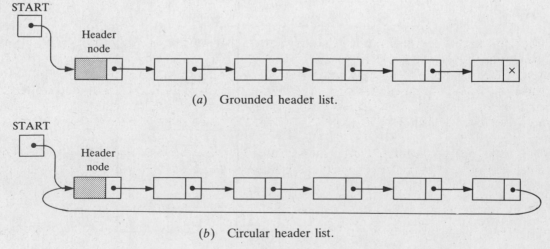

(a) Grounded header list.

(b) Circular header list.

Fig. 5-29

Although our data may be maintained by header lists in memory, the AVAIL list will always be maintained as an ordinary linked list.

EXAMPLE 5.18

Consider the personnel file in Fig. 5-11. The data may be organized as a header list as in Fig. 5-30. Observe that LOC = 5 is now the location of the header record. Therefore, START = 5, and since Rubin is the last employee, LINK[10] = 5. The header record may also be used to store information about the entire file. For example, we let SSN[5] = 9 indicate the number of employees, and we let SALARY[5] = 191 600 indicate the total salary paid to the employees.

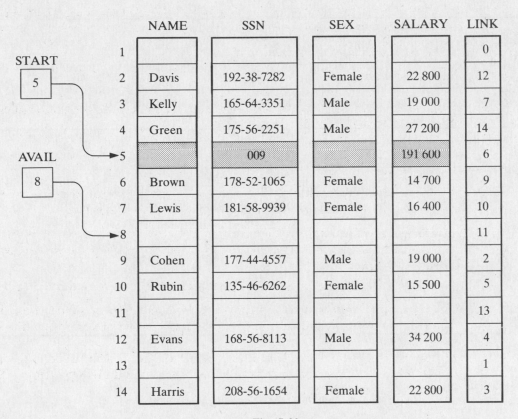

		NAME	SSN	SEX	SALARY	LINK
	1					0
START	2	Davis	192-38-7282	Female	22 800	12
5	3	Kelly	165-64-3351	Male	19 000	7
	4	Green	175-56-2251	Male	27 200	14
AVAIL	5		009		191 600	6
8	6	Brown	178-52-1065	Female	14 700	9
	7	Lewis	181-58-9939	Female	16 400	10
	8					11
	9	Cohen	177-44-4557	Male	19 000	2
	10	Rubin	135-46-6262	Female	15 500	5
	11					13
	12	Evans	168-56-8113	Male	34 200	4
	13					1
	14	Harris	208-56-1654	Female	22 800	3

Fig. 5-30

The term "node," by itself, normally refers to an ordinary node, not the header node, when used with header lists. Thus the *first node* in a header list is the node following the header node, and the location of the first node is LINK[START], not START, as with ordinary linked lists.

Algorithm 5.11, which uses a pointer variable PTR to traverse a circular header list, is essentially the same as Algorithm 5.1, which traverses an ordinary linked list, except that now the algorithm (1) begins with PTR = LINK[START] (not PTR = START) and (2) ends when PTR = START (not PTR = NULL).

Circular header lists are frequently used instead of ordinary linked lists because many operations are much easier to state and implement using header lists. This comes from the following two properties of circular header lists:

(1) The null pointer is not used, and hence all pointers contain valid addresses.

(2) Every (ordinary) node has a predecessor, so the first node may not require a special case.

The next example illustrates the usefulness of these properties.

> **Algorithm 5.11:** (Traversing a Circular Header List) Let LIST be a circular header list in memory. This algorithm traverses LIST, applying an operation PROCESS to each node of LIST.
>
> 1. Set PTR := LINK[START]. [Initializes the pointer PTR.]
> 2. Repeat Steps 3 and 4 while PTR ≠ START:
> 3.   Apply PROCESS to INFO[PTR].
> 4.   Set PTR := LINK[PTR]. [PTR now points to the next node.]
>   [End of Step 2 loop.]
> 5. Exit.

EXAMPLE 5.19

Suppose LIST is a linked list in memory, and suppose a specific ITEM of information is given.

(a) Algorithm 5.2 finds the location LOC of the first node in LIST which contains ITEM when LIST is an ordinary linked list. The following is such an algorithm when LIST is a circular header list.

> **Algorithm 5.12:** SRCHHL(INFO, LINK, START, ITEM, LOC)
> LIST is a circular header list in memory. This algorithm finds the location LOC of the node where ITEM first appears in LIST or sets LOC = NULL.
>
> 1. Set PTR := LINK[START].
> 2. Repeat while INFO[PTR] ≠ ITEM and PTR ≠ START:
>   Set PTR := LINK[PTR]. [PTR now points to the next node.]
>   [End of loop.]
> 3. If INFO[PTR] = ITEM, then:
>   Set LOC := PTR.
>   Else:
>   Set LOC := NULL.
>   [End of If structure.]
> 4. Exit.

The two tests which control the searching loop (Step 2 in Algorithm 5.12) were not performed at the same time in the algorithm for ordinary linked lists; that is, we did not let Algorithm 5.2 use the analogous statement

Repeat while INFO[PTR] ≠ ITEM and PTR ≠ NULL:

because for ordinary linked lists INFO[PTR] is not defined when PTR = NULL.

(b) Procedure 5.9 finds the location LOC of the first node N which contains ITEM and also the location LOCP of the node preceding N when LIST is an ordinary linked list. The following is such a procedure when LIST is a circular header list.

> **Procedure 5.13:** FINDBHL(INFO, LINK, START, ITEM, LOC, LOCP)
> 1. Set SAVE := START and PTR := LINK[START]. [Initializes pointers.]
> 2. Repeat while INFO[PTR] ≠ ITEM and PTR ≠ START.
>   Set SAVE := PTR and PTR := LINK[PTR]. [Updates pointers.]
>   [End of loop.]
> 3. If INFO[PTR] = ITEM, then:
>   Set LOC := PTR and LOCP := SAVE.
>   Else:
>   Set LOC := NULL and LOCP := SAVE.
>   [End of If structure.]
> 4. Exit.

Observe the simplicity of this procedure compared with Procedure 5.9. Here we did not have to consider the special case when ITEM appears in the first node, and here we can perform at the same time the two tests which control the loop.

(c) Algorithm 5.10 deletes the first node N which contains ITEM when LIST is an ordinary linked list. The following is such an algorithm when LIST is a circular header list.

Algorithm 5.14:   DELLOCHL(INFO, LINK, START, AVAIL, ITEM)

1. [Use Procedure 5.13 to find the location of N and its preceding node.]
    Call LINDBHL(INFO, LINK, START, ITEM, LOC, LOCP).
2. If LOC = NULL, then: Write: ITEM not in list, and Exit.
3. Set LINK[LOCP] := LINK[LOC]. [Deletes node.]
4. [Return deleted node to the AVAIL list.]
    Set LINK[LOC] := AVAIL and AVAIL := LOC.
5. Exit.

Again we did not have to consider the special case when ITEM appears in the first node, as we did in Algorithm 5.10.

Remark: There are two other variations of linked lists which sometimes appear in the literature:

(1) A linked list whose last node points back to the first node instead of containing the null pointer, called a *circular list*

(2) A linked list which contains both a special header node at the beginning of the list and a special trailer node at the end of the list

Figure 5-31 contains schematic diagrams of these lists.

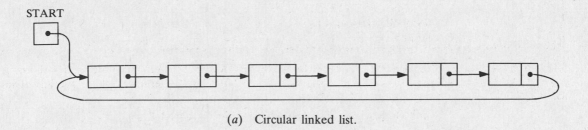

(a) Circular linked list.

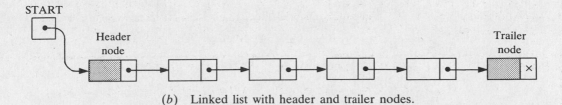

(b) Linked list with header and trailer nodes.

Fig. 5-31

Polynomials

Header linked lists are frequently used for maintaining polynomials in memory. The header node plays an important part in this representation, since it is needed to represent the zero polynomial. This representation of polynomials will be presented in the context of a specific example.

EXAMPLE 5.20

Let $p(x)$ denote the following polynomial in one variable (containing four nonzero terms):

$$p(x) = 2x^8 - 5x^7 - 3x^2 + 4$$

Then $p(x)$ may be represented by the header list pictured in Fig. 5-32(a), where each node corresponds to a nonzero term of $p(x)$. Specifically, the information part of the node is divided into two fields representing, respectively, the coefficient and the exponent of the corresponding term, and the nodes are linked according to decreasing degree.

Observe that the list pointer variable POLY points to the header node, whose exponent field is assigned a negative number, in this case -1. Here the array representation of the list will require three linear arrays, which we will call COEF, EXP and LINK. One such representation appears in Fig. 5-32(b).

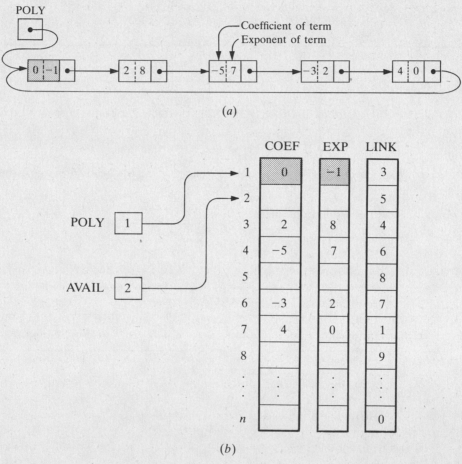

Fig. 5-32 $p(x) = 2x^8 - 5x^7 - 3x^2 + 4$.

5.10 TWO-WAY LISTS

Each list discussed above is called a one-way list, since there is only one way that the list can be traversed. That is, beginning with the list pointer variable START, which points to the first node or the header node, and using the nextpointer field LINK to point to the next node in the list, we can traverse the list in only one direction. Furthermore, given the location LOC of a node N in such a list, one has immediate access to the next node in the list (by evaluating LINK[LOC]), but one does not have access to the preceding node without traversing part of the list. This means, in particular, that one must traverse that part of the list preceding N in order to delete N from the list.

This section introduces a new list structure, called a *two-way list*, which can be traversed in two directions: in the usual forward direction from the beginning of the list to the end, or in the backward direction from the end of the list to the beginning. Furthermore, given the location LOC of a node N in the list, one now has immediate access to both the next node and the preceding node in the list. This means, in particular, that one is able to delete N from the list without traversing any part of the list.

A *two-way list* is a linear collection of data elements, called *nodes*, where each node N is divided into three parts:

(1)   An information field INFO which contains the data of N

(2)   A pointer field FORW which contains the location of the next node in the list

(3)   A pointer field BACK which contains the location of the preceding node in the list

The list also requires two list pointer variables: FIRST, which points to the first node in the list, and LAST, which points to the last node in the list. Figure 5-33 contains a schematic diagram of such a list. Observe that the null pointer appears in the FORW field of the last node in the list and also in the BACK field of the first node in the list.

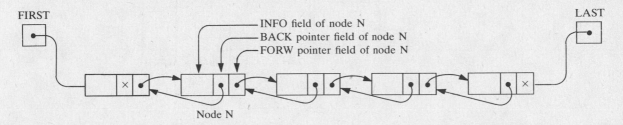

Fig. 5-33   Two-way list.

Observe that, using the variable FIRST and the pointer field FORW, we can traverse a two-way list in the forward direction as before. On the other hand, using the variable LAST and the pointer field BACK, we can also traverse the list in the backward direction.

Suppose LOCA and LOCB are the locations, respectively, of nodes A and B in a two-way list. Then the way that the pointers FORW and BACK are defined gives us the following:

Pointer property: FORW[LOCA] = LOCB   if and only if   BACK[LOCB] = LOCA

In other words, the statement that node B follows node A is equivalent to the statement that node A precedes node B.

Two-way lists may be maintained in memory by means of linear arrays in the same way as one-way lists except that now we require two pointer arrays, FORW and BACK, instead of one pointer array LINK, and we require two list pointer variables, FIRST and LAST, instead of one list pointer variable START. On the other hand, the list AVAIL of available space in the arrays will still be maintained as a one-way list—using FORW as the pointer field—since we delete and insert nodes only at the beginning of the AVAIL list.

EXAMPLE 5.21

Consider again the data in Fig. 5-9, the 9 patients in a ward with 12 beds. Figure 5-34 shows how the alphabetical listing of the patients can be organized into a two-way list. Observe that the values of FIRST and the pointer field FORW are the same, respectively, as the values of START and the array LINK; hence the list can be traversed alphabetically as before. On the other hand, using LAST and the pointer array BACK, the list can also be traversed in reverse alphabetical order. That is, LAST points to Samuels, the pointer field BACK of Samuels points to Nelson, the pointer field BACK of Nelson points to Maxwell, and so on.

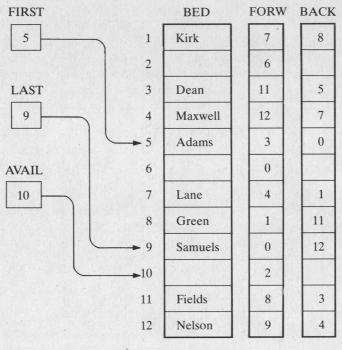

Fig. 5-34

Two-Way Header Lists

The advantages of a two-way list and a circular header list may be combined into a two-way circular header list as pictured in Fig. 5-35. The list is circular because the two end nodes point back to the header node. Observe that such a two-way list requires only one list pointer variable START, which points to the header node. This is because the two pointers in the header node point to the two ends of the list.

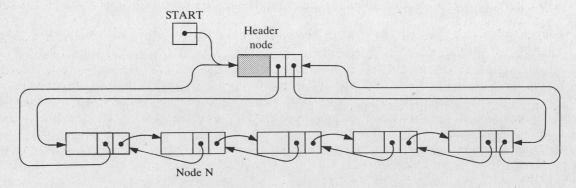

Fig. 5-35 Two-way circular header list.

EXAMPLE 5.22

Consider the personnel file in Fig. 5-30, which is organized as a circular header list. The data may be organized into a two-way circular header list by simply adding another array BACK which gives the locations of preceding nodes. Such a structure is pictured in Fig. 5-36, where LINK has been renamed FORW. Again the AVAIL list is maintained only as a one-way list.

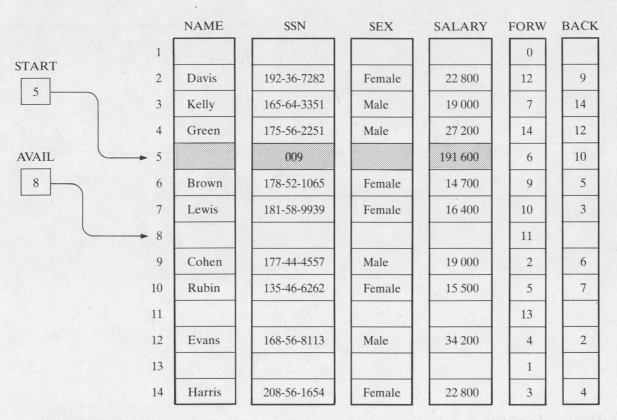

START

5

AVAIL

8

	NAME	SSN	SEX	SALARY	FORW	BACK
1					0	
2	Davis	192-36-7282	Female	22 800	12	9
3	Kelly	165-64-3351	Male	19 000	7	14
4	Green	175-56-2251	Male	27 200	14	12
5		009		191 600	6	10
6	Brown	178-52-1065	Female	14 700	9	5
7	Lewis	181-58-9939	Female	16 400	10	3
8					11	
9	Cohen	177-44-4557	Male	19 000	2	6
10	Rubin	135-46-6262	Female	15 500	5	7
11					13	
12	Evans	168-56-8113	Male	34 200	4	2
13					1	
14	Harris	208-56-1654	Female	22 800	3	4

Fig. 5-36

Operations on Two-Way Lists

Suppose LIST is a two-way list in memory. This subsection discusses a number of operations on LIST.

Traversing. Suppose we want to traverse LIST in order to process each node exactly once. Then we can use Algorithm 5.1 if LIST is an ordinary two-way list, or we can use Algorithm 5.11 if LIST contains a header node. Here it is of no advantage that the data are organized as a two-way list rather than as a one-way list.

Searching. Suppose we are given an ITEM of information—a key value—and we want to find the location LOC of ITEM in LIST. Then we can use Algorithm 5.2 if LIST is an ordinary two-way list, or we can use Algorithm 5.12 if LIST has a header node. Here the main advantage is that we can search for ITEM in the backward direction if we have reason to suspect that ITEM appears near the end of the list. For example, suppose LIST is a list of names sorted alphabetically. If ITEM = Smith, then we would search LIST in the backward direction, but if ITEM = Davis, then we would search LIST in the forward direction.

Deleting. Suppose we are given the location LOC of a node N in LIST, and suppose we want to delete N from the list. We assume that LIST is a two-way circular header list. Note that BACK[LOC] and FORW[LOC] are the locations, respectively, of the nodes which precede and follow node N. Accordingly, as pictured in Fig. 5-37, N is deleted from the list by changing the following pair of pointers:

$$\text{FORW[BACK[LOC]]} := \text{FORW[LOC]} \quad \text{and} \quad \text{BACK[FORW[LOC]]} := \text{BACK[LOC]}$$

The deleted node N is then returned to the AVAIL list by the assignments:

$$\text{FORW[LOC]} := \text{AVAIL} \quad \text{and} \quad \text{AVAIL} := \text{LOC}$$

The formal statement of the algorithm follows.

Algorithm 5.15:   DELTWL(INFO, FORW, BACK, START, AVAIL, LOC)

1. [Delete node.]
   Set FORW[BACK[LOC]] := FORW[LOC] and
   BACK[FORW[LOC]] := BACK[LOC].
2. [Return node to AVAIL list.]
   Set FORW[LOC] := AVAIL and AVAIL := LOC.
3. Exit.

Here we see one main advantage of a two-way list: If the data were organized as a one-way list, then, in order to delete N, we would have to traverse the one-way list to find the location of the node preceding N.

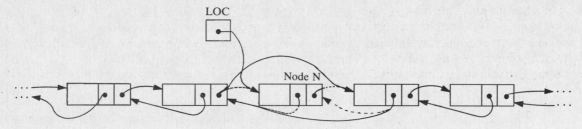

Fig. 5-37   Deleting node N.

Inserting.   Suppose we are given the locations LOCA and LOCB of adjacent nodes A and B in LIST, and suppose we want to insert a given ITEM of information between nodes A and B. As with a one-way list, first we remove the first node N from the AVAIL list, using the variable NEW to keep track of its location, and then we copy the data ITEM into the node N; that is, we set:

$$NEW := AVAIL, \qquad AVAIL := FORW[AVAIL], \qquad INFO[NEW] := ITEM$$

Now, as pictured in Fig. 5-38, the node N with contents ITEM is inserted into the list by changing the following four pointers:

$$FORW[LOCA] := NEW, \qquad FORW[NEW] := LOCB$$
$$BACK[LOCB] := NEW, \qquad BACK[NEW] := LOCA$$

The formal statement of our algorithm follows.

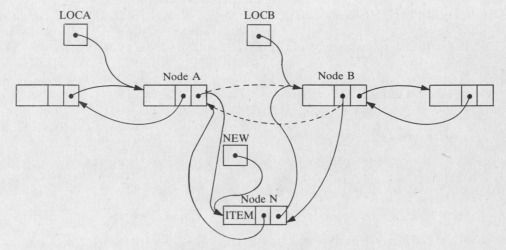

Fig. 5-38   Inserting node N.

Algorithm 5.16:   INSTWL(INFO, FORW, BACK, START, AVAIL, LOCA, LOCB, ITEM)

    1.   [OVERFLOW?] If AVAIL = NULL, then: Write: OVERFLOW, and Exit.
    2.   [Remove node from AVAIL list and copy new data into node.]
        Set NEW := AVAIL, AVAIL := FORW[AVAIL], INFO[NEW] := ITEM.
    3.   [Insert node into list.]
        Set FORW[LOCA] := NEW, FORW[NEW] := LOCB,
        BACK[LOCB] := NEW, BACK[NEW] := LOCA.
    4.   Exit.

Algorithm 5.16 assumes that LIST contains a header node. Hence LOCA or LOCB may point to the header node, in which case N will be inserted as the first node or the last node. If LIST does not contain a header node, then we must consider the case that LOCA = NULL and N is inserted as the first node in the list, and the case that LOCB = NULL and N is inserted as the last node in the list.

Remark: Generally speaking, storing data as a two-way list, which requires extra space for the backward pointers and extra time to change the added pointers, rather than as a one-way list is not worth the expense unless one must frequently find the location of the node which precedes a given node N, as in the deletion above.

Solved Problems

LINKED LISTS

5.1   Find the character strings stored in the four linked lists in Fig. 5-39.

    Here the four list pointers appear in an array CITY. Beginning with CITY[1], traverse the list, by following the pointers, to obtain the string PARIS. Beginning with CITY[2], traverse the list to obtain the string LONDON. Since NULL appears in CITY[3], the third list is empty, so it denotes Λ, the empty string. Beginning with CITY[4], traverse the list to obtain the string ROME. In other words, PARIS, LONDON, Λ and ROME are the four strings.

5.2   The following list of names is assigned (in order) to a linear array INFO:

  Mary, June, Barbara, Paula, Diana, Audrey, Karen, Nancy, Ruth, Eileen, Sandra, Helen

That is, INFO[1] = Mary, INFO[2] = June, . . . , INFO[12] = Helen. Assign values to an array LINK and a variable START so that INFO, LINK and START form an alphabetical listing of the names.

    The alphabetical listing of the names follows:

    Audrey, Barbara, Diana, Eileen, Helen, June, Karen, Mary, Nancy, Paula, Ruth, Sandra

The values of START and LINK are obtained as follows:

  (*a*)   INFO[6] = Audrey, so assign START = 6.
  (*b*)   INFO[3] = Barbara, so assign LINK[6] = 3.
  (*c*)   INFO[5] = Diana, so assign LINK[3] = 5.
  (*d*)   INFO[10] = Eileen, so assign LINK[5] = 10.

And so on. Since INFO[11] = Sandra is the last name, assign LINK[11] = NULL. Figure 5-40 shows the data structure where, assuming INFO has space for only 12 elements, we set AVAIL = NULL.

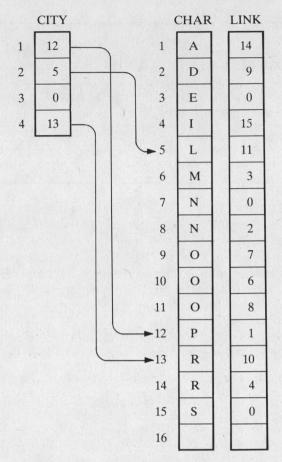

Fig. 5-39

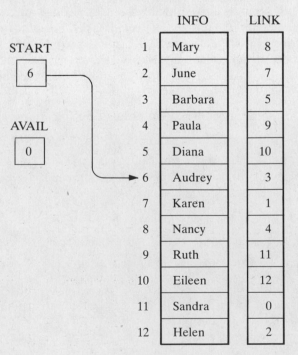

Fig. 5-40

5.3   Let LIST be a linked list in memory. Write a procedure which

    (*a*)   Finds the number NUM of times a given ITEM occurs in LIST

    (*b*)   Finds the number NUM of nonzero elements in LIST

    (*c*)   Adds a given value K to each element in LIST

       Each procedure uses Algorithm 5.1 to traverse the list.

    (*a*)   **Procedure P5.3A:** 1. Set NUM := 0. [Initializes counter.]
                               2. Call Algorithm 5.1, replacing the processing step by:
                                        If INFO[PTR] = ITEM, then: Set NUM := NUM + 1.
                               3. Return

    (*b*)   **Procedure P5.3B:** 1. Set NUM := 0. [Initializes counter.]
                                 2. Call Algorithm 5.1, replacing the processing step by:
                                        If INFO[PTR] $\neq$ 0, then: Set NUM := NUM + 1.
                               3. Return.

    (*c*)   **Procedure P5.3C:** 1. Call Algorithm 5.1, replacing the processing step by:
                                        Set INFO[PTR] := INFO[PTR] + K.
                               2. Return.

5.4   Consider the alphabetized list of patients in Fig. 5-9. Determine the changes in the data structure if (*a*) Walters is added to the list and then (*b*) Kirk is deleted from the list.

    (*a*)   Observe that Walters is put in bed 10, the first available bed, and Walters is inserted after Samuels, who is the last patient on the list. The three changes in the pointer fields follow:

        1. LINK[9] = 10. [Now Samuels points to Walters.]
        2. LINK[10] = 0. [Now Walters is the last patient in the list.]
        3. AVAIL = 2. [Now AVAIL points to the next available bed.]

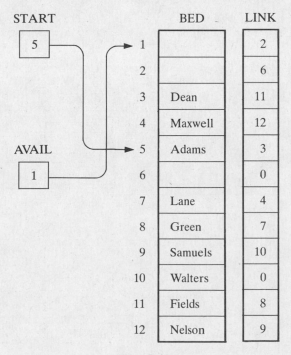

Fig. 5-41

(*b*) Since Kirk is discharged, BED[1] is now empty. The following three changes in the pointer fields must be executed:

$$LINK[8] = 7 \qquad LINK[1] = 2 \qquad AVAIL = 1$$

By the first change, Green, who originally preceded Kirk, now points to Lane, who originally followed Kirk. The second and third changes add the new empty bed to the AVAIL list. We emphasize that before making the deletion, we had to find the node BED[8], which originally pointed to the deleted node BED[1].

Figure 5-41 shows the new data structure.

5.5 Suppose LIST is in memory. Write an algorithm which deletes the last node from LIST.

The last node can be deleted only when one also knows the location of the next-to-last node. Accordingly, traverse the list using a pointer variable PTR, and keep track of the preceding node using a pointer variable SAVE. PTR points to the last node when LINK[PTR] = NULL, and in such a case, SAVE points to the next to last node. The case that LIST has only one node is treated separately, since SAVE can be defined only when the list has 2 or more elements. The algorithm follows.

Algorithm P5.5: DELLST(INFO, LINK, START, AVAIL)

1. [List empty?] If START = NULL, then Write: UNDERFLOW, and Exit.
2. [List contains only one element?]
    If LINK[START] = NULL, then:
    (*a*) Set START := NULL. [Removes only node from list.]
    (*b*) Set LINK[START] := AVAIL and AVAIL := START.
           [Returns node to AVAIL list.]
    (*c*) Exit.
    [End of If structure.]
3. Set PTR := LINK[START] and SAVE := START. [Initializes pointers.]
4. Repeat while LINK[PTR] ≠ NULL. [Traverses list, seeking last node.]
        Set SAVE := PTR and PTR := LINK[PTR]. [Updates SAVE and PTR.]
    [End of loop.]
5. Set LINK[SAVE] := LINK[PTR]. [Removes last node.]
6. Set LINK[PTR] := AVAIL and AVAIL := PTR. [Returns node to AVAIL list.]
7. Exit.

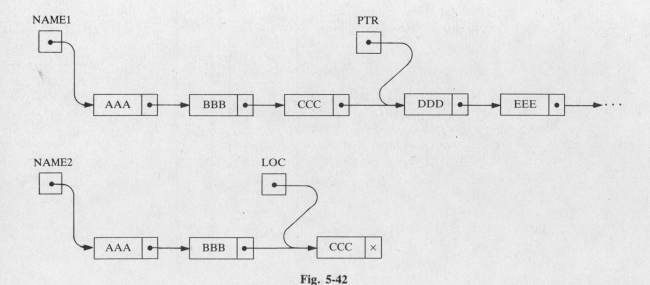

Fig. 5-42

5.6   Suppose NAME1 is a list in memory. Write an algorithm which copies NAME1 into a list NAME2.

First set NAME2 := NULL to form an empty list. Then traverse NAME1 using a pointer variable PTR, and while visiting each node of NAME1, copy its contents INFO[PTR] into a new node, which is then inserted at the end of NAME2. Use LOC to keep track of the last node of NAME2 during the traversal. (Figure 5-42 pictures PTR and LOC before the fourth node is added to NAME2.) Inserting the first node into NAME2 must be treated separately, since LOC is not defined until NAME2 has at least one node. The algorithm follows:

Algorithm P5.6:   COPY(INFO, LINK, NAME1, NAME2, AVAIL)
　　　　　　　　This algorithm makes a copy of a list NAME1 using NAME2 as the list pointer variable of the new list.

1. Set NAME2 := NULL. [Forms empty list.]
2. [NAME1 empty?] If NAME1 = NULL, then: Exit.
3. [Insert first node of NAME1 into NAME2.]
　　Call INSLOC(INFO, LINK, NAME2, AVAIL, NULL, INFO[NAME1]) or:
　　(a)   If AVAIL = NULL, then: Write: OVERFLOW, and Exit.
　　(b)   Set NEW := AVAIL and AVAIL := LINK[AVAIL]. [Removes first node from AVAIL list.]
　　(c)   Set INFO[NEW] := INFO[NAME1]. [Copies data into new node.]
　　(d)   [Insert new node as first node in NAME2.]
　　　　Set LINK[NEW] := NAME2 and NAME2 := NEW.
4. [Initializes pointers PTR and LOC.]
　　Set PTR := LINK[NAME1] and LOC := NAME2.
5. Repeat Steps 6 and 7 while PTR ≠ NULL:
6. 　　Call INSLOC(INFO, LINK, NAME2, AVAIL, LOC, INFO[PTR]) or:
　　(a)   If AVAIL = NULL, then: Write: OVERFLOW, and Exit.
　　(b)   Set NEW := AVAIL and AVAIL := LINK[AVAIL].
　　(c)   Set INFO[NEW] := INFO[PTR]. [Copies data into new node.]
　　(d)   [Insert new node into NAME2 after the node with location LOC.]
　　　　Set LINK[NEW] := LINK[LOC], and LINK[LOC] := NEW.
7. 　　Set PTR := LINK[PTR] and LOC := LINK[LOC]. [Updates PTR and LOC.]
　　[End of Step 5 loop.]
8. Exit.

HEADER LISTS, TWO-WAY LISTS

5.7   Form header (circular) lists from the one-way lists in Fig. 5-11.

Choose TEST[1] as a header node for the list ALG, and TEST[16] as a header node for the list GEOM. Then, for each list:

(a)   Change the list pointer variable so that it points to the header node.

(b)   Change the header node so that it points to the first node in the list.

(c)   Change the last node so that it points back to the header node.

Finally, reorganize the AVAIL list. Figure 5-43 shows the updated data structure.

5.8   Find the polynomials POLY1 and POLY2 stored in Fig. 5-44.

Beginning with POLY1, traverse the list by following the pointers to obtain the polynomial

$$p_1(x) = 3x^5 - 4x^3 + 6x - 5$$

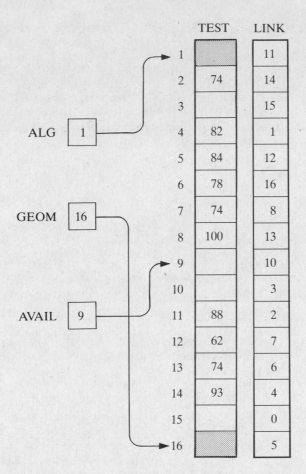

Fig. 5-43

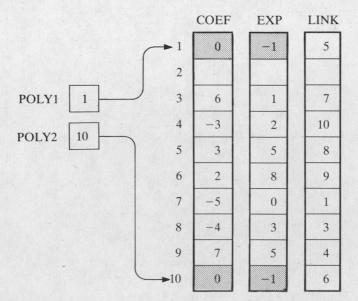

Fig. 5-44

Beginning with POLY2, traverse the list by following the pointers to obtain the polynomial

$$p_2(x) = 2x^8 + 7x^5 - 3x^2$$

Here COEF[K] and EXP[K] contain, respectively, the coefficient and exponent of a term of the polynomial. Observe that the header nodes are assigned -1 in the EXP field.

5.9   Consider a polynomial $p(x, y, z)$ in variables x, y and z. Unless otherwise stated, the terms in $p(x, y, z)$ will be ordered *lexicographically*. That is, first we order the terms according to decreasing degrees in x; those with the same degree in x we order according to decreasing degrees in y; those with the same degrees in x and y we order according to decreasing degrees in z. Suppose

$$p(x, y, z) = 8x^2y^2z - 6yz^8 + 3x^3yz + 2xy^7z - 5x^2y^3 - 4xy^7z^3$$

(*a*)   Rewrite the polynomial so that the terms are ordered.

(*b*)   Suppose the terms are stored in the order shown in the problem statement in the linear arrays COEF, XEXP, YEXP and ZEXP, with the HEAD node first. Assign values to LINK so that the linked list contains the ordered sequence of terms.

(*a*)   Note that $3x^3yz$ comes first, since it has the highest degree in x. Note that $8x^2y^2z$ and $-5x^2y^3$ both have the same degree in x but $-5x^2y^3$ comes before $8x^2y^2z$, since its degree in y is higher. And so on. Finally we have

$$p(x, y, z) = 3x^3yz - 5x^2y^3 + 8x^2y^2z - 4xy^7z^3 + 2xy^7z - 6yz^8$$

(*b*)   Figure 5-45 shows the desired data structure.

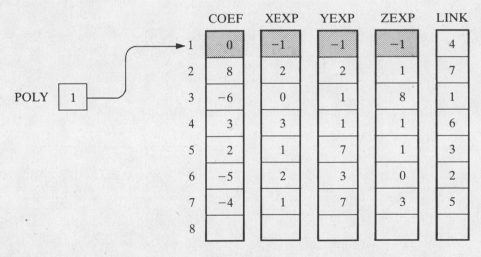

Fig. 5-45

5.10   Discuss the advantages, if any, of a two-way list over a one-way list for each of the following operations:

(*a*)   Traversing the list to process each node

(*b*)   Deleting a node whose location LOC is given

(*c*)   Searching an unsorted list for a given element ITEM

(*d*)   Searching a sorted list for a given element ITEM

(*e*)   Inserting a node before the node with a given location LOC

(*f*)   Inserting a node after the node with a given location LOC

(a)   There is no advantage.

(b)   The location of the preceding node is needed. The two-way list contains this information, whereas with a one-way list we must traverse the list.

(c)   There is no advantage.

(d)   There is no advantage unless we know that ITEM must appear at the end of the list, in which case we traverse the list backward. For example, if we are searching for Walker in an alphabetical listing, it may be quicker to traverse the list backward.

(e)   As in part (b), the two-way list is more efficient.

(f)   There is no advantage.

Remark: Generally speaking, a two-way list is not much more useful than a one-way list except in special circumstances.

5.11   Suppose LIST is a header (circular) list in memory. Write an algorithm which deletes the last node from LIST. (Compare with Prob. 5.5.)

   The algorithm is the same as Algorithm P5.5, except now we can omit the special case when LIST has only one node. That is, we can immediately define SAVE when LIST is not empty.

Algorithm P5.11:   DELLSTH(INFO, LINK, START, AVAIL)
                   This algorithm deletes the last node from the header list.

1.   [List empty?] If LINK[START] = NULL, then: Write: UNDERFLOW, and Exit.
2.   Set PTR := LINK[START] and SAVE := START. [Initializes pointers.]
3.   Repeat while LINK[PTR] ≠ START: [Traverses list seeking last node.]
           Set SAVE := PTR and PTR := LINK[PTR]. [Updates SAVE and PTR.]
     [End of loop.]
4.   Set LINK[SAVE] := LINK[PTR]. [Removes last node.]
5.   Set LINK[PTR] := AVAIL and AVAIL := PTR. [Returns node to AVAIL list.]
6.   Exit.

5.12   Form two-way lists from the one-way header lists in Fig. 5-43.

   Traverse the list ALG in the forward direction to obtain:

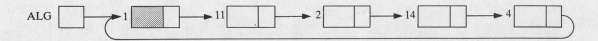

We require the backward pointers. These are calculated node by node. For example, the last node (with location LOC = 4) must point to the next-to-last node (with location LOC = 14). Hence

$$BACK[4] = 14$$

The next-to-last node (with location LOC = 14) must point to the preceding node (with location LOC = 2). Hence

$$BACK[14] = 2$$

And so on. The header node (with location LOC = 1) must point to the last node (with location 4). Hence

$$BACK[1] = 4$$

A similar procedure is done with the list GEOM. Figure 5-46 pictures the two-way lists. Note that there is no difference between the arrays LINK and FORW. That is, only the array BACK need be calculated.

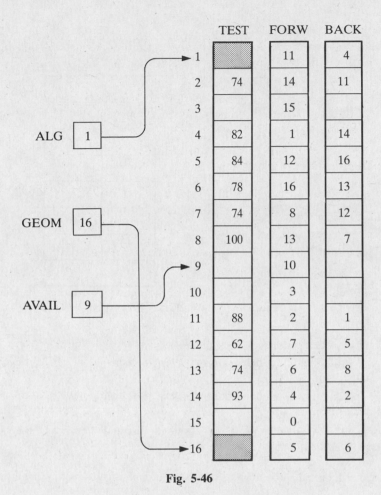

Fig. 5-46

Supplementary Problems

LINKED LISTS

5.13 Figure 5-47 is a list of five hospital patients and their room numbers. (*a*) Fill in values for NSTART and NLINK so that they form an alphabetical listing of the names. (*b*) Fill in values for RSTART and RLINK so that they form an ordering of the room numbers.

NSTART

RSTART

	NAME	ROOM	NLINK	RLINK
1	Brown	650		
2	Smith	422		
3	Adams	704		
4	Jones	462		
5	Burns	632		

Fig. 5-47

5.14 Figure 5-48 pictures a linked list in memory.

START

4

AVAIL

3

	INFO	LINK
1	A	2
2	B	8
3		6
4	C	7
5	D	0
6		0
7	E	1
8	F	5

Fig. 5-48

(a) Find the sequence of characters in the list.

(b) Suppose F and then C are deleted from the list and then G is inserted at the beginning of the list. Find the final structure.

(c) Suppose C and then F are deleted from the list and then G is inserted at the beginning of the list. Find the final structure.

(d) Suppose G is inserted at the beginning of the list and then F and then C are deleted from the structure. Find the final structure.

5.15 Suppose LIST is a linked list in memory consisting of numerical values. Write a procedure for each of the following:

(a) Finding the maximum MAX of the values in LIST

(b) Finding the average MEAN of the values in LIST

(c) Finding the product PROD of the elements in LIST

5.16 Given an integer K, write a procedure which deletes the Kth element from a linked list.

5.17 Write a procedure which adds a given ITEM of information at the end of a list.

5.18 Write a procedure which removes the first element of a list and adds it to the end of the list without changing any values in INFO. (Only START and LINK may be changed.)

5.19 Write a procedure SWAP(INFO, LINK, START, K) which interchanges the Kth and K + 1st elements in the list without changing any values in INFO.

5.20 Write a procedure SORT(INFO, LINK, START) which sorts a list without changing any values in INFO. (*Hint*: Use the procedure SWAP in Prob. 5.19 together with a bubble sort.)

5.21 Suppose AAA and BBB are sorted linked lists with distinct elements, both maintained in INFO and LINK. Write a procedure which combines the lists into a single sorted linked list CCC without changing any values in INFO.

Problems 5.22 to 5.24 refer to character strings which are stored as linked lists with one character per node and use the same arrays INFO and LINK.

5.22   Suppose STRING is a character string in memory.

   (*a*)   Write a procedure which prints SUBSTRING(STRING, K, N), which is the substring of STRING beginning with the Kth character and of length N.

   (*b*)   Write a procedure which creates a new string SUBKN in memory where

$$SUBKN = SUBSTRING(STRING, K, N)$$

5.23   Suppose STR1 and STR2 are character strings in memory. Write a procedure which creates a new string STR3 which is the concatenation of STR1 and STR2.

5.24   Suppose TEXT and PATTERN are strings in memory. Write a procedure which finds the value of INDEX(TEXT, PATTERN), the position where PATTERN first occurs as a substring of TEXT.

HEADER LISTS; TWO-WAY LISTS

5.25   Character strings are stored in the three linked lists in Fig. 5-49. (*a*) Find the three strings. (*b*) Form circular header lists from the one-way lists using CHAR[20], CHAR[19] and CHAR[18] as header nodes.

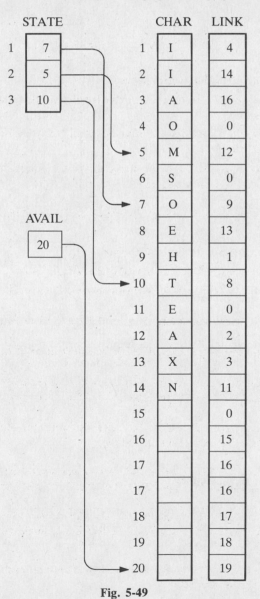

Fig. 5-49

5.26   Find the polynomials stored in the three header lists in Fig. 5-50.

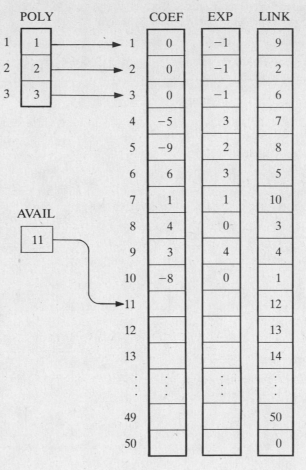

Fig. 5-50

5.27   Consider the following polynomial:

$$p(x, y, z) = 2xy^2z^3 + 3x^2yz^2 + 4xy^3z + 5x^2y^2 + 6y^3z + 7x^3z + 8xy^2z^5 + 9$$

   (*a*)   Rewrite the polynomial so that the terms are ordered lexicographically.

   (*b*)   Suppose the terms are stored in the order shown here in parallel arrays COEF, XEXP, YEXP and ZEXP with the header node first. (Thus COEF[K] = K for K = 2, 3, . . . , 9.) Assign values to an array LINK so that the linked list contains the ordered sequence of terms. (See Prob. 5.9.)

5.28   Write a procedure HEAD(INFO, LINK, START, AVAIL) which forms a header circular list from an ordinary one-way list.

5.29   Redo Probs. 5.16–5.20 using a header circular list rather than an ordinary one-way list. (Observe that the algorithms are now much simpler.)

5.30   Suppose POLY1 and POLY2 are polynomials (in one variable) which are stored as header circular lists using the same parallel arrays COEF, EXP and LINK. Write a procedure

            ADD(COEF, EXP, LINK, POLY1, POLY2, AVAIL, SUMPOLY)

which finds the sum SUMPOLY of POLY1 and POLY2 (and which is also stored in memory using COEF, EXP and LINK).

5.31   For the polynomials POLY1 and POLY2 in Prob. 5.30, write a procedure

MULT(COEF, EXP, LINK, POLY1, POLY2, AVAIL, PRODPOLY)

which finds the product PRODPOLY of the polynomials POLY1 and POLY2.

5.32   Form two-way circular header lists from the one-way lists in Fig. 5-49 using, as in Prob. 5.25, CHAR[20], CHAR[19] and CHAR[18] as header nodes.

5.33   Given an integer K, write a procedure

DELK(INFO, FORW, BACK, START, AVAIL, K)

which deletes the Kth element from a two-way circular header list.

5.34   Suppose LIST(INFO, LINK, START, AVAIL) is a one-way circular header list in memory. Write a procedure

TWOWAY(INFO, LINK, BACK, START)

which assigns values to a linear array BACK to form a two-way list from the one-way list.

Programming Problems

Problems 5.35 to 5.40 refer to the data structure in Fig. 5-51, which consists of four alphabetized lists of clients and their respective lawyers.

5.35   Write a program which reads an integer K and prints the list of clients of lawyer K. Test the program for each K.

5.36   Write a program which prints the name and lawyer of each client whose age is L or higher. Test the program using (a) L = 41 and (b) L = 48.

5.37   Write a program which reads the name LLL of a lawyer and prints the lawyer's list of clients. Test the program using (a) Rogers, (b) Baker and (c) Levine.

5.38   Write a program which reads the NAME of a client and prints the client's name, age and lawyer. Test the program using (a) Newman, (b) Ford, (c) Rivers and (d) Hall.

5.39   Write a program which reads the NAME of the client and deletes the client's record from the structure. Test the program using (a) Lewis, (b) Klein and (c) Parker.

5.40   Write a program which reads the record of a new client, consisting of the client's name, age and lawyer, and inserts the record into the structure. Test the program using (a) Jones, 36, Levine; and (b) Olsen, 44, Nelson.

Problems 5.41 to 5.46 refer to the alphabetized list of employee records in Fig. 5-30, which are stored as a circular header list.

5.41   Write a program which prints out the entire alphabetized list of employee records.

5.42   Write a program which reads the name NNN of an employee and prints the employee's record. Test the program using (a) Evans, (b) Smith and (c) Lewis.

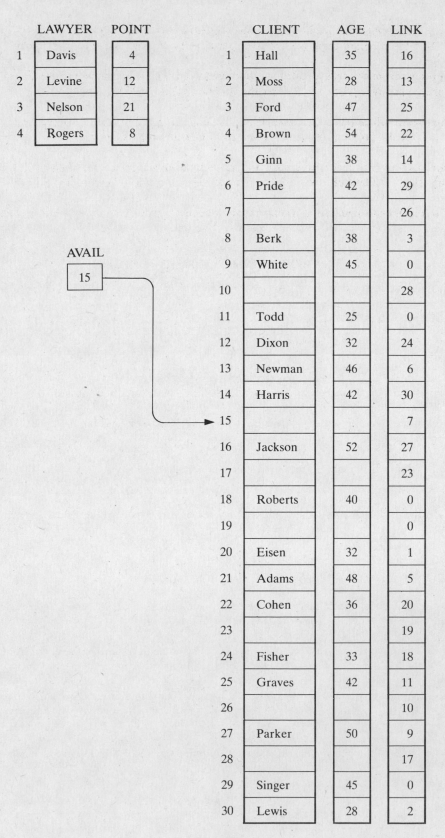

Fig. 5-51

5.43   Write a program which reads the social security number SSS of an employee and prints the employee's record. Test the program using (*a*) 165-64-3351, (*b*) 136-46-6262 and (*c*) 177-44-5555.

5.44   Write a program which reads an integer K and prints the name of each male employee when K = 1 or of each female employee when K = 2. Test the program using (*a*) K = 2, (*b*) K = 5 and (*c*) K = 1.

5.45   Write a program which reads the name NNN of an employee and deletes the employee's record from the structure. Test the program using (*a*) Davis, (*b*) Jones and (*c*) Rubin.

5.46   Write a program which reads the record of a new employee and inserts the record into the file. Test the program using (*a*) Fletcher, 168-52-3388, Female, 21 000; and (*b*) Nelson, 175-32-2468, Male, 19 000.

Remark: Remember to update the header record whenever there is an insertion or a deletion.

Chapter 6

Stacks, Queues, Recursion

6.1 INTRODUCTION

The linear lists and linear arrays discussed in the previous chapters allowed one to insert and delete elements at any place in the list—at the beginning, at the end, or in the middle. There are certain frequent situations in computer science when one wants to restrict insertions and deletions so that they can take place only at the beginning or the end of the list, not in the middle. Two of the data structures that are useful in such situations are *stacks* and *queues*.

A stack is a linear structure in which items may be added or removed only at one end. Figure 6-1 pictures three everyday examples of such a structure: a stack of dishes, a stack of pennies and a stack of folded towels. Observe that an item may be added or removed only from the top of any of the stacks. This means, in particular, that the last item to be added to a stack is the first item to be removed. Accordingly, stacks are also called last-in first-out (LIFO) lists. Other names used for stacks are "piles" and "push-down lists." Although the stack may seem to be a very restricted type of data structure, it has many important applications in computer science.

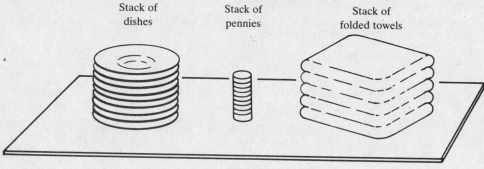

Stack of dishes   Stack of pennies   Stack of folded towels

Fig. 6-1

A queue is a linear list in which items may be added only at one end and items may be removed only at the other end. The name "queue" likely comes from the everyday use of the term. Consider a queue of people waiting at a bus stop, as pictured in Fig. 6-2. Each new person who comes takes his or her place at the end of the line, and when the bus comes, the people at the front of the line board first. Clearly, the first person in the line is the first person to leave. Thus queues are also called first-in first-out (FIFO) lists. Another example of a queue is a batch of jobs waiting to be processed, assuming no job has higher priority than the others.

The notion of *recursion* is fundamental in computer science. This topic is introduced in this chapter because one way of simulating recursion is by means of a stack structure.

Fig. 6-2 Queue waiting for a bus.

6.2 STACKS

A *stack* is a list of elements in which an element may be inserted or deleted only at one end, called the *top* of the stack. This means, in particular, that elements are removed from a stack in the reverse order of that in which they were inserted into the stack.

Special terminology is used for two basic operations associated with stacks:

(*a*) "Push" is the term used to insert an element into a stack.

(*b*) "Pop" is the term used to delete an element from a stack.

We emphasize that these terms are used only with stacks, not with other data structures.

EXAMPLE 6.1

Suppose the following 6 elements are pushed, in order, onto an empty stack:

AAA, BBB, CCC, DDD, EEE, FFF

Figure 6-3 shows three ways of picturing such a stack. For notational convenience, we will frequently designate the stack by writing:

STACK: AAA, BBB, CCC, DDD, EEE, FFF

The implication is that the right-most element is the top element. We emphasize that, regardless of the way a stack is described, its underlying property is that insertions and deletions can occur only at the top of the stack. This means EEE cannot be deleted before FFF is deleted, DDD cannot be deleted before EEE and FFF are deleted, and so on. Consequently, the elements may be popped from the stack only in the reverse order of that in which they were pushed onto the stack.

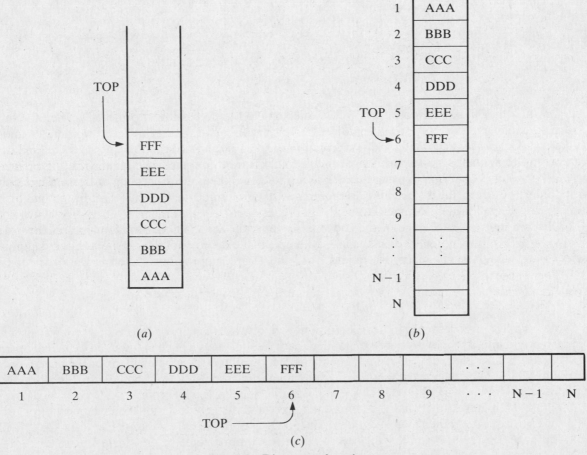

(a)   (b)

(c)

Fig. 6-3 Diagrams of stacks.

Consider again the AVAIL list of available nodes discussed in Chap. 5. Recall that free nodes were removed only from the beginning of the AVAIL list, and that new available nodes were inserted only at the beginning of the AVAIL list. In other words, the AVAIL list was implemented as a stack. This implementation of the AVAIL list as a stack is only a matter of convenience rather than an inherent part of the structure. In the following subsection we discuss an important situation where the stack is an essential tool of the processing algorithm itself.

Postponed Decisions

Stacks are frequently used to indicate the order of the processing of data when certain steps of the processing must be postponed until other conditions are fulfilled. This is illustrated as follows.

Suppose that while processing some project A we are required to move on to project B, whose completion is required in order to complete project A. Then we place the folder containing the data of A onto a stack, as pictured in Fig. 6-4(a), and begin to process B. However, suppose that while processing B we are led to project C, for the same reason. Then we place B on the stack above A, as pictured in Fig. 6-4(b), and begin to process C. Furthermore, suppose that while processing C we are likewise led to project D. Then we place C on the stack above B, as pictured in Fig. 6-4(c), and begin to process D.

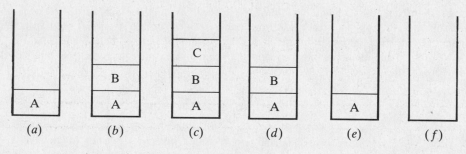

Fig. 6-4

On the other hand, suppose we are able to complete the processing of project D. Then the only project we may continue to process is project C, which is on top of the stack. Hence we remove folder C from the stack, leaving the stack as pictured in Fig. 6-4(d), and continue to process C. Similarly, after completing the processing of C, we remove folder B from the stack, leaving the stack as pictured in Fig. 6-4(e), and continue to process B. Finally, after completing the processing of B, we remove the last folder, A, from the stack, leaving the empty stack pictured in Fig. 6-4(f), and continue the processing of our original project A.

Observe that, at each stage of the above processing, the stack automatically maintains the order that is required to complete the processing. An important example of such a processing in computer science is where A is a main program and B, C and D are subprograms called in the order given.

6.3 ARRAY REPRESENTATION OF STACKS

Stacks may be represented in the computer in various ways, usually by means of a one-way list or a linear array. Unless otherwise stated or implied, each of our stacks will be maintained by a linear array STACK; a pointer variable TOP, which contains the location of the top element of the stack; and a variable MAXSTK which gives the maximum number of elements that can be held by the stack. The condition TOP = 0 or TOP = NULL will indicate that the stack is empty.

Figure 6-5 pictures such an array representation of a stack. (For notational convenience, the array is drawn horizontally rather than vertically.) Since TOP = 3, the stack has three elements, XXX, YYY and ZZZ; and since MAXSTK = 8, there is room for 5 more items in the stack.

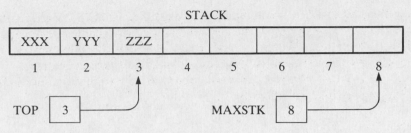

Fig. 6-5

The operation of adding (pushing) an item onto a stack and the operation of removing (popping) an item from a stack may be implemented, respectively, by the following procedures, called PUSH and POP. In executing the procedure PUSH, one must first test whether there is room in the stack for the new item; if not, then we have the condition known as overflow. Analogously, in executing the procedure POP, one must first test whether there is an element in the stack to be deleted; if not, then we have the condition known as underflow.

Procedure 6.1: PUSH(STACK, TOP, MAXSTK, ITEM)
This procedure pushes an ITEM onto a stack.

1. [Stack already filled?]
   If TOP = MAXSTK, then: Print: OVERFLOW, and Return.
2. Set TOP := TOP + 1. [Increases TOP by 1.]
3. Set STACK[TOP] := ITEM. [Inserts ITEM in new TOP position.]
4. Return.

Procedure 6.2: POP(STACK, TOP, ITEM)
This procedure deletes the top element of STACK and assigns it to the variable ITEM.

1. [Stack has an item to be removed?]
   If TOP = 0, then: Print: UNDERFLOW, and Return.
2. Set ITEM := STACK[TOP]. [Assigns TOP element to ITEM.]
3. Set TOP := TOP − 1. [Decreases TOP by 1.]
4. Return.

Frequently, TOP and MAXSTK are global variables; hence the procedures may be called using only

$$\text{PUSH(STACK, ITEM)} \quad \text{and} \quad \text{POP(STACK, ITEM)}$$

respectively. We note that the value of TOP is changed before the insertion in PUSH but the value of TOP is changed after the deletion in POP.

EXAMPLE 6.2

(a) Consider the stack in Fig. 6-5. We simulate the operation PUSH(STACK, WWW):

1. Since TOP = 3, control is transferred to Step 2.
2. TOP = 3 + 1 = 4.
3. STACK[TOP] = STACK[4] = WWW.
4. Return.

Note that WWW is now the top element in the stack.

(*b*) Consider again the stack in Fig. 6-5. This time we simulate the operation POP(STACK, ITEM):

1. Since TOP = 3, control is transferred to Step 2.
2. ITEM = ZZZ.
3. TOP = 3 − 1 = 2.
4. Return.

Observe that STACK[TOP] = STACK[2] = YYY is now the top element in the stack.

Minimizing Overflow

There is an essential difference between underflow and overflow in dealing with stacks. Underflow depends exclusively upon the given algorithm and the given input data, and hence there is no direct control by the programmer. Overflow, on the other hand, depends upon the arbitrary choice of the programmer for the amount of memory space reserved for each stack, and this choice does influence the number of times overflow may occur.

Generally speaking, the number of elements in a stack fluctuates as elements are added to or removed from a stack. Accordingly, the particular choice of the amount of memory for a given stack involves a time-space tradeoff. Specifically, initially reserving a great deal of space for each stack will decrease the number of times overflow may occur; however, this may be an expensive use of the space if most of the space is seldom used. On the other hand, reserving a small amount of space for each stack may increase the number of times overflow occurs; and the time required for resolving an overflow, such as by adding space to the stack, may be more expensive than the space saved.

Various techniques have been developed which modify the array representation of stacks so that the amount of space reserved for more than one stack may be more efficiently used. Most of these techniques lie beyond the scope of this text. We do illustrate one such technique in the following example.

EXAMPLE 6.3

Suppose a given algorithm requires two stacks, A and B. One can define an array STACKA with n_1 elements for stack A and an array STACKB with n_2 elements for stack B. Overflow will occur when either stack A contains more than n_1 elements or stack B contains more than n_2 elements.

Suppose instead that we define a single array STACK with $n = n_1 + n_2$ elements for stacks A and B together. As pictured in Fig. 6-6, we define STACK[1] as the bottom of stack A and let A "grow" to the right, and we define STACK[n] as the bottom of stack B and let B "grow" to the left. In this case, overflow will occur only when A and B together have more than $n = n_1 + n_2$ elements. This technique will usually decrease the number of times overflow occurs even though we have not increased the total amount of space reserved for the two stacks. In using this data structure, the operations of PUSH and POP will need to be modified.

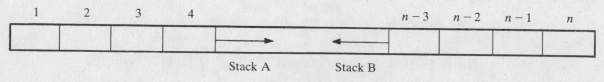

Fig. 6-6

6.4 ARITHMETIC EXPRESSIONS; POLISH NOTATION

Let Q be an arithmetic expression involving constants and operations. This section gives an algorithm which finds the value of Q by using reverse Polish (postfix) notation. We will see that the stack is an essential tool in this algorithm.

Recall that the binary operations in Q may have different levels of precedence. Specifically, we assume the following three levels of precedence for the usual five binary operations:

$$\begin{array}{ll} \text{Highest:} & \text{Exponentiation } (\uparrow) \\ \text{Next highest:} & \text{Multiplication } (*) \text{ and division } (/) \\ \text{Lowest:} & \text{Addition } (+) \text{ and subtraction } (-) \end{array}$$

(Observe that we use the BASIC symbol for exponentiation.) For simplicity, we assume that Q contains no unary operation (e.g., a leading minus sign). We also assume that in any parenthesis-free expression, the operations on the same level are performed from left to right. (This is not standard, since some languages perform exponentiations from right to left.)

EXAMPLE 6.4

Suppose we want to evaluate the following parenthesis-free arithmetic expression:

$$2 \uparrow 3 + 5 * 2 \uparrow 2 - 12 / 6$$

First we evaluate the exponentiations to obtain

$$8 + 5 * 4 - 12 / 6$$

Then we evaluate the multiplication and division to obtain $8 + 20 - 2$. Last, we evaluate the addition and subtraction to obtain the final result, 26. Observe that the expression is traversed three times, each time corresponding to a level of precedence of the operations.

Polish Notation

For most common arithmetic operations, the operator symbol is placed between its two operands. For example,

$$A + B \qquad C - D \qquad E * F \qquad G/H$$

This is called *infix notation*. With this notation, we must distinguish between

$$(A + B) * C \qquad \text{and} \qquad A + (B * C)$$

by using either parentheses or some operator-precedence convention such as the usual precedence levels discussed above. Accordingly, the order of the operators and operands in an arithmetic expression does not uniquely determine the order in which the operations are to be performed.

Polish notation, named after the Polish mathematician Jan Lukasiewicz, refers to the notation in which the operator symbol is placed before its two operands. For example,

$$+AB \qquad -CD \qquad *EF \qquad /GH$$

We translate, step by step, the following infix expressions into Polish notation using brackets [ ] to indicate a partial translation:

$$(A + B) * C = [+AB] * C = *+ABC$$
$$A + (B * C) = A + [*BC] = +A*BC$$
$$(A + B)/(C - D) = [+AB]/[-CD] = /+AB-CD$$

The fundamental property of Polish notation is that the order in which the operations are to be performed is completely determined by the positions of the operators and operands in the expression. Accordingly, one never needs parentheses when writing expressions in Polish notation.

Reverse Polish notation refers to the analogous notation in which the operator symbol is placed after its two operands:

$$AB+ \qquad CD- \qquad EF* \qquad GH/$$

Again, one never needs parentheses to determine the order of the operations in any arithmetic expression written in reverse Polish notation. This notation is frequently called *postfix* (or *suffix*) *notation*, whereas *prefix notation* is the term used for Polish notation, discussed in the preceding paragraph.

The computer usually evaluates an arithmetic expression written in infix notation in two steps. First, it converts the expression to postfix notation, and then it evaluates the postfix expression. In each step, the stack is the main tool that is used to accomplish the given task. We illustrate these applications of stacks in reverse order. That is, first we show how stacks are used to evaluate postfix expressions, and then we show how stacks are used to transform infix expressions into postfix expressions.

Evaluation of a Postfix Expression

Suppose P is an arithmetic expression written in postfix notation. The following algorithm, which uses a STACK to hold operands, evaluates P.

Algorithm 6.3: This algorithm finds the VALUE of an arithmetic expression P written in postfix notation.

1. Add a right parenthesis ")" at the end of P. [This acts as a sentinel.]
2. Scan P from left to right and repeat Steps 3 and 4 for each element of P until the sentinel ")" is encountered.
3.   If an operand is encountered, put it on STACK.
4.   If an operator $\otimes$ is encountered, then:
    (a)   Remove the two top elements of STACK, where A is the top element and B is the next-to-top element.
    (b)   Evaluate $B \otimes A$.
    (c)   Place the result of (b) back on STACK.
    [End of If structure.]
    [End of Step 2 loop.]
5. Set VALUE equal to the top element on STACK.
6. Exit.

We note that, when Step 5 is executed, there should be only one number on STACK.

EXAMPLE 6.5

Consider the following arithmetic expression P written in postfix notation:

$$P: \quad 5, \quad 6, \quad 2, \quad +, \quad *, \quad 12, \quad 4, \quad /, \quad -$$

(Commas are used to separate the elements of P so that 5, 6, 2 is not interpreted as the number 562.) The

Symbol Scanned		STACK
(1)	5	5
(2)	6	5, 6
(3)	2	5, 6, 2
(4)	+	5, 8
(5)	*	40
(6)	12	40, 12
(7)	4	40, 12, 4
(8)	/	40, 3
(9)	–	37
(10)	)	

Fig. 6-7

equivalent infix expression Q follows:

$$Q: \quad 5 * (6 + 2) - 12 / 4$$

Note that parentheses are necessary for the infix expression Q but not for the postfix expression P.

We evaluate P by simulating Algorithm 6.3. First we add a sentinel right parenthesis at the end of P to obtain

$$
\begin{array}{ccccccccccc}
P: & 5, & 6, & 2, & +, & *, & 12, & 4, & /, & -, &) \\
   & (1) & (2) & (3) & (4) & (5) & (6) & (7) & (8) & (9) & (10)
\end{array}
$$

The elements of P have been labeled from left to right for easy reference. Figure 6-7 shows the contents of STACK as each element of P is scanned. The final number in STACK, 37, which is assigned to VALUE when the sentinel ")" is scanned, is the value of P.

Transforming Infix Expressions into Postfix Expressions

Let Q be an arithmetic expression written in infix notation. Besides operands and operators, Q may also contain left and right parentheses. We assume that the operators in Q consist only of exponentiations ($\uparrow$), multiplications ($*$), divisions ($/$), additions ($+$) and subtractions ($-$), and that they have the usual three levels of precedence as given above. We also assume that operators on the same level, including exponentiations, are performed from left to right unless otherwise indicated by parentheses. (This is not standard, since expressions may contain unary operators and some languages perform the exponentiations from right to left. However, these assumptions simplify our algorithm.)

The following algorithm transforms the infix expression Q into its equivalent postfix expression P. The algorithm uses a stack to temporarily hold operators and left parentheses. The postfix expression P will be constructed from left to right using the operands from Q and the operators which are removed from STACK. We begin by pushing a left parenthesis onto STACK and adding a right parenthesis at the end of Q. The algorithm is completed when STACK is empty.

Algorithm 6.4:   POLISH(Q, P)

Suppose Q is an arithmetic expression written in infix notation. This algorithm finds the equivalent postfix expression P.

1. Push "(" onto STACK, and add ")" to the end of Q.
2. Scan Q from left to right and repeat Steps 3 to 6 for each element of Q until the STACK is empty:
3.   If an operand is encountered, add it to P.
4.   If a left parenthesis is encountered, push it onto STACK.
5.   If an operator $\otimes$ is encountered, then:
   (a)   Repeatedly pop from STACK and add to P each operator (on the top of STACK) which has the same precedence as or higher precedence than $\otimes$.
   (b)   Add $\otimes$ to STACK.
   [End of If structure.]
6.   If a right parenthesis is encountered, then:
   (a)   Repeatedly pop from STACK and add to P each operator (on the top of STACK) until a left parenthesis is encountered.
   (b)   Remove the left parenthesis. [Do not add the left parenthesis to P.]
   [End of If structure.]
   [End of Step 2 loop.]
7. Exit.

The terminology sometimes used for Step 5 is that $\otimes$ will "sink" to its own level.

EXAMPLE 6.6

Consider the following arithmetic infix expression Q:

$$Q: \quad A + (B * C - (D / E \uparrow F) * G) * H$$

We simulate Algorithm 6.4 to transform Q into its equivalent postfix expression P.
First we push "(" onto STACK, and then we add ")" to the end of Q to obtain:

Q: A + (B * C − (D / E ↑ F) * G) * H)
     (1) (2) (3) (4) (5) (6) (7) (8) (9) (10) (11) (12) (13) (14) (15) (16) (17) (18) (19) (20)

The elements of Q have now been labeled from left to right for easy reference. Figure 6-8 shows the status of STACK and of the string P as each element of Q is scanned. Observe that

(1) Each operand is simply added to P and does not change STACK.

(2) The subtraction operator (−) in row 7 sends * from STACK to P before it (−) is pushed onto STACK.

(3) The right parenthesis in row 14 sends ↑ and then / from STACK to P, and then removes the left parenthesis from the top of STACK.

(4) The right parenthesis in row 20 sends * and then + from STACK to P, and then removes the left parenthesis from the top of STACK.

After Step 20 is executed, the STACK is empty and

$$P: \quad A \ B \ C * D \ E \ F \uparrow / \ G * - H * +$$

which is the required postfix equivalent of Q.

Symbol Scanned	STACK	Expression P
(1) A	(	A
(2) +	(+	A
(3) (	(+ (	A
(4) B	(+ (	A B
(5) *	(+ (*	A B
(6) C	(+ (*	A B C
(7) −	(+ (−	A B C *
(8) (	(+ (− (	A B C *
(9) D	(+ (− (	A B C * D
(10) /	(+ (− (/	A B C * D
(11) E	(+ (− (/	A B C * D E
(12) ↑	(+ (− (/ ↑	A B C * D E
(13) F	(+ (− (/ ↑	A B C * D E F
(14))	(+ (−	A B C * D E F ↑ /
(15) *	(+ (− *	A B C * D E F ↑ /
(16) G	(+ (− *	A B C * D E F ↑ / G
(17))	(+	A B C * D E F ↑ / G * −
(18) *	(+ *	A B C * D E F ↑ / G * −
(19) H	(+ *	A B C * D E F ↑ / G * − H
(20))		A B C * D E F ↑ / G * − H * +

Fig. 6-8

6.5 QUICKSORT, AN APPLICATION OF STACKS

Let A be a list of n data items. "Sorting A" refers to the operation of rearranging the elements of A so that they are in some logical order, such as numerically ordered when A contains numerical data, or alphabetically ordered when A contains character data. The subject of sorting, including various sorting algorithms, is treated mainly in Chap. 9. This section gives only one sorting algorithm, called *quicksort*, in order to illustrate an application of stacks.

Quicksort is an algorithm of the divide-and-conquer type. That is, the problem of sorting a set is reduced to the problem of sorting two smaller sets. We illustrate this "reduction step" by means of a specific example.

Suppose A is the following list of 12 numbers:

(44,)   33,   11,   55,   77,   90,   40,   60,   99,   22,   88,   (66)

The reduction step of the quicksort algorithm finds the final position of one of the numbers; in this illustration, we use the first number, 44. This is accomplished as follows. Beginning with the last number, 66, scan the list from right to left, comparing each number with 44 and stopping at the first number less than 44. The number is 22. Interchange 44 and 22 to obtain the list

(22,)   33,   11,   55,   77,   90,   40,   60,   99,   (44,)   88,   66

(Observe that the numbers 88 and 66 to the right of 44 are each greater than 44.) Beginning with 22, next scan the list in the opposite direction, from left to right, comparing each number with 44 and stopping at the first number greater than 44. The number is 55. Interchange 44 and 55 to obtain the list

22,   33,   11,   (44,)   77,   90,   40,   60,   99,   (55,)   88,   66

(Observe that the numbers 22, 33 and 11 to the left of 44 are each less than 44.) Beginning this time with 55, now scan the list in the original direction, from right to left, until meeting the first number less than 44. It is 40. Interchange 44 and 40 to obtain the list

22,   33,   11,   (40,)   77,   90,   (44,)   60,   99,   55,   88,   66

(Again, the numbers to the right of 44 are each greater than 44.) Beginning with 40, scan the list from left to right. The first number greater than 44 is 77. Interchange 44 and 77 to obtain the list

22,   33,   11,   40,   (44,)   90,   (77,)   60,   99,   55,   88,   66

(Again, the numbers to the left of 44 are each less than 44.) Beginning with 77, scan the list from right to left seeking a number less than 44. We do not meet such a number before meeting 44. This means all numbers have been scanned and compared with 44. Furthermore, all numbers less than 44 now form the sublist of numbers to the left of 44, and all numbers greater than 44 now form the sublist of numbers to the right of 44, as shown below:

22,   33,   11,   40,   (44,)   90,   77,   60,   99,   55,   88,   66
First sublist   Second sublist

Thus 44 is correctly placed in its final position, and the task of sorting the original list A has now been reduced to the task of sorting each of the above sublists.

The above reduction step is repeated with each sublist containing 2 or more elements. Since we can process only one sublist at a time, we must be able to keep track of some sublists for future processing. This is accomplished by using two stacks, called LOWER and UPPER, to temporarily "hold" such sublists. That is, the addresses of the first and last elements of each sublist, called its *boundary values*, are pushed onto the stacks LOWER and UPPER, respectively; and the reduction step is applied to a sublist only after its boundary values are removed from the stacks. The following example illustrates the way the stacks LOWER and UPPER are used.

EXAMPLE 6.7

Consider the above list A with $n = 12$ elements. The algorithm begins by pushing the boundary values 1 and 12 of A onto the stacks to yield

$$\text{LOWER: } 1 \qquad \text{UPPER: } 12$$

In order to apply the reduction step, the algorithm first removes the top values 1 and 12 from the stacks, leaving

$$\text{LOWER: (empty)} \qquad \text{UPPER: (empty)}$$

and then applies the reduction step to the corresponding list A[1], A[2], . . . , A[12]. The reduction step, as executed above, finally places the first element, 44, in A[5]. Accordingly, the algorithm pushes the boundary values 1 and 4 of the first sublist and the boundary values 6 and 12 of the second sublist onto the stacks to yield

$$\text{LOWER: } 1, 6 \qquad \text{UPPER: } 4, 12$$

In order to apply the reduction step again, the algorithm removes the top values, 6 and 12, from the stacks, leaving

$$\text{LOWER: } 1 \qquad \text{UPPER: } 4$$

and then applies the reduction step to the corresponding sublist A[6], A[7], . . . , A[12]. The reduction step changes this list as in Fig. 6-9. Observe that the second sublist has only one element. Accordingly, the algorithm pushes only the boundary values 6 and 10 of the first sublist onto the stacks to yield

$$\text{LOWER: } 1, 6 \qquad \text{UPPER: } 4, 10$$

And so on. The algorithm ends when the stacks do not contain any sublist to be processed by the reduction step.

A[6],	A[7],	A[8],	A[9],	A[10],	A[11],	A[12],
(90,)	77,	60,	99,	55,	88,	(66)
66,	77,	60,	(99,)	55,	88,	(90)
66,	77,	60,	(90,)	55,	(88,)	99
66,	77,	60,	88,	55,	(90,)	99

First sublist   Second sublist

Fig. 6-9

The formal statement of our quicksort algorithm follows (on page 175). For notational convenience and pedagogical considerations, the algorithm is divided into two parts. The first part gives a procedure, called QUICK, which executes the above reduction step of the algorithm, and the second part uses QUICK to sort the entire list.

Observe that Step 2(c) (iii) is unnecessary. It has been added to emphasize the symmetry between Step 2 and Step 3. The procedure does not assume the elements of A are distinct. Otherwise, the condition LOC $\neq$ RIGHT in Step 2(a) and the condition LEFT $\neq$ LOC in Step 3(a) could be omitted.

The second part of the algorithm follows (on page 175). As noted above, LOWER and UPPER are stacks on which the boundary values of the sublists are stored. (As usual, we use NULL = 0.)

Procedure 6.5: QUICK(A, N, BEG, END, LOC)

Here A is an array with N elements. Parameters BEG and END contain the boundary values of the sublist of A to which this procedure applies. LOC keeps track of the position of the first element A[BEG] of the sublist during the procedure. The local variables LEFT and RIGHT will contain the boundary values of the list of elements that have not been scanned.

1. [Initialize.] Set LEFT := BEG, RIGHT := END and LOC := BEG.
2. [Scan from right to left.]
   - (a) Repeat while A[LOC] ≤ A[RIGHT] and LOC ≠ RIGHT:
     - RIGHT := RIGHT − 1.
     - [End of loop.]
   - (b) If LOC = RIGHT, then: Return.
   - (c) If A[LOC] > A[RIGHT], then:
     - (i) [Interchange A[LOC] and A[RIGHT].]
       - TEMP := A[LOC], A[LOC] := A[RIGHT],
       - A[RIGHT] := TEMP.
     - (ii) Set LOC := RIGHT.
     - (iii) Go to Step 3.
     - [End of If structure.]
3. [Scan from left to right.]
   - (a) Repeat while A[LEFT] ≤ A[LOC] and LEFT ≠ LOC:
     - LEFT := LEFT + 1.
     - [End of loop.]
   - (b) If LOC = LEFT, then: Return.
   - (c) If A[LEFT] > A[LOC], then
     - (i) [Interchange A[LEFT] and A[LOC].]
       - TEMP := A[LOC], A[LOC] := A[LEFT],
       - A[LEFT] := TEMP.
     - (ii) Set LOC := LEFT.
     - (iii) Go to Step 2.
     - [End of If structure.]

Algorithm 6.6: (Quicksort) This algorithm sorts an array A with N elements.

1. [Initialize.] TOP := NULL.
2. [Push boundary values of A onto stacks when A has 2 or more elements.]
   If N > 1, then: TOP := TOP + 1, LOWER[1] := 1, UPPER[1] := N.
3. Repeat Steps 4 to 7 while TOP ≠ NULL.
4. [Pop sublist from stacks.]
   Set BEG := LOWER[TOP], END := UPPER[TOP],
   TOP := TOP − 1.
5. Call QUICK(A, N, BEG, END, LOC). [Procedure 6.5.]
6. [Push left sublist onto stacks when it has 2 or more elements.]
   If BEG < LOC − 1, then:
   TOP := TOP + 1, LOWER[TOP] := BEG,
   UPPER[TOP] = LOC − 1.
   [End of If structure.]
7. [Push right sublist onto stacks when it has 2 or more elements.]
   If LOC + 1 < END, then:
   TOP := TOP + 1, LOWER[TOP] := LOC + 1,
   UPPER[TOP] := END.
   [End of If structure.]
   [End of Step 3 loop.]
8. Exit.

175

Complexity of the Quicksort Algorithm

The running time of a sorting algorithm is usually measured by the number $f(n)$ of comparisons required to sort n elements. The quicksort algorithm, which has many variations, has been studied extensively. Generally speaking, the algorithm has a worst-case running time of order $n^2/2$, but an average-case running time of order $n \log n$. The reason for this is indicated below.

The worst case occurs when the list is already sorted. Then the first element will require n comparisons to recognize that it remains in the first position. Furthermore, the first sublist will be empty, but the second sublist will have $n - 1$ elements. Accordingly, the second element will require $n - 1$ comparisons to recognize that it remains in the second position. And so on. Consequently, there will be a total of

$$f(n) = n + (n - 1) + \cdots + 2 + 1 = \frac{n(n + 1)}{2} = \frac{n^2}{2} + O(n) = O(n^2)$$

comparisons. Observe that this is equal to the complexity of the bubble sort algorithm (Sec. 4.6).

The complexity $f(n) = O(n \log n)$ of the average case comes from the fact that, on the average, each reduction step of the algorithm produces two sublists. Accordingly:

(1) Reducing the initial list places 1 element and produces two sublists.
(2) Reducing the two sublists places 2 elements and produces four sublists.
(3) Reducing the four sublists places 4 elements and produces eight sublists.
(4) Reducing the eight sublists places 8 elements and produces sixteen sublists.

And so on. Observe that the reduction step in the kth level finds the location of 2^{k-1} elements; hence there will be approximately $\log_2 n$ levels of reductions steps. Furthermore, each level uses at most n comparisons, so $f(n) = O(n \log n)$. In fact, mathematical analysis and empirical evidence have both shown that

$$f(n) \approx 1.4 \lceil n \log n \rceil$$

is the expected number of comparisons for the quicksort algorithm.

6.6 RECURSION

Recursion is an important concept in computer science. Many algorithms can be best described in terms of recursion. This section introduces this powerful tool, and Sec. 6.8 will show how recursion may be implemented by means of stacks.

Suppose P is a procedure containing either a Call statement to itself or a Call statement to a second procedure that may eventually result in a Call statement back to the original procedure P. Then P is called a *recursive procedure*. So that the program will not continue to run indefinitely, a recursive procedure must have the following two properties:

(1) There must be certain criteria, called *base criteria*, for which the procedure does not call itself.

(2) Each time the procedure does call itself (directly or indirectly), it must be closer to the base criteria.

A recursive procedure with these two properties is said to be *well-defined*.

Similarly, a function is said to be *recursively defined* if the function definition refers to itself. Again, in order for the definition not to be circular, it must have the following two properties:

(1) There must be certain arguments, called *base values*, for which the function does not refer to itself.

(2)   Each time the function does refer to itself, the argument of the function must be closer to a base value.

A recursive function with these two properties is also said to be well-defined.

The following examples should help clarify these ideas.

Factorial Function

The product of the positive integers from 1 to n, inclusive, is called "n factorial" and is usually denoted by $n!$:

$$n! = 1 \cdot 2 \cdot 3 \cdots (n-2)(n-1)n$$

It is also convenient to define $0! = 1$, so that the function is defined for all nonnegative integers. Thus we have

$$0! = 1 \qquad 1! = 1 \qquad 2! = 1 \cdot 2 = 2 \qquad 3! = 1 \cdot 2 \cdot 3 = 6 \qquad 4! = 1 \cdot 2 \cdot 3 \cdot 4 = 24$$
$$5! = 1 \cdot 2 \cdot 3 \cdot 4 \cdot 5 = 120 \qquad 6! = 1 \cdot 2 \cdot 3 \cdot 4 \cdot 5 \cdot 6 = 720$$

and so on. Observe that

$$5! = 5 \cdot 4! = 5 \cdot 24 = 120 \qquad \text{and} \qquad 6! = 6 \cdot 5! = 6 \cdot 120 = 720$$

This is true for every positive integer n; that is,

$$n! = n \cdot (n-1)!$$

Accordingly, the factorial function may also be defined as follows:

Definition 6.1:   (Factorial Function)

        (a)   If $n = 0$, then $n! = 1$.

        (b)   If $n > 0$, then $n! = n \cdot (n-1)!$

Observe that this definition of $n!$ is recursive, since it refers to itself when it uses $(n-1)!$ However, (a) the value of $n!$ is explicitly given when $n = 0$ (thus 0 is the base value); and (b) the value of $n!$ for arbitrary n is defined in terms of a smaller value of n which is closer to the base value 0. Accordingly, the definition is not circular, or in other words, the procedure is well-defined.

EXAMPLE 6.8

Let us calculate $4!$ using the recursive definition. This calculation requires the following nine steps:

(1) $4! = 4 \cdot 3!$

(2) $3! = 3 \cdot 2!$

(3) $2! = 2 \cdot 1!$

(4) $1! = 1 \cdot 0!$

(5) $0! = 1$

(6) $1! = 1 \cdot 1 = 1$

(7) $2! = 2 \cdot 1 = 2$

(8) $3! = 3 \cdot 2 = 6$

(9) $4! = 4 \cdot 6 = 24$

That is:

Step 1.   This defines $4!$ in terms of $3!$, so we must postpone evaluating $4!$ until we evaluate $3!$ This postponement is indicated by indenting the next step.

Step 2.   Here $3!$ is defined in terms of $2!$, so we must postpone evaluating $3!$ until we evaluate $2!$

Step 3.   This defines $2!$ in terms of $1!$

Step 4.   This defines 1! in terms of 0!

Step 5.   This step can explicitly evaluate 0!, since 0 is the base value of the recursive definition.

Steps 6 to 9.   We backtrack, using 0! to find 1!, using 1! to find 2!, using 2! to find 3!, and finally using 3! to find 4! This backtracking is indicated by the "reverse" indention.

Observe that we backtrack in the reverse order of the original postponed evaluations. Recall that this type of postponed processing lends itself to the use of stacks. (See Sec. 6.2.)

The following are two procedures that each calculate n factorial.

Procedure 6.7A: FACTORIAL(FACT, N)

This procedure calculates N! and returns the value in the variable FACT.

1. If N = 0, then: Set FACT := 1, and Return.
2. Set FACT := 1. [Initializes FACT for loop.]
3. Repeat for K = 1 to N.
   Set FACT := K * FACT.
   [End of loop.]
4. Return.

Procedure 6.7B: FACTORIAL(FACT, N)

This procedure calculates N! and returns the value in the variable FACT.

1. If N = 0, then: Set FACT := 1, and Return.
2. Call FACTORIAL(FACT, N − 1).
3. Set FACT := N * FACT.
4. Return.

Observe that the first procedure evaluates N! using an iterative loop process. The second procedure, on the other hand, is a recursive procedure, since it contains a call to itself. Some programming languages, notably FORTRAN, do not allow such recursive subprograms.

Suppose P is a recursive procedure. During the running of an algorithm or a program which contains P, we associate a *level number* with each given execution of procedure P as follows. The original execution of procedure P is assigned level 1; and each time procedure P is executed because of a recursive call, its level is 1 more than the level of the execution that has made the recursive call. In Example 6.8, Step 1 belongs to level 1. Hence Step 2 belongs to level 2, Step 3 to level 3, Step 4 to level 4 and Step 5 to level 5. On the other hand, Step 6 belongs to level 4, since it is the result of a return from level 5. In other words, Step 6 and Step 4 belong to the same level of execution. Similarly, Step 7 belongs to level 3, Step 8 to level 2, and the final step, Step 9, to the original level 1.

The *depth* of recursion of a recursive procedure P with a given set of arguments refers to the maximum level number of P during its execution.

Fibonacci Sequence

The celebrated Fibonacci sequence (usually denoted by $F_0, F_1, F_2, \ldots$) is as follows:

$$0, 1, 1, 2, 3, 5, 8, 13, 21, 34, 55, \ldots$$

That is, $F_0 = 0$ and $F_1 = 1$ and each succeeding term is the sum of the two preceding terms. For example, the next two terms of the sequence are

$$34 + 55 = 89 \qquad \text{and} \qquad 55 + 89 = 144$$

A formal definition of this function follows:

Definition 6.2:   (Fibonacci Sequence)

     (*a*)   If $n = 0$ or $n = 1$, then $F_n = n$.

     (*b*)   If $n > 1$, then $F_n = F_{n-2} + F_{n-1}$.

This is another example of a recursive definition, since the definition refers to itself when it uses F_{n-2} and F_{n-1}. Here (a) the base values are 0 and 1, and (b) the value of F_n is defined in terms of smaller values of n which are closer to the base values. Accordingly, this function is well-defined.

A procedure for finding the nth term F_n of the Fibonacci sequence follows.

Procedure 6.8:   FIBONACCI(FIB, N)

This procedure calculates F_N and returns the value in the first parameter FIB.

   1.   If $N = 0$ or $N = 1$, then: Set FIB := N, and Return.
   2.   Call FIBONACCI(FIBA, N − 2).
   3.   Call FIBONACCI(FIBB, N − 1).
   4.   Set FIB := FIBA + FIBB.
   5.   Return.

This is another example of a recursive procedure, since the procedure contains a call to itself. In fact, this procedure contains two calls to itself. We note (see Prob. 6.16) that one can also write an iterative procedure to calculate F_n which does not use recursion.

Divide-and-Conquer Algorithms

Consider a problem P associated with a set S. Suppose A is an algorithm which partitions S into smaller sets such that the solution of the problem P for S is reduced to the solution of P for one or more of the smaller sets. Then A is called a divide-and-conquer algorithm.

Two examples of divide-and-conquer algorithms, previously treated, are the quicksort algorithm in Sec. 6.5 and the binary search algorithm in Sec. 4.7. Recall that the quicksort algorithm uses a reduction step to find the location of a single element and to reduce the problem of sorting the entire set to the problem of sorting smaller sets. The binary search algorithm divides the given sorted set into two halves so that the problem of searching for an item in the entire set is reduced to the problem of searching for the item in one of the two halves.

A divide-and-conquer algorithm A may be viewed as a recursive procedure. The reason for this is that the algorithm A may be viewed as calling itself when it is applied to the smaller sets. The base criteria for these algorithms are usually the one-element sets. For example, with a sorting algorithm, a one-element set is automatically sorted; and with a searching algorithm, a one-element set requires only a single comparison.

Ackermann Function

The Ackermann function is a function with two arguments each of which can be assigned any nonnegative integer: 0, 1, 2, ... This function is defined as follows:

Definition 6.3:   (Ackermann Function)

   (a)   If $m = 0$, then $A(m, n) = n + 1$.

   (b)   If $m \neq 0$ but $n = 0$, then $A(m, n) = A(m − 1, 1)$.

   (c)   If $m \neq 0$ and $n \neq 0$, then $A(m, n) = A(m − 1, A(m, n − 1))$.

Once more, we have a recursive definition, since the definition refers to itself in parts (b) and (c). Observe that $A(m, n)$ is explicitly given only when $m = 0$. The base criteria are the pairs

$$(0, 0), \quad (0, 1), \quad (0, 2), \quad (0, 3), \ldots , (0, n), \ldots$$

Although it is not obvious from the definition, the value of any $A(m, n)$ may eventually be expressed in terms of the value of the function on one or more of the base pairs.

The value of $A(1, 3)$ is calculated in Prob. 6.17. Even this simple case requires 15 steps. Generally speaking, the Ackermann function is too complex to evaluate on any but a trivial example. Its importance comes from its use in mathematical logic. The function is stated here mainly to give another example of a classical recursive function and to show that the recursion part of a definition may be complicated.

6.7 TOWERS OF HANOI

The preceding section gave examples of some recursive definitions and procedures. This section shows how recursion may be used as a tool in developing an algorithm to solve a particular problem. The problem we pick is known as the Towers of Hanoi problem.

Suppose three pegs, labeled A, B and C, are given, and suppose on peg A there are placed a finite number n of disks with decreasing size. This is pictured in Fig. 6-10 for the case $n = 6$. The object of the game is to move the disks from peg A to peg C using peg B as an auxiliary. The rules of the game are as follows:

(a)   Only one disk may be moved at a time. Specifically, only the top disk on any peg may be moved to any other peg.

(b)   At no time can a larger disk be placed on a smaller disk.

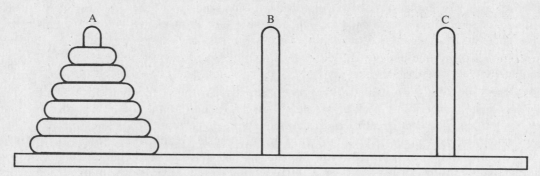

Fig. 6-10   Initial setup of Towers of Hanoi with $n = 6$.

Sometimes we will write $X \rightarrow Y$ to denote the instruction "Move top disk from peg X to peg Y," where X and Y may be any of the three pegs.

The solution to the Towers of Hanoi problem for $n = 3$ appears in Fig. 6-11. Observe that it consists of the following seven moves:

$n = 3$:   Move top disk from peg A to peg C.
Move top disk from peg A to peg B.
Move top disk from peg C to peg B.
Move top disk from peg A to peg C.
Move top disk from peg B to peg A.
Move top disk from peg B to peg C.
Move top disk from peg A to peg C.

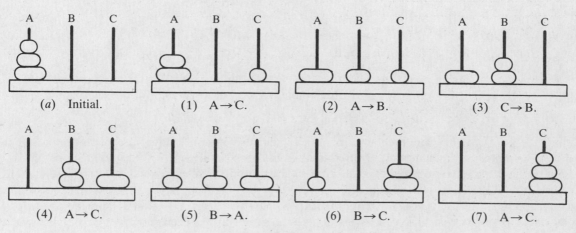

Fig. 6-11

In other words,

$$n = 3: \quad A \rightarrow C, \quad A \rightarrow B, \quad C \rightarrow B, \quad A \rightarrow C, \quad B \rightarrow A, \quad B \rightarrow C, \quad A \rightarrow C$$

For completeness, we also give the solution to the Towers of Hanoi problem for $n = 1$ and $n = 2$:

$$n = 1: \quad A \rightarrow C$$
$$n = 2: \quad A \rightarrow B, \quad A \rightarrow C, \quad B \rightarrow C$$

Note that $n = 1$ uses only one move and that $n = 2$ uses three moves.

Rather than finding a separate solution for each n, we use the technique of recursion to develop a general solution. First we observe that the solution to the Towers of Hanoi problem for $n > 1$ disks may be reduced to the following subproblems:

(1) Move the top $n - 1$ disks from peg A to peg B.
(2) Move the top disk from peg A to peg C: $A \rightarrow C$.
(3) Move the top $n - 1$ disks from peg B to peg C.

This reduction is illustrated in Fig. 6-12 for $n = 6$. That is, first we move the top five disks from peg A to peg B, then we move the large disk from peg A to peg C, and then we move the top five disks from peg B to peg C.

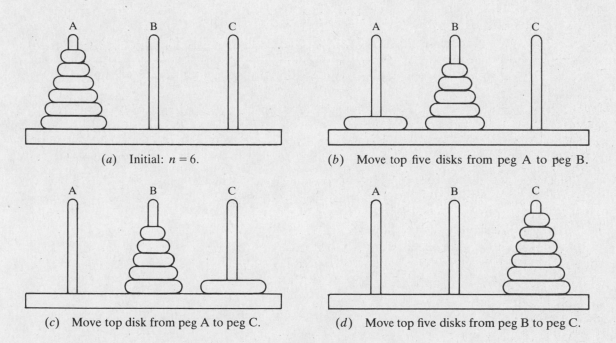

(a) Initial: $n = 6$.

(b) Move top five disks from peg A to peg B.

(c) Move top disk from peg A to peg C.

(d) Move top five disks from peg B to peg C.

Fig. 6-12

Let us now introduce the general notation

TOWER(N, BEG, AUX, END)

to denote a procedure which moves the top n disks from the initial peg BEG to the final peg END using the peg AUX as an auxiliary. When $n = 1$, we have the following obvious solution:

TOWER(1, BEG, AUX, END)   consists of the single instruction   BEG → END

Furthermore, as discussed above, when $n > 1$, the solution may be reduced to the solution of the following three subproblems:

(1)   TOWER(N − 1, BEG, END, AUX)

(2)   TOWER(1, BEG, AUX, END) or BEG → END

(3)   TOWER(N − 1, AUX, BEG, END)

Observe that each of these three subproblems may be solved directly or is essentially the same as the original problem using fewer disks. Accordingly, this reduction process does yield a recursive solution to the Towers of Hanoi problem.

Figure 6-13 contains a schematic diagram of the above recursive solution for

$$\text{TOWER}(4, A, B, C)$$

Observe that the recursive solution for $n = 4$ disks consists of the following 15 moves:

A→B	A→C	B→C	A→B	C→A	C→B	A→B	A→C
B→C	B→A	C→A	B→C	A→B	A→C	B→C	

In general, this recursive solution requires $f(n) = 2^n - 1$ moves for n disks.

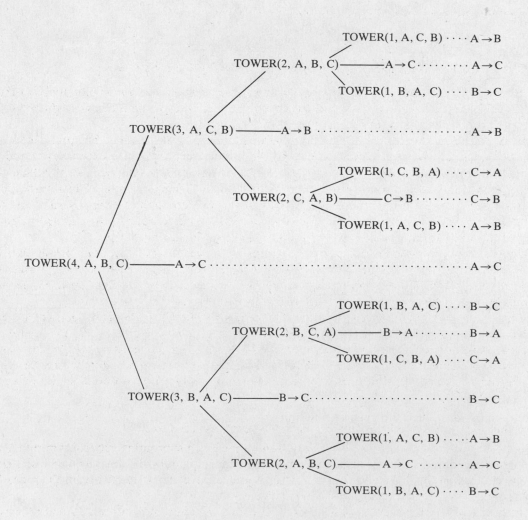

Fig. 6-13   Recursive solution to Towers of Hanoi problem for $n = 4$.

We summarize our investigation with the following formally written procedure.

Procedure 6.9:   TOWER(N, BEG, AUX, END)
This procedure gives a recursive solution to the Towers of Hanoi problem for N disks.

1.   If N = 1, then:
     (*a*)   Write: BEG → END.
     (*b*)   Return.
     [End of If structure.]
2.   [Move N − 1 disks from peg BEG to peg AUX.]
     Call TOWER(N − 1, BEG, END, AUX).
3.   Write: BEG → END.
4.   [Move N − 1 disks from peg AUX to peg END.]
     Call TOWER(N − 1, AUX, BEG, END).
5.   Return.

One can view this solution as a divide-and-conquer algorithm, since the solution for n disks is reduced to a solution for $n − 1$ disks and a solution for $n = 1$ disk.

6.8   IMPLEMENTATION OF RECURSIVE PROCEDURES BY STACKS

The preceding sections showed how recursion may be a useful tool in developing algorithms for specific problems. This section shows how stacks may be used to implement recursive procedures. It is instructive to first discuss subprograms in general.

Recall that a subprogram can contain both parameters and local variables. The parameters are the variables which receive values from objects in the calling program, called arguments, and which transmit values back to the calling program. Besides the parameters and local variables, the subprogram must also keep track of the return address in the calling program. This return address is essential, since control must be transferred back to its proper place in the calling program. At the time that the subprogram is finished executing and control is transferred back to the calling program, the values of the local variables and the return address are no longer needed.

Suppose our subprogram is a recursive program. Then each level of execution of the subprogram may contain different values for the parameters and local variables and for the return address. Furthermore, if the recursive program does call itself, then these current values must be saved, since they will be used again when the program is reactivated.

Suppose a programmer is using a high-level language which admits recursion, such as Pascal. Then the computer handles the bookkeeping that keeps track of all the values of the parameters, local variables and return addresses. On the other hand, if a programmer is using a high-level language which does not admit recursion, such as FORTRAN, then the programmer must set up the necessary bookkeeping by translating the recursive procedure into a nonrecursive one. This bookkeeping is discussed below.

Translation of a Recursive Procedure into a Nonrecursive Procedure

Suppose P is a recursive procedure. We assume that P is a subroutine subprogram rather than a function subprogram. (This is no loss in generality, since function subprograms can easily be written as subroutine subprograms.) We also assume that a recursive call to P comes only from the procedure P. (The treatment of indirect recursion lies beyond the scope of this text.)

The translation of the recursive procedure P into a nonrecursive procedure works as follows. First of all, one defines:

(1)   A stack STPAR for each parameter PAR

(2)   A stack STVAR for each local variable VAR

(3)   A local variable ADD and a stack STADD to hold return addresses

Each time there is a recursive call to P, the current values of the parameters and local variables are pushed onto the corresponding stacks for future processing, and each time there is a recursive return to P, the values of parameters and local variables for the current execution of P are restored from the stacks. The handling of the return addresses is more complicated; it is done as follows.

Suppose the procedure P contains a recursive Call P in Step K. Then there are two return addresses associated with the execution of this Step K:

(1)   There is the current return address of the procedure P, which will be used when the current level of execution of P is finished executing.

(2)   There is the new return address K + 1, which is the address of the step following the Call P and which will be used to return to the current level of execution of procedure P.

Some texts push the first of these two addresses, the current return address, onto the return address stack STADD, whereas some texts push the second address, the new return address K + 1, onto STADD. We will choose the latter method, since the translation of P into a nonrecursive procedure will then be simpler. This also means, in particular, that an empty stack STADD will indicate a return to the main program that initially called the recursive procedure P. (The alternative translation which pushes the current return address onto the stack is discussed in Prob. 6.20.)

The algorithm which translates the recursive procedure P into a nonrecursive procedure follows. It consists of three parts: (1) preparation, (2) translating each recursive Call P in procedure P and (3) translating each Return in procedure P.

(1)   Preparation.
   (a)   Define a stack STPAR for each parameter PAR, a stack STVAR for each local variable VAR, and a local variable ADD and a stack STADD to hold return addresses.
   (b)   Set TOP := NULL.

(2)   Translation of "Step K. Call P."
   (a)   Push the current values of the parameters and local variables onto the appropriate stacks, and push the new return address [Step] K + 1 onto STADD.
   (b)   Reset the parameters using the new argument values.
   (c)   Go to Step 1. [The beginning of the procedure P.]

(3)   Translation of "Step J. Return."
   (a)   If STADD is empty, then: Return. [Control is returned to the main program.]
   (b)   Restore the top values of the stacks. That is, set the parameters and local variables equal to the top values on the stacks, and set ADD equal to the top value on the stack STADD.
   (c)   Go to Step ADD.

Observe that the translation of "Step K. Call P" does depend on the value of K, but that the translation of "Step J. Return" does not depend on the value of J. Accordingly, one need translate only one Return statement, for example, by using

Step L. Return.

as above and then replace every other Return statement by

Go to Step L.

This will simplify the translation of the procedure.

Towers of Hanoi, Revisited

Consider again the Towers of Hanoi problem. Procedure 6.9 is a recursive solution to the problem for n disks. We translate the procedure into a nonrecursive solution. In order to keep the steps analogous, we label the beginning statement TOP := NULL as Step 0. Also, only the Return statement in Step 5 will be translated, as in (3) on the preceding page.

Procedure 6.10:   TOWER(N, BEG, AUX, END)

This is a nonrecursive solution to the Towers of Hanoi problem for N disks which is obtained by translating the recursive solution. Stacks STN, STBEG, STAUX, STEND and STADD will correspond, respectively, to the variables N, BEG, AUX, END and ADD.

0. Set TOP := NULL.
1. If N = 1, then:
    (a) Write: BEG → END.
    (b) Go to Step 5.
    [End of If structure.]
2. [Translation of "Call TOWER(N − 1, BEG, END, AUX)."]
    (a) [Push current values and new return address onto stacks.]
        (i)   Set TOP := TOP + 1.
        (ii) Set STN[TOP] := N, STBEG[TOP] := BEG,
              STAUX[TOP] := AUX, STEND[TOP] := END,
              STADD[TOP] := 3.
    (b) [Reset parameters.]
        Set N := N − 1, BEG := BEG, AUX := END, END := AUX.
    (c) Go to Step 1.
3. Write: BEG → END.
4. [Translation of "Call TOWER(N − 1, AUX, BEG, END)."]
    (a) [Push current values and new return address onto stacks.]
        (i)   Set TOP := TOP + 1.
        (ii) Set STN[TOP] := N, STBEG[TOP] := BEG,
              STAUX[TOP] := AUX, STEND[TOP] := END,
              STADD[TOP] := 5.
    (b) [Reset parameters.]
        Set N := N − 1, BEG := AUX, AUX := BEG, END := END.
    (c) Go to Step 1.
5. [Translation of "Return."]
    (a) If TOP := NULL, then: Return.
    (b) [Restore top values on stacks.]
        (i)   Set N := STN[TOP], BEG := STBEG[TOP],
              AUX := STAUX[TOP], STEND[TOP],
              ADD := STADD[TOP].
        (ii) Set TOP := TOP − 1.
    (c) Go to Step ADD.

Suppose that a main program does contain the following statement:

$$\text{Call TOWER}(3, A, B, C)$$

We simulate the execution of the solution of the problem in Procedure 6.10, emphasizing the different levels of execution of the procedure. Each level of execution will begin with an initialization step where the parameters are assigned the argument values from the initial calling statement or from the

STN:	3	3, 2	3	3, 2	3		3	3, 2	3	3, 2	3	
STBEG:	A	A, A	A	A, A	A		A	A, B	A	A, B	A	
STAUX:	B	B, C	B	B, C	B		B	B, A	B	B, A	B	
STEND:	C	C, B	C	C, B	C		C	C, C	C	C, C	C	
STADD:	3	3, 3	3	3, 5	3		5	5, 3	5	5, 5	5	
	(a)	(b)	(c)	(d)	(e)	(f)	(g)	(h)	(i)	(j)	(k)	(l)

Fig. 6-14 Stacks for TOWER(3, A, B, C).

recursive call in Step 2 or Step 4. (Hence each new return address is either Step 3 or Step 5.) Figure 6-14 shows the different stages of the stacks.

(a) (Level 1) The initial Call TOWER(3, A, B, C) assigns the following values to the parameters:

$$N := 3, \quad BEG := A, \quad AUX := B, \quad END := C$$

Step 1. Since $N \neq 1$, control is transferred to Step 2.
Step 2. This is a recursive call. Hence the current values of the variables and the new return address (Step 3) are pushed onto the stacks as pictured in Fig. 6-14(a).

(b) (Level 2) The Step 2 recursive call [TOWER(N − 1, BEG, END, AUX)] assigns the following values to the parameters:

$$N := N - 1 = 2, \quad BEG := BEG = A, \quad AUX := END = C, \quad END := AUX = B$$

Step 1. Since $N \neq 1$, control is transferred to Step 2.
Step 2. This is a recursive call. Hence the current values of the variables and the new return address (Step 3) are pushed onto the stacks as pictured in Fig. 6-14(b).

(c) (Level 3) The Step 2 recursive call [TOWER(N − 1, BEG, END, AUX)] assigns the following values to the parameters:

$$N := N - 1 = 1, \quad BEG := BEG = A, \quad AUX := END = B, \quad END := AUX = C$$

Step 1. Now $N = 1$. The operation BEG → END implements the move

$$A \to C$$

Then control is transferred to Step 5. [For the Return.]
Step 5. The stacks are not empty, so the top values on the stacks are removed, leaving Fig. 6-14(c), and are assigned as follows:

$$N := 2, \quad BEG := A, \quad AUX := C, \quad END := B, \quad ADD := 3$$

Control is transferred to the preceding Level 2 at Step ADD.

(d) (Level 2) [Reactivated at Step ADD = 3.]
Step 3. The operation BEG → END implements the move

$$A \to B$$

Step 4. This is a recursive call. Hence the current values of the variables and the new return address (Step 5) are pushed onto the stacks as pictured in Fig. 6-14(d).

(e) (Level 3) The Step 4 recursive call [TOWER(N − 1, AUX, BEG, END)] assigns the following values to the parameters:

$$N := N - 1 = 1, \quad BEG := AUX = C, \quad AUX := BEG = A,$$

$$END := END = B$$

Step 1. Now N = 1. The operation BEG → END implements the move

$$C \to B$$

Then control is transferred to Step 5. [For the Return.]

Step 5. The stacks are not empty; hence the top values on the stacks are removed, leaving Fig. 6-14(e), and they are assigned as follows:

$$N := 2, \quad BEG := A, \quad AUX := C, \quad END := B, \quad ADD := 5$$

Control is transferred to the preceding Level 2 at Step ADD.

(f) (Level 2)   [Reactivation at Step ADD = 5.]

Step 5. The stacks are not empty; hence the top values on the stacks are removed, leaving Fig. 6-14(f), and they are assigned as follows:

$$N := 3, \quad BEG := A, \quad AUX := B, \quad END := C, \quad ADD := 3$$

Control is transferred to the preceding Level 1 at Step ADD.

(g) (Level 1)   [Reactivation at Step ADD = 3.]

Step 3. The operation BEG → END implements the move

$$A \to C$$

Step 4. This is a recursive call. Hence the current values of the variables and the new return address (Step 5) are pushed onto the stacks as pictured in Fig. 6-14(g).

(h) (Level 2)   The Step 4 recursive call [TOWER(N − 1, AUX, BEG, END)] assigns the following values to the parameters:

$$N := N - 1 = 2, \quad BEG := AUX = B, \quad AUX := BEG = A, \quad END := END = C$$

Step 1. Since N ≠ 1, control is transferred to Step 2.

Step 2. This is a recursive call. Hence the current values of the variables and the new return address (Step 3) are pushed onto the stacks as pictured in Fig. 6-14(h).

(i) (Level 3)   The Step 2 recursive call [TOWER(N − 1, BEG, END, AUX)] assigns the following values to the parameters:

$$N := N - 1 = 1, \quad BEG := BEG = B, \quad AUX := END = C, \quad END := AUX = A$$

Step 1. Now N = 1. The operation BEG → END implements the move

$$B \to A$$

Then control is transferred to Step 5. [For the Return.]

Step 5. The stacks are not empty; hence the top values on the stacks are removed, leaving Fig. 6-14(i), and they are assigned as follows:

$$N := 2, \quad BEG := B, \quad AUX := A, \quad END := C, \quad ADD := 3$$

Control is transferred to the preceding Level 2 at Step ADD.

(j) (Level 2)   [Reactivation at Step ADD = 3.]

Step 3. The operation BEG → END implements the move

$$B \to C$$

Step 4. This is a recursive call. Hence the current values of the variables and the new return address (Step 5) are pushed onto the stacks as pictured in Fig. 6-14(j).

(k) (Level 3)   The Step 4 recursive call [TOWER(N − 1, AUX, BEG, END)] assigns the following values to the parameters:

$$N := N - 1 = 1, \quad BEG := AUX = C, \quad AUX := BEG = B, \quad END := END = C$$

Step 1.   Now N = 1. The operation BEG → END implements the move

$$A \to C$$

Then control is transferred to Step 5. [For the Return.]

Step 5.   The stacks are not empty; hence the top values on the stacks are removed, leaving Fig. 6-14(k), and they are assigned as follows:

$$N := 2, \quad BEG := B, \quad AUX := A, \quad END := C, \quad ADD := 5$$

Control is transferred to the preceding Level 2 at Step ADD.

(l)   (Level 2)   [Reactivation at Step ADD = 5.]

Step 5.   The stacks are not empty; hence the top values on the stacks are removed, leaving Fig. 6-14(l), and they are assigned as follows:

$$N := 3, \quad BEG := A, \quad AUX := B, \quad END := C, \quad ADD := 5$$

Control is transferred to the preceding Level 1 at Step ADD.

(m)   (Level 1)   [Reactivation at Step ADD = 5.]

Step 5.   The stacks are now empty. Accordingly, control is transferred to the original main program containing the statement

$$\text{Call TOWER}(3, A, B, C)$$

Observe that the output consists of the following seven moves:

$$A \to C, \quad A \to B, \quad C \to B, \quad A \to C, \quad B \to A, \quad B \to C, \quad A \to C$$

This agrees with the solution in Fig. 6-11.

Summary

The Towers of Hanoi problem illustrates the power of recursion in the solution of various algorithmic problems. This section has shown how to implement recursion by means of stacks when using a programming language—notably FORTRAN or COBOL—which does not allow recursive programs. In fact, even when using a programming language—such as Pascal—which does support recursion, the programmer may want to use the nonrecursive solution, since it may be much less expensive than using the recursive solution.

6.9   QUEUES

A *queue* is a linear list of elements in which deletions can take place only at one end, called the *front*, and insertions can take place only at the other end, called the *rear*. The terms "front" and "rear" are used in describing a linear list only when it is implemented as a queue.

Queues are also called first-in first-out (FIFO) lists, since the first element in a queue will be the first element out of the queue. In other words, the order in which elements enter a queue is the order in which they leave. This contrasts with stacks, which are last-in first-out (LIFO) lists.

Queues abound in everyday life. The automobiles waiting to pass through an intersection form a queue, in which the first car in line is the first car through; the people waiting in line at a bank form a queue, where the first person in line is the first person to be waited on; and so on. An important example of a queue in computer science occurs in a timesharing system, in which programs with the same priority form a queue while waiting to be executed. (Another structure, called a priority queue, is discussed in Sec. 6.11.)

EXAMPLE 6.9

Figure 6-15(a) is a schematic diagram of a queue with 4 elements, where AAA is the front element and DDD is the rear element. Observe that the front and rear elements of the queue are also, respectively, the first and last elements of the list. Suppose an element is deleted from the queue. Then it must be AAA. This yields the queue in Fig. 6-15(b), where BBB is now the front element. Next, suppose EEE is added to the queue and then FFF is added to the queue. Then they must be added at the rear of the queue, as pictured in Fig. 6-15(c). Note that FFF is now the rear element. Now suppose another element is deleted from the queue; then it must be BBB, to yield the queue in Fig. 6-15(d). And so on. Observe that in such a data structure, EEE will be deleted before FFF because it has been placed in the queue before FFF. However, EEE will have to wait until CCC and DDD are deleted.

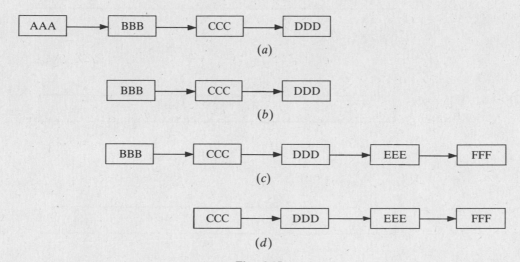

Fig. 6-15

Representation of Queues

Queues may be represented in the computer in various ways, usually by means of one-way lists or linear arrays. Unless otherwise stated or implied, each of our queues will be maintained by a linear array QUEUE and two pointer variables: FRONT, containing the location of the front element of the queue; and REAR, containing the location of the rear element of the queue. The condition FRONT = NULL will indicate that the queue is empty.

Figure 6-16 shows the way the array in Fig. 6-15 will be stored in memory using an array QUEUE with N elements. Figure 6-16 also indicates the way elements will be deleted from the queue and the way new elements will be added to the queue. Observe that whenever an element is deleted from the queue, the value of FRONT is increased by 1; this can be implemented by the assignment

$$FRONT := FRONT + 1$$

Similarly, whenever an element is added to the queue, the value of REAR is increased by 1; this can be implemented by the assignment

$$REAR := REAR + 1$$

This means that after N insertions, the rear element of the queue will occupy QUEUE[N] or, in other words, eventually the queue will occupy the last part of the array. This occurs even though the queue itself may not contain many elements.

Suppose we want to insert an element ITEM into a queue at the time the queue does occupy the last part of the array, i.e., when REAR = N. One way to do this is to simply move the entire queue to the beginning of the array, changing FRONT and REAR accordingly, and then inserting ITEM as above. This procedure may be very expensive. The procedure we adopt is to assume that the array

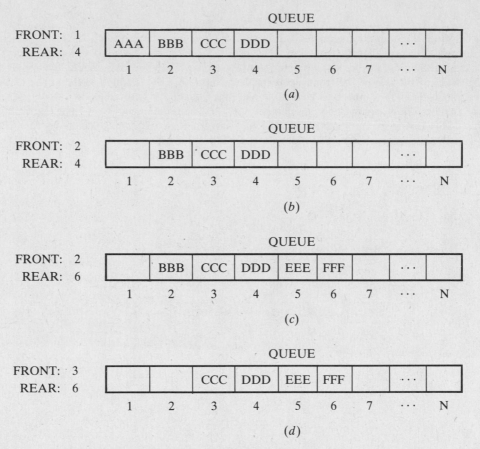

Fig. 6-16. Array representation of a queue.

QUEUE is circular, that is, that QUEUE[1] comes after QUEUE[N] in the array. With this assumption, we insert ITEM into the queue by assigning ITEM to QUEUE[1]. Specifically, instead of increasing REAR to N + 1, we reset REAR = 1 and then assign

$$\text{QUEUE[REAR]} := \text{ITEM}$$

Similarly, if FRONT = N and an element of QUEUE is deleted, we reset FRONT = 1 instead of increasing FRONT to N + 1. (Some readers may recognize this as modular arithmetic, discussed in Sec. 2.2.)

Suppose that our queue contains only one element, i.e., suppose that

$$\text{FRONT} = \text{REAR} \neq \text{NULL}$$

and suppose that the element is deleted. Then we assign

$$\text{FRONT} := \text{NULL} \quad \text{and} \quad \text{REAR} := \text{NULL}$$

to indicate that the queue is empty.

EXAMPLE 6.10

Figure 6-17 shows how a queue may be maintained by a circular array QUEUE with N = 5 memory locations. Observe that the queue always occupies consecutive locations except when it occupies locations at the beginning and at the end of the array. If the queue is viewed as a circular array, this means that it still occupies consecutive locations. Also, as indicated by Fig. 6-17(m), the queue will be empty only when FRONT = REAR and an element is deleted. For this reason, NULL is assigned to FRONT and REAR in Fig. 6-17(m).

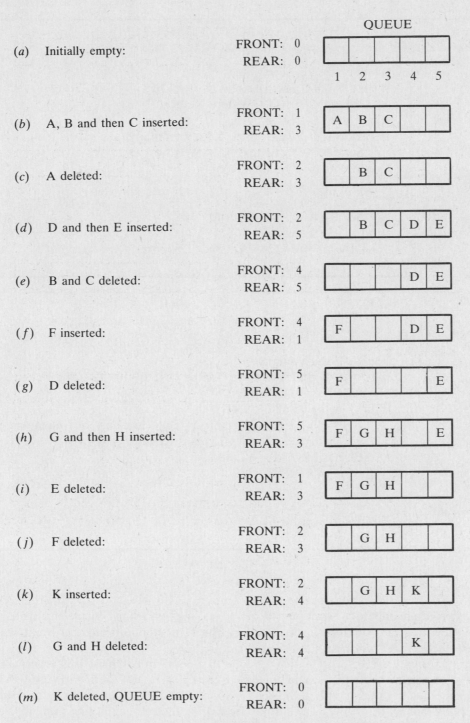

Fig. 6-17

We are now prepared to formally state our procedure QINSERT (Procedure 6.11), which inserts a data ITEM into a queue. The first thing we do in the procedure is to test for overflow, that is, to test whether or not the queue is filled.

Next we give a procedure QDELETE (Procedure 6.12), which deletes the first element from a queue, assigning it to the variable ITEM. The first thing we do is to test for underflow, i.e., to test whether or not the queue is empty.

Procedure 6.11:   QINSERT(QUEUE, N, FRONT, REAR, ITEM)
This procedure inserts an element ITEM into a queue.

1. [Queue already filled?]
   If FRONT = 1 and REAR = N, or if FRONT = REAR + 1, then:
      Write: OVERFLOW, and Return.
2. [Find new value of REAR.]
   If FRONT := NULL, then: [Queue initially empty.]
      Set FRONT := 1 and REAR := 1.
   Else if REAR = N, then:
      Set REAR := 1.
   Else:
      Set REAR := REAR + 1.
   [End of If structure.]
3. Set QUEUE[REAR] := ITEM. [This inserts new element.]
4. Return.

Procedure 6.12:   QDELETE(QUEUE, N, FRONT, REAR, ITEM)
This procedure deletes an element from a queue and assigns it to the variable ITEM.

1. [Queue already empty?]
   If FRONT := NULL, then: Write: UNDERFLOW, and Return.
2. Set ITEM := QUEUE[FRONT].
3. [Find new value of FRONT.]
      If FRONT = REAR, then: [Queue has only one element to start.]
         Set FRONT := NULL and REAR := NULL.
      Else if FRONT = N, then:
         Set FRONT := 1.
      Else:
         Set FRONT := FRONT + 1.
   [End of If structure.]
4. Return.

6.10 DEQUES

A *deque* (pronounced either "deck" or "dequeue") is a linear list in which elements can be added or removed at either end but not in the middle. The term deque is a contraction of the name *double-ended queue*.

There are various ways of representing a deque in a computer. Unless it is otherwise stated or implied, we will assume our deque is maintained by a circular array DEQUE with pointers LEFT and RIGHT, which point to the two ends of the deque. We assume that the elements extend from the left end to the right end in the array. The term "circular" comes from the fact that we assume that DEQUE[1] comes after DEQUE[N] in the array. Figure 6-18 pictures two deques, each with 4 elements maintained in an array with N = 8 memory locations. The condition LEFT = NULL will be used to indicate that a deque is empty.

There are two variations of a deque—namely, an input-restricted deque and an output-restricted deque—which are intermediate between a deque and a queue. Specifically, an *input-restricted deque* is a deque which allows insertions at only one end of the list but allows deletions at both ends of the list; and an *output-restricted deque* is a deque which allows deletions at only one end of the list but allows insertions at both ends of the list.

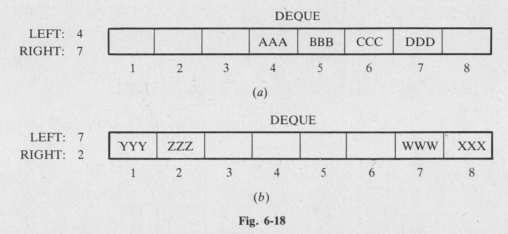

Fig. 6-18

The procedures which insert and delete elements in deques and the variations on those procedures are given as supplementary problems. As with queues, a complication may arise (*a*) when there is overflow, that is, when an element is to be inserted into a deque which is already full, or (*b*) when there is underflow, that is, when an element is to be deleted from a deque which is empty. The procedures must consider these possibilities.

6.11 PRIORITY QUEUES

A *priority queue* is a collection of elements such that each element has been assigned a priority and such that the order in which elements are deleted and processed comes from the following rules:

(1) An element of higher priority is processed before any element of lower priority.

(2) Two elements with the same priority are processed according to the order in which they were added to the queue.

A prototype of a priority queue is a timesharing system: programs of high priority are processed first, and programs with the same priority form a standard queue.

There are various ways of maintaining a priority queue in memory. We discuss two of them here: one uses a one-way list, and the other uses multiple queues. The ease or difficulty in adding elements to or deleting them from a priority queue clearly depends on the representation that one chooses.

One-Way List Representation of a Priority Queue

One way to maintain a priority queue in memory is by means of a one-way list, as follows:

(*a*) Each node in the list will contain three items of information: an information field INFO, a priority number PRN and a link number LINK.

(*b*) A node X precedes a node Y in the list (1) when X has higher priority than Y or (2) when both have the same priority but X was added to the list before Y. This means that the order in the one-way list corresponds to the order of the priority queue.

Priority numbers will operate in the usual way: the lower the priority number, the higher the priority.

EXAMPLE 6.11

Figure 6-19 shows a schematic diagram of a priority queue with 7 elements. The diagram does not tell us whether BBB was added to the list before or after DDD. On the other hand, the diagram does tell us that BBB was inserted before CCC, because BBB and CCC have the same priority number and BBB appears before CCC in the list. Figure 6-20 shows the way the priority queue may appear in memory using linear arrays INFO, PRN and LINK. (See Sec. 5.2.)

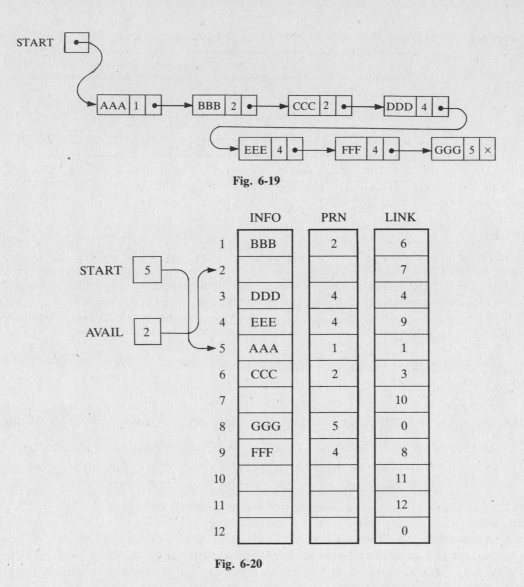

Fig. 6-19

Fig. 6-20

The main property of the one-way list representation of a priority queue is that the element in the queue that should be processed first always appears at the beginning of the one-way list. Accordingly, it is a very simple matter to delete and process an element from our priority queue. The outline of the algorithm follows.

Algorithm 6.13: This algorithm deletes and processes the first element in a priority queue which appears in memory as a one-way list.

    1. Set ITEM := INFO[START]. [This saves the data in the first node.]
    2. Delete first node from the list.
    3. Process ITEM.
    4. Exit.

The details of the algorithm, including the possibility of underflow, are left as an exercise.

    Adding an element to our priority queue is much more complicated than deleting an element from the queue, because we need to find the correct place to insert the element. An outline of the algorithm follows.

Algorithm 6.14: This algorithm adds an ITEM with priority number N to a priority queue which is maintained in memory as a one-way list.

   (*a*) Traverse the one-way list until finding a node X whose priority number exceeds N. Insert ITEM in front of node X.

   (*b*) If no such node is found, insert ITEM as the last element of the list.

The above insertion algorithm may be pictured as a weighted object "sinking" through layers of elements until it meets an element with a heavier weight.

   The details of the above algorithm are left as an exercise. The main difficulty in the algorithm comes from the fact that ITEM is inserted before node X. This means that, while traversing the list, one must also keep track of the address of the node preceding the node being accessed.

EXAMPLE 6.12

   Consider the priority queue in Fig. 6-19. Suppose an item XXX with priority number 2 is to be inserted into the queue. We traverse the list, comparing priority numbers. Observe that DDD is the first element in the list whose priority number exceeds that of XXX. Hence XXX is inserted in the list in front of DDD, as pictured in Fig. 6-21. Observe that XXX comes after BBB and CCC, which have the same priority as XXX. Suppose now that an element is to be deleted from the queue. It will be AAA, the first element in the list. Assuming no other insertions, the next element to be deleted will be BBB, then CCC, then XXX, and so on.

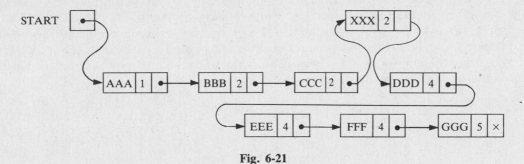

Fig. 6-21

Array Representation of a Priority Queue

   Another way to maintain a priority queue in memory is to use a separate queue for each level of priority (or for each priority number). Each such queue will appear in its own circular array and must have its own pair of pointers, FRONT and REAR. In fact, if each queue is allocated the same amount of space, a two-dimensional array QUEUE can be used instead of the linear arrays. Figure 6-22 indicates this representation for the priority queue in Fig. 6-21. Observe that FRONT[K] and REAR[K] contain, respectively, the front and rear elements of row K of QUEUE, the row that maintains the queue of elements with priority number K.

	FRONT	REAR			1	2	3	4	5	6
1	2	2		1		AAA				
2	1	3		2	BBB	CCC	XXX			
3	0	0		3						
4	5	1		4	FFF				DDD	EEE
5	4	4		5				GGG		

Fig. 6-22

The following are outlines of algorithms for deleting and inserting elements in a priority queue that is maintained in memory by a two-dimensional array QUEUE, as above. The details of the algorithms are left as exercises.

Algorithm 6.15: This algorithm deletes and processes the first element in a priority queue maintained by a two-dimensional array QUEUE.

    1. [Find the first nonempty queue.]
        Find the smallest K such that FRONT[K] $\neq$ NULL.
    2. Delete and process the front element in row K of QUEUE.
    3. Exit.

Algorithm 6.16: This algorithm adds an ITEM with priority number M to a priority queue maintained by a two-dimensional array QUEUE.

    1. Insert ITEM as the rear element in row M of QUEUE.
    2. Exit.

Summary

Once again we see the time-space tradeoff when choosing between different data structures for a given problem. The array representation of a priority queue is more time-efficient than the one-way list. This is because when adding an element to a one-way list, one must perform a linear search on the list. On the other hand, the one-way list representation of the priority queue may be more space-efficient than the array representation. This is because in using the array representation, overflow occurs when the number of elements in any single priority level exceeds the capacity for that level, but in using the one-way list, overflow occurs only when the total number of elements exceeds the *total* capacity. Another alternative is to use a linked list for each priority level.

Solved Problems

STACKS

6.1   Consider the following stack of characters, where STACK is allocated N = 8 memory cells:

$$\text{STACK:}\qquad \text{A, C, D, F, K, \_\_, \_\_, \_\_}$$

(For notational convenience, we use "__" to denote an empty memory cell.) Describe the stack as the following operations take place:

(a)	POP(STACK, ITEM)	(e)	POP(STACK, ITEM)
(b)	POP(STACK, ITEM)	(f)	PUSH(STACK, R)
(c)	PUSH(STACK, L)	(g)	PUSH(STACK, S)
(d)	PUSH(STACK, P)	(h)	POP(STACK, ITEM)

The POP procedure always deletes the top element from the stack, and the PUSH procedure always adds the new element to the top of the stack. Accordingly:

(a)	STACK:	A, C, D, F, __, __, __, __	(e)	STACK:	A, C, D, L, __, __, __, __
(b)	STACK:	A, C, D, __, __, __, __, __	(f)	STACK:	A, C, D, L, R, __, __, __
(c)	STACK:	A, C, D, L, __, __, __, __	(g)	STACK:	A, C, D, L, R, S, __, __
(d)	STACK:	A, C, D, L, P, __, __, __	(h)	STACK:	A, C, D, L, R, __, __, __

6.2 Consider the data in Prob. 6.1. (*a*) When will overflow occur? (*b*) When will C be deleted before D?

(*a*) Since STACK has been allocated N = 8 memory cells, overflow will occur when STACK contains 8 elements and there is a PUSH operation to add another element to STACK.

(*b*) Since STACK is implemented as a stack, C will never be deleted before D.

6.3 Consider the following stack, where STACK is allocated N = 6 memory cells:

$$\text{STACK:} \quad \text{AAA, DDD, EEE, FFF, GGG, _____}$$

Describe the stack as the following operations take place: (*a*) PUSH(STACK, KKK), (*b*) POP(STACK, ITEM), (*c*) PUSH(STACK, LLL), (*d*) PUSH(STACK, SSS), (*e*) POP(STACK, ITEM) and (*f*) PUSH(STACK, TTT).

(*a*) KKK is added to the top of STACK, yielding

$$\text{STACK:} \quad \text{AAA, DDD, EEE, FFF, GGG, KKK}$$

(*b*) The top element is removed from STACK, yielding

$$\text{STACK:} \quad \text{AAA, DDD, EEE, FFF, GGG, _____}$$

(*c*) LLL is added to the top of STACK, yielding

$$\text{STACK:} \quad \text{AAA, DDD, EEE, FFF, GGG, LLL}$$

(*d*) Overflow occurs, since STACK is full and another element SSS is to be added to STACK.

No further operations can take place until the overflow is resolved—by adding additional space for STACK, for example.

6.4 Suppose STACK is allocated N = 6 memory cells and initially STACK is empty, or, in other words, TOP = 0. Find the output of the following module:

1. Set AAA := 2 and BBB := 5.
2. Call PUSH(STACK, AAA).
   Call PUSH(STACK, 4).
   Call PUSH(STACK, BBB + 2).
   Call PUSH(STACK, 9).
   Call PUSH(STACK, AAA + BBB).
3. Repeat while TOP ≠ 0:
       Call POP(STACK, ITEM).
       Write: ITEM.
   [End of loop.]
4. Return.

Step 1. Sets AAA = 2 and BBB = 5.
Step 2. Pushes AAA = 2, 4, BBB + 2 = 7, 9 and AAA + BBB = 7 onto STACK, yielding

$$\text{STACK:} \quad 2, 4, 7, 9, 7, \_\_$$

Step 3. Pops and prints the elements of STACK until STACK is empty. Since the top element is always popped, the output consists of the following sequence:

$$7, 9, 7, 4, 2$$

Observe that this is the reverse of the order in which the elements were added to STACK.

6.5   Suppose a given space S of N contiguous memory cells is allocated to K = 6 stacks. Describe ways that the stacks may be maintained in S.

Suppose no prior data indicate that any one stack will grow more rapidly than any of the other stacks. Then one may reserve N/K cells for each stack, as in Fig. 6-23(a), where $B_1, B_2, \ldots, B_6$ denote, respectively, the bottoms of the stacks. Alternatively, one can partition the stacks into pairs and reserve 2N/K cells for each pair of stacks, as in Fig. 6-23(b). The second method may decrease the number of times overflow will occur.

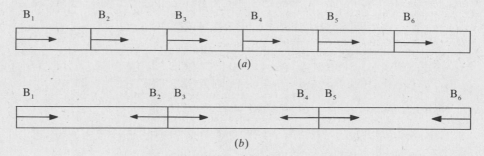

(a)

(b)

Fig. 6-23

POLISH NOTATION

6.6   Translate, by inspection and hand, each infix expression into its equivalent postfix expression:

$$(a) \quad (A - B) * (D/E) \qquad (b) \quad (A + B \uparrow D)/(E - F) + G$$
$$(c) \quad A * (B + D)/E - F * (G + H/K)$$

Using the order in which the operators are executed, translate each operator from infix to postfix notation. (We use brackets [ ] to denote a partial translation.)

(a) $\qquad\qquad\qquad (A - B) * (D/E) = [AB-] * [DE/] = AB-DE/*$

(b) $\qquad (A + B \uparrow D)/(E - F) + G = (A + [BD\uparrow])/[EF-] + G = [ABD\uparrow+]/[EF-] + G$

$$= [ABD\uparrow+EF-/] + G = ABD\uparrow+EF-/G+$$

(c) $\qquad A * (B + D)/E - F * (G + H/K) = A * [BD+]/E - F * (G + [HK/])$

$$= [ABD+*]/E - F * [GHK/+]$$
$$= [ABD+*E/] - [FGHK/+*]$$
$$= ABD+*E/FGHK/+*-$$

Observe that we did translate more than one operator in a single step when the operands did not overlap.

6.7   Consider the following arithmetic expression P, written in postfix notation:

$$P: \qquad 12, 7, 3, -, /, 2, 1, 5, +, *, +$$

(a) Translate P, by inspection and hand, into its equivalent infix expression.

(b) Evaluate the infix expression.

(a) Scanning from left to right, translate each operator from postfix to infix notation. (We use brackets [ ] to denote a partial translation.)

$$P = 12, [7 - 3], /, 2, 1, 5, +, *, +$$
$$= [12/(7 - 3)], 2, 1, 5, +, *, +$$
$$= [12/(7 - 3)], 2, [1 + 5], *, +$$
$$= [12/(7 - 3)], [2 * (1 + 5)], +$$
$$= 12/(7 - 3) + 2 * (1 + 5)$$

(b)   Using the infix expression, we obtain:

$$P = 12/(7-3) + 2*(1+5) = 12/4 + 2*6 = 3 + 12 = 15$$

6.8   Consider the postfix expression P in Prob. 6.7. Evaluate P using Algorithm 6.3.

First add a sentinel right parenthesis at the end of P to obtain:

P: 12, 7, 3, −, /, 2, 1, 5, +, *, +,)

Scan P from left to right. If a constant is encountered, put it on a stack, but if an operator is encountered, evaluate the two top constants on the stack. Figure 6-24 shows the contents of STACK as each element of P is scanned. The final number, 15, in STACK, when the sentinel right parenthesis is scanned, is the value of P. This agrees with the result in Prob. 6.7(b).

Symbol	STACK
12	12
7	12, 7
3	12, 7, 3
−	12, 4
/	3
2	3, 2
1	3, 2, 1
5	3, 2, 1, 5
+	3, 2, 6
*	3, 12
+	15
)	15

Fig. 6-24

6.9   Consider the following infix expression Q:

Q: $((A + B) * D) \uparrow (E - F)$

Use Algorithm 6.4 to translate Q into its equivalent postfix expression P.

First push a left parenthesis onto STACK, and then add a right parenthesis to the end of Q to obtain

Q: ((A + B) * D) $\uparrow$ (E − F))

(Note that Q now contains 16 elements.) Scan Q from left to right. Recall that (1) if a constant is encountered, it is added to P; (2) if a left parenthesis is encountered, it is put on the stack; (3) if an operator is encountered, it "sinks" to its own level; and (4) if a right parenthesis is encountered, it "sinks" to the first left parenthesis. Figure 6-25 shows pictures of STACK and the string P as each element of Q is scanned. When STACK is empty, the final right parenthesis has been scanned and the result is

P: A B + D * E F − $\uparrow$

which is the required postfix equivalent of Q.

6.10   Translate, by inspection and hand, each infix expression into its equivalent prefix expression:

(a)   (A − B) * (D / E)

(b)   (A + B $\uparrow$ D)/(E − F) + G

Symbol	STACK	Expression P
(	((	
(	(((	
A	(((	A
+	(((+	A
B	(((+	A B
)	((	A B +
*	((*	A B +
D	((*	A B + D
)	(	A B + D *
↑	(↑	A B + D *
(	(↑ (	A B + D *
E	(↑ (	A B + D * E
−	(↑ (−	A B + D * E
F	(↑ (−	A B + D * E F
)	(↑	A B + D * E F −
)		A B + D * E F − ↑

Fig. 6-25

Is there any relationship between the prefix expressions and the equivalent postfix expressions obtained in Prob. 6.6.

Using the order in which the operators are executed, translate each operator from infix to prefix notation.

(a)
$$(A - B) * (D/E) = [-AB] * [/DE] = \quad * \quad - \quad A \quad B \quad / \quad D \quad E$$

(b)
$$(A + B \uparrow D)/(E - F) + G = (A + [\uparrow BD])/[-EF] + G$$
$$= [+A\uparrow BD]/[-EF] + G$$
$$= [/+A\uparrow BD - EF] + G$$
$$= \quad + \quad / \quad + \quad A \quad \uparrow \quad B \quad D \quad - \quad E \quad F \quad G$$

The prefix expression is not the reverse of the postfix expression. However, the order of the operands—A, B, D and E in part (a) and A, B, D, E, F and G in part (b)—is the same for all three expressions, infix, postfix and prefix.

QUICKSORT

6.11 Suppose S is the following list of 14 alphabetic characters:

$$\boxed{D} \; A \; T \; A \; S \; T \; R \; U \; C \; T \; U \; R \; E \; \boxed{S}$$

Suppose the characters in S are to be sorted alphabetically. Use the quicksort algorithm to find the final position of the first character D.

Beginning with the last character S, scan the list from right to left until finding a character which precedes D alphabetically. It is C. Interchange D and C to obtain the list:

$$\boxed{C} \; A \; T \; A \; S \; T \; R \; U \; \boxed{D} \; T \; U \; R \; E \; S$$

Beginning with this C, scan the list toward D, i.e., from left to right, until finding a character which succeeds D alphabetically. It is T. Interchange D and T to obtain the list:

$$\text{C A \textcircled{D} A S \textcircled{T} R U T T U R E S}$$

Beginning with this T, scan the list toward D until finding a character which precedes D. It is A. Interchange D and A to obtain the list:

$$\text{C A \textcircled{A} \textcircled{D} S T R U T T U R E \'S}$$

Beginning with this A, scan the list toward D until finding a character which succeeds D. There is no such letter. This means D is in its final position. Furthermore, the letters before D form a sublist consisting of all letters preceding D alphabetically, and the letters after D form a sublist consisting of all the letters succeeding D alphabetically, as follows:

$$\underbrace{\text{C A A}}_{\text{Sublist}} \textcircled{D} \underbrace{\text{S T R U T T U R E S}}_{\text{Sublist}}$$

Sorting S is now reduced to sorting each sublist.

6.12 Suppose S consists of the following $n = 5$ letters:

$$\textcircled{A} \text{ B C D } \textcircled{E}$$

Find the number C of comparisons to sort S using quicksort. What general conclusion can one make, if any?

Beginning with E, it takes $n - 1 = 4$ comparisons to recognize that the first letter A is already in its correct position. Sorting S is now reduced to sorting the following sublist with $n - 1 = 4$ letters:

$$\text{A } \textcircled{B} \text{ C D } \textcircled{E}$$

Beginning with E, it takes $n - 2 = 3$ comparisons to recognize that the first letter B in the sublist is already in its correct position. Sorting S is now reduced to sorting the following sublist with $n - 2 = 3$ letters:

$$\text{A B } \textcircled{C} \text{ D } \textcircled{E}$$

Similarly, it takes $n - 3 = 2$ comparisons to recognize that the letter C is in its correct position, and it takes $n - 4 = 1$ comparison to recognize that the letter D is in its correct position. Since only one letter is left, the list is now known to be sorted. Altogether we have:

$$C = 4 + 3 + 2 + 1 = 10 \text{ comparisons}$$

Similarly, using quicksort, it takes

$$C = (n - 1) + (n - 2) + \cdots + 2 + 1 = \frac{n(n - 1)}{2} = \frac{n^2}{2} + 0(n) = O(n^2)$$

comparisons to sort a list with n elements when the list is already sorted. (This can be shown to be the worst case for quicksort.)

6.13 Consider the quicksort algorithm. (*a*) Can the arrays LOWER and UPPER be implemented as queues rather than as stacks? Why? (*b*) How much extra space is needed for the quicksort algorithm, or, in other words, what is the space complexity of the algorithm?

(*a*)   Since the order in which the subsets are sorted does not matter, LOWER and UPPER can be implemented as queues, or even deques, rather than as stacks.

(*b*)   Quicksort algorithm is an "in-place" algorithm; that is, the elements remain in their places except for interchanges. The extra space is required mainly for the stacks LOWER and UPPER. On the average, the extra space required for the algorithm is proportional to log n, where n is the number of elements to be sorted.

RECURSION

6.14 Let a and b denote positive integers. Suppose a function Q is defined recursively as follows:

$$Q(a, b) = \begin{cases} 0 & \text{if } a < b \\ Q(a - b, b) + 1 & \text{if } b \leq a \end{cases}$$

(a) Find the value of $Q(2, 3)$ and $Q(14, 3)$.

(b) What does this function do? Find $Q(5861, 7)$.

(a)
$$Q(2, 3) = 0 \quad \text{since} \quad 2 < 3$$
$$\begin{aligned} Q(14, 3) &= Q(11, 3) + 1 \\ &= [Q(8, 3) + 1] + 1 = Q(8, 3) + 2 \\ &= [Q(5, 3) + 1] + 2 = Q(5, 3) + 3 \\ &= [Q(2, 3) + 1] + 3 = Q(2, 3) + 4 \\ &= 0 + 4 = 4 \end{aligned}$$

(b) Each time b is subtracted from a, the values of Q is increased by 1. Hence $Q(a, b)$ finds the quotient when a is divided by b. Thus,

$$Q(5861, 7) = 837$$

6.15 Let n denote a positive integer. Suppose a function L is defined recursively as follows:

$$L(n) = \begin{cases} 0 & \text{if } n = 1 \\ L(\lfloor n/2 \rfloor) + 1 & \text{if } n > 1 \end{cases}$$

(Here $\lfloor k \rfloor$ denotes the "floor" of k, that is, the greatest integer which does not exceed k. See Sec. 2.2.)

(a) Find $L(25)$.

(b) What does this function do?

(a)
$$\begin{aligned} L(25) &= L(12) + 1 \\ &= [L(6) + 1] + 1 = L(6) + 2 \\ &= [L(3) + 1] + 2 = L(3) + 3 \\ &= [L(1) + 1] + 3 = L(1) + 4 \\ &= 0 + 4 = 4 \end{aligned}$$

(b) Each time n is divided by 2, the value of L is increased by 1. Hence L is the greatest integer such that

$$2^L \leq n$$

Accordingly, this function finds

$$L = \lfloor \log_2 n \rfloor$$

6.16 Suppose the Fibonacci numbers $F_{11} = 89$ and $F_{12} = 144$ are given.

(a) Should one use recursion or iteration to obtain F_{16}? Find F_{16}.

(b) Write an iterative procedure to obtain the first N Fibonacci numbers F[1], F[2], . . . , F[N], where N > 2. (Compare this with the recursive Procedure 6.8.)

(a) The Fibonacci numbers should be evaluated by using iteration (that is, by evaluating from the bottom up), rather than by using recursion (that is, evaluating from the top down).

Recall that each Fibonacci number is the sum of the two preceding Fibonacci numbers. Beginning with F_{11} and F_{12} we have

$$F_{13} = 89 + 144 = 233, \qquad F_{14} = 144 + 233 = 377, \qquad F_{15} = 233 + 377 = 610$$

and hence

$$F_{16} = 377 + 610 = 987$$

(b) **Procedure P6.16:**   FIBONACCI(F, N)

This procedure finds the first N Fibonacci numbers and assigns them to an array F.

1. Set F[1] := 1 and F[2] := 1.
2. Repeat for L = 3 to N:
     Set F[L] := F[L − 1] + F[L − 2].
   [End of loop.]
3. Return.

(We emphasize that this iterative procedure is much more efficient than the recursive Procedure 6.8.)

6.17 Use the definition of the Ackermann function (Definition 6.3) to find $A(1, 3)$.

We have the following 15 steps:

(1) $A(1, 3) = A(0, A(1, 2))$

(2) $A(1, 2) = A(0, A(1, 1))$

(3) $A(1, 1) = A(0, A(1, 0))$

(4) $A(1, 0) = A(0, 1)$

(5) $A(0, 1) = 1 + 1 = 2$

(6) $A(1, 0) = 2$

(7) $A(1, 1) = A(0, 2)$

(8) $A(0, 2) = 2 + 1 = 3$

(9) $A(1, 1) = 3$

(10) $A(1, 2) = A(0, 3)$

(11) $A(0, 3) = 3 + 1 = 4$

(12) $A(1, 2) = 4$

(13) $A(1, 3) = A(0, 4)$

(14) $A(0, 4) = 4 + 1 = 5$

(15) $A(1, 3) = 5$

The forward indention indicates that we are postponing an evaluation and are recalling the definition, and the backward indention indicates that we are backtracking.

Observe that the first formula in Definition 6.3 is used in Steps 5, 8, 11 and 14, the second formula in Step 4 and the third formula in Steps 1, 2 and 3. In the other Steps we are backtracking with substitutions.

6.18 Suppose a recursive procedure P contains only one recursive call:

Step K. Call P.

Indicate the reason that the stack STADD (for the return addresses) is not necessary.

Since there is only one recursive call, control will always be transferred to Step K + 1 on a Return, except for the final Return to the main program. Accordingly, instead of maintaining the stack STADD (and the local variable ADD), we simply write

      (*c*) Go to Step K + 1

instead of

      (*c*) Go to Step ADD

in the translation of "Step J. Return." (See Sec. 6.8.)

6.19 Rewrite the solution to the Towers of Hanoi problem so it uses only one recursive call instead of two.

One may view the pegs A and B symmetrically. That is, we apply the steps

Move N − 1 disks from A to B, and then apply A → C

Move N − 2 disks from B to A, and then apply B → C

Move N − 3 disks from A to B, and then apply A → C

Move N − 4 disks from B to A, and then apply B → C

and so on. Accordingly, we can iterate a single recursive call, interchanging BEG and AUX after each iteration, as follows:

Procedure P6.19: TOWER(N, BEG, AUX, END)

    1. If N = 0, then: Return.
    2. Repeat Steps 3 to 5 for K = N, N − 1, N − 2, . . . , 1.
    3.   Call TOWER(K − 1, BEG, END, AUX).
    4.   Write: BEG → END.
    5.   [Interchange BEG and AUX.]
            Set TEMP := BEG, BEG := AUX, AUX := TEMP.
      [End of Step 2 loop.]
    6. Return.

Observe that we use N = 0 as a base value for the recursion instead of N = 1. Either one may be used to yield a solution.

6.20 Consider the stack implementation algorithm in Sec. 6.8 for translating a recursive procedure into a nonrecursive procedure. Recall that, at the time of a recursive call, we pushed the new return address rather than the current return address onto the stack STADD. Suppose we decide to push the current return address onto the stack STADD. (Many texts do this.) What changes must then take place in the translation algorithm?

The main change is that, at the time of a Return to the preceding execution level, the current value of ADD determines the location of the Return, not the value of ADD after the stack values have been popped. Accordingly, the value of ADD must be saved, by setting SAVE := ADD, then the stack values are popped, and then control is transferred to Step SAVE. Another change is that one must initially assign ADD := Main and then Return to the main calling program when ADD = Main, not when the stacks are empty. The formal algorithm follows.

(1) Preparation.
    (*a*) Define a stack STPAR for each parameter PAR, a stack STVAR for each local variable VAR and a local variable ADD and a stack STADD to hold return addresses.
    (*b*) Set TOP := NULL and ADD := Main.

(2) Translation of "Step K. Call P."
    (*a*) Push the current values of the parameters and local variables and the current return address ADD onto the appropriate stacks.
    (*b*) Reset the parameters using the new argument values, and set ADD := [Step] K + 1.
    (*c*) Go to Step 1. [The beginning of the procedure P.]

(3) Translation of "Step J. Return."
   (a) If ADD = Main, then: Return. [Control is transferred to the main program.]
   (b) Set SAVE := ADD.
   (c) Restore the top values of the stacks. That is, set the parameters and local variables equal to the
       top values on the stacks, and set ADD equal to the top value on the stack STADD.
   (d) Go to Step SAVE.

(Compare this translation algorithm with the algorithm in Sec. 6.8.)

QUEUES, DEQUES

6.21 Consider the following queue of characters, where QUEUE is a circular array which is allocated six memory cells:

$$FRONT = 2, \quad REAR = 4 \qquad QUEUE: \quad \_, A, C, D, \_, \_$$

(For notational convenience, we use "_" to denote an empty memory cell.) Describe the queue as the following operations take place:

(a) F is added to the queue.   (f) two letters are deleted.
(b) two letters are deleted.   (g) S is added to the queue.
(c) K, L and M are added to the queue.   (h) two letters are deleted.
(d) two letters are deleted.   (i) one letter is deleted.
(e) R is added to the queue.   (j) one letter is deleted.

(a) F is added to the rear of the queue, yielding

$$FRONT = 2, \quad REAR = 5 \qquad QUEUE: \quad \_, A, C, D, F, \_$$

Note that REAR is increased by 1.

(b) The two letters, A and C, are deleted, leaving

$$FRONT = 4, \quad REAR = 5 \qquad QUEUE: \quad \_, \_, \_, D, F, \_$$

Note that FRONT is increased by 2.

(c) K, L and M are added to the rear of the queue. Since K is placed in the last memory cell of QUEUE, L and M are placed in the first two memory cells. This yields

$$FRONT = 4, \quad REAR = 2 \qquad QUEUE: \quad L, M, \_, D, F, K$$

Note that REAR is increased by 3 but the arithmetic is modulo 6:

$$REAR = 5 + 3 = 8 = 2 \ (mod \ 6)$$

(d) The two front letters, D and F are deleted, leaving

$$FRONT = 6, \quad REAR = 2 \qquad QUEUE: \quad L, M, \_, \_, \_, K$$

(e) R is added to the rear of the queue, yielding

$$FRONT = 6, \quad REAR = 3 \qquad QUEUE: \quad L, M, R, \_, \_, K$$

(f) The two front letters, K and L, are deleted, leaving

$$FRONT = 2, \quad REAR = 3 \qquad QUEUE: \quad \_, M, R, \_, \_, \_$$

Note that FRONT is increased by 2 but the arithmetic is modulo 6:

$$FRONT = 6 + 2 = 8 = 2 \ (mod \ 6)$$

(g) S is added to the rear of the queue, yielding

$$FRONT = 2, \quad REAR = 4 \qquad QUEUE: \quad \_, M, R, S, \_, \_$$

(h)   The two front letters, M and R, are deleted, leaving

$$\text{FRONT} = 4, \quad \text{REAR} = 4 \qquad \text{QUEUE:} \quad \_, \_, \_, S, \_, \_$$

(i)   The front letter S is deleted. Since FRONT = REAR, this means that the queue is empty; hence we assign NULL to FRONT and REAR. Thus

$$\text{FRONT} = 0, \quad \text{REAR} = 0 \qquad \text{QUEUE:} \quad \_, \_, \_, \_, \_, \_$$

(j)   Since FRONT = NULL, no deletion can take place. That is, underflow has occurred.

6.22   Suppose each data structure is stored in a circular array with N memory cells.

(a)   Find the number NUMB of elements in a queue in terms of FRONT and REAR.

(b)   Find the number NUMB of elements in a deque in terms of LEFT and RIGHT.

(c)   When will the array be filled?

(a)   If FRONT ≤ REAR, then NUMB = REAR − FRONT + 1. For example, consider the following queue with N = 12:

$$\text{FRONT} = 3, \quad \text{REAR} = 9 \qquad \text{QUEUE:} \quad \_, \_, *, *, *, *, *, *, *, \_, \_, \_$$

Then NUMB = 9 − 3 + 1 = 7, as pictured.

If REAR < FRONT, then FRONT − REAR − 1 is the number of empty cells, so

$$\text{NUMB} = N - (\text{FRONT} - \text{REAR} - 1) = N + \text{REAR} - \text{FRONT} + 1$$

For example, consider the following queue with N = 12:

$$\text{FRONT} = 9, \quad \text{REAR} = 4 \qquad \text{QUEUE:} \quad *, *, *, *, \_, \_, \_, \_, *, *, *, *$$

Then NUMB = 12 + 4 − 9 + 1 = 8, as pictured.

Using arithmetic modulo N, we need only one formula, as follows:

$$\text{NUMB} = \text{REAR} - \text{FRONT} + 1 \pmod{N}$$

(b)   The same result holds for deques except that FRONT is replaced by RIGHT. That is,

$$\text{NUMB} = \text{RIGHT} - \text{LEFT} + 1 \pmod{N}$$

(c)   With a queue, the array is full when

$$\text{(i)} \quad \text{FRONT} = 1 \text{ and } \text{REAR} = N \qquad \text{or} \qquad \text{(ii)} \quad \text{FRONT} = \text{REAR} + 1$$

Similarly, with a deque, the array is full when

$$\text{(i)} \quad \text{LEFT} = 1 \text{ and } \text{RIGHT} = N \qquad \text{or} \qquad \text{(ii)} \quad \text{LEFT} = \text{RIGHT} + 1$$

Each of these conditions implies NUMB = N.

6.23   Consider the following deque of characters where DEQUE is a circular array which is allocated six memory cells:

$$\text{LEFT} = 2, \quad \text{RIGHT} = 4 \qquad \text{DEQUE:} \quad \_, A, C, D, \_, \_$$

Describe the deque while the following operations take place.

(a)   F is added to the right of the deque.

(b)   Two letters on the right are deleted.

(c)   K, L and M are added to the left of the deque.

(d)   One letter on the left is deleted.

(e)   R is added to the left of the deque.

(*f*) S is added to the right of the deque.

(*g*) T is added to the right of the deque.

(*a*) F is added on the right, yielding

$$LEFT = 2, \quad RIGHT = 5 \qquad DEQUE: \quad \_\_, A, C, D, F, \_\_$$

Note that RIGHT is increased by 1.

(*b*) The two right letters, F and D, are deleted, yielding

$$LEFT = 2, \quad RIGHT = 3 \qquad DEQUE: \quad \_\_, A, C, \_\_, \_\_, \_\_$$

Note that RIGHT is decreased by 2.

(*c*) K, L and M are added on the left. Since K is placed in the first memory cell, L is placed in the last memory cell and M is placed in the next-to-last memory cell. This yields

$$LEFT = 5, \quad RIGHT = 3 \qquad DEQUE: \quad K, A, C, \_\_, M, L$$

Note that LEFT is decreased by 3 but the arithmetic is modulo 6:

$$LEFT = 2 - 3 = -1 = 5 \ (\text{mod } 6)$$

(*d*) The left letter, M, is deleted, leaving

$$LEFT = 6, \quad RIGHT = 3 \qquad DEQUE: \quad K, A, C, \_\_, \_\_, L$$

Note that LEFT is increased by 1.

(*e*) R is added on the left, yielding

$$LEFT = 5, \quad RIGHT = 3 \qquad DEQUE: \quad K, A, C, \_\_, R, L$$

Note that LEFT is decreased by 1.

(*f*) S is added on the right, yielding

$$LEFT = 5, \quad RIGHT = 4 \qquad DEQUE: \quad K, A, C, S, R, L$$

(*g*) Since LEFT = RIGHT + 1, the array is full, and hence T cannot be added to the deque. That is, overflow has occurred.

6.24 Consider a deque maintained by a circular array with N memory cells.

(*a*) Suppose an element is added to the deque. How is LEFT or RIGHT changed?

(*b*) Suppose an element is deleted. How is LEFT or RIGHT changed?

(*a*) If the element is added on the left, then LEFT is decreased by 1 (mod N). On the other hand, if the element is added on the right, then RIGHT is increased by 1 (mod N).

(*b*) If the element is deleted from the left, then LEFT is increased by 1 (mod N). However if the element is deleted from the right, then RIGHT is decreased by 1 (mod N). In the case that LEFT = RIGHT before the deletion (that is, when the deque has only one element), then LEFT and RIGHT are both assigned NULL to indicate that the deque is empty.

PRIORITY QUEUES

6.25 Consider the priority queue in Fig. 6-20, which is maintained as a one-way list. (*a*) Describe the structure after (XXX, 2), (YYY, 3), (ZZZ, 2) and (WWW, 1) are added to the queue. (*b*) Describe the structure if, after the preceding insertions, three elements are deleted.

(*a*) Traverse the list to find the first element whose priority number exceeds that of XXX. It is DDD, so insert XXX before DDD (after CCC) in the first empty cell, INFO[2]. Then traverse the list to find the first element whose priority number exceeds that of YYY. Again it is DDD. Hence insert YYY before DDD (after XXX) in the next empty cell, INFO[7]. Then traverse the list to find the first element whose priority number exceeds that of ZZZ. It is YYY. Hence insert ZZZ before YYY (after XXX) in the next empty cell, INFO[10]. Last, traverse the list to find the first element whose priority number exceeds that of WWW. It is BBB. Hence insert WWW before BBB (after AAA) in the next empty cell, INFO[11]. This finally yields the structure in Fig. 6-26(a).

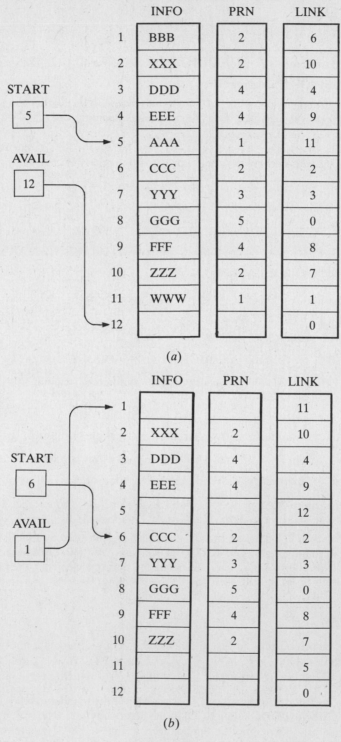

Fig. 6-26

(b)   The first three elements in the one-way list are deleted. Specifically, first AAA is deleted and its memory cell INFO[5] is added to the AVAIL list. Then WWW is deleted and its memory cell INFO[11] is added to the AVAIL list. Last, BBB is deleted and its memory cell INFO[1] is added to the AVAIL list. This finally yields the structure in Fig. 6-26(b).

Remark: Observe that START and AVAIL are changed accordingly.

6.26   Consider the priority queue in Fig. 6-22, which is maintained by a two-dimensional array QUEUE. (a) Describe the structure after (RRR, 3), (SSS, 4), (TTT, 1), (UUU, 4) and (VVV, 2) are added to the queue. (b) Describe the structure if, after the preceding insertions, three elements are deleted.

(a)   Insert each element in its priority row. That is, add RRR as the rear element in row 3, add SSS as the rear element in row 4, add TTT as the rear element in row 1, add UUU as the rear element in row 4 and add VVV as the rear element in row 2. This yields the structure in Fig. 6-27(a). (As noted previously, insertions with this array representation are usually simpler than insertions with the one-way list representation.)

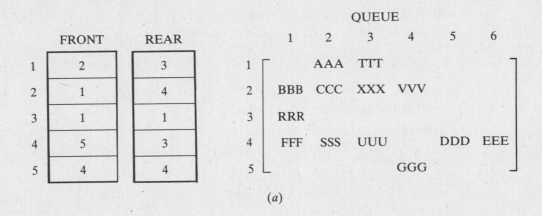

(a)

(b)

Fig. 6-27

(b)   First delete the elements with the highest priority in row 1. Since row 1 contains only two elements, AAA and TTT, then the front element in row 2, BBB, must also be deleted. This finally leaves the structure in Fig. 6-27(b).

Remark: Observe that, in both cases, FRONT and REAR are changed accordingly.

Supplementary Problems

STACKS

6.27   Consider the following stack of city names:

STACK: London, Berlin, Rome, Paris, _____, _____

(*a*)   Describe the stack as the following operations take place:

  (i) PUSH(STACK, Athens),   (iii) POP(STACK, ITEM)   (v) PUSH(STACK, Moscow)
  (ii) POP(STACK, ITEM)   (iv) PUSH(STACK, Madrid) (vi) POP(STACK, ITEM)

(*b*)   Describe the stack if the operation POP(STACK, ITEM) deletes London.

6.28   Consider the following stack where STACK is allocated N = 4 memory cells:

STACK: AAA, BBB, _____, _____

Describe the stack as the following operations take place:

(*a*) POP(STACK, ITEM)   (*c*) PUSH(STACK, EEE)   (*e*) POP(STACK, ITEM)
(*b*) POP(STACK, ITEM)   (*d*) POP(STACK, ITEM)   (*f*) PUSH(STACK, GGG)

6.29   Suppose the following stack of integers is in memory where STACK is allocated N = 6 memory cells:

TOP = 3   STACK: 5, 2, 3, __, __, __

Find the output of the following program segment:

   1.   Call POP(STACK, ITEMA).
       Call POP(STACK, ITEMB).
       Call PUSH(STACK, ITEMB + 2).
       Call PUSH(STACK, 8).
       Call PUSH(STACK, ITEMA + ITEMB).

   2.   Repeat while TOP ≠ 0:
       Call POP(STACK, ITEM).
       Write: ITEM.
     [End of loop.]

6.30   Suppose stacks A[1] and A[2] are stored in a linear array STACK with N elements, as pictured in Fig. 6-28. Assume TOP[K] denotes the top of stack A[K].

(*a*)   Write a procedure PUSH(STACK, N, TOP, ITEM, K) which pushes ITEM onto stack A[K].

(*b*)   Write a procedure POP(STACK, TOP, ITEM, K) which deletes the top element from stack A[K] and assigns the element to the variable ITEM.

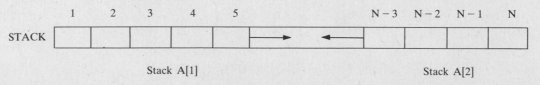

Fig. 6-28

ARITHMETIC EXPRESSIONS; POLISH EXPRESSIONS

6.31   Translate, by inspection and hand, each infix expression into its equivalent postfix expression:

(*a*) $(A - B)/((D + E) * F)$ (*b*) $((A + B)/D) \uparrow ((E - F) * G)$

6.32   Translate, by inspection and hand, each infix expression in Prob. 6.31 into its equivalent prefix expression.

6.33   Evaluate each of the following parenthesis-free arithmetic expressions:

(*a*) $5 \;+\; 3 \;\uparrow\; 2 \;-\; 8 \;/\; 4 \;*\; 3 \;+\; 6$

(*b*) $6 \;+\; 2 \;\uparrow\; 3 \;+\; 9 \;/\; 3 \;-\; 4 \;*\; 5$

6.34   Consider the following parenthesis-free arithmetic expression:

$$E: \quad 6 \;+\; 2 \;\uparrow\; 3 \;\uparrow\; 2 \;-\; 4 \;*\; 5$$

Evaluate the expression E, (*a*) assuming that exponentiation is performed from left to right, as are the other operations, and (*b*) assuming that exponentiation is performed from right to left.

6.35   Consider each of the following postfix expressions:

$$P_1: \quad 5, \;3, \;+, \;2, \;*, \;6, \;9, \;7, \;-, \;/, \;-$$
$$P_2: \quad 3, \;5, \;+, \;6, \;4, \;-, \;*, \;4, \;1, \;-, \;2, \;\uparrow, \;+$$
$$P_3: \quad 3, \;1, \;+, \;2, \;\uparrow, \;7, \;4, \;-, \;2, \;*, \;+, \;5, \;-$$

Translate, by inspection and hand, each expression into infix notation and then evaluate.

6.36   Evaluate each postfix expression in Prob. 6.35, using Algorithm 6.3.

6.37   Use Algorithm 6.4 to translate each infix expression into its equivalent postfix expression:

(*a*) $(A - B)/((D + E) * F)$ 　　　 (*b*) $((A + B)/D)\uparrow((E - F) * G)$

(Compare with Prob. 6.31.)

RECURSION

6.38   Let J and K be integers and suppose Q(J, K) is recursively defined by

$$Q(J, K) = \begin{cases} 5 & \text{if } J < K \\ Q(J - K, K + 2) + J & \text{if } J \geq K \end{cases}$$

Find Q(2, 7), Q(5, 3) and Q(15, 2).

6.39   Let A and B be nonnegative integers. Suppose a function GCD is recursively defined as follows:

$$GCD(A, B) = \begin{cases} GCD(B, A) & \text{if } A < B \\ A & \text{if } B = 0 \\ GCD(B, MOD(A, B)) & \text{otherwise} \end{cases}$$

(Here MOD(A, B), read "A modulo B," denotes the remainder when A is divided by B.) (*a*) Find GCD(6, 15), GCD(20, 28) and GCD(540, 168). (*b*) What does this function do?

6.40   Let N be an integer and suppose H(N) is recursively defined by

$$H(N) = \begin{cases} 3 * N & \text{if } N < 5 \\ 2 * H(N - 5) + 7 & \text{otherwise} \end{cases}$$

(*a*) Find the base criteria of H and (*b*) find H(2), H(8) and H(24).

6.41   Use Definition 6.3 (of the Ackermann function) to find $A(2, 2)$.

6.42 Let M and N be integers and suppose F(M, N) is recursively defined by

$$F(M, N) = \begin{cases} 1 & \text{if } M = 0 \text{ or } M \geq N \geq 1 \\ F(M-1, N) + F(M-1, N-1) & \text{otherwise} \end{cases}$$

(a) Find F(4, 2), F(1, 5) and F(2, 4). (b) When is F(M, N) undefined?

6.43 Let A be an integer array with N elements. Suppose X is an integer function defined by

$$X(K) = X(A, N, K) = \begin{cases} 0 & \text{if } K = 0 \\ X(K-1) + A(K) & \text{if } 0 < K \leq N \\ X(K-1) & \text{if } K > N \end{cases}$$

Find X(5) for each of the following arrays:

(a) N = 8,   A: 3, 7, −2, 5, 6, −4, 2, 7   (b)   N = 3,   A: 2, 7,   −4

What does this function do?

6.44 Show that the recursive solution to the Towers of Hanoi problem in Sec. 6.7 requires $f(n) = 2^n - 1$ moves for *n* disks. Show that no other solution uses fewer than $f(n)$ moves.

6.45 Suppose S is a string with N characters. Let SUB(S, J, L) denote the substring of S beginning in the position J and having length L. Let A//B denote the concatenation of strings A and B. Suppose REV(S, N) is recursively defined by

$$REV(S, N) = \begin{cases} S & \text{if } N = 1 \\ SUB(S, N, 1) \,/\!/\, REV(SUB(S, 1, N-1), N-1) & \text{otherwise} \end{cases}$$

(a) Find REV(S, N) when (i) N = 3, S = *abc* and (ii) N = 5, S = *ababc*. (b) What does this function do?

QUEUES; DEQUES

6.46 Consider the following queue where QUEUE is allocated 6 memory cells:

       FRONT = 2, REAR = 5   QUEUE: _____, London, Berlin, Rome, Paris, _____

Describe the queue, including FRONT and REAR, as the following operations take place: (a) Athens is added, (b) two cities are deleted, (c) Madrid is added, (d) Moscow is added, (e) three cities are deleted and (f) Oslo is added.

6.47 Consider the following deque where DEQUE is allocated 6 memory cells:

       LEFT = 2, RIGHT = 5   DEQUE: _____, London, Berlin, Rome, Paris, _____

Describe the deque, including LEFT and RIGHT, as the following operations take place:

(a) Athens is added on the left.   (e) Two cities are deleted from the right.
(b) Two cities are deleted from the right.   (f) A city is deleted from the left.
(c) Madrid is added on the left.   (g) Oslo is added on the left.
(d) Moscow is added on the right.

6.48 Suppose a queue is maintained by a circular array QUEUE with N = 12 memory cells. Find the number of elements in QUEUE if (a) FRONT = 4, REAR = 8; (b) FRONT = 10, REAR = 3; and (c) FRONT = 5, REAR = 6 and then two elements are deleted.

6.49 Consider the priority queue in Fig. 6-26(b), which is maintained as a one-way list.

(a) Describe the structure if two elements are deleted.
(b) Describe the structure if, after the preceding deletions, the elements (RRR, 3), (SSS, 1), (TTT, 3) and (UUU, 2) are added to the queue.
(c) Describe the structure if, after the preceding insertions, three elements are deleted.

6.50   Consider the priority queue in Fig. 6-27(*b*), which is maintained by a two-dimensional array QUEUE.

    (*a*)   Describe the structure if two elements are deleted.
    (*b*)   Describe the structure if, after the preceding deletions, the elements (JJJ, 3), (KKK, 1), (LLL, 4) and (MMM, 5) are added to the queue.
    (*c*)   Describe the structure if, after the preceding insertions, six elements are deleted.

Programming Problems

6.51   Translate Quicksort into a subprogram QUICK(A, N) which sorts the array A with N elements. Test the program using

    (*a*)   44, 33, 11, 55, 77, 90, 40, 60, 99, 22, 88, 66
    (*b*)   D, A, T, A, S, T, R, U, C, T, U, R, E, S

6.52   Write a program which gives the solution to the Towers of Hanoi problem for *n* disks. Test the program using (*a*) *n* = 3 and (*b*) *n* = 4.

6.53   Translate Algorithm 6.4 into a subprogram POLISH(Q, P) which transforms an infix expression Q into its equivalent postfix expression P. Assume each operand is a single alphabetic character, and use the usual symbols for addition ($+$), subtraction ($-$), multiplication ($*$) and division ($/$), but use the symbol $\uparrow$ or \$ for exponentiation. (Some programming languages do not accept $\uparrow$.) Test the program using
    (*a*)   ((A + B) $*$ D) \$ (E $-$ F)   (*b*) A + (B $*$ C $-$ (D / E \$ F) $*$ G) $*$ H

6.54   Suppose a priority queue is maintained as a one-way list as illustrated in Fig. 6-20.

    (*a*)   Write a procedure

$$INSPQL(INFO, PRN, LINK, START, AVAIL, ITEM, N)$$

        which adds an ITEM with priority number N to the queue. (See Algorithm 6.14.)

    (*b*)   Write a procedure

$$DELPQL(INFO, PRN, LINK, START, AVAIL, ITEM)$$

        which removes an element from the queue and assigns the element to the variable ITEM. (See Algorithm 6.13.)

    Test the procedures, using the data in Prob. 6.25.

6.55   Suppose a priority queue is maintained by a two-dimensional array as illustrated in Fig. 6-22.

    (*a*)   Write a procedure

$$INSPQA(QUEUE, FRONT, REAR, ITEM, M)$$

        which adds an ITEM with priority number M to the queue. (See Algorithm 6.16.)

    (*b*)   Write a procedure

$$DELPQA(QUEUE, FRONT, REAR, ITEM)$$

        which removes an element from the queue and assigns the element to the variable ITEM. (See Algorithm 6.15.)

    Test the procedures, using the data in Prob. 6.26. (Assume that QUEUE has ROW number of rows and COL number of columns, where ROW and COL are global variables.)

Chapter 7

Trees

7.1 INTRODUCTION

So far, we have been studying mainly linear types of data structures: strings, arrays, lists, stacks and queues. This chapter defines a nonlinear data structure called a *tree*. This structure is mainly used to represent data containing a hierarchical relationship between elements, e.g., records, family trees and tables of contents.

First we investigate a special kind of tree, called a *binary tree*, which can be easily maintained in the computer. Although such a tree may seem to be very restrictive, we will see later in the chapter that more general trees may be viewed as binary trees.

7.2 BINARY TREES

A *binary tree* T is defined as a finite set of elements, called *nodes*, such that:

(a)　T is empty (called the *null tree* or *empty tree*), or

(b)　T contains a distinguished node R, called the *root* of T, and the remaining nodes of T form an ordered pair of disjoint binary trees T_1 and T_2.

If T does contain a root R, then the two trees T_1 and T_2 are called, respectively, the *left* and *right subtrees* of R. If T_1 is nonempty, then its root is called the *left successor* of R; similarly, if T_2 is nonempty, then its root is called the *right successor* of R.

A binary tree T is frequently presented by means of a diagram. Specifically, the diagram in Fig. 7-1 represents a binary tree T as follows. (i) T consists of 11 nodes, represented by the letters A through L, excluding I. (ii) The root of T is the node A at the top of the diagram. (iii) A left-downward slanted line from a node N indicates a left successor of N, and a right-downward slanted line from N indicates a right successor of N. Observe that:

(a)　B is a left successor and C is a right successor of the node A.

(b)　The left subtree of the root A consists of the nodes B, D, E and F, and the right subtree of A consists of the nodes C, G, H, J, K and L.

Any node N in a binary tree T has either 0, 1 or 2 successors. The nodes A, B, C and H have two successors, the nodes E and J have only one successor, and the nodes D, F, G, L and K have no successors. The nodes with no successors are called *terminal nodes*.

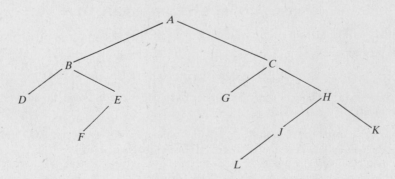

Fig. 7-1

The above definition of the binary tree T is recursive since T is defined in terms of the binary subtrees T_1 and T_2. This means, in particular, that every node N of T contains a left and a right subtree. Moreover, if N is a terminal node, then both its left and right subtrees are empty.

Binary trees T and T' are said to be *similar* if they have the same structure or, in other words, if they have the same shape. The trees are said to be *copies* if they are similar and if they have the same contents at corresponding nodes.

EXAMPLE 7.1

· Consider the four binary trees in Fig. 7-2. The three trees (a), (c) and (d) are similar. In particular, the trees (a) and (c) are copies since they also have the same data at corresponding nodes. The tree (b) is neither similar nor a copy of the tree (d) because, in a binary tree, we distinguish between a left successor and a right successor even when there is only one successor.

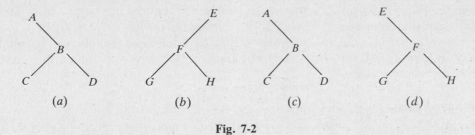

Fig. 7-2

EXAMPLE 7.2   Algebraic Expressions

Consider any algebraic expression E involving only binary operations, such as

$$E = (a - b)/((c * d) + e)$$

E can be represented by means of the binary tree T pictured in Fig. 7-3. That is, each variable or constant in E appears as an "internal" node in T whose left and right subtrees correspond to the operands of the operation. For example:

(a) In the expression E, the operands of $+$ are $c * d$ and e.

(b) In the tree T, the subtrees of the node $+$ correspond to the subexpressions $c * d$ and e.

Clearly every algebraic expression will correspond to a unique tree, and vice versa.

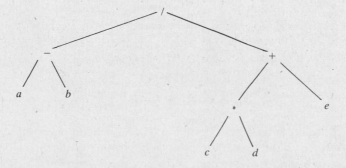

Fig. 7-3 $E = (a - b)/((c * d) + e)$.

Terminology

Terminology describing family relationships is frequently used to describe relationships between the nodes of a tree T. Specifically, suppose N is a node in T with left successor S_1 and right successor S_2. Then N is called the *parent* (or *father*) of S_1 and S_2. Analogously, S_1 is called the *left child* (or *son*) of N, and S_2 is called the *right child* (or *son*) of N. Furthermore, S_1 and S_2 are said to be *siblings* (or *brothers*). Every node N in a binary tree T, except the root, has a unique parent, called the *predecessor* of N.

The terms descendant and ancestor have their usual meaning. That is, a node L is called a *descendant* of a node N (and N is called an *ancestor* of L) if there is a succession of children from N to L. In particular, L is called a *left* or *right descendant* of N according to whether L belongs to the left or right subtree of N.

Terminology from graph theory and horticulture is also used with a binary tree T. Specifically, the line drawn from a node N of T to a successor is called an *edge*, and a sequence of consecutive edges is called a *path*. A terminal node is called a *leaf*, and a path ending in a leaf is called a *branch*.

Each node in a binary tree T is assigned a *level number*, as follows. The root R of the tree T is assigned the level number 0, and every other node is assigned a level number which is 1 more than the level number of its parent. Furthermore, those nodes with the same level number are said to belong to the same *generation*.

The *depth* (or *height*) of a tree T is the maximum number of nodes in a branch of T. This turns out to be 1 more than the largest level number of T. The tree T in Fig. 7-1 has depth 5.

Binary trees T and T' are said to be *similar* if they have the same structure or, in other words, if they have the same shape. The trees are said to be *copies* if they are similar and if they have the same contents at corresponding nodes.

Complete Binary Trees

Consider any binary tree T. Each node of T can have at most two children. Accordingly, one can show that level r of T can have at most 2^r nodes. The tree T is said to be *complete* if all its levels, except possibly the last, have the maximum number of possible nodes, and if all the nodes at the last level appear as far left as possible. Thus there is a unique complete tree T_n with exactly n nodes (we are, of course, ignoring the contents of the nodes). The complete tree T_{26} with 26 nodes appears in Fig. 7-4.

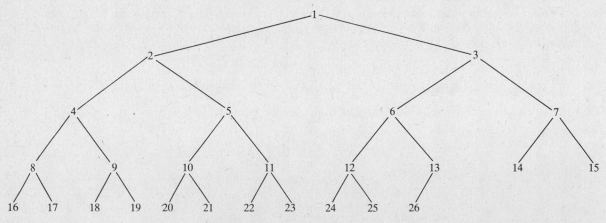

Fig. 7-4   Complete tree T_{26}.

The nodes of the complete binary tree T_{26} in Fig. 7-4 have been purposely labeled by the integers 1, 2, ..., 26, from left to right, generation by generation. With this labeling, one can easily determine the children and parent of any node K in any complete tree T_n. Specifically, the left and right children of the node K are, respectively, $2 * K$ and $2 * K + 1$, and the parent of K is the node $\lfloor K/2 \rfloor$. For example, the children of node 9 are the nodes 18 and 19, and its parent is the node $\lfloor 9/2 \rfloor = 4$. The depth d_n of the complete tree T_n with n nodes is given by

$$D_n = \lfloor \log_2 n + 1 \rfloor$$

This is a relatively small number. For example, if the complete tree T_n has $n = 1\,000\,000$ nodes, then its depth $D_n = 21$.

Extended Binary Trees: 2-Trees

A binary tree tree T is said to be a *2-tree* or an *extended binary tree* if each node N has either 0 or 2 children. In such a case, the nodes with 2 children are called *internal nodes*, and the nodes with 0 children are called *external nodes*. Sometimes the nodes are distinguished in diagrams by using circles for internal nodes and squares for external nodes.

The term "extended binary tree" comes from the following operation. Consider any binary tree T, such as the tree in Fig. 7-5(a). Then T may be "converted" into a 2-tree by replacing each empty subtree by a new node, as pictured in Fig. 7-5(b). Observe that the new tree is, indeed, a 2-tree. Furthermore, the nodes in the original tree T are now the internal nodes in the extended tree, and the new nodes are the external nodes in the extended tree.

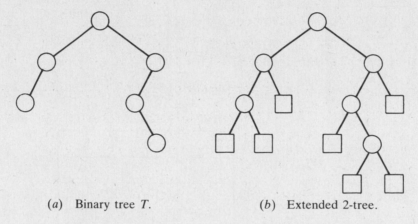

(a) Binary tree T.   (b) Extended 2-tree.

Fig. 7-5 Converting a binary tree T into a 2-tree.

An important example of a 2-tree is the tree T corresponding to any algebraic expression E which uses only binary operations. As illustrated in Fig. 7-3, the variables in E will appear as the external nodes, and the operations in E will appear as internal nodes.

7.3 REPRESENTING BINARY TREES IN MEMORY

Let T be a binary tree. This section discusses two ways of representing T in memory. The first and usual way is called the link representation of T and is analogous to the way linked lists are represented in memory. The second way, which uses a single array, called the sequential representation of T. The main requirement of any representation of T is that one should have direct access to the root R of T and, given any node N of T, one should have direct access to the children of N.

Linked Representation of Binary Trees

Consider a binary tree T. Unless otherwise stated or implied, T will be maintained in memory by means of a *linked representation* which uses three parallel arrays, INFO, LEFT and RIGHT, and a pointer variable ROOT as follows. First of all, each node N of T will correspond to a location K such that:

(1)   INFO[K] contains the data at the node N.

(2)   LEFT[K] contains the location of the left child of node N.

(3)   RIGHT[K] contains the location of the right child of node N.

Furthermore, ROOT will contain the location of the root R of T. If any subtree is empty, then the corresponding pointer will contain the null value; if the tree T itself is empty, then ROOT will contain the null value.

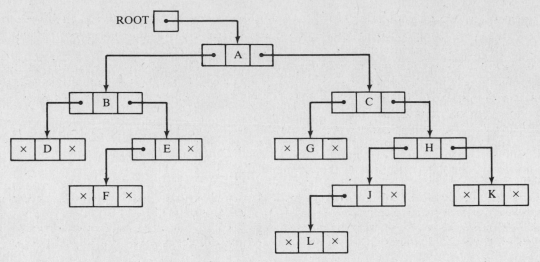

Fig. 7-6

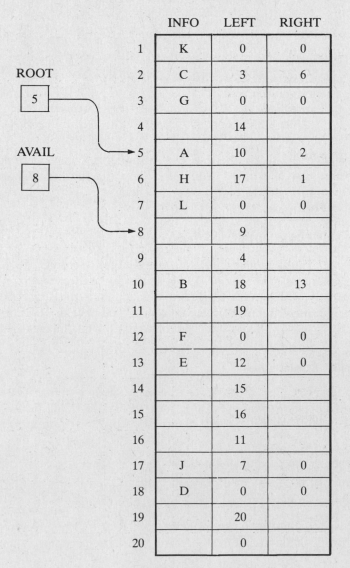

Fig. 7-7

Remark 1:   Most of our examples will show a single item of information at each node N of a binary tree T. In actual practice, an entire record may be stored at the node N. In other words, INFO may actually be a linear array of records or a collection of parallel arrays.

Remark 2:   Since nodes may be inserted into and deleted from our binary trees, we also implicitly assume that the empty locations in the arrays INFO, LEFT and RIGHT form a linked list with pointer AVAIL, as discussed in relation to linked lists in Chap. 5. We will usually let the LEFT array contain the pointers for the AVAIL list.

Remark 3:   Any invalid address may be chosen for the null pointer denoted by NULL. In actual practice, 0 or a negative number is used for NULL. (See Sec. 5.2.)

EXAMPLE 7.3

Consider the binary tree *T* in Fig. 7-1. A schematic diagram of the linked representation of *T* appears in Fig. 7-6. Observe that each node is pictured with its three fields, and that the empty subtrees are pictured by using × for the null entries. Figure 7-7 shows how this linked representation may appear in memory. The choice of 20 elements for the arrays is arbitrary. Observe that the AVAIL list is maintained as a one-way list using the array LEFT.

EXAMPLE 7.4

Suppose the personnel file of a small company contains the following data on its nine employees:

Name,   Social Security Number,   Sex,   Monthly Salary

Figure 7-8 shows how the file may be maintained in memory as a binary tree. Compare this data structure with Fig. 5-12, where the exact same data are organized as a one-way list.

	NAME	SSN	SEX	SALARY	LEFT	RIGHT
1					0	
2	Davis	192-38-7282	Female	22 800	0	12
3	Kelly	165-64-3351	Male	19 000	0	0
4	Green	175-56-2251	Male	27 200	2	0
5					1	
6	Brown	178-52-1065	Female	14 700	0	0
7	Lewis	181-58-9939	Female	16 400	3	10
8					11	
9	Cohen	177-44-4557	Male	19 000	6	4
10	Rubin	135-46-6262	Female	15 500	0	0
11					13	
12	Evans	168-56-8113	Male	34 200	0	0
13					5	
14	Harris	208-56-1654	Female	22 800	9	7

ROOT

14

AVAIL

8

Fig. 7-8

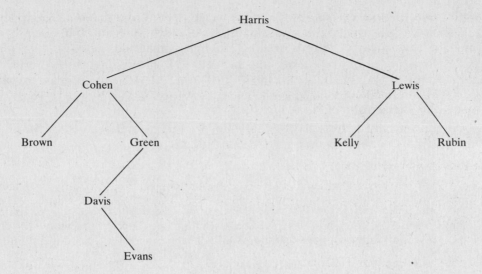

Fig. 7-9

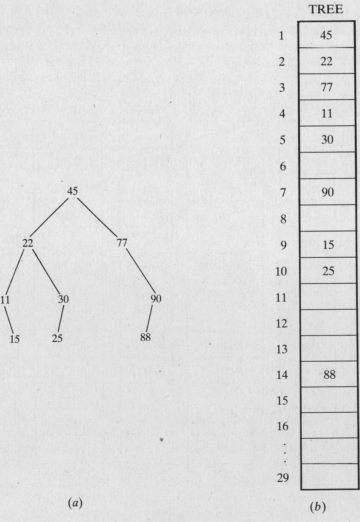

(a)   (b)

Fig. 7-10

Suppose we want to draw the tree diagram which corresponds to the binary tree in Fig. 7-8. For notational convenience, we label the nodes in the tree diagram only by the key values NAME. We construct the tree as follows:

(a)   The value ROOT = 14 indicates that Harris is the root of the tree.

(b)   LEFT[14] = 9 indicates that Cohen is the left child of Harris, and RIGHT[14] = 7 indicates that Lewis is the right child of Harris.

Repeating Step (b) for each new node in the diagram, we obtain Fig. 7-9.

Sequential Representation of Binary Trees

Suppose T is a binary tree that is complete or nearly complete. Then there is an efficient way of maintaining T in memory called the *sequential representation* of T. This representation uses only a single linear array TREE as follows:

(a)   The root R of T is stored in TREE[1].

(b)   If a node N occupies TREE[K], then its left child is stored in TREE[2 * K] and its right child is stored in TREE[2 * K + 1].

Again, NULL is used to indicate an empty subtree. In particular, TREE[1] = NULL indicates that the tree is empty.

The sequential representation of the binary tree T in Fig. 7-10(a) appears in Fig. 7-10(b). Observe that we require 14 locations in the array TREE even though T has only 9 nodes. In fact, if we included null entries for the successors of the terminal nodes, then we would actually require TREE[29] for the right successor of TREE[14]. Generally speaking, the sequential representation of a tree with depth d will require an array with approximately 2^{d+1} elements. Accordingly, this sequential representation is usually inefficient unless, as stated above, the binary tree T is complete or nearly complete. For example, the tree T in Fig. 7-1 has 11 nodes and depth 5, which means it would require an array with approximately $2^6 = 64$ elements.

7.4 TRAVERSING BINARY TREES

There are three standard ways of traversing a binary tree T with root R. These three algorithms, called preorder, inorder and postorder, are as follows:

Preorder: (1)   Process the root R.

               (2)   Traverse the left subtree of R in preorder.

               (3)   Traverse the right subtree of R in preorder.

Inorder: (1)   Traverse the left subtree of R in inorder.

             (2)   Process the root R.

             (3)   Traverse the right subtree of R in inorder.

Postorder: (1)   Traverse the left subtree of R in postorder.

               (2)   Traverse the right subtree of R in postorder.

               (3)   Process the root R.

Observe that each algorithm contains the same three steps, and that the left subtree of R is always traversed before the right subtree. The difference between the algorithms is the time at which the root R is processed. Specifically, in the "pre" algorithm, the root R is processed before the subtrees are traversed; in the "in" algorithm, the root R is processed between the traversals of the subtrees; and in the "post" algorithm, the root R is processed after the subtrees are traversed.

The three algorithms are sometimes called, respectively, the node-left-right (NLR) traversal, the left-node-right (LNR) traversal and the left-right-node (LRN) traversal.

Observe that each of the above traversal algorithms is recursively defined, since the algorithm involves traversing subtrees in the given order. Accordingly, we will expect that a stack will be used when the algorithms are implemented on the computer.

EXAMPLE 7.5

Consider the binary tree T in Fig. 7-11. Observe that A is the root, that its left subtree L_T consists of nodes B, D and E and that its right subtree R_T consists of nodes C and F.

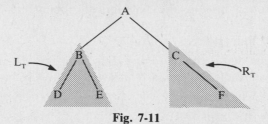

Fig. 7-11

(a) The preorder traversal of T processes A, traverses L_T and traverses R_T. However, the preorder traversal of L_T processes the root B and then D and E, and the preorder traversal of R_T processes the root C and then F. Hence ABDECF is the preorder traversal of T.

(b) The inorder traversal of T traverses L_T, processes A and traverses R_T. However, the inorder traversal of L_T processes D, B and then E, and the inorder traversal of R_T processes C and then F. Hence DBEACF is the inorder traversal of T.

(c) The postorder traversal of T traverses L_T, traverses R_T, and processes A. However, the postorder traversal of L_T processes D, E and then B, and the postorder traversal of R_T processes F and then C. Accordingly, DEBFCA is the postorder traversal of T.

EXAMPLE 7.6

Consider the tree T in Fig. 7-12. The preorder traversal of T is ABDEFCGHJLK. This order is the same as the one obtained by scanning the tree from the left as indicated by the path in Fig. 7-12. That is, one "travels" down the left-most branch until meeting a terminal node, then one backtracks to the next branch, and so on. In the preorder traversal, the right-most terminal node, node K, is the last node scanned. Observe that the left subtree of the root A is traversed before the right subtree, and both are traversed after A. The same is true for any other node having subtrees, which is the underlying property of a preorder traversal.

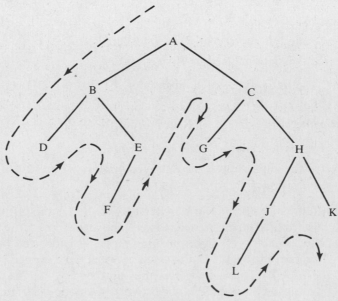

Fig. 7-12

The reader can verify by inspection that the other two ways of traversing the binary tree in Fig. 7-12 are as follows:

$$\text{(Inorder)} \quad D \ B \ F \ E \ A \ G \ C \ L \ J \ H \ K$$
$$\text{(Postorder)} \quad D \ F \ E \ B \ G \ L \ J \ K \ H \ C \ A$$

Observe that the terminal nodes, D, F, G, L and K, are traversed in the same order, from left to right, in all three traversals. We emphasize that this is true for any binary tree T.

EXAMPLE 7.7

Let E denote the following algebraic expression:

$$[a + (b - c)] * [(d - e)/(f + g - h)]$$

The corresponding binary tree T appears in Fig. 7-13. The reader can verify by inspection that the preorder and postorder traversals of T are as follows:

$$\text{(Preorder)} \quad * \ + \ a \ - \ b \ c \ / \ - \ d \ e \ - \ + \ f \ g \ h$$
$$\text{(Postorder)} \quad a \ b \ c \ - \ + \ d \ e \ - \ f \ g \ + \ h \ - \ / \ *$$

The reader can also verify that these orders correspond precisely to the prefix and postfix Polish notation of E as discussed in Sec. 6.4. We emphasize that this is true for any algebraic expression E.

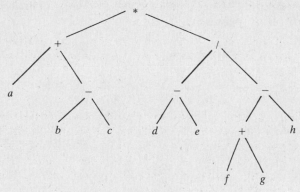

Fig. 7-13

EXAMPLE 7.8

Consider the binary tree T in Fig. 7-14. The reader can verify that the postorder traversal of T is as follows:

$$S_3, \ S_6, \ S_4, \ S_1, \ S_7, \ S_8, \ S_5, \ S_2, \ M$$

One main property of this traversal algorithm is that every descendant of any node N is processed before the node N. For example, S_6 comes before S_4, S_6 and S_4 come before S_1. Similarly, S_7 and S_8 come before S_5, and S_7, S_8 and S_5 come before S_2. Moreover, all the nodes $S_1, S_2, \ldots, S_8$ come before the root M.

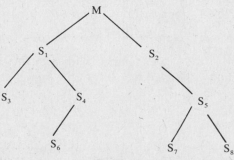

Fig. 7-14

Remark: The reader may be able to implement by inspection the three different traversals of a binary tree T if the tree has a relatively small number of nodes, as in the above two examples. Implementation by inspection may not be possible when T contains hundreds or thousands of nodes. That is, we need some systematic way of implementing the recursively defined traversals. The stack is the natural structure for such an implementation. The discussion of stack-oriented algorithms for this purpose is covered in the next section.

7.5   TRAVERSAL ALGORITHMS USING STACKS

Suppose a binary tree T is maintained in memory by some linked representation

TREE(INFO, LEFT, RIGHT, ROOT)

This section discusses the implementation of the three standard traversals of T, which were defined recursively in the last section, by means of nonrecursive procedures using stacks. We discuss the three traversals separately.

Preorder Traversal

The preorder traversal algorithm uses a variable PTR (pointer) which will contain the location of the node N currently being scanned. This is pictured in Fig. 7-15, where L(N) denotes the left child of node N and R(N) denotes the right child. The algorithm also uses an array STACK, which will hold the addresses of nodes for future processing.

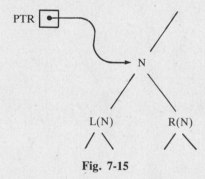

Fig. 7-15

Algorithm: Initially push NULL onto STACK and then set PTR := ROOT. Then repeat the following steps until PTR = NULL or, equivalently, while PTR ≠ NULL.

(*a*)   Proceed down the left-most path rooted at PTR, processing each node N on the path and pushing each right child R(N), if any, onto STACK. The traversing ends after a node N with no left child L(N) is processed. (Thus PTR is updated using the assignment PTR := LEFT[PTR], and the traversing stops when LEFT[PTR] = NULL.)

(*b*)   [Backtracking.] Pop and assign to PTR the top element on STACK. If PTR ≠ NULL, then return to Step (*a*); otherwise Exit.

(We note that the initial element NULL on STACK is used as a sentinel.)

We simulate the algorithm in the next example. Although the example works with the nodes themselves, in actual practice the locations of the nodes are assigned to PTR and are pushed onto the STACK.

EXAMPLE 7.9

Consider the binary tree T in Fig. 7-16. We simulate the above algorithm with T, showing the contents of STACK at each step.

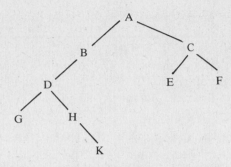

Fig. 7-16

1. Initially push NULL onto STACK:
      STACK: Ø.
    Then set PTR := A, the root of T.
2. Proceed down the left-most path rooted at PTR = A as follows:
      (i)   Process A and push its right child C onto STACK:
              STACK: Ø, C.
      (ii) Process B. (There is no right child.)
      (iii) Process D and push its right child H onto STACK:
              STACK: Ø, C, H.
      (iv) Process G. (There is no right child.)
    No other node is processed, since G has no left child.
3. [Backtracking.] Pop the top element H from STACK, and set PTR := H. This leaves:
      STACK: Ø, C.
    Since PTR ≠ NULL, return to Step (a) of the algorithm.
4. Proceed down the left-most path rooted at PTR = H as follows:
      (v)   Process H and push its right child K onto STACK:
              STACK: Ø, C, K.
    No other node is processed, since H has no left child.
5. [Backtracking.] Pop K from STACK, and set PTR := K. This leaves:
      STACK: Ø, C.
    Since PTR ≠ NULL, return to Step (a) of the algorithm.
6. Proceed down the left-most path rooted at PTR = K as follows:
      (vi) Process K. (There is no right child.)
    No other node is processed, since K has no left child.
7. [Backtracking.] Pop C from STACK, and set PTR := C. This leaves:
      STACK: Ø.
    Since PTR ≠ NULL, return to Step (a) of the algorithm.
8. Proceed down the leftmost path rooted at PTR = C as follows:
      (vii) Process C and push its right child F onto STACK:
              STACK: Ø, F.
      (viii) Process E. (There is no right child.)
9. [Backtracking.] Pop F from STACK, and set PTR := F. This leaves:
      STACK: Ø.
    Since PTR ≠ NULL, return to Step (a) of the algorithm.
10. Proceed down the left-most path rooted at PTR = F as follows:
      (ix) Process F. (There is no right child.)
    No other node is processed, since F has no left child.
11. [Backtracking.] Pop the top element NULL from STACK, and set PTR := NULL. Since PTR = NULL,
    the algorithm is completed.

As seen from Steps 2, 4, 6, 8 and 10, the nodes are processed in the order A, B, D, G, H, K, C, E, F. This is the
required preorder traversal of T.

A formal presentation of our preorder traversal algorithm follows:

Algorithm 7.1: PREORD(INFO, LEFT, RIGHT, ROOT)

A binary tree T is in memory. The algorithm does a preorder traversal of T, applying an operation PROCESS to each of its nodes. An array STACK is used to temporarily hold the addresses of nodes.

1.   [Initially push NULL onto STACK, and initialize PTR.]
     Set TOP := 1, STACK[1] := NULL and PTR := ROOT.
2.   Repeat Steps 3 to 5 while PTR ≠ NULL:
3.   Apply PROCESS to INFO[PTR].
4.   [Right child?]
          If RIGHT[PTR] ≠ NULL, then: [Push on STACK.]
               Set TOP := TOP + 1, and STACK[TOP] := RIGHT[PTR].
          [End of If structure.]
5.   [Left child?]
          If LEFT[PTR] ≠ NULL, then:
               Set PTR := LEFT[PTR].
          Else: [Pop from STACK.]
               Set PTR := STACK[TOP] and TOP := TOP − 1.
          [End of If structure.]
     [End of Step 2 loop.]
6.   Exit.

Inorder Traversal

The inorder traversal algorithm also uses a variable pointer PTR, which will contain the location of the node N currently being scanned, and an array STACK, which will hold the addresses of nodes for future processing. In fact, with this algorithm, a node is processed only when it is popped from STACK.

Algorithm: Initially push NULL onto STACK (for a sentinel) and then set PTR := ROOT. Then repeat the following steps until NULL is popped from STACK.

(a)   Proceed down the left-most path rooted at PTR, pushing each node N onto STACK and stopping when a node N with no left child is pushed onto STACK.
(b)   [Backtracking.] Pop and process the nodes on STACK. If NULL is popped, then Exit. If a node N with a right child R(N) is processed, set PTR = R(N) (by assigning PTR := RIGHT[PTR]) and return to Step (a).

We emphasize that a node N is processed only when it is popped from STACK.

EXAMPLE 7.10

Consider the binary tree T in Fig. 7-17. We simulate the above algorithm with T, showing the contents of STACK.

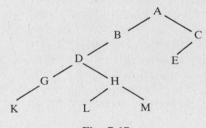

Fig. 7-17

1. Initially push NULL onto STACK:
     STACK: Ø.
   Then set PTR := A, the root of T.
2. Proceed down the left-most path rooted at PTR = A, pushing the nodes A, B, D, G and K onto STACK:
     STACK: Ø, A, B, D, G, K.
   (No other node is pushed onto STACK, since K has no left child.)
3. [Backtracking.] The nodes K, G and D are popped and processed, leaving:
     STACK: Ø, A, B.
   (We stop the processing at D, since D has a right child.) Then set PTR := H, the right child of D.
4. Proceed down the left-most path rooted at PTR = H, pushing the nodes H and L onto STACK:
     STACK: Ø, A, B, H, L.
   (No other node is pushed onto STACK, since L has no left child.)
5. [Backtracking.] The nodes L and H are popped and processed, leaving:
     STACK: Ø, A, B.
   (We stop the processing at H, since H has a right child.) Then set PTR := M, the right child of H.
6. Proceed down the left-most path rooted at PTR = M, pushing node M onto STACK:
     STACK; Ø, A, B, M.
   (No other node is pushed onto STACK, since M has no left child.)
7. [Backtracking.] The nodes M, B and A are popped and processed, leaving:
     STACK; Ø.
   (No other element of STACK is popped, since A does have a right child.) Set PTR := C, the right child of A.
8. Proceed down the left-most path rooted at PTR = C, pushing the nodes C and E onto STACK:
     STACK: Ø, C, E.
9. [Backtracking.] Node E is popped and processed. Since E has no right child, node C is popped and processed. Since C has no right child, the next element, NULL, is popped from STACK.

The algorithm is now finished, since NULL is popped from STACK. As seen from Steps 3, 5, 7 and 9, the nodes are processed in the order K, G, D, L, H, M, B, A, E, C. This is the required inorder traversal of the binary tree T.

A formal presentation of our inorder traversal algorithm follows:

Algorithm 7.2: INORD(INFO, LEFT, RIGHT, ROOT)
A binary tree is in memory. This algorithm does an inorder traversal of T, applying an operation PROCESS to each of its nodes. An array STACK is used to temporarily hold the addresses of nodes.

1. [Push NULL onto STACK and initialize PTR.]
   Set TOP := 1, STACK[1] := NULL and PTR := ROOT.
2. Repeat while PTR ≠ NULL: [Pushes left-most path onto STACK.]
     (a) Set TOP := TOP + 1 and STACK[TOP] := PTR. [Saves node.]
     (b) Set PTR := LEFT[PTR]. [Updates PTR.]
   [End of loop.]
3. Set PTR := STACK[TOP] and TOP := TOP − 1. [Pops node from STACK.]
4. Repeat Steps 5 to 7 while PTR ≠ NULL: [Backtracking.]
5.   Apply PROCESS to INFO[PTR].
6.   [Right child?] If RIGHT[PTR] ≠ NULL, then:
         (a) Set PTR := RIGHT[PTR].
         (b) Go to Step 3.
       [End of If structure.]
7.   Set PTR := STACK[TOP] and TOP := TOP − 1. [Pops node.]
   [End of Step 4 loop.]
8. Exit.

Postorder Traversal

The postorder traversal algorithm is more complicated than the preceding two algorithms, because here we may have to save a node N in two different situations. We distinguish between the two cases by pushing either N or its negative, −N, onto STACK. (In actual practice, the location of N is pushed onto STACK, so −N has the obvious meaning.) Again, a variable PTR (pointer) is used which contains the location of the node N that is currently being scanned, as in Fig. 7-15.

Algorithm: Initially push NULL onto STACK (as a sentinel) and then set PTR := ROOT. Then repeat the following steps until NULL is popped from STACK.

> (a) Proceed down the left-most path rooted at PTR. At each node N of the path, push N onto STACK and, if N has a right child R(N), push −R(N) onto STACK.
>
> (b) [Backtracking.] Pop and process positive nodes on STACK. If NULL is popped, then Exit. If a negative node is popped, that is, if PTR = −N for some node N, set PTR = N (by assigning PTR := −PTR) and return to Step (a).

We emphasize that a node N is processed only when it is popped from STACK and it is positive.

EXAMPLE 7.11

Consider again the binary tree T in Fig. 7-17. We simulate the above algorithm with T, showing the contents of STACK.

1. Initially, push NULL onto STACK and set PTR := A, the root of T:
   STACK: ∅.
2. Proceed down the left-most path rooted at PTR = A, pushing the nodes A, B, D, G and K onto STACK. Furthermore, since A has a right child C, push −C onto STACK after A but before B, and since D has a right child H, push −H onto STACK after D but before G. This yields:
   STACK: ∅, A, −C, B, D, −H, G, K.
3. [Backtracking.] Pop and process K, and pop and process G. Since −H is negative, only pop −H. This leaves:
   STACK: ∅, A, −C, B, D.
   Now PTR = −H. Reset PTR = H and return to Step (a).
4. Proceed down the left-most path rooted at PTR = H. First push H onto STACK. Since H has a right child M, push −M onto STACK after H. Last, push L onto STACK. This gives:
   STACK: ∅, A, −C, B, D, H, −M, L.
5. [Backtracking.] Pop and process L, but only pop −M . This leaves:
   STACK: ∅, A, −C, B, D, H.
   Now PTR = −M. Reset PTR = M and return to Step (a).
6. Proceed down the left-most path rooted at PTR = M. Now, only M is pushed onto STACK. This yields:
   STACK: ∅, A, −C, B, D, H, M.
7. [Backtracking.] Pop and process M, H, D and B, but only pop −C. This leaves:
   STACK: ∅, A.
   Now PTR = −C. Reset PTR = C, and return to Step (a).
8. Proceed down the left-most path rooted at PTR = C. First C is pushed onto STACK and then E, yielding:
   STACK: ∅, A, C, E.
9. [Backtracking.] Pop and process E, C and A. When NULL is popped, STACK is empty and the algorithm is completed.

As seen from Steps 3, 5, 7 and 9, the nodes are processed in the order K, G, L, M, H, D, B, E, C, A. This is the required postorder traversal of the binary tree T.

A formal presentation of our postorder traversal algorithm follows:

Algorithm 7.3: POSTORD(INFO, LEFT, RIGHT, ROOT)
A binary tree T is in memory. This algorithm does a postorder traversal of T, applying an operation PROCESS to each of its nodes. An array STACK is used to temporarily hold the addresses of nodes.

1. [Push NULL onto STACK and initialize PTR.]
   Set TOP := 1, STACK[1] := NULL and PTR := ROOT.
2. [Push left-most path onto STACK.]
   Repeat Steps 3 to 5 while PTR ≠ NULL:
3.   Set TOP := TOP + 1 and STACK[TOP] := PTR.
       [Pushes PTR on STACK.]
4.   If RIGHT[PTR] ≠ NULL, then: [Push on STACK.]
           Set TOP := TOP + 1 and STACK[TOP] := −RIGHT[PTR].
       [End of If structure.]
5.   Set PTR := LEFT[PTR]. [Updates pointer PTR.]
   [End of Step 2 loop.]
6. Set PTR := STACK[TOP] and TOP := TOP − 1.
   [Pops node from STACK.]
7. Repeat while PTR > 0:
   (*a*)   Apply PROCESS to INFO[PTR].
   (*b*)   Set PTR := STACK[TOP] and TOP := TOP − 1.
           [Pops node from STACK.]
   [End of loop.]
8. If PTR < 0, then:
   (*a*)   Set PTR := −PTR.
   (*b*)   Go to Step 2.
   [End of If structure.]
9. Exit.

7.6 HEADER NODES; THREADS

Consider a binary tree T. Variations of the linked representation of T are frequently used because certain operations on T are easier to implement by using the modifications. Some of these variations, which are analogous to header and circular linked lists, are discussed in this section.

Header Nodes

Suppose a binary tree T is maintained in memory by means of a linked representation. Sometimes an extra, special node, called a *header node*, is added to the beginning of T. When this extra node is used, the tree pointer variable, which we will call HEAD (instead of ROOT), will point to the header node, and the left pointer of the header node will point to the root of T. Figure 7-18 shows a schematic picture of the binary tree in Fig. 7-1 that uses a linked representation with a header node. (Compare with Fig. 7-6.)

Suppose a binary tree T is empty. Then T will still contain a header node, but the left pointer of the header node will contain the null value. Thus the condition

$$LEFT[HEAD] = NULL$$

will indicate an empty tree.

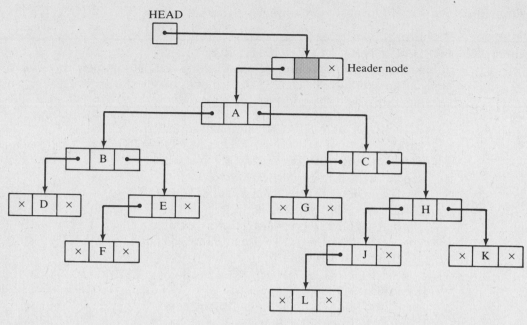

Fig. 7-18

Another variation of the above representation of a binary tree T is to use the header node as a sentinel. That is, if a node has an empty subtree, then the pointer field for the subtree will contain the address of the header node instead of the null value. Accordingly, no pointer will ever contain an invalid address, and the condition

$$LEFT[HEAD] = HEAD$$

will indicate an empty subtree.

Threads; Inorder Threading

Consider again the linked representation of a binary tree T. Approximately half of the entries in the pointer fields LEFT and RIGHT will contain null elements. This space may be more efficiently used by replacing the null entries by some other type of information. Specifically, we will replace certain null entries by special pointers which point to nodes higher in the tree. These special pointers are called *threads*, and binary trees with such pointers are called *threaded trees*.

The threads in a threaded tree must be distinguished in some way from ordinary pointers. The threads in a diagram of a threaded tree are usually indicated by dotted lines. In computer memory, an extra 1-bit TAG field may be used to distinguish threads from ordinary pointers, or, alternatively, threads may be denoted by negative integers when ordinary pointers are denoted by positive integers.

There are many ways to thread a binary tree T, but each threading will correspond to a particular traversal of T. Also, one may choose a one-way threading or a two-way threading. Unless otherwise stated, our threading will correspond to the inorder traversal of T. Accordingly, in the one-way threading of T, a thread will appear in the right field of a node and will point to the next node in the inorder traversal of T; and in the two-way threading of T, a thread will also appear in the LEFT field of a node and will point to the preceding node in the inorder traversal of T. Furthermore, the left pointer of the first node and the right pointer of the last node (in the inorder traversal of T) will contain the null value when T does not have a header node, but will point to the header node when T does have a header node.

There is an analogous one-way threading of a binary tree T which corresponds to the preorder traversal of T. (See Prob. 7.13.) On the other hand, there is no threading of T which corresponds to the postorder traversal of T.

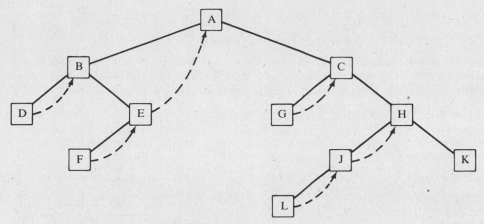

(a)   One-way inorder threading.

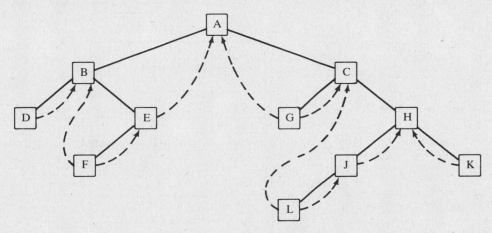

(b)   Two-way inorder threading.

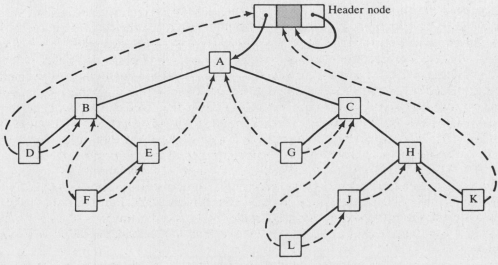

(c)   Two-way threading with header node.

Fig. 7-19

EXAMPLE 7.12

Consider the binary tree T in Fig. 7-1.

(a) The one-way inorder threading of T appears in Fig. 7-19(a). There is a thread from node E to node A, since A is accessed after E in the inorder traversal of T. Observe that every null right pointer has been replaced by a thread except for the node K, which is the last node in the inorder traversal of T.

(b) The two-way inorder threading of T appears in Fig. 7-19(b). There is a left thread from node L to node C, since L is accessed after C in the inorder traversal of T. Observe that every null left pointer has been replaced by a thread except for node D, which is the first node in the inorder traversal of T. All the right threads are the same as in Fig. 7-19(a).

(c) The two-way inorder threading of T when T has a header node appears in Fig. 7-19(c). Here the left thread of D and the right thread of K point to the header node. Otherwise the picture is the same as that in Fig. 7-19(b).

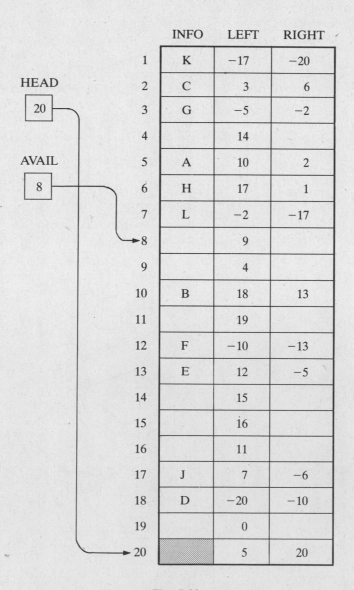

	INFO	LEFT	RIGHT
1	K	−17	−20
2	C	3	6
3	G	−5	−2
4		14	
5	A	10	2
6	H	17	1
7	L	−2	−17
8		9	
9		4	
10	B	18	13
11		19	
12	F	−10	−13
13	E	12	−5
14		15	
15		16	
16		11	
17	J	7	−6
18	D	−20	−10
19		0	
20		5	20

HEAD
20

AVAIL
8

Fig. 7-20

(d) Figure 7-7 shows how T may be maintained in memory by using a linked representation. Figure 7-20 shows how the representation should be modified so that T is a two-way inorder threaded tree using INFO[20] as a header node. Observe that LEFT[12] = −10, which means there is a left thread from node F to node B. Analogously, RIGHT[17] = −6 means there is a right thread from node J to node H. Last, observe that RIGHT[20] = 20, which means there is an ordinary right pointer from the header node to itself. If T were empty, then we would set LEFT[20] = −20, which would mean there is a left thread from the header node to itself.

7.7 BINARY SEARCH TREES

This section discusses one of the most important data structures in computer science, a binary search tree. This structure enables one to search for and find an element with an average running time $f(n) = O(\log_2 n)$. It also enables one to easily insert and delete elements. This structure contrasts with the following structures:

(a) *Sorted linear array.* Here one can search for and find an element with a running time $f(n) = O(\log_2 n)$, but it is expensive to insert and delete elements.

(b) *Linked list.* Here one can easily insert and delete elements, but it is expensive to search for and find an element, since one must use a linear search with running time $f(n) = O(n)$.

Although each node in a binary search tree may contain an entire record of data, the definition of the binary tree depends on a given field whose values are distinct and may be ordered.

Suppose T is a binary tree. Then T is called a *binary search tree* (or *binary sorted tree*) if each node N of T has the following property: *The value at N is greater than every value in the left subtree of N and is less than every value in the right subtree of N.* (It is not difficult to see that this property guarantees that the inorder traversal of T will yield a sorted listing of the elements of T.)

EXAMPLE 7.13

(a) Consider the binary tree T in Fig. 7-21. T is a binary search tree; that is, every node N in T exceeds every number in its left subtree and is less than every number in its right subtree. Suppose the 23 were replaced by 35. Then T would still be a binary search tree. On the other hand, suppose the 23 were replaced by 40. Then T would not be a binary search tree, since the 38 would not be greater than the 40 in its left subtree.

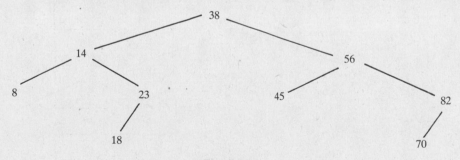

Fig. 7-21

(b) Consider the file in Fig. 7-8. As indicated by Fig. 7-9, the file is a binary search tree with respect to the key NAME. On the other hand, the file is not a binary search tree with respect to the social security number key SSN. This situation is similar to an array of records which is sorted with respect to one key but is unsorted with respect to another key.

The definition of a binary search tree given in this section assumes that all the node values are distinct. There is an analogous definition of a binary search tree which admits duplicates, that is, in which each node N has the following property: *The value at N is greater than every value in the left subtree of N and is less than or equal to every value in the right subtree of N.* When this definition is used, the operations in the next section must be modified accordingly.

7.8 SEARCHING AND INSERTING IN BINARY SEARCH TREES

Suppose T is a binary search tree. This section discusses the basic operations of searching and inserting with respect to T. In fact, the searching and inserting will be given by a single search and insertion algorithm. The operation of deleting is treated in the next section. Traversing in T is the same as traversing in any binary tree; this subject has been covered in Sec. 7.4.

Suppose an ITEM of information is given. The following algorithm finds the location of ITEM in the binary search tree T, or inserts ITEM as a new node in its appropriate place in the tree.

(a)   Compare ITEM with the root node N of the tree.
    (i)   If ITEM < N, proceed to the left child of N.
    (ii)   If ITEM > N, proceed to the right child of N.

(b)   Repeat Step (a) until one of the following occurs:
    (i)   We meet a node N such that ITEM = N. In this case the search is successful.
    (ii)   We meet an empty subtree, which indicates that the search is unsuccessful, and we insert ITEM in place of the empty subtree.

In other words, proceed from the root R down through the tree T until finding ITEM in T or inserting ITEM as a terminal node in T.

EXAMPLE 7.14

(a)   Consider the binary search tree T in Fig. 7-21. Suppose ITEM = 20 is given. Simulating the above algorithm, we obtain the following steps:

1.   Compare ITEM = 20 with the root, 38, of the tree T. Since 20 < 38, proceed to the left child of 38, which is 14.
2.   Compare ITEM = 20 with 14. Since 20 > 14, proceed to the right child of 14, which is 23.
3.   Compare ITEM = 20 with 23. Since 20 < 23, proceed to the left child of 23, which is 18.
4.   Compare ITEM = 20 with 18. Since 20 > 18 and 18 does not have a right child, insert 20 as the right child of 18.

Figure 7-22 shows the new tree with ITEM = 20 inserted. The shaded edges indicate the path down through the tree during the algorithm.

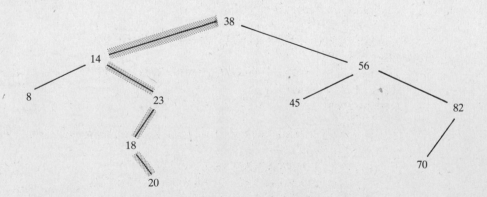

Fig. 7-22   ITEM = 20 inserted.

(b)   Consider the binary search tree T in Fig. 7-9. Suppose ITEM = Davis is given. Simulating the above algorithm, we obtain the following steps:

1.   Compare ITEM = Davis with the root of the tree, Harris. Since Davis < Harris, proceed to the left child of Harris, which is Cohen.
2.   Compare ITEM = Davis with Cohen. Since Davis > Cohen, proceed to the right child of Cohen, which is Green.

3. Compare ITEM = Davis with Green. Since Davis < Green, proceed to the left child of Green, which is Davis.

4. Compare ITEM = Davis with the left child, Davis. We have found the location of Davis in the tree.

EXAMPLE 7.15

Suppose the following six numbers are inserted in order into an empty binary search tree:

$$40, 60, 50, 33, 55, 11$$

Figure 7-23 shows the six stages of the tree. We emphasize that if the six numbers were given in a different order, then the tree might be different and we might have a different depth.

The formal presentation of our search and insertion algorithm will use the following procedure, which finds the locations of a given ITEM and its parent. The procedure traverses down the tree using the pointer PTR and the pointer SAVE for the parent node. This procedure will also be used in the next section, on deletion.

Procedure 7.4: FIND(INFO, LEFT, RIGHT, ROOT, ITEM, LOC, PAR)

A binary search tree T is in memory and an ITEM of information is given. This procedure finds the location LOC of ITEM in T and also the location PAR of the parent of ITEM. There are three special cases:

  (i)   LOC = NULL and PAR = NULL will indicate that the tree is empty.

  (ii) LOC ≠ NULL and PAR = NULL will indicate that ITEM is the root of T.

  (iii) LOC = NULL and PAR ≠ NULL will indicate that ITEM is not in T and can be added to T as a child of the node N with location PAR.

1. [Tree empty?]
   If ROOT = NULL, then: Set LOC := NULL and PAR := NULL, and Return.

2. [ITEM at root?]
   If ITEM = INFO[ROOT], then: Set LOC := ROOT and PAR := NULL, and Return.

3. [Initialize pointers PTR and SAVE.]
   If ITEM < INFO[ROOT], then:
       Set PTR := LEFT[ROOT] and SAVE := ROOT.
   Else:
       Set PTR := RIGHT[ROOT] and SAVE := ROOT.
   [End of If structure.]

4. Repeat Steps 5 and 6 while PTR ≠ NULL:

5.   [ITEM found?]
       If ITEM = INFO[PTR], then: Set LOC := PTR and PAR := SAVE, and Return.

6.   If ITEM < INFO[PTR], then:
           Set SAVE := PTR and PTR := LEFT[PTR].
       Else:
           Set SAVE := PTR and PTR := RIGHT[PTR].
       [End of If structure.]
   [End of Step 4 loop.]

7. [Search unsuccessful.] Set LOC := NULL and PAR := SAVE.

8. Exit.

Observe that, in Step 6, we move to the left child or the right child according to whether ITEM < INFO[PTR] or ITEM > INFO[PTR].

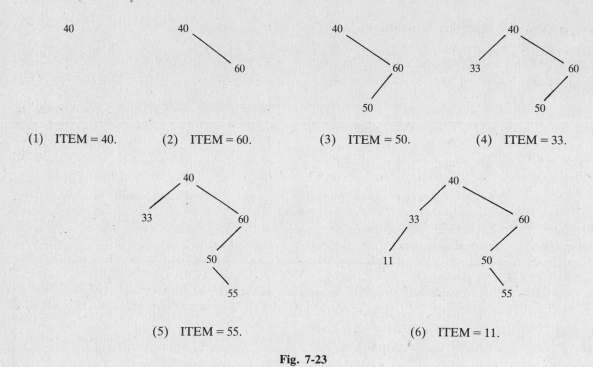

(1)   ITEM = 40.   (2)   ITEM = 60.   (3)   ITEM = 50.   (4)   ITEM = 33.

(5)   ITEM = 55.   (6)   ITEM = 11.

Fig. 7-23

The formal statement of our search and insertion algorithm follows.

Algorithm 7.5:   INSBST(INFO, LEFT, RIGHT, ROOT, AVAIL, ITEM, LOC)
A binary search tree T is in memory and an ITEM of information is given. This algorithm finds the location LOC of ITEM in T or adds ITEM as a new node in T at location LOC.

1. Call FIND(INFO, LEFT, RIGHT, ROOT, ITEM, LOC, PAR).
   [Procedure 7.4.]
2. If LOC ≠ NULL, then Exit.
3. [Copy ITEM into new node in AVAIL list.]
   (a)   If AVAIL = NULL, then: Write: OVERFLOW, and Exit.
   (b)   Set NEW := AVAIL, AVAIL := LEFT[AVAIL] and INFO[NEW] := ITEM.
   (c)   Set LOC := NEW, LEFT[NEW] := NULL and RIGHT[NEW] := NULL.
4. [Add ITEM to tree.]
   If PAR = NULL, then:
        Set ROOT := NEW.
   Else if ITEM < INFO[PAR], then:
        Set LEFT[PAR] := NEW.
   Else:
        Set RIGHT[PAR] := NEW.
   [End of If structure.]
5. Exit.

Observe that, in Step 4, there are three possibilities: (1) the tree is empty, (2) ITEM is added as a left child and (3) ITEM is added as a right child.

Complexity of the Searching Algorithm

Suppose we are searching for an item of information in a binary search tree T. Observe that the number of comparisons is bounded by the depth of the tree. This comes from the fact that we proceed down a single path of the tree. Accordingly, the running time of the search will be proportional to the depth of the tree.

Suppose we are given n data items, $A_1, A_2, \ldots, A_N$, and suppose the items are inserted in order into a binary search tree T. Recall that there are $n!$ permutations of the n items (Sec. 2.2). Each such permutation will give rise to a corresponding tree. It can be shown that the average depth of the $n!$ trees is approximately $c \log_2 n$, where $c = 1.4$. Accordingly, the average running time $f(n)$ to search for an item in a binary tree T with n elements is proportional to $\log_2 n$, that is, $f(n) = O(\log_2 n)$.

Application of Binary Search Trees

Consider a collection of n data items, $A_1, A_2, \ldots, A_N$. Suppose we want to find and delete all duplicates in the collection. One straightforward way to do this is as follows:

Algorithm A: Scan the elements from A_1 to A_N (that is, from left to right).

  (a)   For each element A_K, compare A_K with $A_1, A_2, \ldots, A_{K-1}$, that is, compare A_K with those elements which precede A_K.
  (b)   If A_K does occur among $A_1, A_2, \ldots, A_{K-1}$, then delete A_K.

After all elements have been scanned, there will be no duplicates.

EXAMPLE 7.16

Suppose Algorithm A is applied to the following list of 15 numbers:

$$14, 10, 17, 12, 10, 11, 20, 12, 18, 25, 20, 8, 22, 11, 23$$

Observe that the first four numbers (14, 10, 17 and 12) are not deleted. However,

$A_5 = 10$	is deleted, since	$A_5 = A_2$
$A_8 = 12$	is deleted, since	$A_8 = A_4$
$A_{11} = 20$	is deleted, since	$A_{11} = A_7$
$A_{14} = 11$	is deleted, since	$A_{14} = A_6$

When Algorithm A is finished running, the 11 numbers

$$14, 10, 17, 12, 11, 20, 18, 25, 8, 22, 23$$

which are all distinct, will remain.

Consider now the time complexity of Algorithm A, which is determined by the number of comparisons. First of all, we assume that the number d of duplicates is very small compared with the number n of data items. Observe that the step involving A_K will require approximately $k - 1$ comparisons, since we compare A_K with items $A_1, A_2, \ldots, A_{K-1}$ (less the few that may already have been deleted). Accordingly, the number $f(n)$ of comparisons required by Algorithm A is approximately

$$0 + 1 + 2 + 3 + \cdots + (n - 2) + (n - 1) = \frac{(n - 1)n}{2} = O(n^2)$$

For example, for $n = 1000$ items, Algorithm A will require approximately 500 000 comparisons. In other words, the running time of Algorithm A is proportional to n^2.

Using a binary search tree, we can give another algorithm to find the duplicates in the set $A_1, A_2, \ldots, A_N$ of n data items.

Algorithm B: Build a binary search tree T using the elements A_1, A_2, . . . , A_N. In building the tree, delete A_K from the list whenever the value of A_K already appears in the tree.

The main advantage of Algorithm B is that each element A_K is compared only with the elements in a single branch of the tree. It can be shown that the average length of such a branch is approximately $c \log_2 k$, where $c = 1.4$. Accordingly, the total number $f(n)$ of comparisons required by Algorithm B is approximately $n \log_2 n$, that is, $f(n) = O(n \log_2 n)$. For example, for $n = 1000$, Algorithm B will require approximately 10 000 comparisons rather than the 500 000 comparisons with Algorithm A. (We note that, for the worst case, the number of comparisons for Algorithm B is the same as for Algorithm A.)

EXAMPLE 7.17

Consider again the following list of 15 numbers:

$$14, \ 10, \ 17, \ 12, \ 10, \ 11, \ 20, \ 12, \ 18, \ 25, \ 20, \ 8, \ 22, \ 11, \ 23$$

Applying Algorithm B to this list of numbers, we obtain the tree in Fig. 7-24. The exact number of comparisons is

$$0 + 1 + 1 + 2 + 2 + 3 + 2 + 3 + 3 + 3 + 3 + 2 + 4 + 4 + 5 = 38$$

On the other hand, Algorithm A requires

$$0 + 1 + 2 + 3 + 2 + 4 + 5 + 4 + 6 + 7 + 6 + 8 + 9 + 5 + 10 = 72$$

comparisons.

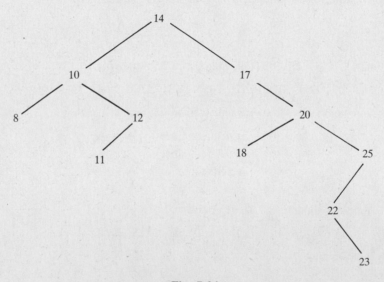

Fig. 7-24

7.9   DELETING IN A BINARY SEARCH TREE

Suppose T is a binary search tree, and suppose an ITEM of information is given. This section gives an algorithm which deletes ITEM from the tree T.

The deletion algorithm first uses Procedure 7.4 to find the location of the node N which contains ITEM and also the location of the parent node P(N). The way N is deleted from the tree depends primarily on the number of children of node N. There are three cases:

Case 1.   N has no children. Then N is deleted from T by simply replacing the location of N in the parent node P(N) by the null pointer.

Case 2. N has exactly one child. Then N is deleted from T by simply replacing the location of N in P(N) by the location of the only child of N.

Case 3. N has two children. Let S(N) denote the inorder successor of N. (The reader can verify that S(N) does not have a left child.) Then N is deleted from T by first deleting S(N) from T (by using Case 1 or Case 2) and then replacing node N in T by the node S(N).

Observe that the third case is much more complicated than the first two cases. In all three cases, the memory space of the deleted node N is returned to the AVAIL list.

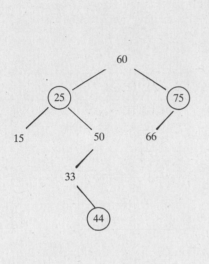

ROOT
3

AVAIL
5

	INFO	LEFT	RIGHT
1	33	0	9
2	25	8	10
3	60	2	7
4	66	0	0
5		6	
6		0	
7	75	4	0
8	15	0	0
9	44	0	0
10	50	1	0

(a) Before deletions. (b) Linked representation.

Fig. 7-25

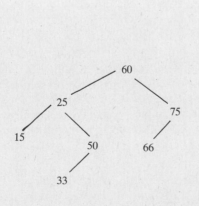

ROOT
3

AVAIL
9

	INFO	LEFT	RIGHT
1	33	0	0
2	25	8	10
3	60	2	7
4	66	0	0
5		6	
6		0	
7	75	4	0
8	15	0	0
9		5	
10	50	1	0

(a) Node 44 is deleted. (b) Linked representation.

Fig. 7-26

EXAMPLE 7.18

Consider the binary search tree in Fig. 7-25(*a*). Suppose T appears in memory as in Fig. 7-25(*b*).

(*a*)   Suppose we delete node 44 from the tree T in Fig. 7-25. Note that node 44 has no children. Figure 7-26(*a*) pictures the tree after 44 is deleted, and Fig. 7-26(*b*) shows the linked representation in memory. The deletion is accomplished by simply assigning NULL to the parent node, 33. (The shading indicates the changes.)

(*b*)   Suppose we delete node 75 from the tree T in Fig. 7-25 instead of node 44. Note that node 75 has only one child. Figure 7-27(*a*) pictures the tree after 75 is deleted, and Fig. 7-27(*b*) shows the linked representation. The deletion is accomplished by changing the right pointer of the parent node 60, which originally pointed to 75, so that it now points to node 66, the only child of 75. (The shading indicates the changes.)

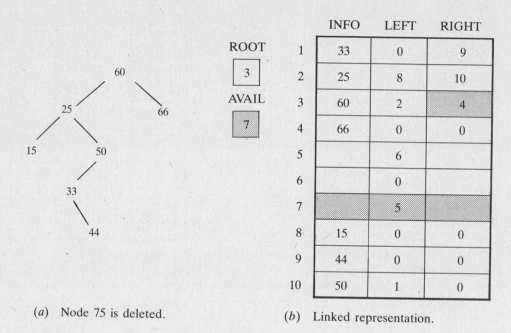

	INFO	LEFT	RIGHT
1	33	0	9
2	25	8	10
3	60	2	4
4	66	0	0
5		6	
6		0	
7		5	
8	15	0	0
9	44	0	0
10	50	1	0

ROOT 3

AVAIL 7

(*a*)   Node 75 is deleted.   (*b*)   Linked representation.

Fig. 7-27

(*c*)   Suppose we delete node 25 from the tree T in Fig. 7-25 instead of node 44 or node 75. Note that node 25 has two children. Also observe that node 33 is the inorder successor of node 25. Figure 7-28(*a*) pictures the tree after 25 is deleted, and Fig. 7-28(*b*) shows the linked representation. The deletion is accomplished by first deleting 33 from the tree and then replacing node 25 by node 33. We emphasize that the replacement of node 25 by node 33 is executed in memory only by changing pointers, not by moving the contents of a node from one location to another. Thus 33 is still the value of INFO[1].

Our deletion algorithm will be stated in terms of Procedures 7.6 and 7.7, which follow. The first procedure refers to Cases 1 and 2, where the deleted node N does not have two children; and the second procedure refers to Case 3, where N does have two children. There are many subcases which reflect the fact that N may be a left child, a right child or the root. Also, in Case 2, N may have a left child or a right child.

Procedure 7.7 treats the case that the deleted node N has two children. We note that the inorder successor of N can be found by moving to the right child of N and then moving repeatedly to the left until meeting a node with an empty left subtree.

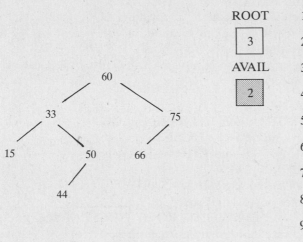

		INFO	LEFT	RIGHT
ROOT	1	33	8	10
3	2		5	
AVAIL	3	60	1	7
2	4	66	0	0
	5		6	
	6		0	
	7	75	4	0
	8	15	0	0
	9	44	0	0
	10	50	9	0

(a)   Node 25 is deleted.   (b)   Linked representation

Fig. 7-28

Procedure 7.6:   CASEA(INFO, LEFT, RIGHT, ROOT, LOC, PAR)
This procedure deletes the node N at location LOC, where N does not have two children. The pointer PAR gives the location of the parent of N, or else PAR = NULL indicates that N is the root node. The pointer CHILD gives the location of the only child of N, or else CHILD = NULL indicates N has no children.

1.   [Initializes CHILD.]
    If LEFT[LOC] = NULL and RIGHT[LOC] = NULL, then:
        Set CHILD := NULL.
    Else if LEFT[LOC] ≠ NULL, then:
        Set CHILD := LEFT[LOC].
    Else
        Set CHILD := RIGHT[LOC].
    [End of If structure.]
2.   If PAR ≠ NULL, then:
        If LOC = LEFT[PAR], then:
            Set LEFT[PAR] := CHILD.
        Else:
            Set RIGHT[PAR] := CHILD.
        [End of If structure.]
    Else:
        Set ROOT := CHILD.
    [End of If structure.]
3.   Return.

Procedure 7.7:   CASEB(INFO, LEFT, RIGHT, ROOT, LOC, PAR)
This procedure will delete the node N at location LOC, where N has two children. The pointer PAR gives the location of the parent of N, or else PAR = NULL indicates that N is the root node. The pointer SUC gives the location of the inorder successor of N, and PARSUC gives the location of the parent of the inorder successor.

1. [Find SUC and PARSUC.]
   (a) Set PTR := RIGHT[LOC] and SAVE := LOC.
   (b) Repeat while LEFT[PTR] ≠ NULL:
           Set SAVE := PTR and PTR := LEFT[PTR].
       [End of loop.]
   (c) Set SUC := PTR and PARSUC := SAVE.
2. [Delete inorder successor, using Procedure 7.6.]
   Call CASEA(INFO, LEFT, RIGHT, ROOT, SUC, PARSUC).
3. [Replace node N by its inorder successor.]
   (a) If PAR ≠ NULL, then:
           If LOC = LEFT[PAR], then:
               Set LEFT[PAR] := SUC.
           Else:
               Set RIGHT[PAR] := SUC.
           [End of If structure.]
       Else:
           Set ROOT := SUC.
       [End of If structure.]
   (b) Set LEFT[SUC] := LEFT[LOC] and
       RIGHT[SUC] := RIGHT[LOC].
4. Return.

We can now formally state our deletion algorithm, using Procedures 7.6 and 7.7 as building blocks.

Algorithm 7.8:   DEL(INFO, LEFT, RIGHT, ROOT, AVAIL, ITEM)
A binary search tree T is in memory, and an ITEM of information is given. This algorithm deletes ITEM from the tree.

1. [Find the locations of ITEM and its parent, using Procedure 7.4.]
   Call FIND(INFO, LEFT, RIGHT, ROOT, ITEM, LOC, PAR).
2. [ITEM in tree?]
   If LOC = NULL, then: Write: ITEM not in tree, and Exit.
3. [Delete node containing ITEM.]
   If RIGHT[LOC] ≠ NULL and LEFT[LOC] ≠ NULL, then:
       Call CASEB(INFO, LEFT, RIGHT, ROOT, LOC, PAR).
   Else:
       Call CASEA(INFO, LEFT, RIGHT, ROOT, LOC, PAR).
   [End of If structure.]
4. [Return deleted node to the AVAIL list.]
   Set LEFT[LOC] := AVAIL and AVAIL := LOC.
5. Exit.

7.10   HEAP; HEAPSORT

This section discusses another tree structure, called a *heap*. The heap is used in an elegant sorting algorithm called *heapsort*. Although sorting will be treated mainly in Chap. 9, we give the heapsort algorithm here and compare its complexity with that of the bubble sort and quicksort algorithms, which were discussed, respectively, in Chaps. 4 and 6.

Suppose H is a complete binary tree with n elements. (Unless otherwise stated, we assume that H is maintained in memory by a linear array TREE using the sequential representation of H, not a linked representation.) Then H is called a *heap*, or a *maxheap*, if each node N of H has the following property: *The value at N is greater than or equal to the value at each of the children of* N. Accordingly, the value at N is greater than or equal to the value at any of the descendants of N. (A *minheap* is defined analogously: The value at N is less than or equal to the value at any of the children of N.)

EXAMPLE 7.19

Consider the complete tree H in Fig. 7-29(*a*). Observe that H is a heap. This means, in particular, that the largest element in H appears at the "top" of the heap, that is, at the root of the tree. Figure 7-29(*b*) shows the sequential representation of H by the array TREE. That is, TREE[1] is the root of the tree H, and the left and right children of node TREE[K] are, respectively, TREE[2K] and TREE[2K + 1]. This means, in particular, that the parent of any nonroot node TREE[J] is the node TREE[J $\div$ 2] (where J $\div$ 2 means integer division). Observe that the nodes of H on the same level appear one after the other in the array TREE.

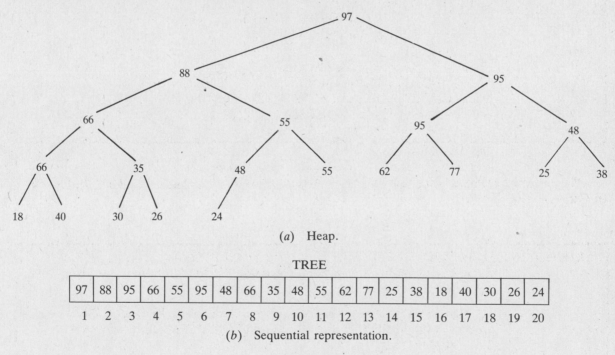

(*a*)   Heap.

TREE

97	88	95	66	55	95	48	66	35	48	55	62	77	25	38	18	40	30	26	24
1	2	3	4	5	6	7	8	9	10	11	12	13	14	15	16	17	18	19	20

(*b*)   Sequential representation.

Fig. 7-29

Inserting into a Heap

Suppose H is a heap with N elements, and suppose an ITEM of information is given. We insert ITEM into the heap H as follows:

(1)   First adjoin ITEM at the end of H so that H is still a complete tree, but not necessarily a heap.

(2)   Then let ITEM rise to its "appropriate place" in H so that H is finally a heap.

We illustrate the way this procedure works before stating the procedure formally.

EXAMPLE 7.20

Consider the heap H in Fig. 7-29. Suppose we want to add ITEM = 70 to H. First we adjoin 70 as the next element in the complete tree; that is, we set TREE[21] = 70. Then 70 is the right child of TREE[10] = 48. The path from 70 to the root of H is pictured in Fig. 7-30(a). We now find the appropriate place of 70 in the heap as follows:

(a)   Compare 70 with its parent, 48. Since 70 is greater than 48, interchange 70 and 48; the path will now look like Fig. 7-30(b).

(b)   Compare 70 with its new parent, 55. Since 70 is greater than 55, interchange 70 and 55; the path will now look like Fig. 7-30(c).

(c)   Compare 70 with its new parent, 88. Since 70 does not exceed 88, ITEM = 70 has risen to its appropriate place in H.

Figure 7-30(d) shows the final tree. A dotted line indicates that an exchange has taken place.

Remark: One must verify that the above procedure does always yield a heap as a final tree, that is, that nothing else has been disturbed. This is easy to see, and we leave this verification to the reader.

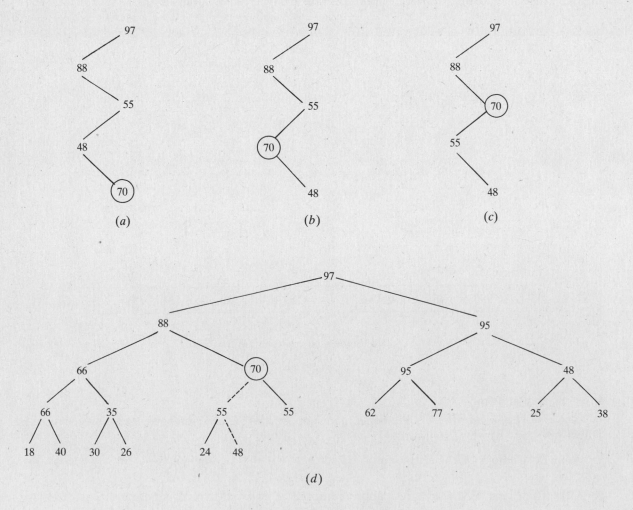

Fig. 7-30   ITEM = 70 is inserted.

EXAMPLE 7.21

Suppose we want to build a heap H from the following list of numbers:

$$44, 30, 50, 22, 60, 55, 77, 55$$

This can be accomplished by inserting the eight numbers one after the other into an empty heap H using the above procedure. Figure 7-31(a) through (h) shows the respective pictures of the heap after each of the eight elements has been inserted. Again, the dotted line indicates that an exchange has taken place during the insertion of the given ITEM of information.

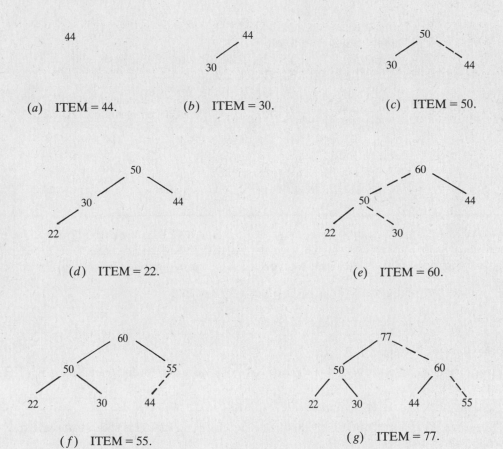

(a) ITEM = 44.   (b) ITEM = 30.   (c) ITEM = 50.

(d) ITEM = 22.   (e) ITEM = 60.

(f) ITEM = 55.   (g) ITEM = 77.

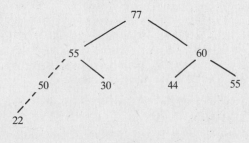

(h) ITEM = 55.

Fig. 7-31 Building a heap.

The formal statement of our insertion procedure follows:

Procedure 7.9:   INSHEAP(TREE, N, ITEM)

A heap H with N elements is stored in the array TREE, and an ITEM of information is given. This procedure inserts ITEM as a new element of H. PTR gives the location of ITEM as it rises in the tree, and PAR denotes the location of the parent of ITEM.

1. [Add new node to H and initialize PTR.]
   Set N := N + 1 and PTR := N.
2. [Find location to insert ITEM.]
   Repeat Steps 3 to 6 while PTR < 1.
3.   Set PAR := $\lfloor PTR/2 \rfloor$. [Location of parent node.]
4.   If ITEM ≤ TREE[PAR], then:
           Set TREE[PTR] := ITEM, and Return.
       [End of If structure.]
5.   Set TREE[PTR] := TREE[PAR]. [Moves node down.]
6.   Set PTR := PAR. [Updates PTR.]
   [End of Step 2 loop.]
7. [Assign ITEM as the root of H.]
   Set TREE[1] := ITEM.
8. Return.

Observe that ITEM is not assigned to an element of the array TREE until the appropriate place for ITEM is found. Step 7 takes care of the special case that ITEM rises to the root TREE[1].

Suppose an array A with N elements is given. By repeatedly applying Procedure 7.9 to A, that is, by executing

$$\text{Call INSHEAP(A, J, A[J + 1])}$$

for J = 1, 2, . . . , N − 1, we can build a heap H out of the array A.

Deleting the Root of a Heap

Suppose H is a heap with N elements, and suppose we want to delete the root R of H. This is accomplished as follows:

(1) Assign the root R to some variable ITEM.

(2) Replace the deleted node R by the last node L of H so that H is still a complete tree, but not necessarily a heap.

(3) (Reheap) Let L sink to its appropriate place in H so that H is finally a heap.

Again we illustrate the way the procedure works before stating the procedure formally.

EXAMPLE 7.22

Consider the heap H in Fig. 7-32(a), where R = 95 is the root and L = 22 is the last node of the tree. Step 1 of the above procedure deletes R = 95, and Step 2 replaces R = 95 by L = 22. This gives the complete tree in Fig. 7-32(b), which is not a heap. Observe, however, that both the right and left subtrees of 22 are still heaps. Applying Step 3, we find the appropriate place of 22 in the heap as follows:

(a) Compare 22 with its two children, 85 and 70. Since 22 is less than the larger child, 85, interchange 22 and 85 so the tree now looks like Fig. 7-32(c).

(b) Compare 22 with its two new children, 55 and 33. Since 22 is less than the larger child, 55, interchange 22 and 55 so the tree now looks like Fig. 7-32(d).

(c) Compare 22 with its new children, 15 and 20. Since 22 is greater than both children, node 22 has dropped to its appropriate place in H.

Thus Fig. 7-32(d) is the required heap H without its original root R.

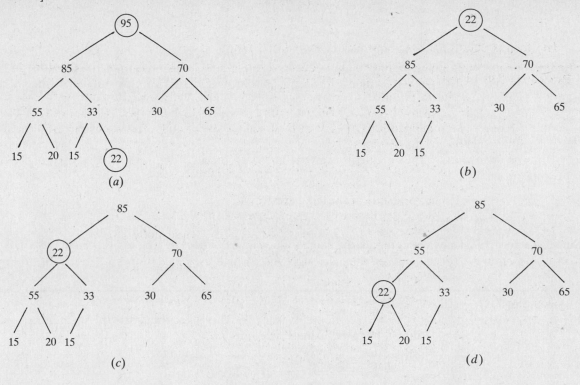

Fig. 7-32 Reheaping.

Remark:　As with inserting an element into a heap, one must verify that the above procedure does always yield a heap as a final tree. Again we leave this verification to the reader. We also note that Step 3 of the procedure may not end until the node L reaches the bottom of the tree, i.e., until L has no children.

The formal statement of our procedure follows.

Procedure 7.10:　DELHEAP(TREE, N, ITEM)

A heap H with N elements is stored in the array TREE. This procedure assigns the root TREE[1] of H to the variable ITEM and then reheaps the remaining elements. The variable LAST saves the value of the original last node of H. The pointers PTR, LEFT and RIGHT give the locations of LAST and its left and right children as LAST sinks in the tree.

1. Set ITEM := TREE[1]. [Removes root of H.]
2. Set LAST := TREE[N] and N := N − 1. [Removes last node of H.]
3. Set PTR := 1, LEFT := 2 and RIGHT := 3. [Initializes pointers.]
4. Repeat Steps 5 to 7 while RIGHT ≤ N:
5. 　　　If LAST ≥ TREE[LEFT] and LAST ≥ TREE[RIGHT], then:
　　　　　　　Set TREE[PTR] := LAST and Return.
　　　　[End of If structure.]
6. 　　　IF TREE[RIGHT] ≤ TREE[LEFT], then:
　　　　　　　Set TREE[PTR] := TREE[LEFT] and PTR := LEFT.
　　　　Else:
　　　　　　　Set TREE[PTR] := TREE[RIGHT] and PTR := RIGHT.
　　　　[End of If structure.]
7. 　　　Set LEFT := 2 * PTR and RIGHT := LEFT + 1.
　　　[End of Step 4 loop.]
8. If LEFT = N and if LAST < TREE[LEFT], then: Set PTR := LEFT.
9. Set TREE[PTR] := LAST.
10. Return.

The Step 4 loop repeats as long as LAST has a right child. Step 8 takes care of the special case in which LAST does not have a right child but does have a left child (which has to be the last node in H). The reason for the two "If" statements in Step 8 is that TREE[LEFT] may not be defined when LEFT > N.

Application to Sorting

Suppose an array A with N elements is given. The heapsort algorithm to sort A consists of the two following phases:

Phase A: Build a heap H out of the elements of A.

Phase B: Repeatedly delete the root element of H.

Since the root of H always contains the largest node in H, Phase B deletes the elements of A in decreasing order. A formal statement of the algorithm, which uses Procedures 7.9 and 7.10, follows.

Algorithm 7.11:   HEAPSORT(A, N)
An array A with N elements is given. This algorithm sorts the elements of A.
1.   [Build a heap H, using Procedure 7.9.]
    Repeat for J = 1 to N − 1:
        Call INSHEAP(A, J, A[J + 1]).
    [End of loop.]
2.   [Sort A by repeatedly deleting the root of H, using Procedure 7.10.]
    Repeat while N > 1:
        (*a*)   Call DELHEAP(A, N, ITEM).
        (*b*)   Set A[N + 1] := ITEM.
    [End of Loop.]
3.   Exit.

The purpose of Step 2(*b*) is to save space. That is, one could use another array B to hold the sorted elements of A and replace Step 2(*b*) by

$$\text{Set } B[N + 1] := \text{ITEM}$$

However, the reader can verify that the given Step 2(*b*) does not interfere with the algorithm, since A[N + 1] does not belong to the heap H.

Complexity of Heapsort

Suppose the heapsort algorithm is applied to an array A with n elements. The algorithm has two phases, and we analyze the complexity of each phase separately.

Phase A. Suppose H is a heap. Observe that the number of comparisons to find the appropriate place of a new element ITEM in H cannot exceed the depth of H. Since H is a complete tree, its depth is bounded by $\log_2 m$ where m is the number of elements in H. Accordingly, the total number $g(n)$ of comparisons to insert the n elements of A into H is bounded as follows:

$$g(n) \le n \log_2 n$$

Consequently, the running time of Phase A of heapsort is proportional to $n \log_2 n$.

Phase B. Suppose H is a complete tree with m elements, and suppose the left and right subtrees of H are heaps and L is the root of H. Observe that reheaping uses 4 comparisons to move the node L one step down the tree H. Since the depth of H does not exceed $\log_2 m$, reheaping uses at most $4 \log_2 m$ comparisons to find the appropriate place of L in the tree H. This means that the total number $h(n)$ of comparisons to delete the n elements of A from H, which requires reheaping n times, is bounded as follows:

$$h(n) \le 4n \log_2 n$$

Accordingly, the running time of Phase B of heapsort is also proportional to $n \log_2 n$.

Since each phase requires time proportional to $n \log_2 n$, the running time to sort the n-element array A using heapsort is proportional to $n \log_2 n$, that is, $f(n) = O(n \log_2 n)$. Observe that this gives a worst-case complexity of the heapsort algorithm. This contrasts with the following two sorting algorithms already studied:

(1) *Bubble sort* (Sec. 4.6). The running time of bubble sort is $O(n^2)$.

(2) *Quicksort* (Sec. 6.5). The average running time of quicksort is $O(n \log_2 n)$, the same as heapsort, but the worst-case running time of quicksort is $O(n^2)$, the same as bubble sort.

Other sorting algorithms are investigated in Chap. 9.

7.11 PATH LENGTHS; HUFFMAN'S ALGORITHM

Recall that an *extended binary tree* or *2-tree* is a binary tree T in which each node has either 0 or 2 children. The nodes with 0 children are called *external nodes*, and the nodes with 2 children are called *internal nodes*. Figure 7-33 shows a 2-tree where the internal nodes are denoted by circles and the external nodes are denoted by squares. In any 2-tree, the number N_E of external nodes is 1 more than the number N_I of internal nodes; that is,

$$N_E = N_I + 1$$

For example, for the 2-tree in Fig. 7-33, $N_I = 6$, and $N_E = N_I + 1 = 7$.

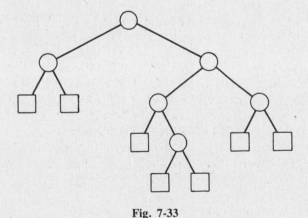

Fig. 7-33

Frequently, an algorithm can be represented by a 2-tree T where the internal nodes represent tests and the external nodes represent actions. Accordingly, the running time of the algorithm may depend on the lengths of the paths in the tree. With this in mind, we define the *external path length* L_E of a 2-tree T to be the sum of all path lengths summed over each path from the root R of T to an external node. The *internal path length* L_I of T is defined analogously, using internal nodes instead of external nodes. For the tree in Fig. 7-33,

$$L_E = 2 + 2 + 3 + 4 + 4 + 3 + 3 = 21 \qquad \text{and} \qquad L_I = 0 + 1 + 1 + 2 + 3 + 2 = 9$$

Observe that

$$L_I + 2n = 9 + 2 \cdot 6 = 9 + 12 = 21 = L_E$$

where $n = 6$ is the number of internal nodes. In fact, the formula

$$L_E = L_I + 2n$$

is true for any 2-tree with n internal nodes.

Suppose T is a 2-tree with n external nodes, and suppose each of the external nodes is assigned a (nonnegative) weight. The (external) *weighted path length* P of the tree T is defined to be the sum of the weighted path lengths; i.e.,

$$P = W_1 L_1 + W_2 L_2 + \cdots + W_n L_n$$

where W_i and L_i denote, respectively, the weight and path length of an external node N_i.

Consider now the collection of all 2-trees with n external nodes. Clearly, the complete tree among them will have a minimal external path length L_E. On the other hand, suppose each tree is given the same n weights for its external nodes. Then it is not clear which tree will give a minimal weighted path length P.

EXAMPLE 7.23

Figure 7-34 shows three 2-trees, T_1, T_2 and T_3, each having external nodes with weights 2, 3, 5 and 11. The weighted path lengths of the three trees are as follows:

$$P_1 = 2 \cdot 2 + 3 \cdot 2 + 5 \cdot 2 + 11 \cdot 2 = 42$$
$$P_2 = 2 \cdot 1 + 3 \cdot 3 + 5 \cdot 3 + 11 \cdot 2 = 48$$
$$P_3 = 2 \cdot 3 + 3 \cdot 3 + 5 \cdot 2 + 11 \cdot 1 = 36$$

The quantities P_1 and P_3 indicate that the complete tree need not give a minimum length P, and the quantities P_2 and P_3 indicate that similar trees need not give the same lengths.

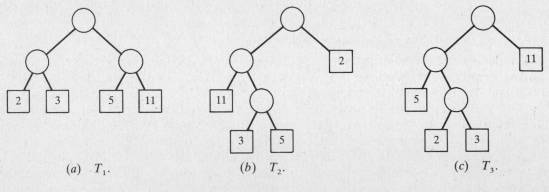

(a) T_1. (b) T_2. (c) T_3.

Fig. 7-34

The general problem that we want to solve is as follows. Suppose a list of n weights is given:

$$w_1, w_2, \ldots, w_n$$

Among all the 2-trees with n external nodes and with the given n weights, find a tree T with a minimum-weighted path length. (Such a tree T is seldom unique.) Huffman gave an algorithm, which we now state, to find such a tree T.

Observe that the Huffman algorithm is recursively defined in terms of the number of weights and the solution for one weight is simply the tree with one node. On the other hand, in practice, we use an equivalent iterated form of the Huffman algorithm constructing the tree from the bottom up rather than from the top down.

Huffman's Algorithm: Suppose w_1 and w_2 are two minimum weights among the n given weights $w_1, w_2, \ldots, w_n$. Find a tree T' which gives a solution for the $n - 1$ weights

$$w_1 + w_2, w_3, w_4, \ldots, w_n$$

Then, in the tree T', replace the external node

$\boxed{w_1 + w_2}$ by the subtree

The new 2-tree T is the desired solution.

EXAMPLE 7.24

Suppose A, B, C, D, E, F, G and H are 8 data items, and suppose they are assigned weights as follows:

Data item:	A	B	C	D	E	F	G	H
Weight:	22	5	11	19	2	11	25	5

Figure 7-35(a) through (h) shows how to construct the tree T with minimum-weighted path length using the above data and Huffman's algorithm. We explain each step separately.

(a)   Here each data item belongs to its own subtree. Two subtrees with the smallest possible combination of weights, the one weighted 2 and one of those weighted 5, are shaded.

(b)   Here the subtrees that were shaded in Fig. 7-35(a) are joined together to form a subtree with weight 7. Again, the current two subtrees of lowest weight are shaded.

(c) to (g)   Each step joins together two subtrees having the lowest existing weights (always the ones that were shaded in the preceding diagram), and again, the two resulting subtree of lowest weight are shaded.

(h)   This is the final desired tree T, formed when the only two remaining subtrees are joined together.

Computer Implementation of Huffman's Algorithm

Consider again the data in Example 7.24. Suppose we want to implement the Huffman algorithm using the computer. First of all, we require an extra array WT to hold the weights of the nodes; i.e., our tree will be maintained by four parallel arrays, INFO, WT, LEFT and RIGHT. Figure 7-36(a) shows how the given data may be stored in the computer initially. Observe that there is sufficient room for the additional nodes. Observe that NULL appears in the left and right pointers for the initial nodes, since these nodes will be terminal in the final tree.

During the execution of the algorithm, one must be able to keep track of all the different subtrees and one must also be able to find the subtrees with minimum weights. This may be accomplished by maintaining an auxiliary minheap, where each node contains the weight and the location of the root of a current subtree. The initial minheap appears in Fig. 7-36(b). (The minheap is used rather than a maxheap since we want the node with the lowest weight to be on the top of the heap.)

The first step in building the required Huffman tree T involves the following substeps:

(i)   Remove the node $N_1 = [2, 5]$ and the node $N_2 = [5, 2]$ from the heap. (Each time a node is deleted, one must reheap.)

(ii)   Use the data in N_1 and N_2 and the first available space AVAIL = 9 to add a new node as follows:

$$\text{WT}[9] = 2 + 5 = 7 \qquad \text{LEFT}[9] = 5 \qquad \text{RIGHT}[9] = 2$$

Thus N_1 is the left child of the new node and N_2 is the right child of the new node.

(iii)   Adjoin the weight and location of the new node, that is, [7, 9], to the heap.

Fig. 7-35 Building a Huffman tree.

	INFO	WT	LEFT	RIGHT
1	A	22	0	0
2	B	5	0	0
3	C	11	0	0
4	D	19	0	0
5	E	2	0	0
6	F	11	0	0
7	G	25	0	0
8	H	5	0	0
9			10	
10			11	
11			12	
12			13	
13			14	
14			15	
15			16	
16			0	

AVAIL = 9

(a)

	INFO	WT	LEFT	RIGHT
1	A	22	0	0
2	B	5	0	0
3	C	11	0	0
4	D	19	0	0
5	E	2	0	0
6	F	11	0	0
7	G	25	0	0
8	H	5	0	0
9		7	5	2
10		12	8	9
11		22	6	3
12		31	10	4
13		44	1	11
14		56	7	12
15		100	13	14
16				

ROOT = 15, AVAIL = 16

(c)

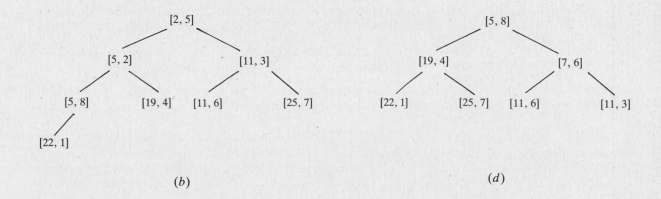

(b)

(d)

Fig. 7-36 Implementation of Huffman's algorithmn.

The shaded area in Fig. 7-36(c) shows the new node, and Fig. 7-36(d) shows the new heap, which has one less element than the heap in Fig. 7-36(b).

Repeating the above step until the heap is empty, we obtain the required tree T in Fig. 7-36(c). We must set ROOT = 15, since this is the location of the last node added to the tree.

Application to Coding

Suppose a collection of n data items, $A_1, A_2, \ldots, A_N$, are to be coded by means of strings of bits. One way to do this is to code each item by an r-bit string where

$$2^{r-1} < n \le 2^r$$

For example, a 48-character set is frequently coded in memory by using 6-bit strings. One cannot use 5-bit strings, since $2^5 < 48 < 2^6$.

Suppose the data items do not occur with the same probability. Then memory space may be conserved by using variable-length strings, where items which occur frequently are assigned shorter strings and items which occur infrequently are assigned longer strings. This section discusses a coding using variable-length strings that is based on the Huffman tree T for weighted data items.

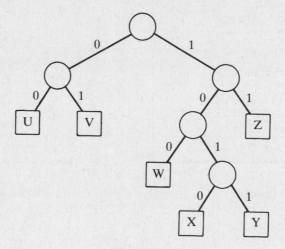

Fig. 7-37

Consider the extended binary tree T in Fig. 7-37 whose external nodes are the items U, V, W, X, Y and Z. Observe that each edge from an internal node to a left child is labeled by the bit 0 and each edge to a right child is labeled by the bit 1. The Huffman code assigns to each external node the sequence of bits from the root to the node. Thus the tree T in Fig. 7-37 determines the following code for the external nodes:

U: 00   V: 01   W: 100   X: 1010   Y: 1011   Z: 11

This code has the "prefix" property; i.e., the code of any item is not an initial substring of the code of any other item. This means there cannot be any ambiguity in decoding any message using a Huffman code.

Consider again the 8 data items A, B, C, D, E, F, G and H in Example 7-24. Suppose the weights represent the percentage probabilities that the items will occur. Then the tree T of minimum-weighted path length constructed in Fig. 7-35, appearing with the bit labels in Fig. 7-38, will yield an efficient coding of the data items. The reader can verify that the tree T yields the following code:

A: 00   B: 11011   C: 011   D: 111

E: 11010   F: 010   G: 10   H: 1100

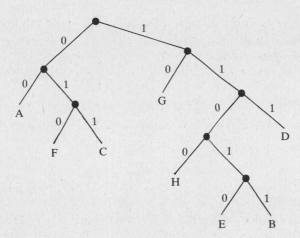

Fig. 7-38

7.12 GENERAL TREES

A *general tree* (sometimes called a *tree*) is defined to be a nonempty finite set T of elements, called *nodes*, such that:

(1) T contains a distinguished element R, called the *root* of T.

(2)   The remaining elements of T form an ordered collection of zero or more disjoint trees $T_1, T_2, \ldots, T_m$.

The trees $T_1, T_2, \ldots, T_m$ are called *subtrees* of the root R, and the roots of $T_1, T_2, \ldots, T_m$ are called *successors* of R.

Terminology from family relationships, graph theory and horticulture is used for general trees in the same way as for binary trees. In particular, if N is a node with successors $S_1, S_2, \ldots, S_m$, then N is called the *parent* of the S_i's, the S_i's are called *children* of N, and the S_i's are called *siblings* of each other.

The term "tree" comes up, with slightly different meanings, in many different areas of mathematics and computer science. Here we assume that our general tree T is *rooted*, that is, that T has a distinguished node R called the root of T; and that T is *ordered*, that is, that the children of each node N of T have a specific order. These two properties are not always required for the definition of a tree.

EXAMPLE 7.25

Figure 7-39 pictures a general tree T with 13 nodes,

$$A, B, C, D, E, F, G, H, J, K, L, M, N$$

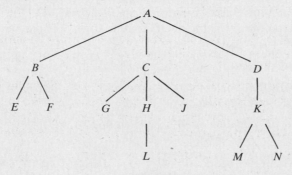

Fig. 7-39

Unless otherwise stated, the root of a tree T is the node at the top of the diagram, and the children of a node are ordered from left to right. Accordingly, A is the root of T, and A has three children; the first child B, the second child C and the third child D. Observe that:

(a) The node C has three children.

(b) Each of the nodes B and K has two children.

(c) Each of the nodes D and H has only one child.

(d) The nodes E, F, G, L, J, M and N have no children.

The last group of nodes, those with no children, are called *terminal nodes*.

A binary tree T' is not a special case of a general tree T: binary trees and general trees are different objects. The two basic differences follow:

(1) A binary tree T' may be empty, but a general tree T is nonempty.

(2) Suppose a node N has only one child. Then the child is distinguished as a left child or right child in a binary tree T', but no such distinction exists in a general tree T.

The second difference is illustrated by the trees T_1 and T_2 in Fig. 7-40. Specifically, as binary trees, T_1 and T_2 are distinct trees, since B is the left child of A in the tree T_1 but B is the right child of A in the tree T_2. On the other hand, there is no difference between the trees T_1 and T_2 as general trees.

(a) Tree T_1.   (b) Tree T_2.

Fig. 7-40

A *forest F* is defined to be an ordered collection of zero or more distinct trees. Clearly, if we delete the root R from a general tree T, then we obtain the forest F consisting of the subtrees of R (which may be empty). Conversely, if F is a forest, then we may adjoin a node R to F to form a general tree T where R is the root of T and the subtrees of R consist of the original trees in F.

Computer Representation of General Trees

Suppose T is a general tree. Unless otherwise stated or implied, T will be maintained in memory by means of a linked representation which uses three parallel arrays INFO, CHILD (or DOWN) and SIBL (or HORZ), and a pointer variable ROOT as follows. First of all, each node N of T will correspond to a location K such that:

(1) INFO[K] contains the data at node N.

(2) CHILD[K] contains the location of the first child of N. The condition CHILD[K] = NULL indicates that N has no children.

(3) SIBL[K] contains the location of the next sibling of N. The condition SIBL[K] = NULL indicates that N is the last child of its parent.

Furthermore, ROOT will contain the location of the root R of T. Although this representation may seem artificial, it has the important advantage that each node N of T, regardless of the number of children of N, will contain exactly three fields.

The above representation may easily be extended to represent a forest F consisting of trees $T_1, T_2, \ldots, T_m$ by assuming the roots of the trees are siblings. In such a case, ROOT will contain the location of the root R_1 of the first tree T_1; or when F is empty, ROOT will equal NULL.

EXAMPLE 7.26

Consider the general tree T in Fig. 7-39. Suppose the data of the nodes of T are stored in an array INFO as in Fig. 7-41(a). The structural relationships of T are obtained by assigning values to the pointer ROOT and the arrays CHILD and SIBL as follows:

(a) Since the root A of T is stored in INFO[2], set ROOT := 2.

(b) Since the first child of A is the node B, which is stored in INFO[3], set CHILD[2] := 3. Since A has no sibling, set SIBL[2] := NULL.

(c) Since the first child of B is the node E, which is stored in INFO[15], set CHILD[3] := 15. Since node C is the next sibling of B and C is stored in INFO[4], set SIBL[3] := 4.

And so on. Figure 7-41(b) gives the final values in CHILD and SIBL. Observe that the AVAIL list of empty nodes is maintained by the first array, CHILD, where AVAIL = 1.

	INFO		CHILD	SIBL
1		1	5	
2	A	2	3	0
3	B	3	15	4
4	C	4	6	16
5		5	13	
6	G	6	0	7
7	H	7	11	8
8	J	8	0	0
9	N	9	0	0
10	M	10	0	9
11	L	11	0	0
12	K	12	10	0
13		13	0	
14	F	14	0	0
15	E	15	0	14
16	D	16	12	0

ROOT = 2, AVAIL = 13

(a)   (b)

Fig. 7-41

Correspondence between General Trees and Binary Trees

Suppose T is a general tree. Then we may assign a unique binary tree T' to T as follows. First of all, the nodes of the binary tree T' will be the same as the nodes of the general tree T, and the root of

T' will be the root of T. Let N be an arbitrary node of the binary tree T'. Then the left child of N in T' will be the first child of the node N in the general tree T and the right child of N in T' will be the next sibling of N in the general tree T.

EXAMPLE 7.27

Consider the general tree T in Fig. 7-39. The reader can verify that the binary tree T' in Fig. 7-42 corresponds to the general tree T. Observe that by rotating counterclockwise the picture of T' in Fig. 7-42 until the edges pointing to right children are horizontal, we obtain a picture in which the nodes occupy the same relative position as the nodes in Fig. 7-39.

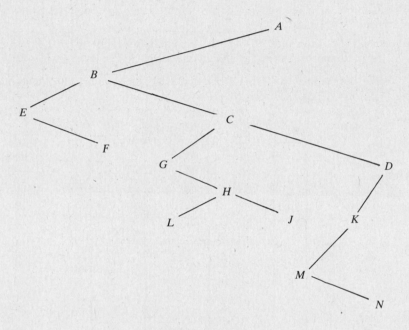

Fig. 7-42 Binary tree T'.

The computer representation of the general tree T and the linked representation of the corresponding binary tree T' are exactly the same except that the names of the arrays CHILD and SIBL for the general tree T will correspond to the names of the arrays LEFT and RIGHT for the binary tree T'. The importance of this correspondence is that certain algorithms that applied to binary trees, such as the traversal algorithms, may now apply to general trees.

Solved Problems

BINARY TREES

7.1   Suppose T is the binary tree stored in memory as in Fig. 7-43. Draw the diagram of T.

The tree T is drawn from its root R downward as follows:

(*a*) The root R is obtained from the value of the pointer ROOT. Note that ROOT = 5. Hence INFO[5] = 60 is the root R of T.

	INFO	LEFT	RIGHT
1	20	0	0
2	30	1	13
3	40	0	0
4	50	0	0
5	60	2	6
6	70	0	8
7	80	0	0
8	90	7	14
9		10	
10		0	
11	35	0	12
12	45	3	4
13	55	11	0
14	95	0	0

ROOT

5

AVAIL

9

Fig. 7-43

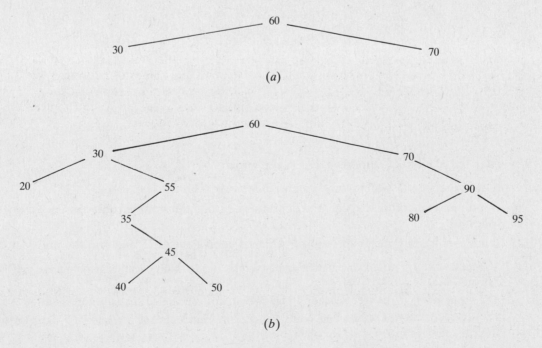

(a)

(b)

Fig. 7-44

(b)   The left child of R is obtained from the left pointer field of R. Note that LEFT[5] = 2. Hence
       INFO[2] = 30 is the left child of R.

(c)   The right child of R is obtained from the right pointer field of R. Note that RIGHT[5] = 6. Hence
       INFO[6] = 70 is the right child of R.

We can now draw the top part of the tree as pictured in Fig. 7-44(a). Repeating the above process with
each new node, we finally obtain the required tree T in Fig. 7-44(b).

7.2   A binary tree T has 9 nodes. The inorder and preorder traversals of T yield the following
       sequences of nodes:

$$\text{Inorder:} \quad E \ A \ C \ K \ F \ H \ D \ B \ G$$
$$\text{Preorder:} \quad F \ A \ E \ K \ C \ D \ H \ G \ B$$

Draw the tree T.

The tree T is drawn from its root downward as follows.

(a)   The root of T is obtained by choosing the first node in its preorder. Thus F is the root of T.

(b)   The left child of the node F is obtained as follows. First use the inorder of T to find the nodes in the
       left subtree T_1 of F. Thus T_1 consists of the nodes E, A, C and K. Then the left child of F is obtained
       by choosing the first node in the preorder of T_1 (which appears in the preorder of T). Thus A is the
       left son of F.

(c)   Similarly, the right subtree T_2 of F consists of the nodes H, D, B and G, and D is the root of T_2, that
       is, D is the right child of F.

Repeating the above process with each new node, we finally obtain the required tree in Fig. 7-45.

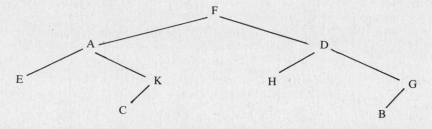

Fig. 7-45

7.3   Consider the algebraic expression $E = (2x + y)(5a - b)^3$.

(a)   Draw the tree T which corresponds to the expression E.

(b)   Find the *scope* of the exponential operator; i.e., find the subtree rooted at the exponential
       operator.

(c)   Find the prefix Polish expression P which is equivalent to E, and find the preorder of T.

(a)   Use an arrow (↑) for exponentiation and an asterisk (∗) for multiplication to obtain the tree shown
       in Fig. 7-46.

(b)   The scope of ↑ is the tree shaded in Fig. 7-46. It corresponds to the subexpression $(5a - b)^3$.

(c)   There is no difference between the prefix Polish expression P and the preorder of T. Scan the tree T
       from the left, as in Fig. 7-12, to obtain:

$$∗ \ + \ ∗ \ 2 \ x \ y \ ↑ \ - \ ∗ \ 5 \ a \ b \ 3$$

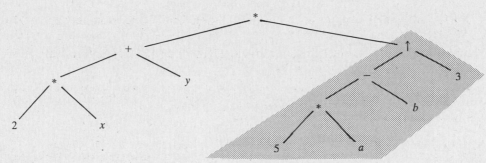

Fig. 7-46

7.4 Suppose a binary tree T is in memory. Write a recursive procedure which finds the number NUM of nodes in T.

The number NUM of nodes in T is 1 more than the number NUML of nodes in the left subtree of T plus the number NUMR of nodes in the right subtree of T. Accordingly:

Procedure P7.4: COUNT(LEFT, RIGHT, ROOT, NUM)
This procedure finds the number NUM of nodes in a binary tree T in memory.

1. If ROOT = NULL, then: Set NUM := 0, and Return.
2. Call COUNT(LEFT, RIGHT, LEFT[ROOT], NUML).
3. Call COUNT(LEFT, RIGHT, RIGHT[ROOT], NUMR).
4. Set NUM := NUML + NUMR + 1.
5. Return.

(Observe that the array INFO does not play any role in this procedure.)

7.5 Suppose a binary tree T is in memory. Write a recursive procedure which finds the depth DEP of T.

The depth DEP of T is 1 more than the maximum of the depths of the left and right subtrees of T. Accordingly:

Procedure P7.5: DEPTH(LEFT, RIGHT, ROOT, DEP)
This procedure finds the depth DEP of a binary tree T in memory.

1. If ROOT = NULL, then: Set DEP := 0, and Return.
2. Call DEPTH(LEFT, RIGHT, LEFT[ROOT], DEPL).
3. Call DEPTH(LEFT, RIGHT, RIGHT[ROOT], DEPR).
4. If DEPL ≥ DEPR, then:
         Set DEP := DEPL + 1.
    Else:
         Set DEP := DEPR + 1.
    [End of If structure.]
5. Return.

(Observe that the array INFO does not play any role in this procedure.)

7.6 Draw all the possible nonsimilar trees T where:

(*a*) T is a binary tree with 3 nodes.

(*b*) T is a 2-tree with 4 external nodes.

(*a*) There are five such trees, which are pictured in Fig. 7-47(*a*).

(*b*) Each 2-tree with 4 external nodes is determined by a binary tree with 3 nodes, i.e., by a tree in part (*a*). Thus there are five such trees, which are pictured in Fig. 7-47(*b*).

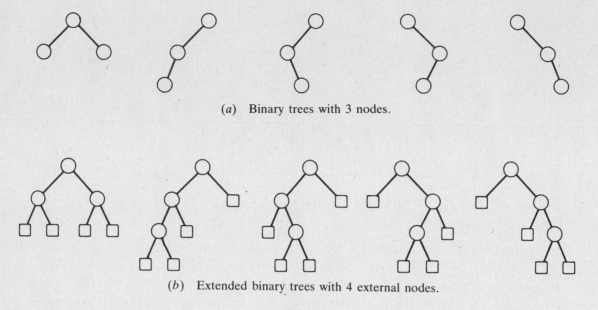

(a) Binary trees with 3 nodes.

(b) Extended binary trees with 4 external nodes.

Fig. 7-47

BINARY SEARCH TREES; HEAPS

7.7   Consider the binary search tree T in Fig. 7-44(b), which is stored in memory as in Fig. 7-43.
Suppose ITEM = 33 is added to the tree T. (a) Find the new tree T. (b) Which changes occur in
Fig. 7-43?

(a)   Compare ITEM = 33 with the root, 60. Since $33 < 60$, move to the left child, 30. Since $33 > 30$, move
to the right child, 55. Since $33 < 55$, move to the left child, 35. Now $33 < 35$, but 35 has no left child.
Hence add ITEM = 33 as a left child of the node 35 to give the tree in Fig. 7-48. The shaded edges
indicate the path down through the tree during the insertion algorithm.

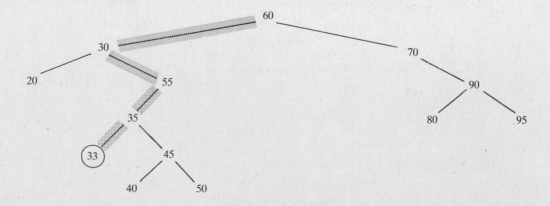

Fig. 7-48

(b)   First, ITEM = 33 is assigned to the first available node. Since AVAIL = 9, set INFO[9] := 33 and set
LEFT[9] := 0 and RIGHT[9] := 0. Also, set AVAIL := 10, the next available node. Finally, set
LEFT[11] := 9 so that ITEM = 33 is the left child of INFO[11] = 35. Figure 7-49 shows the updated
tree T in memory. The shading indicates the changes from the original picture.

	INFO	LEFT	RIGHT
1	20	0	0
2	30	1	13
3	40	0	0
4	50	0	0
5	60	2	6
6	70	0	8
7	80	0	0
8	90	7	14
9	33	0	0
10		0	
11	35	9	12
12	45	3	4
13	55	11	0
14	95	0	0

ROOT

5

AVAIL

10

Fig. 7-49

7.8   Suppose the following list of letters is inserted in order into an empty binary search tree:

$$J, R, D, G, T, E, M, H, P, A, F, Q$$

(a)   Find the final tree T and (b) find the inorder traversal of T.

(a)   Insert the nodes one after the other to obtain the tree in Fig. 7-50.

(b)   The inorder traversal of T follows:

$$A, D, E, F, G, H, J, M, P, Q, R, T$$

Observe that this is the alphabetical listing of the letters.

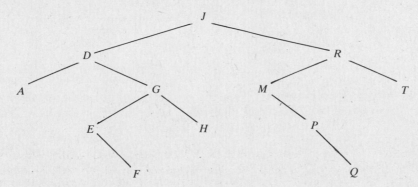

Fig. 7-50

7.9 Consider the binary search tree T in Fig. 7-50. Describe the tree after (*a*) the node *M* is deleted and (*b*) the node *D* is also deleted.

(*a*) The node *M* has only one child, *P*. Hence delete *M* and let *P* become the left child of *R* in place of *M*.

(*b*) The node *D* has two children. Find the inorder successor of *D*, which is the node *E*. First delete *E* from the tree, and then replace *D* by the node *E*.

Figure 7-51 shows the updated tree.

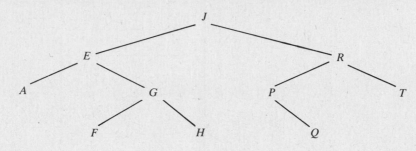

Fig. 7-51

7.10 Suppose *n* data items $A_1, A_2, \ldots, A_N$ are already sorted, i.e.,

$$A_1 < A_2 < \cdots < A_N$$

(*a*) Assuming the items are inserted in order into an empty binary search tree, describe the final tree T.

(*b*) What is the depth D of the tree T?

(*c*) Compare D with the average depth AD of a binary search tree with *n* nodes for (i) $n = 50$, (ii) $n = 100$ and (iii) $n = 500$.

(*a*) The tree will consist of one branch which extends to the right, as pictured in Fig. 7-52.

(*b*) Since T has a branch with all *n* nodes, $D = n$.

(*c*) It is known that $AD = c \log_2 n$, where $c \approx 1.4$. Hence $D(50) = 50$, $AD(50) \approx 9$; $D(100) = 100$, $AD(100) \approx 10$; $D(500) = 500$, $AD(500) \approx 12$.

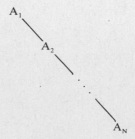

Fig. 7-52

7.11 Consider the minheap H in Fig. 7-53(*a*). (H is a minheap, since the smaller elements are on top of the heap, rather than the larger elements.) Describe the heap after ITEM = 11 is inserted into H.

First insert ITEM as the next node in the complete tree, that is, as the left child of node 44. Then repeatedly compare ITEM with its parent. Since $11 < 44$, interchange 11 and 44. Since $11 < 22$, interchange 11 and 22. Since $11 > 8$, ITEM = 11 has found its appropriate place in the heap. Figure 7-53(*b*) shows the updated heap H. The shaded edges indicate the path of ITEM up the tree.

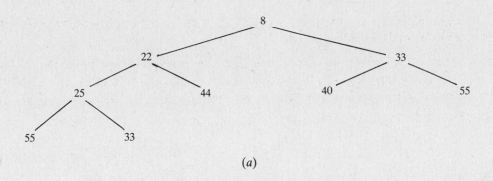

(a)

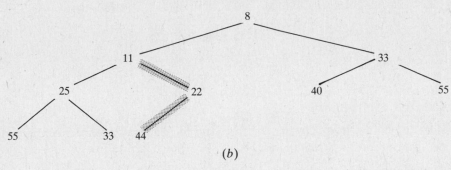

(b)

Fig. 7-53

7.12 Consider the complete tree T with N = 6 nodes in Fig. 7-54. Suppose we form a heap out of T by applying

Call **INSHEAP(A, J, A[J + 1])**

for J = 1, 2, . . . , N − 1. (Here T is stored sequentially in the array A.) Describe the different steps.

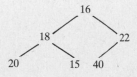

Fig. 7-54

Figure 7-55 shows the different steps. We explain each step separately.

(a) J = 1 and ITEM = A[2] = 18. Since 18 > 16, interchange 18 and 16.

(b) J = 2 and ITEM = A[3] = 22. Since 22 > 18, interchange 22 and 18.

(c) J = 3 and ITEM = A[4] = 20. Since 20 > 16 but 20 < 22, interchange only 20 and 16.

(d) J = 4 and ITEM = A[5] = 15. Since 15 < 20, no interchanges take place.

(e) J = 5 and ITEM = A[6] = 40. Since 40 > 18 and 40 > 22, first interchange 40 and 18 and then interchange 40 and 22.

The tree is now a heap. The dotted edges indicate that an exchange has taken place. The unshaded area indicates that part of the tree which forms a heap. Observe that the heap is created from the top down (although individual elements move up the tree).

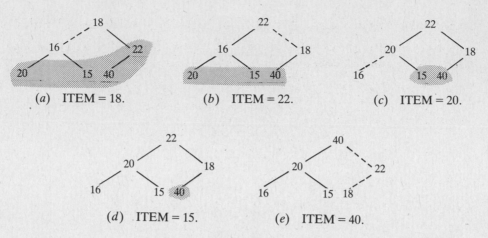

(a)   ITEM = 18.   (b)   ITEM = 22.   (c)   ITEM = 20.

(d)   ITEM = 15.   (e)   ITEM = 40.

Fig. 7-55

MISCELLANEOUS PROBLEMS

7.13   Consider the binary tree T in Fig. 7-1. (a) Find the one-way preorder threading of T. (b) Find the two-way preorder threading of T.

(a)   Replace the right null subtree of a terminal node N by a thread pointing to the successor of N in the preorder traversal of T. Thus there is a thread from D to E, since E is visited after D in the preorder traversal of T. Similarly, there is a thread from F to C, from G to H and from L to K. The threaded tree appears in Fig. 7-56. The terminal node K has no thread, since it is the last node in the preorder traversal of T. (On the other hand, if T had a header node Z, then there would be a thread from K back to Z.)

(b)   There is no two-way preorder threading of T that is analogous to the two-way inorder threading of T.

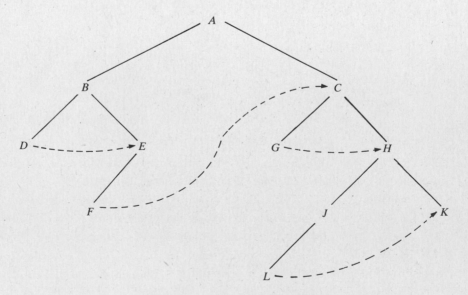

Fig. 7-56   Preorder threaded tree.

7.14   Consider the weighted 2-tree T in Fig. 7-57. Find the weighted path length P of the tree T.

Multiply each weight W_i by the length L_i of the path from the root of T to the node containing the weight, and then sum all such products to obtain P. Thus:

$$P = 4 \cdot 2 + 15 \cdot 4 + 25 \cdot 4 + 5 \cdot 3 + 8 \cdot 2 + 16 \cdot 2 = 8 + 60 + 100 + 15 + 16 + 32 = 231$$

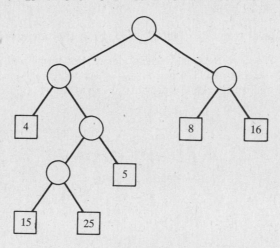

Fig. 7-57

7.15   Suppose the six weights 4, 15, 25, 5, 8, 16 are given. Find a 2-tree T with the given weights and a minimum weighted path length P. (Compare T with the tree in Fig. 7-57.)

Use the Huffman algorithm. That is, repeatedly combine the two subtrees with minimum weights into a single subtree as follows:

(a)   4,   15,   25,   5,   8,   16

(b)   15,   25, ⑨,   8,   16

(c)   15,   25,   ⑰, 16

(d)   25,   17, ㉛

(e)   ㊷, 31

(f)   ⑦³

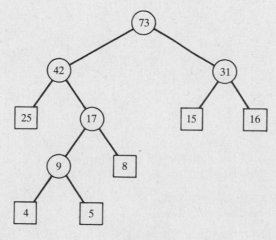

Fig. 7-58

(The circled number indicates the root of the new subtree in the step.) The tree T is drawn from Step (f) backward, yielding Fig. 7-58. With the tree T, compute

$$P = 25 \cdot 2 + 4 \cdot 4 + 5 \cdot 4 + 8 \cdot 3 + 15 \cdot 2 + 16 \cdot 2 = 50 + 16 + 20 + 24 + 30 + 32 = 172$$

(The tree in Fig. 7-57 has weighted path length 231.)

7.16 Consider the general tree T in Fig. 7-59(a). Find the corresponding binary tree T'.

The nodes of T' will be the same as the nodes of the general tree T, and in particular, the root of T' will be the same as the root of T. Furthermore, if N is a node in the binary tree T', then its left child is the first child of N in T and its right child is the next sibling of N in T. Constructing T' from the root down, we obtain the tree in Fig. 7-59(b).

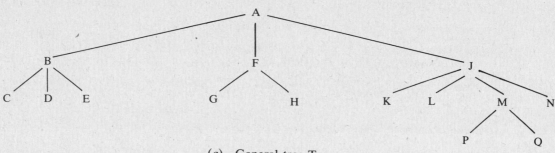

(a)   General tree T.

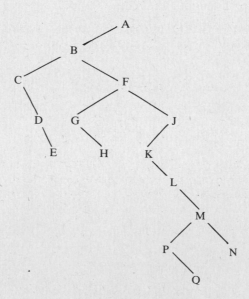

(b)   Binary tree T'.

Fig. 7-59

7.17 Suppose T is a general tree with root R and subtrees $T_1, T_2, \ldots, T_M$. The preorder traversal and the postorder traversal of T are defined as follows:

Preorder: (1)   Process the root R.
               (2)   Traverse the subtrees $T_1, T_2, \ldots, T_M$ in preorder.
Postorder: (1)   Traverse the subtrees $T_1, T_2, \ldots, T_M$ in postorder.
               (2)   Process the root R.

Let T be the general tree in Fig. 7-59(a). (a) Traverse T in preorder. (b) Traverse T in postorder.

Note that T has the root A and subtrees T_1, T_2 and T_3 such that:

T_1 consists of nodes B, C, D and E.

T_2 consists of nodes F, G and H.

T_3 consists of nodes J, K, L, M, N, P and Q.

(a)   The preorder traversal of T consists of the following steps:
   (i)   Process root A.
   (ii) Traverse T_1 in preorder: Process nodes B, C, D, E.
   (iii) Traverse T_2 in preorder: Process nodes F, G, H.
   (iv) Traverse T_3 in preorder: Process nodes J, K, L, M, P, Q, N.

That is, the preorder traversal of T is as follows:

A, B, C, D, E, F, G, H, J, K, L, M, P, Q, N

(b)   The postorder traversal of T consists of the following steps:
   (i)   Traverse T_1 in postorder: Process nodes C, D, E, B.
   (ii) Traverse T_2 in postorder: Process nodes G, H, F.
   (iii) Traverse T_3 in postorder: Process nodes K, L, P, Q, M, N, J.
   (iv) Process root A.

In other words, the postorder traversal of T is as follows:

C, D, E, B, G, H, F, K, L, P, Q, M, N, J, A

7.18   Consider the binary tree T′ in Fig. 7-59(b). Find the preorder, inorder and postorder traversals of T′. Compare them with the preorder and postorder traversals obtained in Prob. 7.17 of the general tree T in Fig. 7-59(a).

Using the binary tree traversal algorithms in Sec. 7.4, we obtain the following traversals of T′:

Preorder: A, B, C, D, E, F, G, H, J, K, L, M, P, Q, N

Inorder: C, D, E, B, G, H, F, K, L, P, Q, M, N, J, A

Postorder: E, D, C, H, G, Q, P, N, M, L, K, J, F, B, A

Observe that the preorder of the binary tree T′ is identical to the preorder of the general T, and that the inorder traversal of the binary tree T′ is identical to the postorder traversal of the general tree T. There is no natural traversal of the general tree T which corresponds to the postorder traversal of its corresponding binary tree T′.

Supplementary Problems

BINARY TREES

7.19   Consider the tree T in Fig. 7-60(a).

(a)   Fill in the values for ROOT, LEFT and RIGHT in Fig. 7-60(b) so that T will be stored in memory.

(b)   Find (i) the depth D of T, (ii) the number of null subtrees and (iii) the descendants of node B.

7.20   List the nodes of the tree T in Fig. 7-60(a) in (a) preorder, (b) inorder and (c) postorder.

7.21   Draw the diagram of the tree T in Fig. 7-61.

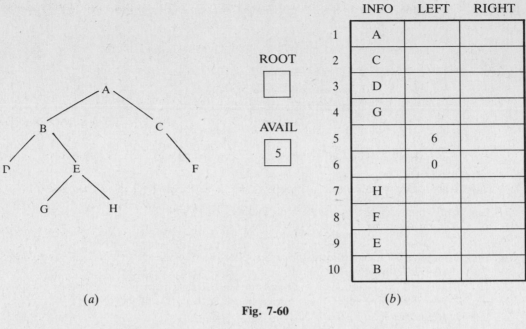

ROOT

[ ]

AVAIL

[5]

	INFO	LEFT	RIGHT
1	A		
2	C		
3	D		
4	G		
5		6	
6		0	
7	H		
8	F		
9	E		
10	B		

(a)   (b)

Fig. 7-60

ROOT

[14]

AVAIL

[8]

	INFO	LEFT	RIGHT
1	H	4	11
2	R	0	0
3		17	
4	P	0	0
5	B	18	7
6		3	
7	E	1	0
8		6	
9	C	0	10
10	F	15	16
11	Q	0	12
12	S	0	0
13		0	
14	A	5	9
15	K	2	0
16	L	0	0
17		13	
18	D	0	0

Fig. 7-61

7.22   Suppose the following sequences list the nodes of a binary tree T in preorder and inorder, respectively:

$$\text{Preorder:} \quad \text{G, B, Q, A, C, K, F, P, D, E, R, H}$$
$$\text{Inorder:} \quad \text{Q, B, K, C, F, A, G, P, E, D, H, R}$$

Draw the diagram of the tree.

7.23   Suppose a binary tree T is in memory and an ITEM of information is given.

(a) Write a procedure which finds the location LOC of ITEM in T (assuming the elements of T are distinct).

(b) Write a procedure which finds the location LOC of ITEM and the location PAR of the parent of ITEM in T.

(c) Write a procedure which finds the number NUM of times ITEM appears in T (assuming the elements of T are not necessarily distinct).

Remark: T is not necessarily a binary search tree.

7.24   Suppose a binary tree T is in memory. Write a nonrecursive procedure for each of the following:

(a) Finding the number of nodes in T.

(b) Finding the depth D of T.

(c) Finding the number of terminal nodes in T.

7.25   Suppose a binary tree T is in memory. Write a procedure which deletes all the terminal nodes in T.

7.26   Suppose ROOTA points to a binary tree T_1 in memory. Write a procedure which makes a copy T_2 of the tree T_1 using ROOTB as a pointer.

BINARY SEARCH TREES

7.27   Suppose the following eight numbers are inserted in order into an empty binary search tree T:

$$50, 33, 44, 22, 77, 35, 60, 40$$

Draw the tree T.

7.28   Consider the binary search tree T in Fig. 7-62. Draw the tree T if each of the following operations is applied to the original tree T. (That is, the operations are applied independently, not successively.)

(a)   Node 20 is added to T.   (d)   Node 22 is deleted from T.

(b)   Node 15 is added to T.   (e)   Node 25 is deleted from T.

(c)   Node 88 is added to T.   (f)   Node 75 is deleted from T.

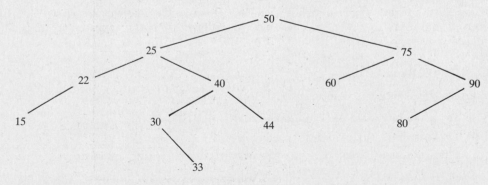

Fig. 7-62

7.29 Consider the binary search tree T in Fig. 7-62. Draw the final tree T if the six operations in Problem 7.28 are applied one after the other (not independently) to T.

7.30 Draw the binary search tree T in Fig. 7-63.

		INFO	LEFT	RIGHT
ROOT	1	Jones	7	0
4	2	Fox	11	1
AVAIL	3		8	
3	4	Murphy	2	15
	5		13	
	6	Thomas	0	0
	7	Green	0	0
	8		9	
	9		10	
	10		5	
	11	Conroy	0	0
	12	Parker	0	0
	13		14	
	14		0	
	15	Rosen	12	6

Fig. 7-63

7.31 Consider the binary search tree T in Fig. 7-63. Describe the changes in INFO, LEFT, RIGHT, ROOT and AVAIL if each of the following operations is applied independently (not successively) to T.

      (a) Davis is added to T.   (d) Parker is deleted from T.

      (b) Harris is added to T.   (e) Fox is deleted from T.

      (c) Smith is added to T.   (f) Murphy is deleted from T.

7.32 Consider the binary search tree T in Fig. 7-63. Describe the final changes in INFO, LEFT, RIGHT, ROOT and AVAIL if the six operations in Problem 7.31 are applied one after the other (not independently) to T.

MISCELLANEOUS PROBLEMS

7.33 Consider the binary tree T in Fig. 7-60(a).

    (a) Draw the one-way inorder threading of T.

    (b) Draw the one-way preorder threading of T.

    (c) Draw the two-way inorder threading of T.

In each case, show how the threaded tree will appear in memory using the data in Fig. 7-60(b).

7.34   Consider the complete tree T with N = 10 nodes in Fig. 7-64. Suppose a maxheap is formed out of T by applying

$$\text{Call INSHEAP}(A, J, A[J + 1])$$

for J = 1, 2, . . . , N − 1. (Assume T is stored sequentially in the array A.) Find the final maxheap.

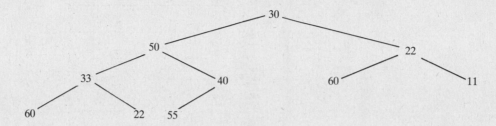

Fig. 7-64

7.35   Repeat Problem 7.34 for the tree T in Fig. 7-64, except now form a minheap out of T instead of a maxheap.

7.36   Draw the 2-tree corresponding to each of the following algebraic expressions:

   (a) $E_1 = (a - 3b)(2x - y)^3$
   (b) $E_2 = (2a + 5b)^3(x - 7y)^4$

7.37   Consider the 2-tree in Fig. 7-65. Find the Huffman coding for the seven letters determined by the tree T.

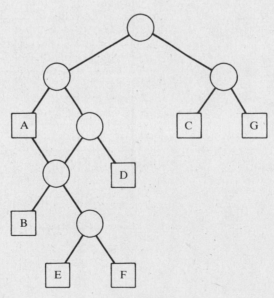

Fig. 7-65

7.38   Suppose the 7 data items A, B, . . . , G are assigned the following weights:

$$(A, 13),\quad (B, 2),\quad (C, 19),\quad (D, 23),\quad (E, 29),\quad (F, 5),\quad (G, 9)$$

Find the weighted path length P of the tree in Fig. 7-65.

7.39   Using the data in Problem 7.38, find a 2-tree with a minimum weighted path length P. What is the Huffman coding for the 7 letters using this new tree?

7.40 Consider the forest F in Fig.7-66, which consists of three trees with roots A, B and C, respectively.

  (*a*) Find the binary tree F′ corresponding to the forest F.

  (*b*) Fill in values for ROOT, CHILD and SIB in Fig. 7-67 so that F will be stored in memory.

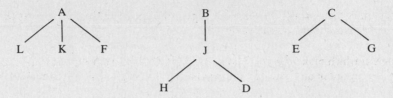

Fig. 7-66   Forest F.

ROOT		INFO	CHILD	SIB
	1	A		
	2	C		
	3	E		
	4	G		
	5	J		
	6	L		
	7	·		
	8	K		
	9	H		
	10	F		
	11	D		
	12	B		

Fig. 7-67

7.41 Suppose T is a complete tree with n nodes and depth D. Prove (*a*) $2^{D-1} - 1 < n \leq 2^D - 1$ and (*b*) $D \approx \log_2 n$.

Hint: Use the following identity with $x = 2$:
$$1 + x + x^2 + x^3 + \cdots + x^n = \frac{x^{n+1} - 1}{x - 1}$$

7.42 Suppose T is an extended binary tree. Prove:

  (*a*) $N_E = N_I + 1$, where N_E is the number of external nodes and N_I is the number of internal nodes.

  (*b*) $L_E = L_I + 2n$, where L_E is the external path length, L_I is the internal path length and n is the number of internal nodes.

Programming Problems

Problems 7.43 to 7.45 refer to the tree T in Fig. 7-1, which is stored in memory as in Fig. 7-68.

7.43   Write a program which prints the nodes of T in (*a*) preorder, (*b*) inorder and (*c*) postorder.

7.44   Write a program which prints the terminal nodes of T in (*a*) preorder (*b*) inorder and (*c*) postorder. (*Note*: All three lists should be the same.)

7.45   Write a program which makes a copy T' of T using ROOTB as a pointer. Test the program by printing the nodes of T' in preorder and inorder and comparing the lists with those obtained in Prob. 7.43.

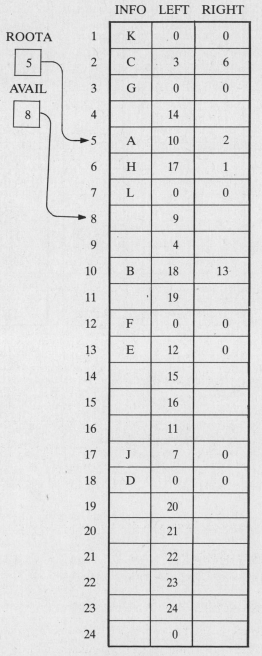

Fig. 7-68

7.46   Translate heapsort into a subprogram HEAPSORT(A, N) which sorts the array A with N elements. Test the program using

   (*a*)   44, 33, 11, 55, 77, 90, 40, 60, 99, 22, 88, 66   (*b*)   D, A, T, A, S, T, R, U, C, T, U, R, E, S

   Problems 7.47 to 7.52 refer to the list of employee records which are stored either as in Fig. 7-8 or as in Fig. 7-69. Each is a binary search tree with respect to the NAME key, but Fig. 7-69 uses a header node, which also acts as a sentinel. (Compare these problems with Probs. 5.41 to 5.46 in Chap. 5.)

		NAME	SSN	SEX	SALARY	LEFT	RIGHT
HEAD	1					0	
5	2	Davis	192-38-7282	Female	22 800	5	12
AVAIL	3	Kelly	165-64-3351	Male	19 000	5	5
8	4	Green	175-56-2251	Male	27 200	2	5
	5		009		191 600	14	5
	6	Brown	178-52-1065	Female	14 700	5	5
	7	Lewis	181-58-9939	Female	16 400	3	10
	8					11	
	9	Cohen	177-44-4557	Male	19 000	6	4
	10	Rubin	135-46-6262	Female	15 500	5	5
	11					13	
	12	Evans	168-56-8113	Male	34 200	5	5
	13					1	
	14	Harris	208-56-1654	Female	22 800	9	7

Fig. 7-69

7.47   Write a program which prints the list of employee records in alphabetical order. (*Hint*: Print the records in inorder.)

7.48   Write a program which reads the name NNN of an employee and prints the employee's record. Test the program using (*a*) Evans, (*b*) Smith and (*c*) Lewis.

7.49   Write a program which reads the social security number SSS of an employee and prints the employee's record. Test the program using (*a*) 165-64-3351, (*b*) 135-46-6262 and (*c*) 177-44-5555.

7.50   Write a program which reads an integer K and prints the name of each male employee when K = 1 or of each female employee when K = 2. Test the program using (*a*) K = 2, (*b*) K = 5 and (*c*) K = 1.

7.51   Write a program which reads the name NNN of an employee and deletes the employee's record from the structure. Test the program using (*a*) Davis, (*b*) Jones and (*c*) Rubin.

7.52   Write a program which reads the record of a new employee and inserts the record into the file. Test the program using:

   (*a*)   Fletcher; 168-52-3388; Female; 21 000
   (*b*)   Nelson; 175-32-2468; Male; 19 000

Chapter 8

Graphs and Their Applications

8.1 INTRODUCTION

This chapter investigates another nonlinear data structure: the *graph*. As we have done with other data structures, we discuss the representation of graphs in memory and present various operations and algorithms on them. In particular, we discuss the breadth-first search and the depth-first search of our graphs. Certain applications of graphs, including topological sorting, are also covered.

8.2 GRAPH THEORY TERMINOLOGY

This section summarizes some of the main terminology associated with the theory of graphs. Unfortunately, there is no standard terminology in graph theory. The reader is warned, therefore, that our definitions may be slightly different from the definitions used by other texts on data structures and graph theory.

Graphs and Multigraphs

A graph G consists of two things:

(1) A set V of elements called *nodes* (or *points* or *vertices*)

(2) A set E of *edges* such that each edge e in E is identified with a unique (unordered) pair $[u, v]$ of nodes in V, denoted by $e = [u, v]$

Sometimes we indicate the parts of a graph by writing $G = (V, E)$.

Suppose $e = [u, v]$. Then the nodes u and v are called the *endpoints* of e, and u and v are said to be *adjacent nodes* or *neighbors*. The *degree* of a node u, written $\deg(u)$, is the number of edges containing u. If $\deg(u) = 0$—that is, if u does not belong to any edge—then u is called an *isolated* node.

A *path* P of *length* n from a node u to a node v is defined as a sequence of $n + 1$ nodes.

$$P = (v_0, v_1, v_2, \ldots, v_n)$$

such that $u = v_0$; v_{i-1} is adjacent to v_i for $i = 1, 2, \ldots, n$; and $v_n = v$. The path P is said to be *closed* if $v_0 = v_n$. The path P is said to be *simple* if all the nodes are distinct, with the exception that v_0 may equal v_n; that is, P is simple if the nodes $v_0, v_1, \ldots, v_{n-1}$ are distinct and the nodes $v_1, v_2, \ldots, v_n$ are distinct. A *cycle* is a closed simple path with length 3 or more. A cycle of length k is called a *k-cycle*.

A *graph* G is said to be *connected* if there is a path between any two of its nodes. We will show (in Prob. 8.18) that if there is a path P from a node u to a node v, then, by eliminating unnecessary edges, one can obtain a simple path Q from u to v; accordingly, we can state the following proposition.

Proposition 8.1: A graph G is connected if and only if there is a simple path between any two nodes in G.

A graph G is said to be *complete* if every node u in G is adjacent to every other node v in G. Clearly such a graph is connected. A complete graph with n nodes will have $n(n - 1)/2$ edges.

A connected graph T without any cycles is called a *tree graph* or *free tree* or, simply, a *tree*. This means, in particular, that there is a unique simple path P between any two nodes u and v in T (Prob. 8.18). Furthermore, if T is a finite tree with m nodes, then T will have $m - 1$ edges (Prob. 8.20).

A graph G is said to be *labeled* if its edges are assigned data. In particular, G is said to be *weighted* if each edge e in G is assigned a nonnegative numerical value $w(e)$ called the *weight* or *length* of e. In such a case, each path P in G is assigned a *weight* or *length* which is the sum of the weights of the edges along the path P. If we are given no other information about weights, we may assume any graph G to be weighted by assigning the weight $w(e) = 1$ to each edge e in G.

The definition of a graph may be generalized by permitting the following:

(1)   *Multiple edges.* Distinct edges e and e' are called *multiple edges* if they connect the same endpoints, that is, if $e = [u, v]$ and $e' = [u, v]$.

(2)   *Loops.* An edge e is called a *loop* if it has identical endpoints, that is, if $e = [u, u]$.

Such a generalization M is called a *multigraph*. In other words, the definition of a graph usually does not allow either multiple edges or loops.

A multigraph M is said to be *finite* if it has a finite number of nodes and a finite number of edges. Observe that a graph G with a finite number of nodes must automatically have a finite number of edges and so must be finite; but this is not necessarily true for a multigraph M, since M may have multiple edges. Unless otherwise specified, graphs and multigraphs in this text shall be finite.

EXAMPLE 8.1

(a)   Figure 8-1(a) is a picture of a connected graph with 5 nodes—A, B, C, D and E—and 7 edges:

$$[A, B], \quad [B, C], \quad [C, D], \quad [D, E], \quad [A, E], \quad [C, E] \quad [A, C]$$

There are two simple paths of length 2 from B to E: (B, A, E) and (B, C, E). There is only one simple path of length 2 from B to D: (B, C, D). We note that (B, A, D) is not a path, since $[A, D]$ is not an edge. There are two 4-cycles in the graph:

$$[A, B, C, E, A] \quad \text{and} \quad [A, C, D, E, A].$$

Note that $\deg(A) = 3$, since A belongs to 3 edges. Similarly, $\deg(C) = 4$ and $\deg(D) = 2$.

(b)   Figure 8-1(b) is not a graph but a multigraph. The reason is that it has multiple edges—$e_4 = [B, C]$ and $e_5 = [B, C]$—and it has a loop, $e_6 = [D, D]$. The definition of a graph usually does not allow either multiple edges or loops.

(c)   Figure 8-1(c) is a tree graph with $m = 6$ nodes and, consequently, $m - 1 = 5$ edges. The reader can verify that there is a unique simple path between any two nodes of the tree graph.

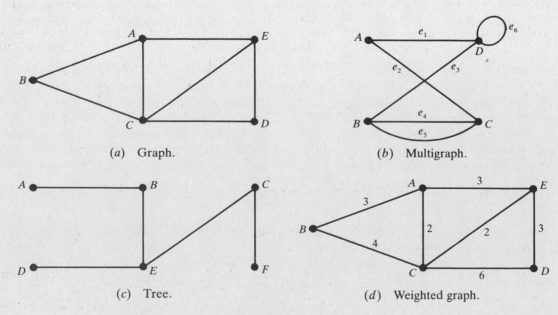

(a)   Graph.   (b)   Multigraph.

(c)   Tree.   (d)   Weighted graph.

Fig. 8-1

(d) Figure 8-1(d) is the same graph as in Fig. 8-1(a), except that now the graph is weighted. Observe that $P_1 = (B, C, D)$ and $P_2 = (B, A, E, D)$ are both paths from node B to node D. Although P_2 contains more edges than P_1, the weight $w(P_2) = 9$ is less than the weight $w(P_1) = 10$.

Directed Graphs

A *directed graph* G, also called a *digraph* or *graph*, is the same as a multigraph except that each edge e in G is assigned a direction, or in other words, each edge e is identified with an ordered pair (u, v) of nodes in G rather than an unordered pair $[u, v]$.

Suppose G is a directed graph with a directed edge $e = (u, v)$. Then e is also called an *arc*. Moreover, the following terminology is used:

(1) *e begins* at u and *ends* at v.

(2) u is the *origin* or *initial point* of e, and v is the *destination* or *terminal point* of e.

(3) u is a *predecessor* of v, and v is a *successor* or *neighbor* of u.

(4) u is *adjacent to* v, and v is *adjacent to* u.

The *outdegree* of a node u in G, written outdeg(u), is the number of edges beginning at u. Similarly, the *indegree* of u, written indeg(u), is the number of edges ending at u. A node u is called a *source* if it has a positive outdegree but zero indegree. Similarly, u is called a *sink* if it has a zero outdegree but a positive indegree.

The notions of *path*, *simple path* and *cycle* carry over from undirected graphs to directed graphs except that now the direction of each edge in a path (cycle) must agree with the direction of the path (cycle). A node v is said to be *reachable* from a node u if there is a (directed) path from u to v.

A directed graph G is said to be *connected*, or *strongly connected*, if for each pair u, v of nodes in G there is a path from u to v and there is also a path from v to u. On the other hand, G is said to be *unilaterally connected* if for any pair u, v of nodes in G there is a path from u to v or a path from v to u.

EXAMPLE 8.2

Figure 8-2 shows a directed graph G with 4 nodes and 7 (directed) edges. The edges e_2 and e_3 are said to be *parallel*, since each begins at B and ends at A. The edge e_7 is a *loop*, since it begins and ends at the same point, B. The sequence $P_1 = (D, C, B, A)$ is not a path, since (C, B) is not an edge—that is, the direction of the edge $e_5 = (B, C)$ does not agree with the direction of the path P_1. On the other hand, $P_2 = (D, B, A)$ is a path from D to A, since (D, B) and (B, A) are edges. Thus A is reachable from D. There is no path from C to any other node, so G is not strongly connected. However, G is unilaterally connected. Note that indeg(D) = 1 and outdeg(D) = 2. Node C is a sink, since indeg(C) = 2 but outdeg(C) = 0. No node in G is a source.

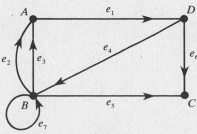

Fig. 8-2

Let T be any nonempty tree graph. Suppose we choose any node R in T. Then T with this designated node R is called a *rooted tree* and R is called its *root*. Recall that there is a unique simple path from the root R to any other node in T. This defines a direction to the edges in T, so the rooted tree T may be viewed as a directed graph. Furthermore, suppose we also order the successors of each node v in T. Then T is called an *ordered rooted tree*. Ordered rooted trees are nothing more than the general trees discussed in Chap. 7.

A directed graph G is said to be *simple* if G has no parallel edges. A simple graph G may have loops, but it cannot have more than one loop at a given node. A nondirected graph G may be viewed as a simple directed graph by assuming that each edge $[u, v]$ in G represents two directed edges, (u, v) and (v, u). (Observe that we use the notation $[u, v]$ to denote an unordered pair and the notation (u, v) to denote an ordered pair.)

Warning: The main subject matter of this chapter is simple directed graphs. Accordingly, unless otherwise stated or implied, the term "graph" shall mean simple directed graph, and the term "edge" shall mean directed edge.

8.3 SEQUENTIAL REPRESENTATION OF GRAPHS; ADJACENCY MATRIX; PATH MATRIX

There are two standard ways of maintaining a graph G in the memory of a computer. One way, called the *sequential representation* of G, is by means of its adjacency matrix A. The other way, called the *linked representation* of G, is by means of linked lists of neighbors. This section covers the first representation, and shows how the adjacency matrix A of G can be used to easily answer certain questions of connectivity in G. The linked representation of G will be covered in Sec. 8.5.

Regardless of the way one maintains a graph G in the memory of the computer, the graph G is normally input into the computer by using its formal definition: a collection of nodes and a collection of edges.

Adjacency Matrix

Suppose G is a simple directed graph with m nodes, and suppose the nodes of G have been ordered and are called $v_1, v_2, \ldots, v_m$. Then the *adjacency matrix* $A = (a_{ij})$ of the graph G is the $m \times m$ matrix defined as follows:

$$a_{ij} = \begin{cases} 1 & \text{if } v_i \text{ is adjacent to } v_j, \text{ that is, if there is an edge } (v_i, v_j) \\ 0 & \text{otherwise} \end{cases}$$

Such a matrix A, which contains entries of only 0 and 1, is called a *bit matrix* or a *Boolean matrix*.

The adjacency matrix A of the graph G does depend on the ordering of the nodes of G; that is, a different ordering of the nodes may result in a different adjacency matrix. However, the matrices resulting from two different orderings are closely related in that one can be obtained from the other by simply interchanging rows and columns. Unless otherwise stated, we will assume that the nodes of our graph G have a fixed ordering.

Suppose G is an undirected graph. Then the adjacency matrix A of G will be a *symmetric matrix*, i.e., one in which $a_{ij} = a_{ji}$ for every i and j. This follows from the fact that each undirected edge $[u, v]$ corresponds to the two directed edges (u, v) and (v, u).

The above matrix representation of a graph may be extended to multigraphs. Specifically, if G is a multigraph, then the *adjacency matrix* of G is the $m \times m$ matrix $A = (a_{ij})$ defined by setting a_{ij} equal to the number of edges from v_i to v_j.

EXAMPLE 8.3

Consider the graph G in Fig. 8-3. Suppose the nodes are stored in memory in a linear array DATA as follows:

DATA: X, Y, Z, W

Then we assume that the ordering of the nodes in G is as follows: $v_1 = X$, $v_2 = Y$, $v_3 = Z$ and $v_4 = W$. The adjacency matrix A of G is as follows:

$$A = \begin{pmatrix} 0 & 0 & 0 & 1 \\ 1 & 0 & 1 & 1 \\ 1 & 0 & 0 & 1 \\ 0 & 0 & 1 & 0 \end{pmatrix}$$

Note that the number of 1's in A is equal to the number of edges in G.

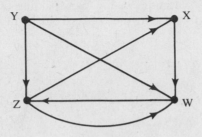

Fig. 8-3

Consider the powers A, A^2, A^3, . . . of the adjacency matrix A of a graph G. Let

$$a_K(i, j) = \text{the } ij \text{ entry in the matrix } A^K$$

Observe that $a_1(i, j) = a_{ij}$ gives the number of paths of length 1 from node v_i to node v_j. One can show that $a_2(i, j)$ gives the number of paths of length 2 from v_i to v_j. In fact, we prove in Prob. 8.19 the following general result.

Proposition 8.2:   Let A be the adjacency matrix of a graph G. Then $a_K(i, j)$, the ij entry in the matrix A^K, gives the number of paths of length K from v_i to v_j.

Consider again the graph G in Fig. 8-3, whose adjacency matrix A is given in Example 8.3. The powers A^2, A^3 and A^4 of the matrix A follow:

$$A^2 = \begin{pmatrix} 0 & 0 & 1 & 0 \\ 1 & 0 & 1 & 2 \\ 0 & 0 & 1 & 1 \\ 1 & 0 & 0 & 1 \end{pmatrix} \qquad A^3 = \begin{pmatrix} 1 & 0 & 0 & 1 \\ 1 & 0 & 2 & 2 \\ 1 & 0 & 1 & 1 \\ 0 & 0 & 1 & 1 \end{pmatrix} \qquad A^4 = \begin{pmatrix} 0 & 0 & 1 & 1 \\ 2 & 0 & 2 & 3 \\ 1 & 0 & 1 & 2 \\ 1 & 0 & 1 & 1 \end{pmatrix}$$

Accordingly, in particular, there is a path of length 2 from v_4 to v_1, there are two paths of length 3 from v_2 to v_3, and there are three paths of length 4 from v_2 to v_4. (Here, $v_1 = \text{X}$, $v_2 = \text{Y}$, $v_3 = \text{Z}$ and $v_4 = \text{W}$.)

Suppose we now define the matrix B_r as follows:

$$B_r = A + A^2 + A^3 + \cdots + A^r$$

Then the ij entry of the matrix B_r gives the number of paths of length r or less from node v_i to v_j.

Path Matrix

Let G be a simple directed graph with m nodes, $v_1, v_2, \ldots, v_m$. The *path matrix* or *reachability matrix* of G is the m-square matrix $P = (p_{ij})$ defined as follows:

$$P_{ij} = \begin{cases} 1 & \text{if there is a path from } v_i \text{ to } v_j \\ 0 & \text{otherwise} \end{cases}$$

Suppose there is a path from v_i to v_j. Then there must be a simple path from v_i to v_j when $v_i \neq v_j$, or there must be a cycle from v_i to v_j when $v_i = v_j$. Since G has only m nodes, such a simple path must have length $m - 1$ or less, or such a cycle must have length m or less. This means that there is a nonzero ij

entry in the matrix B_m, defined at the end of the preceding subsection. Accordingly, we have the following relationship between the path matrix P and the adjacency matrix A.

Proposition 8.3:   Let A be the adjacency matrix and let $P = (p_{ij})$ be the path matrix of a digraph G. Then $p_{ij} = 1$ if and only if there is a nonzero number in the ij entry of the matrix

$$B_m = A + A^2 + A^3 + \cdots + A^m$$

Consider the graph G with $m = 4$ nodes in Fig. 8-3. Adding the matrices A, A^2, A^3 and A^4, we obtain the following matrix B_4, and, replacing the nonzero entries in B_4 by 1, we obtain the path matrix P of the graph G:

$$B_4 = \begin{pmatrix} 1 & 0 & 2 & 3 \\ 5 & 0 & 6 & 8 \\ 3 & 0 & 3 & 5 \\ 2 & 0 & 3 & 3 \end{pmatrix} \quad \text{and} \quad P = \begin{pmatrix} 1 & 0 & 1 & 1 \\ 1 & 0 & 1 & 1 \\ 1 & 0 & 1 & 1 \\ 1 & 0 & 1 & 1 \end{pmatrix}$$

Examining the matrix P, we see that the node v_2 is not reachable from any of the other nodes.

Recall that a directed graph G is said to be *strongly connected* if, for any pair of nodes u and v in G, there are both a path from u to v and a path from v to u. Accordingly, G is strongly connected if and only if the path matrix P of G has no zero entries. Thus the graph G in Fig. 8-3 is not strongly connected.

The *transitive closure* of a graph G is defined to be the graph G' such that G' has the same nodes as G and there is an edge (v_i, v_j) in G' whenever there is a path from v_i to v_j in G. Accordingly, the path matrix P of the graph G is precisely the adjacency matrix of its transitive closure G'. Furthermore, a graph G is strongly connected if and only if its transitive closure is a complete graph.

Remark: The adjacency matrix A and the path matrix P of a graph G may be viewed as logical (Boolean) matrices, where 0 represents "false" and 1 represents "true." Thus, the logical operations of $\wedge$(AND) and $\vee$(OR) may be applied to the entries of A and P. The values of $\wedge$ and $\vee$ appear in Fig. 8-4. These operations will be used in the next section.

$\wedge$	0	1
0	0	0
1	0	1

$\vee$	0	1
0	0	1
1	1	1

(a) AND.   (b) OR.

Fig. 8-4

8.4 WARSHALL'S ALGORITHM; SHORTEST PATHS

Let G be a directed graph with m nodes, $v_1, v_2, \ldots, v_m$. Suppose we want to find the path matrix P of the graph G. Warshall gave an algorithm for this purpose that is much more efficient than calculating the powers of the adjacency matrix A and using Proposition 8.3. This algorithm is described in this section, and a similar algorithm is used to find shortest paths in G when G is weighted.

First we define m-square Boolean matrices $P_0, P_1, \ldots, P_m$ as follows. Let $P_k[i, j]$ denote the ij entry of the matrix P_k. Then we define:

$$P_k[i, j] = \begin{cases} 1 & \text{if there is a simple path from } v_i \text{ to } v_j \\ & \text{which does not use any other nodes} \\ & \text{except possibly } v_1, v_2, \ldots, v_k \\ 0 & \text{otherwise} \end{cases}$$

In other words,

$$P_0[i, j] = 1 \qquad \text{if there is an edge from } v_i \text{ to } v_j$$

$$P_1[i, j] = 1 \qquad \text{if there is a simple path from } v_i \text{ to } v_j$$
which does not use any other nodes
except possibly v_1

$$P_2[i, j] = 1 \qquad \text{if there is a simple path from } v_i \text{ to } v_j$$
which does not use any other nodes
except possibly v_1 and v_2

. . . .

First observe that the matrix $P_0 = A$, the adjacency matrix of G. Furthermore, since G has only m nodes, the last matrix $P_m = P$, the path matrix of G.

Warshall observed that $P_k[i, j] = 1$ can occur only if one of the following two cases occurs:

(1) There is a simple path from v_i to v_j which does not use any other nodes except possibly $v_1, v_2, \ldots, v_{k-1}$; hence

$$P_{k-1}[i, j] = 1$$

(2) There is a simple path from v_i to v_k and a simple path from v_k to v_j where each path does not use any other nodes except possibly $v_1, v_2, \ldots, v_{k-1}$; hence

$$P_{k-1}[i, k] = 1 \qquad \text{and} \qquad P_{k-1}[k, j] = 1$$

These two cases are pictured, respectively, in Fig. 8-5(a) and (b), where

$$\longrightarrow \cdots \longrightarrow$$

denotes part of a simple path which does not use any nodes except possibly $v_1, v_2, \ldots, v_{k-1}$.

$$v_i \longrightarrow \cdots \longrightarrow v_j \qquad\qquad v_i \longrightarrow \cdots \longrightarrow v_k \longrightarrow \cdots \longrightarrow v_j$$

$$(a) \qquad\qquad\qquad\qquad (b)$$

Fig. 8-5

Accordingly, the elements of the matrix P_k can be obtained by

$$P_k[i, j] = P_{k-1}[i, j] \vee (P_{k-1}[i, k] \wedge P_{k-1}[k, j])$$

where we use the logical operations of $\wedge$ (AND) and $\vee$ (OR). In other words we can obtain each entry in the matrix P_k by looking at only three entries in the matrix P_{k-1}. Warshall's algorithm follows.

Algorithm 8.1: (Warshall's Algorithm) A directed graph G with M nodes is maintained in memory by its adjacency matrix A. This algorithm finds the (Boolean) path matrix P of the graph G.

1. Repeat for I, J = 1, 2, . . . , M: [Initializes P.]
     If A[I, J] = 0, then: Set P[I, J] := 0;
     Else: Set P[I, J] := 1.
   [End of loop.]
2. Repeat Steps 3 and 4 for K = 1, 2, . . . , M: [Updates P.]
3.   Repeat Step 4 for I = 1, 2, . . . , M:
4.   Repeat for J = 1, 2, . . . , M:
             Set P[I, J] := P[I, J] ∨ (P[I, K] ∧ P[K, J]).
           [End of loop.]
       [End of Step 3 loop.]
   [End of Step 2 loop.]
5. Exit.

Shortest-Path Algorithm

Let G be a directed graph with m nodes, $v_1, v_2, \ldots, v_m$, Suppose G is *weighted*; that is, suppose each edge e in G is assigned a nonnegative number $w(e)$ called the *weight* or *length* of the edge e. Then G may be maintained in memory by its *weight matrix* $W = (w_{ij})$, defined as follows:

$$w_{ij} = \begin{cases} w(e) & \text{if there is an edge } e \text{ from } v_i \text{ to } v_j \\ 0 & \text{if there is no edge from } v_i \text{ to } v_j \end{cases}$$

The path matrix P tells us whether or not there are paths between the nodes. Now we want to find a matrix Q which will tell us the lengths of the shortest paths between the nodes or, more exactly, a matrix $Q = (q_{ij})$ where

$$q_{ij} = \text{length of a shortest path from } v_i \text{ to } v_j$$

Next we describe a modification of Warshall's algorithm which finds us the matrix Q.

Here we define a sequence of matrices $Q_0, Q_1, \ldots, Q_m$ (analogous to the above matrices $P_0, P_1, \ldots, P_m$) whose entries are defined as follows:

$Q_k[i, j] =$ the smaller of the length of the preceding path from v_i to v_j or the sum of the lengths of the preceding paths from v_i to v_k and from v_k to v_j

More exactly,

$$Q_k[i, j] = \text{MIN}(Q_{k-1}[i, j], \quad Q_{k-1}[i, k] + Q_{k-1}[k, j])$$

The initial matrix Q_0 is the same as the weight matrix W except that each 0 in W is replaced by ∞ (or a very, very large number). The final matrix Q_m will be the desired matrix Q.

EXAMPLE 8.4

Consider the weighted graph G in Fig. 8-6. Assume $v_1 = \text{R}$, $v_2 = \text{S}$, $v_3 = \text{T}$ and $v_4 = \text{U}$. Then the weight matrix W of G is as follows:

$$W = \begin{pmatrix} 7 & 5 & 0 & 0 \\ 7 & 0 & 0 & 2 \\ 0 & 3 & 0 & 0 \\ 4 & 0 & 1 & 0 \end{pmatrix}$$

Applying the modified Warshall's algorithm, we obtain the following matrices Q_0, Q_1, Q_2, Q_3 and $Q_4 = Q$. To the right of each matrix Q_k, we show the matrix of paths which correspond to the lengths in the matrix Q_k.

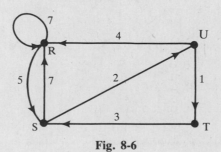

Fig. 8-6

$$Q_0 = \begin{pmatrix} 7 & 5 & \infty & \infty \\ 7 & \infty & \infty & 2 \\ \infty & 3 & \infty & \infty \\ 4 & \infty & 1 & \infty \end{pmatrix} \qquad \begin{pmatrix} RR & RS & - & - \\ SR & - & - & SU \\ - & TS & - & - \\ UR & - & UT & - \end{pmatrix}$$

$$Q_1 = \begin{pmatrix} 7 & 5 & \infty & \infty \\ 7 & 12 & \infty & 2 \\ \infty & 3 & \infty & \infty \\ 4 & ⑨ & 1 & \infty \end{pmatrix} \qquad \begin{pmatrix} RR & RS & - & - \\ SR & SRS & - & SU \\ - & TS & - & - \\ UR & URS & UT & - \end{pmatrix}$$

$$Q_2 = \begin{pmatrix} 7 & 5 & ⊗ & 7 \\ 7 & 12 & \infty & 2 \\ 10 & 3 & \infty & 5 \\ 4 & 9 & 1 & 11 \end{pmatrix} \qquad \begin{pmatrix} RR & RS & - & RSU \\ SR & SRS & - & SU \\ TSR & TS & - & TSU \\ UR & URS & UT & URS \end{pmatrix}$$

$$Q_3 = \begin{pmatrix} 7 & 5 & \infty & 7 \\ 7 & 12 & \infty & 2 \\ 10 & 3 & \infty & 5 \\ 4 & ④ & 1 & 6 \end{pmatrix} \qquad \begin{pmatrix} RR & RS & - & RSU \\ SR & SRS & - & SU \\ TSR & TS & - & TSU \\ UR & UTS & UT & UTSU \end{pmatrix}$$

$$Q_4 = \begin{pmatrix} 7 & 5 & 8 & 7 \\ 7 & 11 & 3 & 2 \\ ⑨ & 3 & 6 & 5 \\ 4 & 4 & 1 & 6 \end{pmatrix} \qquad \begin{pmatrix} RR & RS & RSUT & RSU \\ SR & SURS & SUT & SU \\ TSUR & TS & TSUT & TSU \\ UR & UTS & UT & UTSU \end{pmatrix}$$

We indicate how the circled entries are obtained:

$$Q_1[4, 2] = MIN(Q_0[4, 2], Q_0[4, 1] + Q_0[1, 2]) = MIN(\infty, 4 + 5) = 9$$
$$Q_2[1, 3] = MIN(Q_1[1, 3], Q_1[1, 2] + Q_1[2, 3]) = MIN(\infty, 5 + \infty) = \infty$$
$$Q_3[4, 2] = MIN(Q_2[4, 2], Q_2[4, 3] + Q_2[3, 2]) = MIN(9, 3 + 1) = 4$$
$$Q_4[3, 1] = MIN(Q_3[3, 1], Q_3[3, 4] + Q_3[4, 1]) = MIN(10, 5 + 4) = 9$$

The formal statement of the algorithm follows.

Algorithm 8.2:   (Shortest-Path Algorithm) A weighted graph G with M nodes is maintained in memory by its weight matrix W. This algorithm finds a matrix Q such that Q[I, J] is the length of a shortest path from node V_I to node V_J. INFINITY is a very large number, and MIN is the minimum value function.

1.   Repeat for I, J = 1, 2, . . . , M: [Initializes Q.]
         W[I, J] = 0, then: Set Q[I, J] := INFINITY;
         Else: Set Q[I, J] := W[I, J].
     [End of loop.]
2.   Repeat Steps 3 and 4 for K = 1, 2, . . . , M: [Updates Q.]
3.   Repeat Step 4 for I = 1, 2, . . . , M:
4.   Repeat for J = 1, 2, . . . , M:
                 Set Q[I, J] := MIN(Q[I, J], Q[I, K] + Q[K, J]).
             [End of loop.]
         [End of Step 3 loop.]
     [End of Step 2 loop.]
5.   Exit.

Observe the similarity between Algorithm 8.1 and Algorithm 8.2.

Algorithm 8.2 can also be used for a graph G without weights by simply assigning the weight $w(e) = 1$ to each edge e in G.

8.5 LINKED REPRESENTATION OF A GRAPH

Let G be a directed graph with m nodes. The sequential representation of G in memory—i.e., the representation of G by its adjacency matrix A—has a number of major drawbacks. First of all, it may be difficult to insert and delete nodes in G. This is because the size of A may need to be changed and the nodes may need to be reordered, so there may be many, many changes in the matrix A. Furthermore, if the number of edges is $O(m)$ or $O(m \log_2 m)$, then the matrix A will be sparse (will contain many zeros); hence a great deal of space will be wasted. Accordingly, G is usually represented in memory by a linked *representation*, also called an *adjacency structure*, which is described in this section.

Consider the graph G in Fig. 8-7(a). The table in Fig. 8-7(b) shows each node in G followed by its *adjacency list*, which is its list of adjacent nodes, also called its *successors* or *neighbors*. Figure 8-8 shows a schematic diagram of a linked representation of G in memory. Specifically, the linked representation will contain two lists (or files), a node list NODE and an edge list EDGE, as follows.

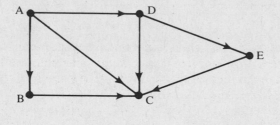

Node	Adjacency List
A	B, C, D
B	C
C	
D	C, E
E	C

(a)   Graph G.   (b)   Adjacency lists of G.

Fig. 8-7

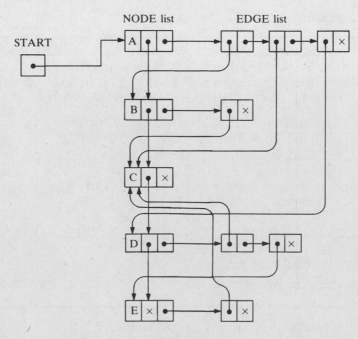

Fig. 8-8

(a) *Node list.* Each element in the list NODE will correspond to a node in *G*, and it will be a record of the form:

NODE	NEXT	ADJ	

Here NODE will be the name or key value of the node, NEXT will be a pointer to the next node in the list NODE and ADJ will be a pointer to the first element in the adjacency list of the node, which is maintained in the list EDGE. The shaded area indicates that there may be other information in the record, such as the indegree INDEG of the node, the outdegree OUTDEG of the node, the STATUS of the node during the execution of an algorithm, and so on. (Alternatively, one may assume that NODE is an array of records containing fields such as NAME, INDEG, OUTDEG, STATUS, ...) The nodes themselves, as pictured in Fig. 8-7, will be organized as a linked list and hence will have a pointer variable START for the beginning of the list and a pointer variable AVAILN for the list of available space. Sometimes, depending on the application, the nodes may be organized as a sorted array or a binary search tree instead of a linked list.

(b) *Edge list.* Each element in the list EDGE will correspond to an edge of *G* and will be a record of the form:

DEST	LINK	

The field DEST will point to the location in the list NODE of the destination or terminal node of the edge. The field LINK will link together the edges with the same initial node, that is, the nodes in the same adjacency list. The shaded area indicates that there may be other information in the record corresponding to the edge, such as a field EDGE containing the labeled data of the edge when *G* is a labeled graph, a field WEIGHT containing the weight of the edge when *G* is a weighted graph, and so on. We also need a pointer variable AVAILE for the list of available space in the list EDGE.

Figure 8-9 shows how the graph *G* in Fig. 8-7(*a*) may appear in memory. The choice of 10 locations for the list NODE and 12 locations for the list EDGE is arbitrary.

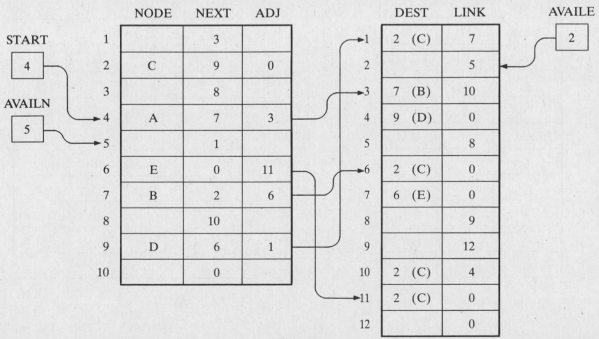

Fig. 8-9

The linked representation of a graph G that we have been discussing may be denoted by

GRAPH(NODE, NEXT, ADJ, START, AVAILN, DEST, LINK, AVAILE)

The representation may also include an array WEIGHT when G is weighted or may include an array EDGE when G is a labeled graph.

EXAMPLE 8.5

Suppose Friendly Airways has nine daily flights, as follows:

103	Atlanta to Houston	203	Boston to Denver	305	Chicago to Miami
106	Houston to Atlanta	204	Denver to Boston	308	Miami to Boston
201	Boston to Chicago	301	Denver to Reno	402	Reno to Chicago

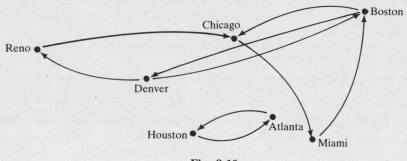

Fig. 8-10

NODE list

	CITY	NEXT	ADJ
1		0	
2	Atlanta	12	1
3	Chicago	11	7
4	Houston	7	2
5		6	
6		8	
7	Miami	10	8
8		9	
9		1	
10	Reno	0	9
11	Denver	4	5
12	Boston	3	3

START = 2, AVAILN = 5

EDGE list

	NUMBER	ORIG	DEST	LINK
1	103	2	4	0
2	106	4	2	0
3	201	12	3	4
4	203	12	11	0
5	204	11	12	6
6	301	11	10	0
7	305	3	7	0
8	308	7	12	0
9	402	10	3	0
10				11
11				12
12				0

AVAILE = 10

Fig. 8-11

Clearly, the data may be stored efficiently in a file where each record contains three fields:

$$\text{Flight Number,} \quad \text{City of Origin,} \quad \text{City of Destination}$$

However, such a representation does not easily answer the following natural questions:

(a) Is there a direct flight from city X to city Y?

(b) Can one fly, with possible stops, from city X to city Y?

(c) What is the most direct route, i.e., the route with the smallest number of stops, from city X to city Y?

To make the answers to these questions more readily available, it may be very useful for the data to be organized also as a graph G with the cities as nodes and with the flights as edges. Figure 8-10 is a picture of the graph G.

Figure 8-11 shows how the graph G may appear in memory using the linked representation. We note that G is a labeled graph, not a weighted graph, since the flight number is simply for identification. Even though the data are organized as a graph, one still would require some type of algorithm to answer questions (b) and (c). Such algorithms are discussed later in the chapter.

8.6 OPERATIONS ON GRAPHS

Suppose a graph G is maintained in memory by the linked representation

GRAPH(NODE, NEXT, ADJ, START, AVAILN, DEST, LINK, AVAILE)

as discussed in the preceding section. This section discusses the operations of searching, inserting and deleting nodes and edges in the graph G. The operation of traversing is treated in the next section.

The operations in this section use certain procedures from Chap. 5, on linked lists. For completeness, we restate these procedures below, but in a slightly different manner than in Chap. 5. Naturally, if a circular linked list or a binary search tree is used instead of a linked list, then the analogous procedures must be used.

Procedure 8.3 (originally Algorithm 5.2) finds the location LOC of an ITEM in a linked list.

Procedure 8.4 (originally Procedure 5.9 and Algorithm 5.10) deletes a given ITEM from a linked list. Here we use a logical variable FLAG to tell whether or not ITEM originally appears in the linked list.

Searching in a Graph

Suppose we want to find the location LOC of a node N in a graph G. This can be accomplished by using Procedure 8.3, as follows:

Call FIND(NODE, NEXT, START, N, LOC)

That is, this Call statement searches the list NODE for the node N.

On the other hand, suppose we want to find the location LOC of an edge (A, B) in the graph G. First we must find the location LOCA of A and the location LOCB of B in the list NODE. Then we must find in the list of successors of A, which has the list pointer ADJ[LOCA], the location LOC of LOCB. This is implemented by Procedure 8.5, which also checks to see whether A and B are nodes in G. Observe that LOC gives the location of LOCB in the list EDGE.

Inserting in a Graph

Suppose a node N is to be inserted in the graph G. Note that N will be assigned to NODE[AVAILN], the first available node. Moreover, since N will be an isolated node, one must also set ADJ[AVAILN] := NULL. Procedure 8.6 accomplishes this task using a logical variable FLAG to indicate overflow.

Clearly, Procedure 8.6 must be modified if the list NODE is maintained as a sorted list or a binary search tree.

Procedure 8.3: FIND(INFO, LINK START, ITEM, LOC) [Algorithm 5.2]
Finds the location LOC of the first node containing ITEM, or sets
LOC := NULL.

1. Set PTR := START.
2. Repeat while PTR ≠ NULL:
        If ITEM = INFO[PTR], then: Set LOC := PTR, and Return.
        Else: Set PTR := LINK[PTR].
    [End of loop.]
3. Set LOC := NULL, and Return.

Procedure 8.4: DELETE(INFO, LINK, START, AVAIL, ITEM, FLAG) [Algorithm 5.10]
Deletes the first node in the list containing ITEM, or sets FLAG := FALSE
when ITEM does not appear in the list.

1. [List empty?] If START = NULL, then: Set FLAG := FALSE, and Return.
2. [ITEM in first node?] If INFO[START] = ITEM, then:
        Set PTR := START, START := LINK[START],
        LINK[PTR] := AVAIL, AVAIL := PTR,
        FLAG := TRUE, and Return.
    [End of If structure.]
3. Set PTR := LINK[START] and SAVE := START. [Initializes pointers.]
4. Repeat Steps 5 and 6 while PTR ≠ NULL:
5.   If INFO[PTR] = ITEM, then:
            Set LINK[SAVE] := LINK[PTR], LINK[PTR] := AVAIL,
            AVAIL := PTR, FLAG := TRUE, and Return.
        [End of If structure.]
6.   Set SAVE := PTR and PTR := LINK[PTR]. [Updates pointers]
    [End of Step 4 loop.]
7. Set FLAG := FALSE, and Return.

Procedure 8.5: FINDEDGE(NODE, NEXT, ADJ, START, DEST, LINK, A, B, LOC)
This procedure finds the location LOC of an edge (A, B) in the graph G, or sets
LOC := NULL.

1. Call FIND(NODE, NEXT, START, A, LOCA).
2. CALL FIND(NODE, NEXT, START, B, LOCB).
3. If LOCA = NULL or LOCB = NULL, then: Set LOC := NULL.
    Else: Call FIND(DEST, LINK, ADJ[LOCA], LOCB, LOC).
4. Return.

Procedure 8.6: INSNODE(NODE, NEXT, ADJ, START, AVAILN, N, FLAG)
This procedure inserts the node N in the graph G.

1. [OVERFLOW?] If AVAILN = NULL, then: Set FLAG := FALSE, and
    Return.
2. Set ADJ[AVAILN] := NULL.
3. [Removes node from AVAILN list.]
    Set NEW := AVAILN and AVAILN := NEXT[AVAILN].
4. [Inserts node N in the NODE list.]
    Set NODE[NEW] := N, NEXT[NEW] := START and START := NEW.
5. Set FLAG := TRUE, and Return.

Suppose an edge (A, B) is to be inserted in the graph G. (The procedure will assume that both A and B are already nodes in the graph G.) The procedure first finds the location LOCA of A and the location LOCB of B in the node list. Then (A, B) is inserted as an edge in G by inserting LOCB in the list of successors of A, which has the list pointer ADJ[LOCA]. Again, a logical variable FLAG is used to indicate overflow. The procedure follows.

Procedure 8.7: INSEDGE(NODE, NEXT, ADJ, START, DEST, LINK, AVAILE, A, B, FLAG)
This procedure inserts the edge (A, B) in the graph G.

1. Call FIND(NODE, NEXT, START, A, LOCA).
2. Call FIND(NODE, NEXT, START, B, LOCB).
3. [OVERFLOW?] If AVAILE = NULL, then: Set FLAG := FALSE, and Return.
4. [Remove node from AVAILE list.] Set NEW := AVAILE and AVAILE := LINK[AVAILE].
5. [Insert LOCB in list of successors of A.]
   Set DEST[NEW] := LOCB, LINK[NEW] := ADJ[LOCA] and ADJ[LOCA] := NEW.
6. Set FLAG := TRUE, and Return.

The procedure must be modified by using Procedure 8.6 if A or B is not a node in the graph G.

Deleting from a Graph

Suppose an edge (A, B) is to be deleted from the graph G. (Our procedure will assume that A and B are both nodes in the graph G.) Again, we must first find the location LOCA of A and the location LOCB of B in the node list. Then we simply delete LOCB from the list of successors of A, which has the list pointer ADJ[LOCA]. A logical variable FLAG is used to indicate that there is no such edge in the graph G. The procedure follows.

Procedure 8.8: DELEDGE(NODE, NEXT, ADJ, START, DEST, LINK, AVAILE, A, B, FLAG)
This procedure deletes the edge (A, B) from the graph G.

1. Call FIND(NODE, NEXT, START, A, LOCA). [Locates node A.]
2. Call FIND(NODE, NEXT, START, B, LOCB). [Locates node B.]
3. Call DELETE(DEST, LINK, ADJ[LOCA], AVAILE, LOCB, FLAG). [Uses Procedure 8.4.]
4. Return.

Suppose a node N is to be deleted from the graph G. This operation is more complicated than the search and insertion operations and the deletion of an edge, because we must also delete all the edges that contain N. Note these edges come in two kinds; those that begin at N and those that end at N. Accordingly, our procedure will consist mainly of the following four steps:

(1) Find the location LOC of the node N in G.

(2) Delete all edges ending at N; that is, delete LOC from the list of successors of each node M in G. (This step requires traversing the node list of G.)

(3)   Delete all the edges beginning at N. This is accomplished by finding the location BEG of the first successor and the location END of the last successor of N, and then adding the successor list of N to the free AVAILE list.

(4)   Delete N itself from the list NODE.

The procedure follows.

Procedure 8.9:   DELNODE(NODE, NEXT, ADJ, START, AVAILN, DEST, LINK, AVAILE, N, FLAG)
This procedure deletes the node N from the graph G.

1.   Call FIND(NODE, NEXT, START, N, LOC). [Locates node N.]
2.   If LOC = NULL, then: Set FLAG := FALSE, and Return.
3.   [Delete edges ending at N.]
   (a)   Set PTR := START.
   (b)   Repeat while PTR ≠ NULL:
       (i)   Call DELETE(DEST, LINK, ADJ[PTR], AVAILE, LOC, FLAG).
       (ii)   Set PTR := NEXT[PTR].
   [End of loop.]
4.   [Successor list empty?] If ADJ[LOC] = NULL, then: Go to Step 7.
5.   [Find the first and last successor of N.]
   (a)   Set BEG := ADJ[LOC], END := ADJ[LOC] and PTR := LINK[END].
   (b)   Repeat while PTR ≠ NULL:
       Set END := PTR and PTR := LINK[PTR].
   [End of loop.]
6.   [Add successor list of N to AVAILE list.]
   Set LINK[END] := AVAILE and AVAILE := BEG.
7.   [Delete N using Procedure 8.4.]
   Call DELETE(NODE, NEXT, START, AVAILN, N, FLAG).
8.   Return.

EXAMPLE 8.6

Consider the (undirected) graph G in Fig. 8-12(a), whose adjacency lists appear in Fig. 8-12(b). Observe that G has 14 directed edges, since there are 7 undirected edges.

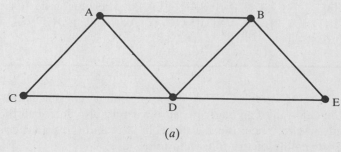

Adjacency Lists
A: B, C, D
B: A, D, E
C: A, D
D: A, B, C, E
E: B, D

(a)   (b)

Fig. 8-12

Suppose G is maintained in memory as in Fig. 8-13(a). Furthermore, suppose node B is deleted from G by using Procedure 8.9. We obtain the following steps:

	NODE	NEXT	ADJ
1	A	2	1
2	Ⓑ	3	4
3	C	4	7
4	D	5	9
5	E	0	13
6		7	
7		8	
8		0	

START = 1
AVAILN = 6

	NODE	NEXT	ADJ
1	A	3	2
2		6	
3	C	4	7
4	D	5	9
5	E	0	14
6		7	
7		8	
8		0	

START = 1
AVAILN = 2

	DEST	LINK
1	②	2
2	3	3
3	4	0
4	①	5
5	④	6
6	⑤	0
7	1	8
8	4	0
9	1	10
10	②	11
11	3	12
12	5	0
13	②	14
14	4	0
15		16
16		0

AVAILE = 16

(a) Before deletion.

	DEST	LINK
1		15
2	3	3
3	4	0
4		5
5		6
6		13
7	1	8
8	4	0
9	1	11
10		1
11	3	12
12	5	0
13		10
14	4	0
15		16
16		0

AVAILE = 4

(b) After deleting B.

Fig. 8-13

Step 1.   Finds LOC = 2, the location of B in the node list.

Step 3.   Deletes LOC = 2 from the edge list, that is, from each list of successors.

Step 5.   Finds BEG = 4 and END = 6, the first and last successors of B.

Step 6.   Deletes the list of successors from the edge list.

Step 7.   Deletes node B from the node list.

Step 8.   Returns.

The deleted elements are circled in Fig. 8-13(a). Figure 8-13(b) shows G in memory after node B (and its edges) are deleted.

8.7 TRAVERSING A GRAPH

Many graph algorithms require one to systematically examine the nodes and edges of a graph G. There are two standard ways that this is done. One way is called a breadth-first search, and the other is called a depth-first search. The breadth-first search will use a queue as an auxiliary structure to hold nodes for future processing, and analogously, the depth-first search will use a stack.

During the execution of our algorithms, each node N of G will be in one of three states, called the *status* of N, as follows:

STATUS = 1:   (Ready state.) The initial state of the node N.

STATUS = 2:   (Waiting state.) The node N is on the queue or stack, waiting to be processed.

STATUS = 3:   (Processed state.) The node N has been processed.

We now discuss the two searches separately.

Breadth-First Search

The general idea behind a breadth-first search beginning at a starting node A is as follows. First we examine the starting node A. Then we examine all the neighbors of A. Then we examine all the neighbors of the neighbors of A. And so on. Naturally, we need to keep track of the neighbors of a node, and we need to guarantee that no node is processed more than once. This is accomplished by using a queue to hold nodes that are waiting to be processed, and by using a field STATUS which tells us the current status of any node. The algorithm follows.

Algorithm A: This algorithm executes a breadth-first search on a graph G beginning at a starting node A.

1.   Initialize all nodes to the ready state (STATUS = 1).
2.   Put the starting node A in QUEUE and change its status to the waiting state (STATUS = 2).
3.   Repeat Steps 4 and 5 until QUEUE is empty:
4.   Remove the front node N of QUEUE. Process N and change the status of N to the processed state (STATUS = 3).
5.   Add to the rear of QUEUE all the neighbors of N that are in the steady state (STATUS = 1), and change their status to the waiting state (STATUS = 2).
     [End of Step 3 loop.]
6.   Exit.

The above algorithm will process only those nodes which are reachable from the starting node A. Suppose one wants to examine all the nodes in the graph G. Then the algorithm must be modified so that it begins again with another node (which we will call B) that is still in the ready state. This node B can be obtained by traversing the list of nodes.

EXAMPLE 8.7

Consider the graph G in Fig. 8-14(a). (The adjacency lists of the nodes appear in Fig. 8-14(b).) Suppose G represents the daily flights between cities of some airline, and suppose we want to fly from city A to city J with the minimum number of stops. In other words, we want the minimum path P from A to J (where each edge has length 1).

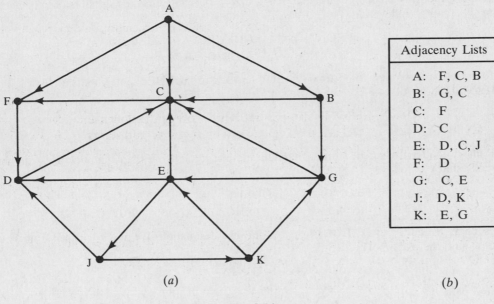

Adjacency Lists
A: F, C, B
B: G, C
C: F
D: C
E: D, C, J
F: D
G: C, E
J: D, K
K: E, G

(a)   (b)

Fig. 8-14

The minimum path P can be found by using a breadth-first search beginning at city A and ending when J is encountered. During the execution of the search, we will also keep track of the origin of each edge by using an array ORIG together with the array QUEUE. The steps of our search follow.

(a)   Initially, add A to QUEUE and add NULL to ORIG as follows:

$$\text{FRONT} = 1 \qquad \text{QUEUE:} \quad A$$
$$\text{REAR} = 1 \qquad \text{ORIG:} \quad \emptyset$$

(b)   Remove the front element A from QUEUE by setting FRONT := FRONT + 1, and add to QUEUE the neighbors of A as follows:

$$\text{FRONT} = 2 \qquad \text{QUEUE:} \quad A, F, C, B$$
$$\text{REAR} = 4 \qquad \text{ORIG:} \quad \emptyset, A, A, A$$

Note that the origin A of each of the three edges is added to ORIG.

(c)   Remove the front element F from QUEUE by setting FRONT := FRONT + 1, and add to QUEUE the neighbors of F as follows:

$$\text{FRONT} = 3 \qquad \text{QUEUE:} \quad A, F, C, B, D$$
$$\text{REAR} = 5 \qquad \text{ORIG:} \quad \emptyset, A, A, A, F$$

(d)   Remove the front element C from QUEUE, and add to QUEUE the neighbors of C (which are in the ready state) as follows:

$$\text{FRONT} = 4 \qquad \text{QUEUE:} \quad A, F, C, B, D$$
$$\text{REAR} = 5 \qquad \text{ORIG:} \quad \emptyset, A, A, A, F$$

Note that the neighbor F of C is not added to QUEUE, since F is not in the ready state (because F has already been added to QUEUE).

(e)   Remove the front element B from QUEUE, and add to QUEUE the neighbors of B (the ones in the ready state) as follows:

FRONT = 5   QUEUE: A, F, C, B, D, G
REAR = 6   ORIG: Ø, A, A, A, F, B

Note that only G is added to QUEUE, since the other neighbor, C is not in the ready state.

(f)   Remove the front element D from QUEUE, and add to QUEUE the neighbors of D (the ones in the ready state) as follows:

FRONT = 6   QUEUE: A, F, C, B, D, G
REAR = 6   ORIG: Ø, A, A, A, F, B

(g)   Remove the front element G from QUEUE and add to QUEUE the neighbors of G (the ones in the ready state) as follows:

FRONT = 7   QUEUE: A, F, C, B, D, G, E
REAR = 7   ORIG: Ø, A, A, A, F, B, G

(h)   Remove the front element E from QUEUE and add to QUEUE the neighbors of E (the ones in the ready state) as follows:

FRONT = 8   QUEUE: A, F, C, B, D, G, E, J
REAR = 8   ORIG: Ø, A, A, A, F, B, G, E

We stop as soon as J is added to QUEUE, since J is our final destination. We now backtrack from J, using the array ORIG to find the path P. Thus

$$J \leftarrow E \leftarrow G \leftarrow B \leftarrow A$$

is the required path P.

Depth-First Search

The general idea behind a depth-first search beginning at a starting node A is as follows. First we examine the starting node A. Then we examine each node N along a path P which begins at A; that is, we process a neighbor of A, then a neighbor of a neighbor of A, and so on. After coming to a "dead end," that is, to the end of the path P, we backtrack on P until we can continue along another path P'. And so on. (This algorithm is similar to the inorder traversal of a binary tree, and the algorithm is also similar to the way one might travel through a maze.) The algorithm is very similar to the breadth-first search except now we use a stack instead of the queue. Again, a field STATUS is used to tell us the current status of a node. The algorithm follows.

Algorithm B: This algorithm executes a depth-first search on a graph G beginning at a starting node A.

1.   Initialize all nodes to the ready state (STATUS = 1).
2.   Push the starting node A onto STACK and change its status to the waiting state (STATUS = 2).
3.   Repeat Steps 4 and 5 until STACK is empty.
4.   Pop the top node N of STACK. Process N and change its status to the processed state (STATUS = 3).
5.   Push onto STACK all the neighbors of N that are still in the ready state (STATUS = 1), and change their status to the waiting state (STATUS = 2).
     [End of Step 3 loop.]
6.   Exit.

Again, the above algorithm will process only those nodes which are reachable from the starting node A. Suppose one wants to examine all the nodes in G. Then the algorithm must be modified so that it begins again with another node which we will call B—that is still in the ready state. This node B can be obtained by traversing the list of nodes.

EXAMPLE 8.8

Consider the graph G in Fig. 8-14(a). Suppose we want to find and print all the nodes reachable from the node J (including J itself). One way to do this is to use a depth-first search of G starting at the node J. The steps of our search follow.

(a)   Initially, push J onto the stack as follows:

STACK: J

(b)   Pop and print the top element J, and then push onto the stack all the neighbors of J (those that are in the ready state) as follows:

Print J   STACK: D, K

(c)   Pop and print the top element K, and then push onto the stack all the neighbors of K (those that are in the ready state) as follows:

Print K   STACK: D, E, G

(d)   Pop and print the top element G, and then push onto the stack all the neighbors of G (those in the ready state) as follows:

Print G   STACK: D, E, C

Note that only C is pushed onto the stack, since the other neighbor, E, is not in the ready state (because E has already been pushed onto the stack).

(e)   Pop and print the top element C, and then push onto the stack all the neighbors of C (those in the ready state) as follows:

Print C   STACK: D, E, F

(f)   Pop and print the top element F, and then push onto the stack all the neighbors of F (those in the ready state) as follows:

Print F   STACK: D, E

Note that the only neighbor D of F is not pushed onto the stack, since D is not in the ready state (because D has already been pushed onto the stack).

(g)   Pop and print the top element E, and push onto the stack all the neighbors of E (those in the ready state) as follows:

Print E   STACK: D

(Note that none of the three neighbors of E is in the ready state.)

(h)   Pop and print the top element D, and push onto the stack all the neighbors of D (those in the ready state) as follows:

Print D   STACK:

The stack is now empty, so the depth-first search of G starting at J is now complete. Accordingly, the nodes which were printed,

J, K, G, C, F, E, D

are precisely the nodes which are reachable from J.

8.8   POSETS; TOPOLOGICAL SORTING

Suppose S is a graph such that each node v_i of S represents a task and each edge (u, v) means that the completion of the task u is a prerequisite for starting the task v. Suppose such a graph S contains a cycle, such as

$$P = (u, v, w, u)$$

This means that we cannot begin v until completing u, we cannot begin w until completing v and we cannot begin u until completing w. Thus we cannot complete any of the tasks in the cycle. Accordingly, such a graph S, representing tasks and a prerequisite relation, cannot have cycles.

Suppose S is a graph without cycles. Consider the relation $<$ on S defined as follows:

$$u < v \qquad \text{if there is a path from } u \text{ to } v$$

This relation has the following three properties:

(1) For each element u in S, we have $u \not< u$. (Irreflexivity.)

(2) If $u < v$, then $v \not< u$. (Asymmetry.)

(3) If $u < v$ and $v < w$, then $u < w$. (Transitivity.)

Such a relation $<$ on S is called a *partial ordering* of S, and S with such an ordering is called a *partially ordered set*, or *poset*. Thus a graph S without cycles may be regarded as a partially ordered set.

On the other hand, suppose S is a partially ordered set with the partial ordering denoted by $<$. Then S may be viewed as a graph whose nodes are the elements of S and whose edges are defined as follows:

$$(u, v) \qquad \text{is an edge in } S \text{ if} \qquad u < v$$

Furthermore, one can show that a partially ordered set S, regarded as a graph, has no cycles.

EXAMPLE 8.9

Let S be the graph in Fig. 8-15. Observe that S has no cycles. Thus S may be regarded as a partially ordered set. Note that $G < C$, since there is a path from G to C. Similarly, $B < F$ and $B < C$. On the other hand, $B \not< A$, since there is no path from B to A. Also, $A \not< B$.

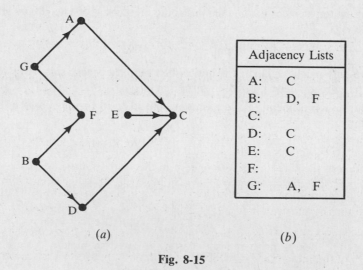

Adjacency Lists	
A:	C
B:	D, F
C:	
D:	C
E:	C
F:	
G:	A, F

(a)   (b)

Fig. 8-15

Topological Sorting

Let S be a directed graph without cycles (or a partially ordered set). A topological sort T of S is a linear ordering of the nodes of S which preserves the original partial ordering of S. That is: *If $u < v$ in S (i.e., if there is a path from u to v in S), then u comes before v in the linear ordering T.* Figure 8-16 shows two different topological sorts of the graph S in Fig. 8-15. We have included the edges in Fig. 8-16 to indicate that they agree with the direction of the linear ordering.

The following is the main theoretical result in this section.

Proposition 8.4:   Let S be a finite directed graph without cycles or a finite partially ordered set. Then there exists a topological sort T of the set S.

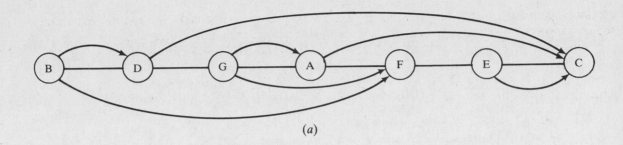

(a)

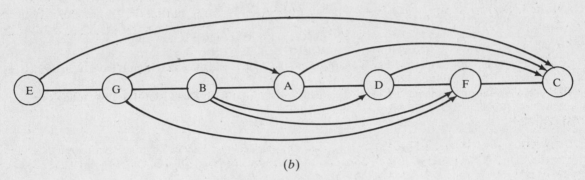

(b)

Fig. 8-16   Two topological sorts.

Note that the proposition states only that a topological sort exists. We now give an algorithm which will find such a topological sort.

The main idea behind our algorithm to find a topological sort T of a graph S without cycles is that any node N with zero indegree, i.e., without any predecessors, may be chosen as the first element in the sort T. Accordingly, our algorithm will repeat the following two steps until the graph S is empty:

(1)   Finding a node N with zero indegree

(2)   Deleting N and its edges from the graph S

The order in which the nodes are deleted from the graph S will use an auxiliary array QUEUE which will temporarily hold all the nodes with zero indegree. The algorithm also uses a field INDEG such that INDEG(N) will contain the current indegree of the node N. The algorithm follows.

Algorithm C: This algorithm finds a topological sort T of a graph S without cycles.

1.   Find the indegree INDEG(N) of each node N of S. (This can be done by traversing each adjacency list as in Prob. 8.15.)
2.   Put in a queue all the nodes with zero indegree.
3.   Repeat Steps 4 and 5 until the queue is empty.
4.   Remove the front node N of the queue (by setting FRONT := FRONT + 1).
5.   Repeat the following for each neighbor M of the node N:
           (a)   Set INDEG(M) := INDEG(M) − 1.
                   [This deletes the edge from N to M.]
           (b)   If INDEG(M) = 0, then: Add M to the rear of the queue.
         [End of loop.]
       [End of Step 3 loop.]
6.   Exit.

EXAMPLE 8.10

Consider the graph S in Fig. 8-15(a). We apply our Algorithm C to find a topological sort T of the graph S. The steps of the algorithm follow.

1. Find the indegree INDEG(N) of each node N of the graph S. This yields:
    $$\text{INDEG(A)} = 1 \qquad \text{INDEG(B)} = 0 \qquad \text{INDEG(C)} = 3 \qquad \text{INDEG(D)} = 1$$
    $$\text{INDEG(E)} = 0 \qquad \text{INDEG(F)} = 2 \qquad \text{INDEG(G)} = 0$$
    [This can be done as in Problem 8.15.]
2. Initially add to the queue each node with zero indegree as follows:
    $$\text{FRONT} = 1, \qquad \text{REAR} = 3, \qquad \text{QUEUE: B, E, G}$$
3a. Remove the front element B from the queue by setting FRONT := FRONT + 1, as follows:
    $$\text{FRONT} = 2, \qquad \text{REAR} = 3 \qquad \text{QUEUE: B, E, G}$$
3b. Decrease by 1 the indegree of each neighbor of B, as follows:
    $$\text{INDEG(D)} = 1 - 1 = 0 \qquad \text{and} \qquad \text{INDEG(F)} = 2 - 1 = 1$$
    [The adjacency list of B in Fig. 8-15(b) is used to find the neighbors D and F of the node B.] The neighbor D is added to the rear of the queue, since its indegree is now zero:
    $$\text{FRONT} = 2, \qquad \text{REAR} = 4 \qquad \text{QUEUE: B, E, G, D}$$
    [The graph S now looks like Fig. 8-17(a), where the node B and the edges from B have been deleted, as indicated by the dotted lines.]
4a. Remove the front element E from the queue by setting FRONT := FRONT + 1, as follows:
    $$\text{FRONT} = 3, \qquad \text{REAR} = 4 \qquad \text{QUEUE: B, E, G, D}$$

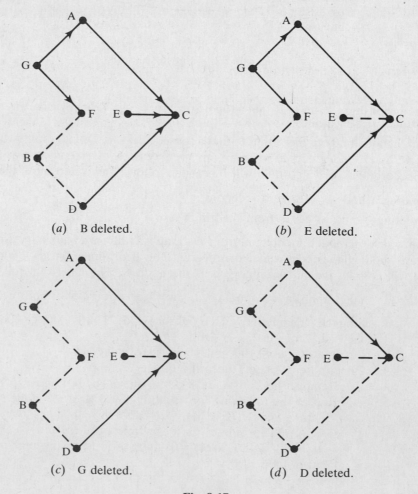

(a)   B deleted.   (b)   E deleted.

(c)   G deleted.   (d)   D deleted.

Fig. 8-17

4b. Decrease by 1 the indegree of each neighbor of E, as follows:
   INDEG(C) = 3 − 1 = 2
   [Since the indegree is nonzero, QUEUE is not changed. The graph S now looks like Fig. 8-17(b), where the node E and its edge have been deleted.]

5a. Remove the front element G from the queue by setting FRONT := FRONT + 1, as follows:
   FRONT = 4,   REAR = 4   QUEUE: B, E, G, D

5b. Decrease by 1 the indegree of each neighbor of G, as follows:
   INDEG(A) = 1 − 1 = 0   and   INDEG(F) = 1 − 1 = 0
   Both A and F are added to the rear of the queue, as follows:
   FRONT = 4,   REAR = 6   QUEUE: B, E, G, D, A, F
   [The graph S now looks like Fig. 8-17(c), where G and its two edges have been deleted.]

6a. Remove the front element D from the queue by setting FRONT := FRONT + 1, as follows:
   FRONT = 5,   REAR = 6   QUEUE: B, E, G, D, A, F

6b. Decrease by 1 the indegree of each neighbor of D, as follows:
   INDEG(C) = 2 − 1 = 1
   [Since the indegree is nonzero, QUEUE is not changed. The graph S now looks like Fig. 8-17(d), where D and its edge have been deleted.]

7a. Remove the front element A from the queue by setting FRONT := FRONT + 1, as follows:
   FRONT = 6,   REAR = 6   QUEUE: B, E, G, D, A, F

7b. Decrease by 1 the indegree of each neighbor of A, as follows:
   INDEG(C) = 1 − 1 = 0
   Add C to the rear of the queue, since its indegree is now zero:
   FRONT = 6,   REAR = 7   QUEUE: B, E, G, D, A, F, C

8a. Remove the front element F from the queue by setting FRONT := FRONT + 1, as follows:
   FRONT = 7,   REAR = 7   QUEUE: B, E, G, D, A, F, C

8b. The node F has no neighbors, so no change takes place.

9a. Remove the front element C from the queue by setting FRONT := FRONT + 1, as follows:
   FRONT = 8,   REAR = 7   QUEUE: B, E, G, D, A, F, C

9b. The node C has no neighbors, so no other changes take place.

The queue now has no front element, so the algorithm is completed. The elements in the array QUEUE give the required topological sort T of S as follows:
   T: B, E, G, D, A, F, C
The algorithm could have stopped in Step 7b, where REAR is equal to the number of nodes in the graph S.

Solved Problems

GRAPH TERMINOLOGY

8.1 Consider the (undirected) graph G in Fig. 8-18. (*a*) Describe G formally in terms of its set V of nodes and its set E of edges. (*b*) Find the degree of each node.

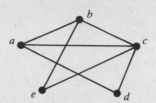

Fig. 8-18

(*a*) There are 5 nodes, a, b, c, d and e; hence $V = \{a, b, c, d, e\}$. There are 7 pairs $[x, y]$ of nodes such that node x is connected with node y; hence

$$E = \{[a, b], [a, c], [a, d], [b, c], [b, e], [c, d], [c, e]\}$$

(*b*) The degree of a node is equal to the number of edges to which it belongs; for example, $\deg(a) = 3$, since a belongs to three edges, $[a, b]$, $[a, c]$ and $[a, d]$. Similarly, $\deg(b) = 3$, $\deg(c) = 4$, $\deg(d) = 2$ and $\deg(e) = 2$.

8.2 Consider the multigraphs in Fig. 8-19. Which of them are (*a*) connected; (*b*) loop-free (i.e., without loops); (*c*) graphs?

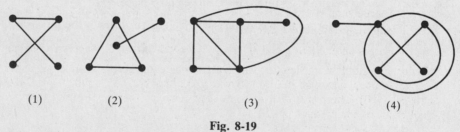

(1)   (2)   (3)   (4)

Fig. 8-19

(*a*) Only multigraphs 1 and 3 are connected.

(*b*) Only multigraph 4 has a loop (i.e., an edge with the same endpoints).

(*c*) Only multigraphs 1 and 2 are graphs. Multigraph 3 has multiple edges, and multigraph 4 has multiple edges and a loop.

8.3 Consider the connected graph G in Fig. 8-20. (*a*) Find all simple paths from node A to node F. (*b*) Find the distance between A and F. (*c*) Find the diameter of G. (The diameter of G is the maximum distance existing between any two of its nodes.)

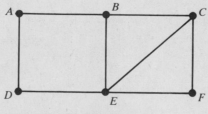

Fig. 8-20

(a)   A simple path from A to F is a path such that no node and hence no edge is repeated. There are seven such simple paths:

$$(A, B, C, F) \qquad (A, B, E, F) \qquad (A, D, E, F) \qquad (A, D, E, C, F)$$
$$(A, B, C, E, F) \qquad (A, B, E, C, F) \qquad (A, D, E, B, C, F)$$

(b)   The distance from A to F equals 3, since there is a simple path, (A, B, C, F), from A to F of length 3 and there is no shorter path from A to F.

(c)   The distance between A and F equals 3, and the distance between any two nodes does not exceed 3; hence the diameter of the graph G equals 3.

8.4   Consider the (directed) graph G in Fig. 8-21. (a) Find all the simple paths from X to Z. (b) Find all the simple paths from Y to Z. (c) Find indeg(Y) and outdeg(Y). (d) Are there any sources or sinks?

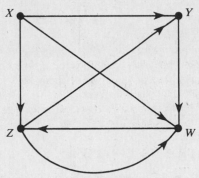

Fig. 8-21

(a)   There are three simple paths from X to Z: (X, Z), (X, W, Z) and (X, Y, W, Z).

(b)   There is only one simple path from Y to Z: (Y, W, Z).

(c)   Since two edges enter Y (i.e., end at Y), we have indeg(Y) = 2. Since only one edge leaves Y (i.e., begins at Y), outdeg(Y) = 1.

(d) X is a source, since no edge enters X (i.e., indeg(X) = 0) but some edges leave X (i.e., outdeg(X) > 0). There are no sinks, since each node has a nonzero outdegree (i.e., each node is the initial point of some edge).

8.5   Draw all (nonsimilar) trees with exactly 6 nodes. (A graph G is *similar* to a graph G' if there is a one-to-one correspondence between the set V of nodes of G and the set V' of nodes of G' such that (u, v) is an edge in G if and only if the corresponding pair (u', v') of nodes is an edge in G'.)

There are six such trees, which are exhibited in Fig. 8-22. The first tree has diameter 5, the next two diameter 4, the next two diameter 3 and the last one diameter 2. Any other tree with 6 nodes will be similar to one of these trees.

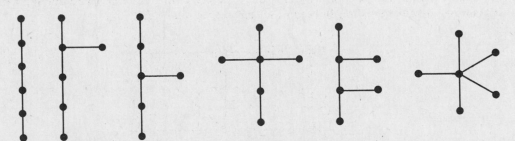

Fig. 8-22

8.6 Find all spanning trees of the graph G shown in Fig. 8-23(a). (A tree T is called a *spanning tree* of a connected graph G if T has the same nodes as G and all the edges of T are contained among the edges of G.)

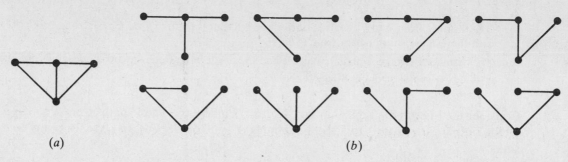

(a)   (b)

Fig. 8-23

There are eight such spanning trees, as shown in Fig. 8-23(b). Since G has 4 nodes, each spanning tree T must have $4 - 1 = 3$ edges. Thus each spanning tree can be obtained by deleting 2 of the 5 edges of G. This can be done in 10 ways, except that two of them lead to disconnected graphs. Hence the eight spanning trees shown are all the spanning trees of G.

SEQUENTIAL REPRESENTATION OF GRAPHS

8.7 Consider the graph G in Fig. 8-21. Suppose the nodes are stored in memory in an array DATA as follows:

$$\text{DATA:} \quad \text{X, Y, Z, W}$$

(a) Find the adjacency matrix A of the graph G.

(b) Find the path matrix P of G using powers of the adjacency matrix A.

(c) Is G strongly connected?

(a) The nodes are normally ordered according to the way they appear in memory; that is, we assume $v_1 = \text{X}$, $v_2 = \text{Y}$, $v_3 = \text{Z}$ and $v_4 = \text{W}$. The adjacency matrix A of G follows:

$$A = \begin{pmatrix} 0 & 1 & 1 & 1 \\ 0 & 0 & 0 & 1 \\ 0 & 1 & 0 & 1 \\ 0 & 0 & 1 & 0 \end{pmatrix}$$

Here $a_{ij} = 1$ if there is a node from v_i to v_j; otherwise, $a_{ij} = 0$.

(b) Since G has 4 nodes, compute A^2, A^3, A^4 and $B_4 = A + A^2 + A^3 + A^4$:

$$A^2 = \begin{pmatrix} 0 & 1 & 1 & 2 \\ 0 & 0 & 1 & 0 \\ 0 & 0 & 1 & 1 \\ 0 & 1 & 0 & 1 \end{pmatrix} \qquad A^3 = \begin{pmatrix} 0 & 1 & 2 & 2 \\ 0 & 1 & 0 & 1 \\ 0 & 1 & 1 & 1 \\ 0 & 0 & 1 & 1 \end{pmatrix}$$

$$A^4 = \begin{pmatrix} 0 & 2 & 2 & 3 \\ 0 & 0 & 1 & 1 \\ 0 & 1 & 1 & 2 \\ 0 & 1 & 1 & 1 \end{pmatrix} \qquad B_4 = \begin{pmatrix} 0 & 5 & 6 & 8 \\ 0 & 1 & 2 & 3 \\ 0 & 3 & 3 & 5 \\ 0 & 2 & 3 & 5 \end{pmatrix}$$

The path matrix P is now obtained by setting $p_{ij} = 1$ wherever there is a nonzero entry in the matrix B_4. Thus

$$P = \begin{pmatrix} 0 & 1 & 1 & 1 \\ 0 & 1 & 1 & 1 \\ 0 & 1 & 1 & 1 \\ 0 & 1 & 1 & 1 \end{pmatrix}$$

(c)   The path matrix shows that there is no path from v_2 to v_1. In fact, there is no path from any node to v_1. Thus G is not strongly connected.

8.8   Consider the graph G in Fig. 8-21 and its adjacency matrix A obtained in Prob. 8.7. Find the path matrix P of G using Warshall's algorithm rather than the powers of A.

Compute the matrices P_0, P_1, P_2, P_3 and P_4 where initially $P_0 = A$ and

$$P_k[i, j] = P_{k-1}[i, j] \vee (P_{k-1}[i, j] \wedge P_{k-1}[k, j])$$

That is,

$$P_k[i, j] = 1 \quad \text{if} \quad P_{k-1}[i, j] = 1 \quad \text{or both} \quad P_{k-1}[i, k] = 1 \quad \text{and} \quad P_{k-1}[k, j] = 1$$

Then:

$$P_1 = \begin{pmatrix} 0 & 1 & 1 & 1 \\ 0 & 0 & 0 & 1 \\ 0 & 1 & 0 & 1 \\ 0 & 0 & 1 & 0 \end{pmatrix} \qquad P_2 = \begin{pmatrix} 0 & 1 & 1 & 1 \\ 0 & 0 & 0 & 1 \\ 0 & 1 & 0 & 1 \\ 0 & 0 & 1 & 0 \end{pmatrix}$$

$$P_3 = \begin{pmatrix} 0 & 1 & 1 & 1 \\ 0 & 0 & 0 & 1 \\ 0 & 1 & 0 & 1 \\ 0 & 1 & 1 & 1 \end{pmatrix} \qquad P_4 = \begin{pmatrix} 0 & 1 & 1 & 1 \\ 0 & 1 & 1 & 1 \\ 0 & 1 & 1 & 1 \\ 0 & 1 & 1 & 1 \end{pmatrix}$$

Observe that $P_0 = P_1 = P_2 = A$. The changes in P_3 occur for the following reasons:

$$P_3(4, 2) = 1 \quad \text{because} \quad P_2(4, 3) = 1 \quad \text{and} \quad P_2(3, 2) = 1$$
$$P_3(4, 4) = 1 \quad \text{because} \quad P_2(4, 3) = 1 \quad \text{and} \quad P_2(3, 4) = 1$$

The changes in P_4 occur similarly. The last matrix, P_4, is the required path matrix P of the graph G.

8.9   Consider the (undirected) weighted graph G in Fig. 8-24. Suppose the nodes are stored in memory in an array DATA as follows:

$$\text{DATA:} \qquad A, B, C, X, Y$$

Find the weight matrix $W = (w_{ij})$ of the graph G.

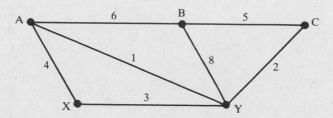

Fig. 8-24

Assuming $v_1 = A$, $v_2 = B$, $v_3 = C$, $v_4 = X$ and $v_5 = Y$, we arrive at the following weight matrix W of G:

$$W = \begin{pmatrix} 0 & 6 & 0 & 4 & 1 \\ 6 & 0 & 5 & 0 & 8 \\ 0 & 5 & 0 & 0 & 2 \\ 4 & 0 & 0 & 0 & 3 \\ 1 & 8 & 2 & 3 & 0 \end{pmatrix}$$

Here w_{ij} denotes the weight of the edge from v_i to v_j. Since G is undirected, W is a symmetric matrix, that is, $w_{ij} = w_{ji}$.

8.10   Suppose G is a graph (undirected) which is cycle-free, that is, without cycles. Let $P = (p_{ij})$ be the path matrix of G.

   (a)   When can an edge $[v_i, v_j]$ be added to G so that G is still cycle-free?

   (b)   How does the path matrix P change when an edge $[v_i, v_j]$ is added to G?

   (a)   The edge $[v_i, v_j]$ will form a cycle when it is added to G if and only if there already is a path between v_i and v_j. Hence the edge may be added to G when $p_{ij} = 0$.

   (b)   First set $p_{ij} = 1$, since the edge is a path from v_i to v_j. Also, set $p_{st} = 1$ if $p_{si} = 1$ and $p_{jt} = 1$. In other words, if there are both a path P_1 from v_s to v_i and a path P_2 from v_j to v_t, then P_1, $[v_i, v_j]$, P_2 will form a path from v_s to v_t.

8.11   A minimum spanning tree T of a weighted graph G is a spanning tree of G (see Prob. 8.6) which has the minimum weight among all the spanning trees of G.

   (a)   Describe an algorithm to find a minimum spanning tree T of a weighted graph G.

   (b)   Find a minimum spanning tree T of the graph in Fig. 8-24.

   (a)   **Algorithm P8.11:**   This algorithm finds a minimum spanning tree T of a weighted graph G.

         1.   Order all the edges of G according to increasing weights.
         2.   Initialize T to be a graph consisting of the same nodes as G and no edges.
         3.   Repeat the following M − 1 times, where M is the number of nodes in G:
                 Add to T an edge E of G with minimum weight such that E does not form a cycle in T.
                 [End of loop.]
         4.   Exit.

Step 3 may be implemented using the results of Prob. 8.10. Problem 8.10(a) tells us which edge e may be added to T so that no cycle is formed—i.e., so that T is still cycle-free—and Prob. 8.10(b) tells us how to keep track of the path matrix P of T as each edge e is added to T.

   (b)   Apply Algorithm P8.11 to obtain the minimum spanning tree T in Fig. 8-25. Although $[A, X]$ has less weight than $[B, C]$, we cannot add $[A, X]$ to T, since it would form a cycle with $[A, Y]$ and $[Y, X]$.

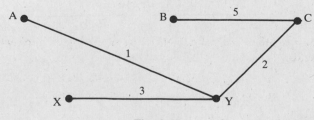

Fig. 8-25

8.12 Suppose a weighted graph G is maintained in memory by a node array DATA and a weight matrix W as follows:

$$\text{DATA:} \quad \text{X, Y, S, T}$$

$$W = \begin{pmatrix} 0 & 0 & 3 & 0 \\ 5 & 0 & 1 & 7 \\ 2 & 0 & 0 & 4 \\ 0 & 6 & 8 & 0 \end{pmatrix}$$

Draw a picture of G.

The picture appears in Fig. 8-26. The nodes are labeled by the entries in DATA. Also, if $w_{ij} \neq 0$, then there is an edge from v_i to v_j with weight w_{ij}. (We assume $v_1 = X$, $v_2 = Y$, $v_3 = S$ and $v_4 = T$, the order in which the nodes appear in the array DATA.)

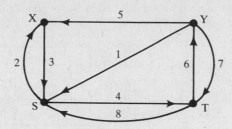

Fig. 8-26

LINKED REPRESENTATION OF GRAPHS

8.13 A graph G is stored in memory as follows:

NODE	A	B		E		D	C	
NEXT	7	4	0	6	8	0	2	3
ADJ	1	2		5		7	9	
	1	2	3	4	5	6	7	8

START = 1, AVAILN = 5

DEST	2	6	4		6	7	4		4	6
LINK	10	3	6	0	0	0	0	4	0	0
	1	2	3	4	5	6	7	8	9	10

AVAILE = 8

Draw the graph G.

First find the neighbors of each NODE[K] by traversing its adjacency list, which has the pointer ADJ[K]. This yields:

A: 2(B) and 6(D)   C: 4(E)   E: 6(D)

B: 6(D), 4(E) and 7(C)   D: 4(E)

Then draw the diagram as in Fig. 8-27.

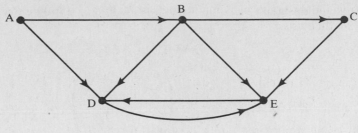

Fig. 8-27

8.14 Find the changes in the linked representation of the graph G in Prob. 8.13 if the following operations occur: (*a*) Node F is added to G. (*b*) Edge (B, E) is deleted from G. (*c*) Edge (A, F) is added to G. Draw the resultant graph G.

(*a*) The node list is not sorted, so F is inserted at the beginning of the list, using the first available free node as follows:

START = 5

AVAILN = 8

NODE	A	B		E	F	D	C	
NEXT	7	4	0	6	1	0	2	3
ADJ	1	2		5	0	7	9	
	1	2	3	4	5	6	7	8

Observe that the edge list does not change.

(*b*) Delete LOC = 4 of node E from the adjacency list of node B as follows:

AVAILE = 3

DEST	2	6			6	7	4		4	6
LINK	10	6	8	0	0	0	0	4	0	0
	1	2	3	4	5	6	7	8	9	10

Observe that the node list does not change.

(*c*) The location LOC = 5 of the node F is inserted at the beginning of the adjacency list of the node A, using the first available free edge. The changes are as follows:

ADJ[1] = 3

AVAILE = 8

DEST	2	6	5		6	7	4		4	6
LINK	10	6	1	0	0	0	0	4	0	0
	1	2	3	4	5	6	7	8	9	10

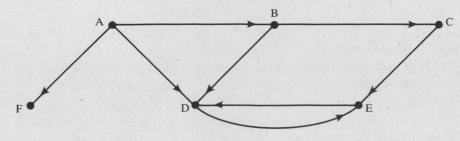

Fig. 8-28

The only change in the node list is the ADJ[1] = 3. (Observe that the shading indicates the changes in the lists.) The updated graph G appears in Fig. 8-28.

8.15 Suppose a graph G is maintained in memory in the form

GRAPH(NODE, NEXT, ADJ, START, DEST, LINK)

Write a procedure which finds the indegree INDEG and the outdegree OUTDEG of each node of G.

First we traverse the node list, using the pointer PTR in order to initialize the arrays INDEG and OUTDEG to zero. Then we traverse the node list, using the pointer PTRA, and for each value of PTRA, we traverse the list of neighbors of NODE[PTRA], using the pointer PTRB. Each time an edge is encountered, PTRA gives the location of its initial node and DEST[PTRB] gives the location of its terminal node. Accordingly, each edge updates the arrays INDEG and OUTDEG as follows:

$$\text{OUTDEG[PTRA]} := \text{OUTDEG[PTRA]} + 1$$

and

$$\text{INDEG[DEST[PTRB]]} := \text{INDEG[DEST[PTRB]]} + 1$$

The formal procedure follows.

Procedure P8.15: DEGREE(NODE, NEXT, ADJ, START, DEST, LINK, INDEG, OUTDEG)
This procedure finds the indegree INDEG and outdegree OUTDEG of each node in the graph G in memory.

1. [Initialize arrays INDEG and OUTDEG.]
   (a) Set PTR := START.
   (b) Repeat while PTR ≠ NULL: [Traverses node list.]
        (i)   Set INDEG[PTR] := 0 and OUTDEG[PTR] := 0.
        (ii) Set PTR := NEXT[PTR].
   [End of loop.]
2. Set PTRA := START.
3. Repeat Steps 4 to 6 while PTRA ≠ NULL: [Traverses node list.]
4.   Set PTRB := ADJ[PTRA].
5.   Repeat while PTRB ≠ NULL: [Traverses list of neighbors.]
        (a) Set OUTDEG[PTRA] := OUTDEG[PTRA] + 1 and
             INDEG[DEST[PTRB]] := INDEG[DEST[PTRB]] + 1.
        (b) Set PTRB := LINK[PTRB].
        [End of inner loop using pointer PTRB.]
6.   Set PTRA := NEXT[PTRA].
   [End of Step 3 outer loop using the pointer PTRA.]
7. Return.

8.16 Suppose G is a finite undirected graph. Then G consists of a finite number of disjoint connected components. Describe an algorithm which finds the number NCOMP of connected components of G. Furthermore, the algorithm should assign a component number COMP(N) to every node N in the same connected component of G such that the component numbers range from 1 to NCOMP.

The general idea of the algorithm is to use a breadth-first or depth-first search to find all nodes N reachable from a starting node A and to assign them the same component number. The algorithm follows.

Algorithm P8.16: Finds the connected components of an undirected graph G.

1. Initially set COMP(N) := 0 for every node N in G, and initially set L := 0.
2. Find a node A such that COMP(A) = 0. If no such node A exists, then:
        Set NCOMP := L, and Exit.
    Else:
        Set L := L + 1 and set COMP(A) := L.
3. Find all nodes N in G which are reachable from A (using a breadth-first search or a depth-first search) and set COMP(N) = L for each such node N.
4. Return to Step 2.

MISCELLANEOUS PROBLEMS

8.17 Suppose G is an undirected graph with m nodes $v_1, v_2, \ldots, v_m$ and n edges $e_1, e_2, \ldots, e_n$. The *incidence matrix* of G is the $m \times n$ matrix $M = (m_{ij})$ where

$$m_{ij} = \begin{cases} 1 & \text{if node } v_i \text{ belongs to edge } e_j \\ 0 & \text{otherwise} \end{cases}$$

Find the incidence matrix M of the graph G in Fig. 8-29.

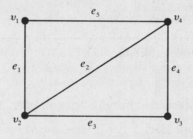

Fig. 8-29

Since G has 4 nodes and 5 edges, M is a 4×5 matrix. Set $m_{ij} = 1$ if v_i belongs to e_j. This yields the following matrix M:

$$M = \begin{pmatrix} 1 & 0 & 0 & 0 & 1 \\ 1 & 1 & 1 & 0 & 0 \\ 0 & 0 & 1 & 1 & 0 \\ 0 & 1 & 0 & 1 & 1 \end{pmatrix}$$

8.18 Suppose u and v are distinct nodes in an undirected graph G. Prove:

(a) If there is a path P from u to v, then there is a simple path Q from u to v.

(b) If there are two distinct paths P_1 and P_2 from u to v, then G contains a cycle.

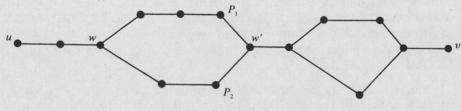

Fig. 8-30

(a) Suppose $P = (v_0, v_1, \ldots, v_n)$ where $u = v_0$ and $v = v_n$. If $v_i = v_j$, then

$$P' = (v_0, \ldots, v_i, v_{j+1}, \ldots, v_n)$$

is a path from u to v which is shorter than P. Repeating this process, we finally obtain a path Q from u to v whose nodes are distinct. Thus Q is a simple path from u to v.

(b) Let w be a node in P_1 and P_2 such that the next nodes in P_1 and P_2 are distinct. Let w' be the first node following w which lies on both P_1 and P_2. (See Fig. 8-30.) Then the subpaths of P_1 and P_2 between w and w' have no nodes in common except w and w'; hence these two subpaths form a cycle.

8.19 Prove Proposition 8.2: Let A be the adjacency matrix of a graph G. Then $a_K(i, j)$, the ij entry in the matrix A^K, gives the number of paths of length K from v_i to v_j.

The proof is by induction on K. Note first that a path of length 1 from v_i to v_j is precisely an edge (v_i, v_j). By definition of the adjacency matrix A, $a_1(i, j) = a_{ij}$ gives the number of edges from v_i to v_j. Hence the proposition is true for $K = 1$.

Supose $K > 1$. (Assume G has m nodes.) Since $A^K = A^{K-1}A$,

$$a_K(i, j) = \sum_{s=1}^{m} a_{K-1}(i, s)a_1(s, j)$$

By induction, $a_{K-1}(i, s)$ gives the number of paths of length $K - 1$ from v_i to v_s, and $a_1(s, j)$ gives the number of paths of length 1 from v_s to v_j. Thus $a_{K-1}(i, s)a_1(s, j)$ gives the number of paths of length K from v_i to v_j where v_s is the next-to-last node. Thus all the paths of length K from v_i to v_j can be obtained by summing up the $a_{K-1}(i, s)a_1(s, j)$ for all s. That is, $a_K(i, j)$ is the number of paths of length K from v_i to v_j. Thus the proposition is proved.

8.20 Suppose G is a finite undirected graph without cycles. Prove each of the following:

(a) If G has at least one edge, then G has a node v with degree 1.

(b) If G is connected—so that G is a tree—and if G has m nodes, then G has $m - 1$ edges.

(c) If G has m nodes and $m - 1$ edges, then G is a tree.

(a) Let $P = (v_0, v_1, \ldots, v_n)$ be a simple path of maximum length. Suppose $\deg(v_0) \neq 1$, and assume $[u, v_0]$ is an edge and $u \neq v_1$. If $u = v_i$ for $i > 1$, then $C = (v_i, v_0, \ldots, v_i)$ is a cycle. If $u \neq v_i$, then $P' = (u, v_0, \ldots, v_n)$ is a simple path with length greater than P. Each case leads to a contradiction. Hence $\deg(v_0) = 1$.

(b) The proof is by induction on m. Suppose $m = 1$. Then G consists of an isolated node and G has $m - 1 = 0$ edges. Hence the result is true for $m = 1$. Suppose $m > 1$. Then G has a node v such that $\deg(v) = 1$. Delete v and its only edge $[v, v']$ from the graph G to obtain the graph G'. Then G is still connected and G is a tree with $m - 1$ nodes. By induction, G' has $m - 2$ edges. Hence G has $m - 1$ edges. Thus the result is true.

(c) Let $T_1, T_2, \ldots, T_s$ denote the connected components of G. Then each T_i is a tree. Hence each T_i has one more node than edges. Hence G has s more nodes than edges. But G has only one more node than edges. Hence $s = 1$ and G is a tree.

Supplementary Problems

GRAPH TERMINOLOGY

8.21   Consider the undirected graph G in Fig. 8-31. Find (*a*) all simple paths from node A to node H, (*b*) the diameter of G and (*c*) the degree of each node.

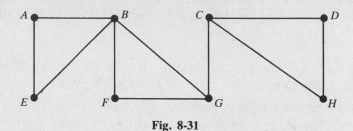

Fig. 8-31

8.22   Which of the multigraphs in Fig. 8-32 are (*a*) connected, (*b*) loop-free (i.e., without loops) and (*c*) graphs?

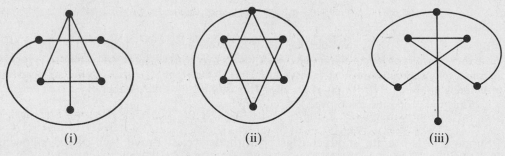

(i)   (ii)   (iii)

Fig. 8-32

8.23   Consider the directed graph G in Fig. 8-33. (*a*) Find the indegree and outdegree of each node. (*b*) Find the number of simple paths from v_1 to v_4. (*c*) Are there any sources or sinks?

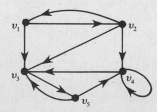

Fig. 8-33

8.24   Draw all (nonsimilar) trees with 5 or fewer nodes. (There are eight such trees.)

8.25   Find the number of spanning trees of the graph G in Fig. 8-34.

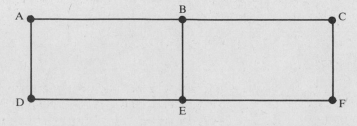

Fig. 8-34

SEQUENTIAL REPRESENTATION OF GRAPHS; WEIGHTED GRAPHS

8.26   Consider the graph G in Fig. 8-35. Suppose the nodes are stored in memory in an array DATA as follows:

$$\text{DATA:} \quad X, Y, Z, S, T$$

(a) Find the adjacency matrix A of G. (b) Find the path matrix P or G. (c) Is G strongly connected?

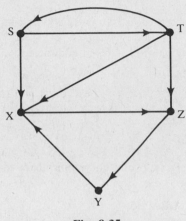

Fig. 8-35

8.27   Consider the weighted graph G in Fig. 8-36. Suppose the nodes are stored in an array DATA as follows:

$$\text{DATA:} \quad X, Y, S, T$$

(a) Find the weight matrix W of G. (b) Find the matrix Q of shortest paths using Warshall's Algorithm 8.2.

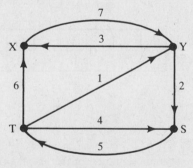

Fig. 8-36

8.28   Find a minimum spanning tree of the graph G in Fig. 8-37.

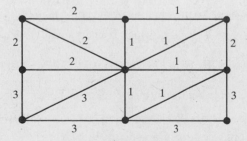

Fig. 8-37

8.29   The following is the incidence matrix M of an undirected graph G:

$$M = \begin{pmatrix} 0 & 0 & 1 & 0 & 0 & 1 & 1 & 1 \\ 0 & 1 & 0 & 1 & 0 & 0 & 1 & 0 \\ 1 & 0 & 1 & 1 & 0 & 0 & 0 & 0 \\ 0 & 0 & 0 & 0 & 1 & 0 & 0 & 1 \\ 1 & 1 & 0 & 0 & 1 & 1 & 0 & 0 \end{pmatrix}$$

(Note that G has 5 nodes and 8 edges.) Draw G and find its adjacency matrix A.

8.30   The following is the adjacency matrix A of an undirected graph G:

$$A = \begin{pmatrix} 0 & 1 & 0 & 1 & 0 \\ 1 & 0 & 0 & 1 & 1 \\ 0 & 0 & 0 & 1 & 1 \\ 1 & 1 & 1 & 0 & 1 \\ 0 & 1 & 1 & 1 & 0 \end{pmatrix}$$

(Note that G has 5 nodes.) Draw G and find its incidence matrix M.

LINKED REPRESENTATION OF GRAPHS

8.31   Suppose a graph G is stored in memory as follows:

NODE	A		C	E		D		B
NEXT	4	0	8	0	7	3	2	1
ADJ	6		1	10		2		9
	1	2	3	4	5	6	7	8

START = 6, AVAILN = 5

DEST	8	8		1	4	3	3		6	3
LINK	5	7	8	0	0	0	0	0	4	0
	1	2	3	4	5	6	7	8	9	10

AVAILE = 3

Draw the graph G.

8.32   Find the changes in the linked representation of the graph G in Prob. 8.31 if edge (C, E) is deleted and edge (D, E) is inserted.

8.33   Find the changes in the linked representation of the graph G in Prob. 8.31 if a node F and the edges (E, F) and (F, D) are inserted into G.

8.34   Find the changes in the linked representation of the graph G in Prob. 8.31 if the node B is deleted from G.

Problems 8.35 to 8.38 refer to a graph G which is maintained in memory by a linked representation:

GRAPH(NODE, NEXT, ADJ, START, AVAILN, DEST, LINK, AVAILE)

8.35   Write a procedure to supplement each of the following:

(*a*)   Print the list of successors of a given node ND.

(*b*)   Print the list of predecessors of a given node ND.

8.36   Write a procedure which determines whether or not G is an undirected graph.

8.37   Write a procedure which finds the number M of nodes of G and then finds the $M \times M$ adjacency matrix A of G. (The nodes are ordered according to their order in the node list of G.)

8.38   Write a procedure which determines whether there are any sources or sinks in G.

Problems 8.39 to 8.40 refer to a weighted graph G which is stored in memory using a linked representation as follows:

GRAPH(NODE, NEXT, ADJ, START, AVAILN, WEIGHT, DEST, LINK, AVAILE)

8.39   Write a procedure which finds the shortest path from a given node NA to a given node NB.

8.40   Write a procedure which finds the longest simple path from a given node NA to a given node NB.

Programming Problems

8.41   Suppose a graph G is input by means of an integer M, representing the nodes $1, 2, \ldots, M$, and a list of N ordered pairs of the integers, representing the edges of G. Write a procedure for each of the following:

(*a*)   To find the $M \times M$ adjacency matrix A of the graph G.

(*b*)   To use the adjacency matrix A and Warshall's algorithm to find the path matrix P of the graph G.

Test the above using the following data:

(i)   M = 5; N = 8; (3, 4), (5, 3), (2, 4), (1, 5), (3, 2), (4, 2), (3, 1), (5, 1),

(ii)   M = 6; N = 10; (1, 6), (2, 1), (2, 3), (3, 5), (4, 5), (4, 2), (2, 6), (5, 3), (4, 3), (6, 4)

8.42   Suppose a weighted graph G is input by means of an integer M, representing the nodes $1, 2, \ldots, M$, and a list of N ordered triplets (a_i, b_i, w_i) of integers such that the pair (a_i, b_i) is an edge of G and w_i is its weight. Write a procedure for each of the following:

(*a*)   To find the $M \times M$ weight matrix W of the graph G.

(*b*)   To use the weight matrix W and Warshall's Algorithm 8.2 to find the matrix Q of shortest paths between the nodes.

Test the above using the following data:

(i)   M = 4; N = 7; (1, 2, 5), (2, 4, 2), (3, 2, 3), (1, 1, 7), (4, 1, 4), (4, 3, 1). (Compare with Example 8.4.)

(ii)   M = 5; N = 8; (3, 5, 3), (4, 1, 2), (5, 2, 2), (1, 5, 5), (1, 3, 1), (2, 4, 1), (3, 4, 4), (5, 4, 4).

8.43   Suppose an empty graph G is stored in memory using the linked representation

GRAPH(NODE, NEXT, ADJ, START, AVAILN, DEST, LINK, AVAILE)

Assume NODE has space for 8 nodes and DEST has space for 12 edges. Write a program which executes the following operations on G:

(*a*)   Inputs nodes A, B, C and D

(*b*)   Inputs edges (A, B), (A, C), (C, B), (D, A), (B, D) and (C, D)

(*c*)   Inputs nodes E and F

	CITY	LEFT	RIGHT	ADJ
1	Atlanta	0	2	12
2	Boston	0	0	1
3	Houston	0	0	14
4	New York	3	8	4
5		6		
6		0		
7	Washington	0	0	10
8	Philadelphia	0	7	6
9	Denver	10	4	8
10	Chicago	1	0	2

START = 9, AVAILN = 5

	NUMBER	PRICE	ORIG	DEST	LINK
1	201	80	2	10	3
2	202	80	10	2	0
3	301	50	2	4	0
4	302	50	4	2	5
5	303	40	4	8	7
6	304	40	8	4	9
7	305	120	4	9	0
8	306	120	9	4	13
9	401	40	8	7	0
10	402	40	7	8	11
11	403	80	7	1	0
12	404	80	1	7	16
13	501	80	9	3	15
14	502	80	3	9	0
15	503	140	9	1	0
16	504	140	1	9	0
17					18
18					19
19					20
20					0

NUM = 16, AVAILE = 17

Fig. 8-38

(d)   Inputs edges (B, E), (F, E), (D, F) and (F, B)

(e)   Deletes edges (D, A) and (B, D)

(f)   Deletes node A

Problems 8.44 to 8.48 refer to the data in Fig. 8-38, where the cities are stored as a binary search tree.

8.44   Write a procedure with input CITYA and CITYB which finds the flight number and cost of the flight from city A to city B, if a flight exists. Test the procedure using (a) CITYA = Chicago, CITYB = Boston; (b) CITYA = Washington, CITYB = Denver; and (c) CITYA = New York, CITYB = Philadelphia.

8.45   Write a procedure with input CITYA and CITYB which finds the way to fly from city A to city B with a minimum number of stops, and also finds its cost. Test the procedure using (a) CITYA = Boston, CITYB = Houston; (b) CITYA = Denver, CITYB = Washington; and (c) CITYA = New York, CITYB = Atlanta.

8.46   Write a procedure with input CITYA and CITYB which finds the cheapest way to fly from city A to city B and also finds the cost. Test the procedure using the data in Prob. 8.45. (Compare the results.)

8.47   Write a procedure which deletes a record from the file given the flight number NUMB. Test the program using (a) NUMB = 503 and NUMB = 504 and (b) NUMB = 303 and NUMB = 304.

8.48   Write a procedure which inputs a record of the form

(NUMBNEW, PRICENEW, ORIGNEW, DESTNEW)

Test the procedure using the following data:

(a)   NUMBNEW = 505,   PRICENEW = 80,   ORIGNEW = Chicago,   DESTNEW = Denver
NUMBNEW = 506,   PRICENEW = 80,   ORIGNEW = Denver,   DESTNEW = Chicago

(b)   NUMBNEW = 601,   PRICENEW = 70,   ORIGNEW = Atlanta,   DESTNEW = Miami
NUMBNEW = 602,   PRICENEW = 70,   ORIGNEW = Miami,   DESTNEW = Atlanta

(Note that a new city may have to be inserted into the binary search tree of cities.)

8.49   Translate the topological sort algorithm into a program which sorts a graph G. Assume G is input by its set V of nodes and its set E of edges. Test the program using the nodes A, B, C, D, X, Y, Z, S and T and the edges

(a)   (A, Z), (S, Z), (X, D), (B, T), (C, B), (Y, X), (Z, X), (S, C) and (Z, B)

(b)   (A, Z), (D, Y), (A, X), (Y, B), (S, Y), (C, T), (X, S), (B, A), (C, S) and (X, T)

(c)   (A, C), (B, Z), (Y, A), (Z, X), (D, Z), (A, S), (B, T), (Z, Y), (T, Y) and (X, A)

8.50   Write a program which finds the number of connected components of an unordered graph G and also assigns a component number to each of its nodes. Assume G is input by its set V of nodes and its set E of (undirected) edges. Test the program using the nodes A, B, C, D, X, Y, Z, S and T and the edges:

(a)   [A, X], [B, T], [Y, C], [S, Z], [D, T], [A, S], [Z, A], [D, B] and [X, S]

(b)   [Z, C], [D, B], [A, X], [S, C], [D, T], [X, S], [Y, B], [T, B] and [S, Z]

Chapter 9

Sorting and Searching

9.1 INTRODUCTION

Sorting and searching are fundamental operations in computer science. *Sorting* refers to the operation of arranging data in some given order, such as increasing or decreasing, with numerical data, or alphabetically, with character data. *Searching* refers to the operation of finding the location of a given item in a collection of items.

There are many sorting and searching algorithms. Some of them, such as heapsort and binary search, have already been discussed throughout the text. The particular algorithm one chooses depends on the properties of the data and the operations one may perform on the data. Accordingly, we will want to know the complexity of each algorithm; that is, we will want to know the running time $f(n)$ of each algorithm as a function of the number n of input items. Sometimes, we will also discuss the space requirements of our algorithms.

Sorting and searching frequently apply to a file of records, so we recall some standard terminology. Each record in a file F can contain many fields, but there may be one particular field whose values uniquely determine the records in the file. Such a field K is called a *primary key*, and the values $k_1, k_2, \ldots$ in such a field are called *keys* or *key values*. Sorting the file F usually refers to sorting F with respect to a particular primary key, and searching in F refers to searching for the record with a given key value.

This chapter will first investigate sorting algorithms and then investigate searching algorithms. Some texts treat searching before sorting.

9.2 SORTING

Let A be a list of n elements $A_1, A_2, \ldots, A_n$ in memory. *Sorting A* refers to the operation of rearranging the contents of A so that they are increasing in order (numerically or lexicographically), that is, so that

$$A_1 \leq A_2 \leq A_3 \leq \cdots \leq A_n$$

Since A has n elements, there are $n!$ ways that the contents can appear in A. These ways correspond precisely to the $n!$ permutations of $1, 2, \ldots, n$. Accordingly, each sorting algorithm must take care of these $n!$ possibilities.

EXAMPLE 9.1

Suppose an array DATA contains 8 elements as follows:

$$\text{DATA:} \quad 77, 33, 44, 11, 88, 22, 66, 55$$

After sorting, DATA must appear in memory as follows:

$$\text{DATA:} \quad 11, 22, 33, 44, 55, 66, 77, 88$$

Since DATA consists of 8 elements, there are $8! = 40\,320$ ways that the numbers $11, 22, \ldots, 88$ can appear in DATA.

Complexity of Sorting Algorithms

The complexity of a sorting algorithm measures the running time as a function of the number n of items to be sorted. We note that each sorting algorithm S will be made up of the following operations, where $A_1, A_2, \ldots, A_n$ contain the items to be sorted and B is an auxiliary location:

(a) Comparisons, which test whether $A_i < A_j$ or test whether $A_i < B$

(b) Interchanges, which switch the contents of A_i and A_j or of A_i and B

(c) Assignments, which set $B := A_i$ and then set $A_j := B$ or $A_j := A_i$

Normally, the complexity function measures only the number of comparisons, since the number of other operations is at most a constant factor of the number of comparisons.

There are two main cases whose complexity we will consider; the worst case and the average case. In studying the average case, we make the probabilistic assumption that all the $n!$ permutations of the given n items are equally likely. (The reader is referred to Sec. 2.5 for a more detailed discussion of complexity.)

Previously, we have studied the bubble sort (Sec. 4.6), quicksort (Sec. 6.5) and heapsort (Sec. 7.10). The approximate number of comparisons and the order of complexity of these algorithms are summarized in the following table:

Algorithm	Worst Case	Average Case
Bubble Sort	$\dfrac{n(n-1)}{2} = O(n^2)$	$\dfrac{n(n-1)}{2} = O(n^2)$
Quicksort	$\dfrac{n(n+3)}{2} = O(n^2)$	$1.4n \log n = O(n \log n)$
Heapsort	$3n \log n = O(n \log n)$	$3n \log n = O(n \log n)$

Note first that the bubble sort is a very slow way of sorting; its main advantage is the simplicity of the algorithm. Observe that the average-case complexity $(n \log n)$ of heapsort is the same as that of quicksort, but its worst-case complexity $(n \log n)$ seems quicker than quicksort (n^2). However, empirical evidence seems to indicate that quicksort is superior to heapsort except on rare occasions.

Lower Bounds

The reader may ask whether there is an algorithm which can sort n items in time of order less than $O(n \log n)$. The answer is no. The reason is indicated below.

Suppose S is an algorithm which sorts n items $a_1, a_2, \ldots, a_n$. We assume there is a *decision tree T* corresponding to the algorithm S such that T is an extended binary search tree where the external nodes correspond to the $n!$ ways that n items can appear in memory and where the internal nodes correspond to the different comparisons that may take place during the execution of the algorithm S. Then the number of comparisons in the worst case for the algorithm S is equal to the length of the longest path in the decision tree T or, in other words, the depth D of the tree, T. Moreover, the average number of comparisons for the algorithm S is equal to the average external path length $\bar{E}$ of the tree T.

Figure 9-1 shows a decision tree T for sorting $n = 3$ items. Observe that T has $n! = 3! = 6$ external nodes. The values of D and $\bar{E}$ for the tree follow:

$$D = 3 \quad \text{and} \quad \bar{E} = \frac{1}{6}(2 + 3 + 3 + 3 + 3 + 2) = 2.667$$

Consequently, the corresponding algorithm S requires at most (worst case) $D = 3$ comparisons and, on the average, $\bar{E} = 2.667$ comparisons to sort the $n = 3$ items.

Accordingly, studying the worst-case and average-case complexity of a sorting algorithm S is reduced to studying the values of D and $\bar{E}$ in the corresponding decision tree T. First, however, we recall some facts about extended binary trees (Sec. 7.11). Suppose T is an extended binary tree with N external nodes, depth D and external path length $E(T)$. Any such tree cannot have more than 2^D external nodes, and so

$$2^D \geq N \quad \text{or equivalently} \quad D \geq \log N$$

Furthermore, T will have a minimum external path length $E(L)$ among all such trees with N nodes when T is a complete tree. In such a case,

$$E(L) = N \log N + O(N) \geq N \log N$$

The $N \log N$ comes from the fact that there are N paths with length $\log N$ or $\log N + 1$, and the $O(N)$ comes from the fact that there are at most N nodes on the deepest level. Dividing $E(L)$ by the number N of external paths gives the average external path length $\bar{E}$. Thus, for any extended binary tree T with N external nodes,

$$\bar{E} = \frac{E(L)}{N} \geq \frac{N \log N}{N} = \log N$$

Now suppose T is the decision tree corresponding to a sorting algorithm S which sorts n items. Then T has $n!$ external nodes. Substituting $n!$ for N in the above formulas yields

$$D \geq \log n! \approx n \log n \quad \text{and} \quad \bar{E} \geq \log n! \approx n \log n$$

The condition $\log n! \approx n \log n$ comes from Stirling's formula, that

$$n! \approx \sqrt{2\pi n}\left(\frac{n}{e}\right)^n\left(1 + \frac{1}{12n} + \cdots\right)$$

Thus $n \log n$ is a lower bound for both the worst case and the average case. In other words, $O(n \log n)$ *is the best possible for any sorting algorithm which sorts n items.*

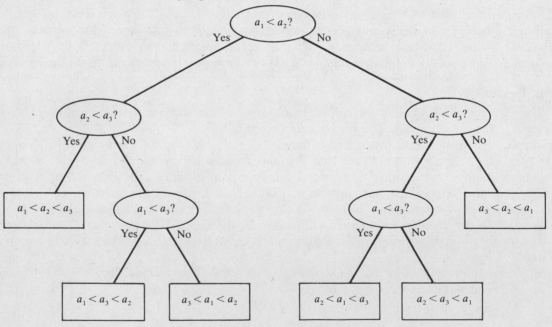

Fig. 9-1 Decision tree T for sorting $n = 3$ items.

Sorting Files; Sorting Pointers

Suppose a file F of records $R_1, R_2, \ldots, R_n$ is stored in memory. "Sorting F" refers to sorting F with respect to some field K with corresponding values $k_1, k_2, \ldots, k_n$. That is, the records are ordered so that

$$k_1 \leq k_2 \leq \cdots \leq k_n$$

The field K is called the *sort key*. (Recall that K is called a *primary key* if its values uniquely determine the records in F.) Sorting the file with respect to another key will order the records in another way.

EXAMPLE 9.2

Suppose the personnel file of a company contains the following data on each of its employees:

Name   Social Security Number   Sex   Monthly Salary

Sorting the file with respect to the Name key will yield a different order of the records than sorting the file with respect to the Social Security Number key. The company may want to sort the file according to the Salary field even though the field may not uniquely determine the employees. Sorting the file with respect to the Sex key will likely be useless; it simply separates the employees into two subfiles, one with the male employees and one with the female employees.

Sorting a file F by reordering the records in memory may be very expensive when the records are very long. Moreover, the records may be in secondary memory, where it is even more time-consuming to move records into different locations. Accordingly, one may prefer to form an auxiliary array POINT containing pointers to the records in memory and then sort the array POINT with respect to a field KEY rather than sorting the records themselves. That is, we sort POINT so that

$$KEY[POINT[1]] \leq KEY[POINT[2]] \leq \cdots \leq KEY[POINT[N]]$$

Note that choosing a different field KEY will yield a different order of the array POINT.

EXAMPLE 9.3

Figure 9-2(a) shows a personnel file of a company in memory. Figure 9-2(b) shows three arrays, POINT, PTRNAME and PTRSSN. The array POINT contains the locations of the records in memory, PTRNAME shows the pointers sorted according to the NAME field, that is,

$$NAME[PTRNAME[1]] < NAME[PTRNAME[2]] < \cdots < NAME[PTRNAME[9]]$$

	NAME	SSN	SEX	SALARY
1				
2	Davis	192-38-7282	Female	22 800
3	Kelly	165-64-3351	Male	19 000
4	Green	175-56-2251	Male	27 200
5				
6	Brown	178-52-1065	Female	14 700
7	Lewis	181-58-9939	Female	16 400
8				
9	Cohen	177-44-4557	Male	19 000
10	Rubin	135-46-6262	Female	15 500
11				
12	Evans	168-56-8113	Male	34 200
13				
14	Harris	208-56-1654	Female	22 800

(a)

	POINT	PTRNAME	PTRSSN
1	2	6	10
2	3	9	3
3	4	2	12
4	6	12	4
5	7	4	9
6	9	14	6
7	10	3	7
8	12	7	2
9	14	10	14

(b)

Fig. 9-2

and PTRSSN shows the pointers sorted according to the SSN field, that is,

$$\text{SSN}[\text{PTRSSN}[1]] < \text{SSN}[\text{PTRSSN}[2]] < \cdots < \text{SSN}[\text{PTRSSN}[9]]$$

Given the name (EMP) of an employee, one can easily find the location of NAME in memory using the array PTRNAME and the binary search algorithm. Similarly, given the social security number NUMB of an employee, one can easily find the location of the employee's record in memory by using the array PTRSSN and the binary search algorithm. Observe, also, that it is not even necessary for the records to appear in successive memory locations. Thus inserting and deleting records can easily be done.

9.3 INSERTION SORT

Suppose an array A with n elements A[1], A[2], . . . , A[N] is in memory. The insertion sort algorithm scans A from A[1] to A[N], inserting each element A[K] into its proper position in the previously sorted subarray A[1], A[2], . . . , A[K−1]. That is:

Pass 1.　A[1] by itself is trivially sorted.

Pass 2.　A[2] is inserted either before or after A[1] so that: A[1], A[2] is sorted.

Pass 3.　A[3] is inserted into its proper place in A[1], A[2], that is, before A[1], between A[1] and A[2], or after A[2], so that: A[1], A[2], A[3] is sorted.

Pass 4.　A[4] is inserted into its proper place in A[1], A[2], A[3] so that:
　　　　　A[1], A[2], A[3], A[4] is sorted.

. . . .

Pass N.　A[N] is inserted into its proper place in A[1], A[2], . . . , A[N − 1] so that:
　　　　　A[1], A[2], . . . , A[N] is sorted.

This sorting algorithm is frequently used when n is small. For example, this algorithm is very popular with bridge players when they are first sorting their cards.

There remains only the problem of deciding how to insert A[K] in its proper place in the sorted subarray A[1], A[2], . . . , A[K−1]. This can be accomplished by comparing A[K] with A[K−1], comparing A[K] with A[K−2], comparing A[K] with A[K−3], and so on, until first meeting an element A[J] such that $A[J] \leq A[K]$. Then each of the elements A[K−1], A[K−2], . . . , A[J+1] is moved forward one location, and A[K] is then inserted in the J+1st position in the array.

The algorithm is simplified if there always is an element A[J] such that $A[J] \leq A[K]$; otherwise we must constantly check to see if we are comparing A[K] with A[1]. This condition can be accomplished by introducing a sentinel element $A[0] = -\infty$ (or a very small number).

Pass	A[0]	A[1]	A[2]	A[3]	A[4]	A[5]	A[6]	A[7]	A[8]
K = 1:	$-\infty$	(77)	33	44	11	88	22	66	55
K = 2:	$-\infty$	77	(33)	44	11	88	22	66	·55
K = 3:	$-\infty$	33	77	(44)	11	88	22	66	55
K = 4:	$-\infty$	33	44	77	(11)	88	22	66	55
K = 5:	$-\infty$	11	33	44	77	(88)	22	66	55
K = 6:	$-\infty$	11	33	44	77	88	(22)	66	55
K = 7:	$-\infty$	11	22	33	44	77	88	(66)	55
K = 8:	$-\infty$	11	22	33	44	66	77	88	(55)
Sorted:	$-\infty$	11	22	33	44	55	66	77	88

Fig. 9-3 Insertion sort for $n = 8$ items.

EXAMPLE 9.4

Suppose an array A contains 8 elements as follows:

$$77, 33, 44, 11, 88, 22, 66, 55$$

Figure 9-3 illustrates the insertion sort algorithm. The circled element indicates the A[K] in each pass of the algorithm, and the arrow indicates the proper place for inserting A[K].

The formal statement of our insertion sort algorithm follows.

Algorithm 9.1: (Insertion Sort) INSERTION(A, N).
This algorithm sorts the array A with N elements.
1. Set A[0] := −∞. [Initializes sentinel element.]
2. Repeat Steps 3 to 5 for K = 2, 3, ... , N:
3.   Set TEMP := A[K] and PTR := K − 1.
4.   Repeat while TEMP < A[PTR]:
        (a) Set A[PTR + 1] := A[PTR]. [Moves element forward.]
        (b) Set PTR := PTR − 1.
        [End of loop.]
5.   Set A[PTR + 1] := TEMP. [Inserts element in proper place.]
    [End of Step 2 loop.]
6. Return.

Observe that there is an inner loop which is essentially controlled by the variable PTR, and there is an outer loop which uses K as an index.

Complexity of Insertion Sort

The number $f(n)$ of comparisons in the insertion sort algorithm can be easily computed. First of all, the worst case occurs when the array A is in reverse order and the inner loop must use the maximum number $K - 1$ of comparisons. Hence

$$f(n) = 1 + 2 + \cdots + (n - 1) = \frac{n(n - 1)}{2} = O(n^2)$$

Furthermore, one can show that, on the average, there will be approximately $(K - 1)/2$ comparisons in the inner loop. Accordingly, for the average case,

$$f(n) = \frac{1}{2} + \frac{2}{2} + \cdots + \frac{n - 1}{2} = \frac{n(n - 1)}{4} = O(n^2)$$

Thus the insertion sort algorithm is a very slow algorithm when n is very large.
The above results are summarized in the following table:

Algorithm	Worst Case	Average Case
Insertion Sort	$\frac{n(n - 1)}{2} = O(n^2)$	$\frac{n(n - 1)}{4} = O(n^2)$

Remark: Time may be saved by performing a binary search, rather than a linear search, to find the location in which to insert A[K] in the subarray A[1], A[2], . . . , A[K − 1]. This requires, on the average, log K comparisons rather than $(K - 1)/2$ comparisons. However, one still needs to move $(K - 1)/2$ elements forward. Thus the order of complexity is not changed. Furthermore, insertion sort is usually used only when n in small, and in such a case, the linear search is about as efficient as the binary search.

9.4 SELECTION SORT

Suppose an array A with *n* elements A[1], A[2], . . . , A[N] is in memory. The selection sort algorithm for sorting A works as follows. First find the smallest element in the list and put it in the first position. Then find the second smallest element in the list and put it in the second position. And so on. More precisely:

Pass 1.   Find the location LOC of the smallest in the list of N elements
          A[1], A[2], . . . , A[N], and then interchange A[LOC] and A[1]. Then:
                                   A[1] is sorted.

Pass 2.   Find the location LOC of the smallest in the sublist of N − 1 elements
          A[2], A[3], . . . , A[N], and then interchange A[LOC] and A[2]. Then:
                          A[1], A[2] is sorted, since A[1] ≤ A[2].

Pass 3.   Find the location LOC of the smallest in the sublist of N − 2 elements
          A[3], A[4], . . . , A[N], and then interchange A[LOC] and A[3]. Then:
                   A[1], A[2], . . . , A[3] is sorted, since A[2] ≤ A[3].

. . .   .
. . .   .

Pass N − 1.   Find the location LOC of the smaller of the elements A[N − 1], A[N], and then
              interchange A[LOC] and A[N − 1]. Then:
                       A[1], A[2], . . . , A[N] is sorted, since A[N − 1] ≤ A[N].

Thus A is sorted after N − 1 passes.

EXAMPLE 9.5

Suppose an array A contains 8 elements as follows:

$$77, 33, 44, 11, 88, 22, 66, 55$$

Applying the selection sort algorithm to A yields the data in Fig. 9-4. Observe that LOC gives the location of the smallest among A[K], A[K + 1], . . . , A[N] during Pass K. The circled elements indicate the elements which are to be interchanged.

There remains only the problem of finding, during the Kth pass, the location LOC of the smallest among the elements A[K], A[K + 1], . . . , A[N]. This may be accomplished by using a variable MIN to hold the current smallest value while scanning the subarray from A[K] to A[N]. Specifically, first set MIN := A[K] and LOC := K, and then traverse the list, comparing MIN with each other element A[J] as follows:

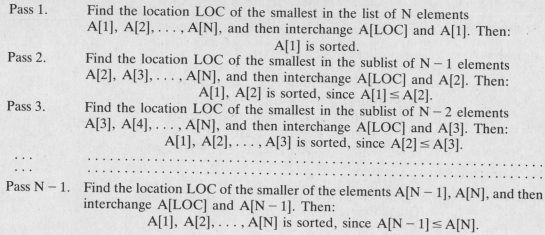

Pass	A[1]	A[2]	A[3]	A[4]	A[5]	A[6]	A[7]	A[8]
K = 1, LOC = 4	(77)	33	44	(11)	88	22	66	55
K = 2, LOC = 6	11	(33)	44	77	88	(22)	66	55
K = 3, LOC = 6	11	22	(44)	77	88	(33)	66	55
K = 4, LOC = 6	11	22	33	(77)	88	(44)	66	55
K = 5, LOC = 8	11	22	33	44	(88)	77	66	(55)
K = 6, LOC = 7	11	22	33	44	55	(77)	(66)	88
K = 7, LOC = 7	11	22	33	44	55	66	(77)	88
Sorted:	11	22	33	44	55	66	77	88

Fig. 9-4   Selection sort for *n* = 8 items.

(a)   If MIN ≤ A[J], then simply move to the next element.

(b)   If MIN > A[J], then update MIN and LOC by setting MIN := A[J] and LOC := J.

After comparing MIN with the last element A[N], MIN will contain the smallest among the elements A[K], A[K + 1], . . . , A[N] and LOC will contain its location.

The above process will be stated separately as a procedure.

Procedure 9.2:   MIN(A, K, N, LOC)
An array A is in memory. This procedure finds the location LOC of the smallest element among A[K], A[K + 1], . . . , A[N].

1.   Set MIN := A[K] and LOC := K. [Initializes pointers.]
2.   Repeat for J = K + 1, K + 2, . . . , N:
         If MIN > A[J], then: Set MIN := A[J] and LOC := A[J] and LOC := J.
     [End of loop.]
3.   Return.

The selection sort algorithm can now be easily stated:

Algorithm 9.3:   (Selection Sort) SELECTION(A, N)
This algorithm sorts the array A with N elements.

1.   Repeat Steps 2 and 3 for K = 1, 2, . . . , N − 1:
2.   Call MIN(A, K, N, LOC).
3.   [Interchange A[K] and A[LOC].]
          Set TEMP := A[K], A[K] := A[LOC] and A[LOC] := TEMP.
     [End of Step 1 loop.]
4.   Exit.

Complexity of the Selection Sort Algorithm

First note that the number $f(n)$ of comparisons in the selection sort algorithm is independent of the original order of the elements. Observe that MIN(A, K, N, LOC) requires $n − K$ comparisons. That is, there are $n − 1$ comparisons during Pass 1 to find the smallest element, there are $n − 2$ comparisons during Pass 2 to find the second smallest element, and so on. Accordingly,

$$f(n) = (n - 1) + (n - 2) + \cdots + 2 + 1 = \frac{n(n - 1)}{2} = O(n^2)$$

The above result is summarized in the following table:

Algorithm	Worst Case	Average Case
Selection Sort	$\frac{n(n - 1)}{2} = O(n^2)$	$\frac{n(n - 1)}{2} = O(n^2)$

Remark: The number of interchanges and assignments does depend on the original order of the elements in the array A, but the sum of these operations does not exceed a factor of n^2.

9.5   MERGING

Suppose A is a sorted list with r elements and B is a sorted list with s elements. The operation that combines the elements of A and B into a single sorted list C with $n = r + s$ elements is called *merging*. One simple way to merge is to place the elements of B after the elements of A and then use some sorting algorithm on the entire list. This method does not take advantage of the fact that A and B are individually sorted. A much more efficient algorithm is Algorithm 9.4 in this section. First, however, we indicate the general idea of the algorithm by means of two examples.

Suppose one is given two sorted decks of cards. The decks are merged as in Fig. 9-5. That is, at each step, the two front cards are compared and the smaller one is placed in the combined deck. When one of the decks is empty, all of the remaining cards in the other deck are put at the end of the combined deck. Similarly, suppose we have two lines of students sorted by increasing heights, and suppose we want to merge them into a single sorted line. The new line is formed by choosing, at each step, the shorter of the two students who are at the head of their respective lines. When one of the lines has no more students, the remaining students line up at the end of the combined line.

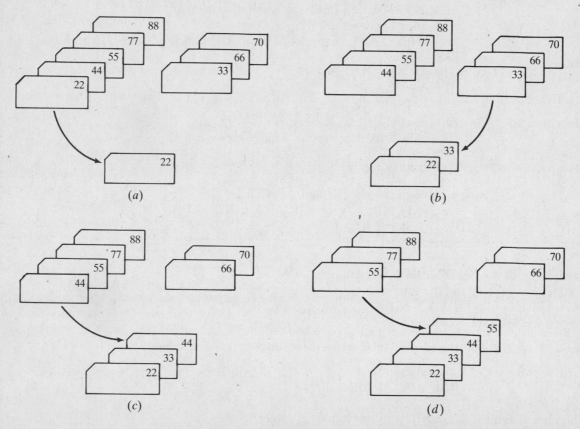

Fig. 9-5

The above discussion will now be translated into a formal algorithm which merges a sorted r-element array A and a sorted s-element array B into a sorted array C, with $n = r + s$ elements. First of all, we must always keep track of the locations of the smallest element of A and the smallest element of B which have not yet been placed in C. Let NA and NB denote these locations, respectively. Also, let PTR denote the location in C to be filled. Thus, initially, we set NA := 1, NB := 1 and PTR := 1. At each step of the algorithm, we compare

$$A[NA] \quad \text{and} \quad B[NB]$$

and assign the smaller element to C[PTR]. Then we increment PTR by setting PTR := PTR + 1, and we either increment NA by setting NA := NA + 1 or increment NB by setting NB := NB + 1, according to whether the new element in C has come from A or from B. Furthermore, if NA > r, then the remaining elements of B are assigned to C; or if NB > s, then the remaining elements of A are assigned to C.

The formal statement of the algorithm follows.

Algorithm 9.4:　MERGING(A, R, B, S, C)

Let A and B be sorted arrays with R and S elements, respectively. This algorithm merges A and B into an array C with N = R + S elements.

1. [Initialize.] Set NA := 1, NB := 1 and PTR := 1.
2. [Compare.] Repeat while NA ≤ R and NB ≤ S:
    If A[NA] < B[NB], then:
        (a) [Assign element from A to C.] Set C[PTR] := A[NA].
        (b) [Update pointers.] Set PTR := PTR + 1 and NA := NA + 1.
    Else:
        (a) [Assign element from B to C.] Set C[PTR] := B[NB].
        (b) [Update pointers.] Set PTR := PTR + 1 and NB := NB + 1.
    [End of If structure.]
    [End of loop.]
3. [Assign remaining elements to C.]
    If NA > R, then:
        Repeat for K = 0, 1, 2, . . . , S − NB:
            Set C[PTR + K] := B[NB + K].
        [End of loop.]
    Else:
        Repeat for K = 0, 1, 2, . . . , R − NA:
            Set C[PTR + K] := A[NA + K].
        [End of loop.]
    [End of If structure.]
4. Exit.

Complexity of the Merging Algorithm

The input consists of the total number $n = r + s$ of elements in A and B. Each comparison assigns an element to the array C, which eventually has n elements. Accordingly, the number $f(n)$ of comparisons cannot exceed n:

$$f(n) \leq n = O(n)$$

In other words, the merging algorithm can be run in linear time.

Nonregular Matrices

Suppose A, B and C are matrices, but not necessarily regular matrices. Assume A is sorted, with r elements and lower bound LBA; B is sorted, with s elements and lower bound LBB; and C has lower bound LBC. Then UBA = LBA + r − 1 and UBB = LBB + s − 1 are, respectively, the upper bounds of A and B. Merging A and B now may be accomplished by modifying the above algorithm as follows.

Procedure 9.5:　MERGE(A, R, LBA, S, LBB, C, LBC)

This procedure merges the sorted arrays A and B into the array C.

1. Set NA := LBA, NB := LBB, PTR := LBC, UBA := LBA + R − 1, UBB := LBB + S − 1.
2. Same as Algorithm 9.4 except R is replaced by UBA and S by UBB.
3. Same as Algorithm 9.4 except R is replaced by UBA and S by UBB.
4. Return.

Observe that this procedure is called MERGE, whereas Algorithm 9.4 is called MERGING. The reason for stating this special case is that this procedure will be used in the next section, on merge-sort.

Binary Search and Insertion Algorithm

Suppose the number r of elements in a sorted array A is much smaller than the number s of elements in a sorted array B. One can merge A with B as follows. For each element A[K] of A, use a binary search on B to find the proper location to insert A[K] into B. Each such search requires at most $\log s$ comparisons; hence this binary search and insertion algorithm to merge A and B requires at most $r \log s$ comparisons. We emphasize that this algorithm is more efficient than the usual merging Algorithm 9.4 only when $r < < s$, that is, when r is much less than s.

EXAMPLE 9.6

Suppose A has 5 elements and suppose B has 100 elements. Then merging A and B by Algorithm 9.4 uses approximately 100 comparisons. On the other hand, only approximately $\log 100 = 7$ comparisons are needed to find the proper place to insert an element of A into B using a binary search. Hence only approximately $5 \cdot 7 = 35$ comparisons are need to merge A and B using the binary search and insertion algorithm.

The binary search and insertion algorithm does not take into account the fact that A is sorted. Accordingly, the algorithm may be improved in two ways as follows. (Here we assume that A has 5 elements and B has 100 elements.)

(1) *Reducing the target set.* Suppose after the first search we find that A[1] is to be inserted after B[16]. Then we need only use a binary search on B[17], . . . , B[100] to find the proper location to insert A[2]. And so on.

(2) *Tabbing.* The expected location for inserting A[1] in B is near B[20] (that is, B[s/r]), not near B[50]. Hence we first use a linear search on B[20], B[40], B[60], B[80] and B[100] to find B[K] such that A[1] $\leq$ B[K], and then we use a binary search on B[K $-$ 20], B[K $-$ 19], . . . , B[K]. (This is analogous to using the tabs in a dictionary which indicate the location of all words with the same first letter.)

The details of the revised algorithm are left to the reader.

9.6 MERGE-SORT

Suppose an array A with n elements A[1], A[2], . . . , A[N] is in memory. The merge-sort algorithm which sorts A will first be described by means of a specific example.

EXAMPLE 9.7

Suppose the array A contains 14 elements as follows:

$$66, 33, 40, 22, 55, 88, 60, 11, 80, 20, 50, 44, 77, 30$$

Each pass of the merge-sort algorithm will start at the beginning of the array A and merge pairs of sorted subarrays as follows:

Pass 1. Merge each pair of elements to obtain the following list of sorted pairs:

$$33, 66 \qquad 22, 40 \qquad 55, 88 \qquad 11, 60 \qquad 20, 80 \qquad 44, 50 \qquad 30, 77$$

Pass 2. Merge each pair of pairs to obtain the following list of sorted quadruplets:

$$22, 33, 40, 66 \qquad 11, 55, 60, 88 \qquad 20, 44, 50, 80 \qquad 30, 77$$

Pass 3. Merge each pair of sorted quadruplets to obtain the following two sorted subarrays:

$$11, 22, 33, 40, 55, 60, 66, 88 \qquad 20, 30, 44, 50, 77, 80$$

Pass 4. Merge the two sorted subarrays to obtain the single sorted array

$$11, 20, 22, 30, 33, 40, 44, 50, 55, 60, 66, 77, 80, 88$$

The original array A is now sorted.

The above merge-sort algorithm for sorting an array A has the following important property. After Pass K, the array A will be partitioned into sorted subarrays where each subarray, except possibly the last, will contain exactly $L = 2^K$ elements. Hence the algorithm requires at most log n passes to sort an n-element array A.

The above informal description of merge-sort will now be translated into a formal algorithm which will be divided into two parts. The first part will be a procedure MERGEPASS, which uses Procedure 9.5 to execute a single pass of the algorithm; and the second part will repeatedly apply MERGEPASS until A is sorted.

The MERGEPASS procedure applies to an n-element array A which consists of a sequence of sorted subarrays. Moreover, each subarray consists of L elements except that the last subarray may have fewer than L elements. Dividing n by $2 * L$, we obtain the quotient Q, which tells the number of pairs of L-element sorted subarrays; that is,

$$Q = INT(N/(2*L))$$

(We use INT(X) to denote the integer value of X.) Setting $S = 2*L*Q$, we get the total number S of elements in the Q pairs of subarrays. Hence $R = N - S$ denotes the number of remaining elements. The procedure first merges the initial Q pairs of L-element subarrays. Then the procedure takes care of the case where there is an odd number of subarrays (when $R \le L$) or where the last subarray has fewer than L elements.

The formal statement of MERGEPASS and the merge-sort algorithm follow:

Procedure 9.6:   MERGEPASS(A, N, L, B)

The N-element array A is composed of sorted subarrays where each subarray has L elements except possibly the last subarray, which may have fewer than L elements. The procedure merges the pairs of subarrays of A and assigns them to the array B.

1. Set Q := INT(N/(2*L)), S := 2*L*Q and R := N − S.
2. [Use Procedure 9.5 to merge the Q pairs of subarrays.]
    Repeat for J = 1, 2, . . . , Q:
        (*a*)   Set LB := 1 + (2*J − 2)*L. [Finds lower bound of first array.]
        (*b*)   Call MERGE(A, L, LB, A, L, LB + L, B, LB).
    [End of loop.]
3. [Only one subarray left?]
    If R ≤ L, then:
        Repeat for J = 1, 2, . . . , R:
            Set B(S + J) := A(S + J).
        [End of loop.]
    Else:
        Call MERGE(A, L, S + 1, A, R, L + S + 1, B, S + 1).
    [End of If structure.]
4. Return.

Algorithm 9.7:   MERGESORT(A, N)

This algorithm sorts the N-element array A using an auxiliary array B.

1. Set L := 1. [Initializes the number of elements in the subarrays.]
2. Repeat Steps 3 to 6 while L < N:
3.   Call MERGEPASS(A, N, L, B).
4.   Call MERGEPASS(B, N, 2 * L, A).
5.   Set L := 4 * L.
    [End of Step 2 loop.]
6. Exit.

Since we want the sorted array to finally appear in the original array A, we must execute the procedure MERGEPASS an even number of times.

Complexity of the Merge-Sort Algorithm

Let $f(n)$ denote the number of comparisons needed to sort an n-element array A using the merge-sort algorithm. Recall that the algorithm requires at most $\log n$ passes. Moreover, each pass merges a total of n elements, and by the discussion on the complexity of merging, each pass will require at most n comparisons. Accordingly, for both the worst case and average case,

$$f(n) \le n \log n$$

Observe that this algorithm has the same order as heapsort and the same average order as quicksort. The main drawback of merge-sort is that it requires an auxiliary array with n elements. Each of the other sorting algorithms we have studied requires only a finite number of extra locations, which is independent of n.

The above results are summarized in the following table:

Algorithm	Worst Case	Average Case	Extra Memory
Merge-Sort	$n \log n = O(n \log n)$	$n \log n = O(n \log n)$	$O(n)$

9.7 RADIX SORT

Radix sort is the method that many people intuitively use or begin to use when alphabetizing a large list of names. (Here the radix is 26, the 26 letters of the alphabet.) Specifically, the list of names is first sorted according to the first letter of each name. That is, the names are arranged in 26 classes, where the first class consists of those names that begin with "A," the second class consists of those names that begin with "B," and so on. During the second pass, each class is alphabetized according to the second letter of the name. And so on. If no name contains, for example, more than 12 letters, the names are alphabetized with at most 12 passes.

The radix sort is the method used by a card sorter. A card sorter contains 13 receiving pockets labeled as follows:

$$9, 8, 7, 6, 5, 4, 3, 2, 1, 0, 11, 12, R \text{ (reject)}$$

Each pocket other than R corresonds to a row on a card in which a hole can be punched. Decimal numbers, where the radix is 10, are punched in the obvious way and hence use only the first 10 pockets of the sorter. The sorter uses a radix reverse-digit sort on numbers. That is, suppose a card sorter is given a collection of cards where each card contains a 3-digit number punched in columns 1 to 3. The cards are first sorted according to the units digit. On the second pass, the cards are sorted according to the tens digit. On the third and last pass, the cards are sorted according to the hundreds digit. We illustrate with an example.

EXAMPLE 9.8

Suppose 9 cards are punched as follows:

$$348, \ 143, \ 361, \ 423, \ 538, \ 128, \ 321, \ 543, \ 366$$

Given to a card sorter, the numbers would be sorted in three phases, as pictured in Fig. 9-6:

(a) In the first pass, the units digits are sorted into pockets. (The pockets are pictured upside down, so 348 is at the bottom of pocket 8.) The cards are collected pocket by pocket, from pocket 9 to pocket 0. (Note that 361 will now be at the bottom of the pile and 128 at the top of the pile.) The cards are now reinput to the sorter.

(b) In the second pass, the tens digits are sorted into pockets. Again the cards are collected pocket by pocket and reinput to the sorter.

Input	0	1	2	3	4	5	6	7	8	9
348									348	
143				143						
361		361								
423				423						
538									538	
128									128	
321		321								
543				543						
366							366			

(a) First pass.

Input	0	1	2	3	4	5	6	7	8	9
361							361			
321			321							
143					143					
423			423							
543					543					
366					543					
366							366			
348					348					
538				538						
128			128							

(b) Second pass.

Input	0	1	2	3	4	5	6	7	8	9
321				321						
423					423					
128		128								
538						538				
143		143								
543						543				
348				348						
361				361						
366				366						

(c) Third pass.

Fig. 9-6

(*c*) In the third and final pass, the hundreds digits are sorted into pockets.

When the cards are collected after the third pass, the numbers are in the following order:

$$128, 143, 321, 348, 361, 366, 423, 538, 543$$

Thus the cards are now sorted.

The number C of comparisons needed to sort nine such 3-digit numbers is bounded as follows:

$$C \leq 9*3*10$$

The 9 comes from the nine cards, the 3 comes from the three digits in each number, and the 10 comes from radix $d = 10$ digits.

Complexity of Radix Sort

Suppose a list A of n items $A_1, A_2, \ldots, A_n$ is given. Let d denote the radix (e.g., $d = 10$ for decimal digits, $d = 26$ for letters and $d = 2$ for bits), and suppose each item A_i is represented by means of s of the digits:

$$A_i = d_{i1} d_{i2} \cdots d_{is}$$

The radix sort algorithm will require s passes, the number of digits in each item. Pass K will compare each d_{iK} with each of the d digits. Hence the number $C(n)$ of comparisons for the algorithm is bounded as follows:

$$C(n) \leq d*s*n$$

Although d is independent of n, the number s does depend on n. In the worst case, $s = n$, so $C(n) = O(n^2)$. In the best case, $s = \log_d n$, so $C(n) = O(n \log n)$. In other words, radix sort performs well only when the number s of digits in the representation of the A_i's is small.

Another drawback of radix sort is that one may need $d*n$ memory locations. This comes from the fact that all the items may be "sent to the same pocket" during a given pass. This drawback may be minimized by using linked lists rather than arrays to store the items during a given pass. However, one will still require $2*n$ memory locations.

9.8 SEARCHING AND DATA MODIFICATION

Suppose S is a collection of data maintained in memory by a table using some type of data structure. Searching is the operation which finds the location LOC in memory of some given ITEM of information or sends some message that ITEM does not belong to S. The search is said to be successful or unsuccessful according to whether ITEM does or does not belong to S. The searching algorithm that is used depends mainly on the type of data structure that is used to maintain S in memory.

Data modification refers to the operations of inserting, deleting and updating. Here data modification will mainly refer to inserting and deleting. These operations are closely related to searching, since usually one must search for the location of the ITEM to be deleted or one must search for the proper place to insert ITEM in the table. The insertion or deletion also requires a certain amount of execution time, which also depends mainly on the type of data structure that is used.

Generally speaking, there is a tradeoff between data structures with fast searching algorithms and data structures with fast modification algorithms. This situation is illustrated below, where we summarize the searching and data modification of three of the data structures previously studied in the text.

(1) *Sorted array*. Here one can use a binary search to find the location LOC of a given ITEM in time $O(\log n)$. On the other hand, inserting and deleting are very slow, since, on the average, $n/2 = O(n)$ elements must be moved for a given insertion or deletion. Thus a sorted array would likely be used when there is a great deal of searching but only very little data modification.

(2) *Linked list.* Here one can only perform a linear search to find the location LOC of a given ITEM, and the search may be very, very slow, possibly requiring time $O(n)$. On the other hand, inserting and deleting requires only a few pointers to be changed. Thus a linked list would be used when there is a great deal of data modification, as in word (string) processing.

(3) *Binary search tree.* This data structure combines the advantages of the sorted array and the linked list. That is, searching is reduced to searching only a certain path P in the tree T, which, on the average, requires only $O(\log n)$ comparisons. Furthermore, the tree T is maintained in memory by a linked representation, so only certain pointers need be changed after the location of the insertion or deletion is found. The main drawback of the binary search tree is that the tree may be very unbalanced, so that the length of a path P may be $O(n)$ rather than $O(\log n)$. This will reduce the searching to approximately a linear search.

Remark: The above worst-case scenario of a binary search tree may be eliminated by using a height-balanced binary search tree that is rebalanced after each insertion or deletion. The algorithms for such rebalancing are rather complicated and lie beyond the scope of this text.

Searching Files, Searching Pointers

Suppose a file F of records $R_1, R_2, \ldots, R_N$ is stored in memory. Searching F usually refers to finding the location LOC in memory of the record with a given key value relative to a primary key field K. One way to simplify the searching is to use an auxiliary sorted array of pointers, as discussed in Sec. 9.2. Then a binary search can be used to quickly find the location LOC of the record with the given key. In the case where there is a great deal of inserting and deleting of records in the file, one might want to use an auxiliary binary search tree rather than an auxiliary sorted array. In any case, the searching of the file F is reduced to the searching of a collection S of items, as discussed above.

9.9 HASHING

The search time of each algorithm discussed so far depends on the number n of elements in the collection S of data. This section discusses a searching technique, called *hashing* or *hash addressing*, which is essentially independent of the number n.

The terminology which we use in our presentation of hashing will be oriented toward file management. First of all, we assume that there is a file F of n records with a set K of keys which uniquely determine the records in F. Secondly, we assume that F is maintained in memory by a table T of m memory locations and that L is the set of memory addresses of the locations in T. For notational convenience, we assume that the keys in K and the addresses in L are (decimal) integers. (Analogous methods will work with binary integers or with keys which are character strings, such as names, since there are standard ways of representing strings by integers.)

The subject of hashing will be introduced by the following example.

EXAMPLE 9.9

Suppose a company with 68 employees assigns a 4-digit employee number to each employee which is used as the primary key in the company's employee file. We can, in fact, use the employee number as the address of the record in memory. The search will require no comparisons at all. Unfortunately, this technique will require space for 10 000 memory locations, whereas space for fewer than 30 such locations would actually be used. Clearly, this tradeoff of space for time is not worth the expense.

The general idea of using the key to determine the address of a record is an excellent idea, but it must be modified so that a great deal of space is not wasted. This modification takes the form of a function H from the set K of keys into the set L of memory addresses. Such a function,

$$H: K \to L$$

is called a *hash function* or *hashing function*. Unfortunately, such a function H may not yield distinct values: it is possible that two different keys k_1 and k_2 will yield the same hash address. This situation is called *collision*, and some method must be used to resolve it. Accordingly, the topic of hashing is divided into two parts: (1) hash functions and (2) collision resolutions. We discuss these two parts separately.

Hash Functions

The two principal criteria used in selecting a hash function $H: K \rightarrow L$ are as follows. First of all, the function H should be very easy and quick to compute. Second the function H should, as far as possible, uniformly distribute the hash addresses throughout the set L so that there are a minimum number of collisions. Naturally, there is no guarantee that the second condition can be completely fulfilled without actually knowing beforehand the keys and addresses. However, certain general techniques do help. One technique is to "chop" a key k into pieces and combine the pieces in some way to form the hash address $H(k)$. (The term "hashing" comes from this technique of "chopping" a key into pieces.)

We next illustrate some popular hash functions. We emphasize that each of these hash functions can be easily and quickly evaluated by the computer.

(a)   *Division method.* Choose a number m larger than the number n of keys in K. (The number m is usually chosen to be a prime number or a number without small divisors, since this frequently minimizes the number of collisions.) The hash function H is defined by

$$H(k) = k \ (\text{mod } m) \qquad \text{or} \qquad H(k) = k \ (\text{mod } m) + 1$$

Here $k \ (\text{mod } m)$ denotes the remainder when k is divided by m. The second formula is used when we want the hash addresses to range from 1 to m rather than from 0 to $m - 1$.

(b)   *Midsquare method.* The key k is squared. Then the hash function H is defined by

$$H(k) = l$$

where l is obtained by deleting digits from both ends of k^2. We emphasize that the same positions of k^2 must be used for all of the keys.

(c)   *Folding method.* The key k is partitioned into a number of parts, $k_1, \ldots, k_r$, where each part, except possibly the last, has the same number of digits as the required address. Then the parts are added together, ignoring the last carry. That is,

$$H(k) = k_1 + k_2 + \cdots + k_r$$

where the leading-digit carries, if any, are ignored. Sometimes, for extra "milling," the even-numbered parts, $k_2, k_4, \ldots$, are each reversed before the addition.

EXAMPLE 9.10

Consider the company in Example 9.9, each of whose 68 employees is assigned a unique 4-digit employee number. Suppose L consists of 100 two-digit addresses: $00, 01, 02, \ldots, 99$. We apply the above hash functions to each of the following employee numbers:

$$3205, \qquad 7148, \qquad 2345$$

(a)   *Division method.* Choose a prime number m close to 99, such as $m = 97$. Then

$$H(3205) = 4, \qquad H(7148) = 67, \qquad H(2345) = 17$$

That is, dividing 3205 by 97 gives a remainder of 4, dividing 7148 by 97 gives a remainder of 67, and dividing 2345 by 97 gives a remainder of 17. In the case that the memory addresses begin with 01 rather than 00, we choose that the function $H(k) = k(\text{mod } m) + 1$ to obtain:

$$H(3205) = 4 + 1 = 5, \qquad H(7148) = 67 + 1 = 68, \qquad H(2345) = 17 + 1 = 18$$

(b) *Midsquare method.* The following calculations are performed:

k:	3205	7148	2345
k^2:	10 272 025	51 093 904	5 499 025
$H(k)$:	72	93	99

Observe that the fourth and fifth digits, counting from the right, are chosen for the hash address.

(c) *Folding method.* Chopping the key k into two parts and adding yields the following hash addresses:

$$H(3205) = 32 + 05 = 37, \qquad H(7148) = 71 + 48 = 19, \qquad H(2345) = 23 + 45 = 68$$

Observe that the leading digit 1 in $H(7148)$ is ignored. Alternatively, one may want to reverse the second part before adding, thus producing the following hash addresses:

$$H(3205) = 32 + 50 = 82, \qquad H(7148) = 71 + 84 + 55, \qquad H(2345) = 23 + 54 = 77$$

Collision Resolution

Suppose we want to add a new record R with key k to our file F, but suppose the memory location address $H(k)$ is already occupied. This situation is called *collision*. This subsection discusses two general ways of resolving collisions. The particular procedure that one chooses depends on many factors. One important factor is the ratio of the number n of keys in K (which is the number of records in F) to the number m of hash addresses in L. This ratio, $\lambda = n/m$, is called the *load factor*.

First we show that collisions are almost impossible to avoid. Specifically, suppose a student class has 24 students and suppose the table has space for 365 records. One random hash function is to choose the student's birthday as the hash address. Although the load factor $\lambda = 24/365 \approx 7\%$ is very small, it can be shown that there is a better than fifty-fifty chance that two of the students have the same birthday.

The efficiency of a hash function with a collision resolution procedure is measured by the average number of *probes* (key comparisons) needed to find the location of the record with a given key k. The efficiency depends mainly on the load factor λ. Specifically, we are interested in the following two quantities:

$$S(\lambda) = \text{average number of probes for a successful search}$$
$$U(\lambda) = \text{average number of probes for an unsuccessful search}$$

These quantities will be discussed for our collision procedures.

Open Addressing: Linear Probing and Modifications

Suppose that a new record R with key k is to be added to the memory table T, but that the memory location with hash address $H(k) = h$ is already filled. One natural way to resolve the collision is to assign R to the first available location following $T[h]$. (We assume that the table T with m locations is circular, so that $T[1]$ comes after $T[m]$.) Accordingly, with such a collision procedure, we will search for the record R in the table T by linearly searching the locations $T[h]$, $T[h+1]$, $T[h+2]$, ... until finding R or meeting an empty location, which indicates an unsuccessful search.

The above collision resolution is called *linear probing*. The average numbers of probes for a successful search and for an unsuccessful search are known to be the following respective quantities:

$$S(\lambda) = \frac{1}{2}\left(1 + \frac{1}{1 - \lambda}\right) \qquad \text{and} \qquad U(\lambda) = \frac{1}{2}\left(1 + \frac{1}{(1 - \lambda)^2}\right)$$

(Here $\lambda = n/m$ is the load factor.)

EXAMPLE 9.11

Suppose the table T has 11 memory locations, $T[1]$, $T[2]$, ..., $T[11]$, and suppose the file F consists of 8 records, A, B, C, D, E, X, Y and Z, with the following hash addresses:

Record:	A,	B,	C,	D,	E,	X,	Y,	Z
$H(k)$:	4,	8,	2,	11,	4,	11,	5,	1

Suppose the 8 records are entered into the table T in the above order. Then the file F will appear in memory as follows:

Table T:	X,	C,	Z,	A,	E,	Y,	_,	B,	_,	_,	D
Address:	1,	2,	3,	4,	5,	6,	7,	8,	9,	10,	11

Although Y is the only record with hash address $H(k) = 5$, the record is not assigned to $T[5]$, since $T[5]$ has already been filled by E because of a previous collision at $T[4]$. Similarly, Z does not appear in $T[1]$.

The average number S of probes for a successful search follows:

$$S = \frac{1+1+1+1+2+2+2+3}{8} = \frac{13}{8} \approx 1.6$$

The average number U of probes for an unsuccessful search follows:

$$U = \frac{7+6+5+4+3+2+1+2+1+1+8}{11} = \frac{40}{11} \approx 3.6$$

The first sum adds the number of probes to find each of the 8 records, and the second sum adds the number of probes to find an empty location for each of the 11 locations.

One main disadvantage of linear probing is that records tend to *cluster*, that is, appear next to one another, when the load factor is greater than 50 percent. Such a clustering substantially increases the average search time for a record. Two techniques to minimize clustering are as follows:

(1) *Quadratic probing.* Suppose a record R with key k has the hash address $H(k) = h$. Then, instead of searching the locations with addresses $h, h+1, h+2, \ldots$, we linearly search the locations with addresses

$$h, h+1, h+4, h+9, h+16, \ldots, h+i^2, \ldots$$

If the number m of locations in the table T is a prime number, then the above sequence will access half of the locations in T.

(2) *Double hashing.* Here a second hash function H' is used for resolving a collision, as follows. Suppose a record R with key k has the hash addresses $H(k) = h$ and $H'(k) = h' \neq m$. Then we linearly search the locations with addresses

$$h, h+h', h+2h', h+3h', \ldots$$

If m is a prime number, then the above sequence will access all the locations in the table T.

Remark: One major disadvantage in any type of open addressing procedure is in the implementation of deletion. Specifically, suppose a record R is deleted from the location $T[r]$. Afterwards, suppose we meet $T[r]$ while searching for another record R'. This does not necessarily mean that the search is unsuccessful. Thus, when deleting the record R, we must label the location $T[r]$ to indicate that it previously did contain a record. Accordingly, open addressing may seldom be used when a file F is constantly changing.

Chaining

Chaining involves maintaining two tables in memory. First of all, as before, there is a table T in memory which contains the records in F, except that T now has an additional field LINK which is used so that all records in T with the same hash address h may be linked together to form a linked list. Second, there is a hash address table LIST which contains pointers to the linked lists in T.

Suppose a new record R with key k is added to the file F. We place R in the first available location in the table T and then add R to the linked list with pointer LIST[$H(k)$]. If the linked lists of records are not sorted, than R is simply inserted at the beginning of its linked list. Searching for a record or deleting a record is nothing more than searching for a node or deleting a node from a linked list, as discussed in Chap. 5.

The average number of probes, using chaining, for a successful search and for an unsuccessful search are known to be the following approximate values:

$$S(\lambda) \approx 1 + \frac{1}{2}\lambda \quad \text{and} \quad U(\lambda) \approx e^{-\lambda} + \lambda$$

Here the load factor $\lambda = n/m$ may be greater than 1, since the number m of hash addresses in L (not the number of locations in T) may be less than the number n of records in F.

EXAMPLE 9.12

Consider again the data in Example 9.11, where the 8 records have the following hash addresses:

Record:	A,	B,	C,	D,	E,	X,	Y,	Z
$H(k)$:	4,	8,	2,	11,	4,	11,	5,	1

Using chaining, the records will appear in memory as pictured in Fig. 9-7. Observe that the location of a record R in table T is not related to its hash address. A record is simply put in the first node in the AVAIL list of table T. In fact, table T need not have the same number of elements as the hash address table.

Table T

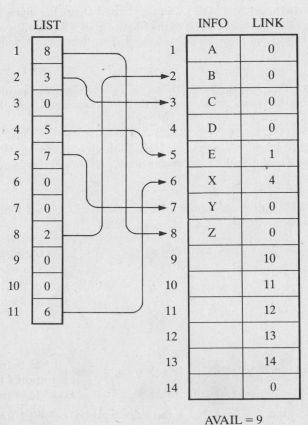

AVAIL = 9

Fig. 9-7

The main disadvantage to chaining is that one needs $3m$ memory cells for the data. Specifically, there are m cells for the information field INFO, there are m cells for the link field LINK, and there are m cells for the pointer array LIST. Suppose each record requires only 1 word for its information field. Then it may be more useful to use open addressing with a table with $3m$ locations, which has the load factor $\lambda \le 1/3$, than to use chaining to resolve collisions.

Supplementary Problems

SORTING

9.1 Write a subprogram RANDOM(DATA, N, K) which assigns N random integers between 1 and K to the array DATA.

9.2 Translate insertion sort into a subprogram INSERTSORT(A, N) which sorts the array A with N elements. Test the program using:

   (*a*)   44, 33, 11, 55, 77, 90, 40, 60, 99, 22, 88, 66

   (*b*)   D, A, T, A, S, T, R, U, C, T, U, R, E, S

9.3 Translate insertion sort into a subprogram INSERTCOUNT(A, N, NUMB) which sorts the array A with N elements and which also counts the number NUMB of comparisons.

9.4 Write a program TESTINSERT(N, AVE) which repeats 500 times the procedure INSERTCOUNT(A, N, NUMB) and which finds the average AVE of the 500 values of NUMB. (Theoretically, $\text{AVE} \approx N^2/4$.) Use RANDOM(A, N, 5*N) from Prob. 9.1 as each input. Test the program using $N = 100$ (so, theoretically, $\text{AVE} \approx N^2/4 = 2500$).

9.5 Translate quicksort into a subprogram QUICKCOUNT(A, N, NUMB) which sorts the array A with N elements and which also counts the number NUMB of comparisons. (See Sec. 6.5.)

9.6 Write a program TESTQUICKSORT(N, AVE) which repeats QUICKCOUNT(A, N, NUMB) 500 times and which finds the average AVE of the 500 values of NUMB. (Theoretically, $\text{AVE} \approx N \log_2 N$.) Use RANDOM(A, N, 5*N) from Prob. 9.1 as each input. Test the program using $N = 100$ (so, theoretically, $\text{AVE} \approx 700$).

9.7 Translate Procedure 9.2 into a subprogram MIN(A, LB, UB, LOC) which finds the location LOC of the smallest elements among A[LB], A[LB + 1], . . . , A[UB].

9.8 Translate selection sort into a subprogram SELECTSORT(A, N) which sorts the array with N elements. Test the program using:

   (*a*)   44, 33, 11, 55, 77, 90, 40, 60, 99, 22, 88, 66

   (*b*)   D, A, T, A, S, T, R, U, C, T, U, R, E, S

SEARCHING, HASHING

9.9 Suppose an unsorted linked list is in memory. Write a procedure

$$\text{SEARCH(INFO, LINK, START, ITEM, LOC)}$$

which (*a*) finds the location LOC of ITEM in the list or sets LOC := NULL for an unsuccessful search and (*b*) when the search is successful, interchanges ITEM with the element in front of it. (Such a list is said to be *self-organizing*. It has the property that elements which are frequently accessed tend to move to the beginning of the list.)

9.10   Consider the following 4-digit employee numbers (see Example 9.10):

$$9614, \qquad 5882, \qquad 6713, \qquad 4409, \qquad 1825$$

Find the 2-digit hash address of each number using (*a*) the division method, with $m = 97$; (*b*) the midsquare method; (*c*) the folding method without reversing; and (*d*) the folding method with reversing.

9.11   Consider the data in Example 9.11. Suppose the 8 records are entered into the table T in the reverse order Z, Y, X, E, D, C, B, A. (*a*) Show how the file F appears in memory. (*b*) Find the average number S of probes for a successful search and the average number U of probes for an unsuccessful search. (Compare with the corresponding results in Example 9.11.)

9.12   Consider the data in Example 9.12 and Fig. 9-7. Suppose the following additional records are added to the file:

$$(P, 2), \qquad (Q, 7), \qquad (R, 4), \qquad (S, 9)$$

(Here the left entry is the record and the right entry is the hash address.) (*a*) Find the updated tables T and LIST. (*b*) Find the average number S of probes for a successful search and the average number U of probes for an unsuccesful search.

9.13   Write a subprogram MID(KEY, HASH) which uses the midsquare method to find the 2-digit hash address HASH of a 4-digit employee number key.

9.14   Write a subprogram FOLD(KEY, HASH) which uses the folding method with reversing to find the 2-digit hash address HASH of a 4-digit employee number key.

Index

Absolute value, 19
Ackermann function, 179
ADJ, 287
Adjacency matrix, 280
Adjacency structure, 286
Adjacent nodes, 277
Algebraic expression, 6, 215
Algorithm, 9, 17
Algorithmic notation, 21
Ancestor, 215
Arithmetic expression, 168
Array, 2, 67
  circular, 190
  jagged, 87
  multidimensional, 81, 84
  parallel, 92
  pointer, 86
Assignment statement, 23
Atoms, 90
Attributes, 1
AVAIL list, 123
Average case, 28

BACK, 145
Base address, 69
Base criteria, 176
Base values, 176
Big O notation, 29
Binary search, 9, 78
  complexity of, 80
Binary search tree, 233
  deleting in, 238
  inserting in, 234
  searching in, 234
Binary tree, 214
  complete, 216
  depth of, 216
  extended, 217
  height of, 216
  traversing, 221
Bit matrix, 280
Boolean matrix, 280
Branch, 215
Breadth-first search, 294
Brothers, 215
Bubble sort, 73–75
  complexity of, 75

Ceiling function, 18
Chaining, 337
Character set, 41
Character type, 31, 46
Child, 215

CHILD, 256
Circular array, 190
Circular list, 140, 143
Coding, 254
Collision resolution, 335
Column, 3, 81, 84
Column-major order, 83, 84
Complete binary tree, 216
Complete graph, 277
Complexity of algorithms, 5, 9, 27
Concatenation, 48
Conditional flow, 24
Connected graph, 279
  strongly, 279, 282
Control, flow of, 23
Copying, 133
Cycle, 277

Data, 1
Data base management, 2
Data modification, 332
Data structure, 2
Decision tree, 319
Degree of a node, 277
Deleting, 8, 50
Dense list, 114
Depth, 178, 216
Depth-first search, 296
Deque, 192
Descendent, 215
DEST, 287
Diagonal, 95
Digraph, 279
Directed graph, 279
Divide-and-conquer, 179
Division method, 334
Double hashing, 336

Edge, 215, 277
Elementary item, 1
Empty string, 41
Entity, 1
Exit, 22
Exponents, 20
Extended binary tree, 217
External node, 217
External path length, 249

Factorial function, 19, 177
Father, 215
Fibonacci sequence, 178
Field, 1, 90
FIFO (first-in-first-out), 7, 164, 188

File, 1, 90
File management, 2
File searching, 333
File sorting, 320
Finite graph, 278
FIRST, 145
Fixed-length records, 2
Fixed-length storage, 42
Floor function, 18
Folding method, 334
FORW, 145
Free-storage list, 123
Front, 7, 188
FRONT, 189
Function subalgorithm, 30

Garbage collection, 127
General tree, 255
    representation of, 256
Generation, 216
Global variables, 32
Graph, 8, 277
    complete, 277
    deleting from, 291
    directed, 279
    inserting in, 289
    labeled, 277
    linked representation of, 286
    searching in, 289
    sequential representation of, 280
    simple, 280
    weighted, 277
Group item, 1
Growth, rate of, 29

Hanoi, Towers of, 180–183
Hash addressing, 333
Hash function, 334
Hashing, 333
    double, 336
Header linked list, 140
Header list, two-way, 146
Header node, 140
Heap, 243
    deleting the root of, 246
    inserting into, 243
    reheaping, 246
Heapsort, 243
    complexity of, 248
Height of a tree, 216
Horner's method, 113
Huffman's algorithm, 249, 251

Identifiers, 96
Identifying numbers, 22
Incedence matrix, 310

Indegree, 279
Index, 67, 82
Indexing, 91
Infix notation, 169
INFO, 116, 217
Initial point, 279
Inorder threading, 230
Inorder traversal, 221, 226
Input-restricted deque, 192
Inserting, 8, 49
Insertion sort, 322
    complexity of, 323
Integer value, 19
Internal node, 217
Internal path length, 249
Isolated node, 277
Item, 1
Iteration logic, 26

Jagged array, 87

Key, 1, 318

Labeled graph, 277
LAST, 145
Leaf, 215
Left child, 215
Left subtree, 214
Left successor, 214
LEFT, 217
Length:
    of path, 249
    of string, 41, 49
Level, 216
LIFO (last-in-first-out), 7, 164
Linear array, 2, 67
    deleting from, 71
    inserting in, 71
    traversing, 70
Linear probing, 335
Linear search, 9, 28, 76
    complexity of, 77
LINK, 116
Link field, 115
Linked list, 4, 114
    circular, 143
    copying, 133
    deleting from, 134
    header, 140, 146
    inserting into, 127
    searching, 121
    traversing, 120
    two-way, 144, 153
Linked storage, 45

List, 4, 114
  AVAIL, 123
  free-storage, 123
Load factor, 335
Local variables, 32
Logarithms, 20
Logic, 23
Logical type, 32
Loop, 278
Lower bound, 67, 82
  for sorting, 319

Matrix, 3, 81, 94
  adjacency, 280
  bit, 280
  Boolean, 280
  incedence, 310
  path, 281
  reachability, 281
  sparse, 97
  triangular, 97
  tridiagonal, 97, 104
  weight, 284
Matrix multiplication, 96
  complexity of, 96–97
Maxheap, 243
Mean, 31
Memory, 2
Memory allocation, 123
Merge-sort, 328
  complexity of, 330
Merging, 8, 325
  algorithm, 327
  complexity of, 327
Midsquare method, 334
Minheap, 243
Modules, 17, 23
Modulus arithmetic, 18
Multidimensional arrays, 81, 84
Multigraph, 278
Multiple edges, 278

Neighbor, 277, 286
NEXT, 287
Nextpointer field, 115
Node, 115, 214, 255, 277
  external, 217
  header, 140, 229
  internal, 217
  isolated, 277
  terminal, 214
  trailer, 143
NODE, 287
Nonlocal variables, 33
NULL, 116, 219
Null pointer, 115

Null string, 41
Null tree, 214
Number, priority, 193

O notation, 29–30
One-dimensional array, 3
One-way list, 115
Open addressing, 335
Operations, 8
  on graphs, 289
  string, 47
Outdegree, 279
Output-restricted deque, 192
Overflow, 127
  stack, 167–168

Page, 84
Parallel arrays, 92
Parent node, 215
Partial ordering, 298
Pass (in an algorithm), 73
Path, 215, 277
  simple, 277
Path length, 249, 271
  external, 249
  internal, 249
  weighted, 250
Path matrix, 281–282
Pattern matching, 53, 55
  complexity of, 57
Permutations, 20
Pointers, 4, 86
  searching, 333
  sorting, 320
Polish notation, 169
Polynomials, 143
POP, 167
Pop operation, 165
Poset, 297
Postfix notation, 169
Postorder traversal, 221, 228
Prefix notation, 169
Preorder traversal, 221, 224
Primary key, 1, 318
Prime number, 37
Priority number, 193
Priority queue, 193
Probe, 335
Probing, 335
  linear, 335
  quadratic, 336
Procedure, 23, 30
PUSH, 167
Push operation, 165
Push-down list, 164

Quadratic probing, 336
Qualification, 92
Queue, 7, 164, 188
   deleting from, 192
   inserting into, 192
   priority, 193
Quicksort, 173, 175, 200
   complexity of, 176

Radix sort, 330
   complexity of, 332
Reachable in a graph, 279
Reachability matrix, 281
Real type, 32
Rear, 7, 188
REAR, 189
Record, 1, 90
   fixed-length, 2
   variable-length, 2
Record structure, 6
Recursion, 176
Recursive procedure, 183
Recursively defined, 176
Regular array, 82
Reheap, 246
Remainder function, 18
Repeat-for loop, 26
Repeat-while loop, 27
Repetitive flow, 26
Replacement, 51
RIGHT, 217
Right son, 216
Right subtree, 214
Right successor, 214
Root, 214, 279
ROOT, 217
Rooted tree, 279
Row, 3, 81, 84
Row-major order, 83, 84

$S(\lambda)$, 335
Scalor, 90
Search:
   binary, 9, 78
   linear, 9, 28, 76
   sequential, 76
Searching, 8, 76, 318, 332
   binary search tree, 234
   files, 333
   graph, 289
   linked list, 121
   pointers, 333
   two-way list, 147
Selection logic, 24
Selection sort, 324
   complexity of, 325

Sequence logic, 23
Sequential sort, 76
Shortest-path algorithm, 284
SIBL, 256
Sibling, 216
Side effect, 33
Sigma (Σ), 19
Similar graphs, 303
Similar trees, 215
Simple graph, 280
Simple path, 277
Son, 215–216
Sorting, 8, 73, 318
   bubble, 73
   heapsort, 243
   insertion, 322
   lower bound complexity, 318–320
   merge-sort, 328
   quicksort, 173
   radix, 330
   selection, 324
   topological, 297
Sparse matrix, 97
Square matrix, 95
Stack, 7, 164
STACK, 166
START, 116
STATUS, 294
Status of a node, 294
Strings, 41
Strongly connected graph, 279
Subalgorithm, 30
Subscript, 2, 68
Substring, 41, 47
Subtree, 214
Successor, 214, 286
Summation symbol (Σ), 19
SWITCH, 31
Symmetric matrix, 97

Table, 3, 81
Terminal node, 214
Terminal point, 279
Text, 49
Thread, 230
Threaded tree, 230
Time-space tradeoff, 10, 15
TOP, 166
Top of a stack, 7, 165
Topological sorting, 297
Towers of Hanoi, 180, 185
Trailer node, 143
Transitive closure, 282
Traversing, 8
   binary tree, 221
   graph, 294

Traversing (*continued*)
   linear array, 70
   linked list, 120
   two-way list, 147
Tree, 5, 214, 255
   binary, 214
   decision, 319
   depth of, 216
   general, 255
   height of, 216
   null, 214
   threaded, 230
Triangular matrix, 97
Tridiagonal matrix, 94, 104
Two-dimensional array, 3
Two-way header list, 146
Two-way list, 144, 153
   deleting from, 147
   inserting into, 148
Type, 31

$U(\lambda)$, 335
Underflow, 127
Upper bound, 67, 82

Variable, 31
   global, 32–33
   local, 32
   subscripted, 2
Variable length, 2
Variable-length records, 2
Variable-length storage, 44
Vertex, 277
Visiting, 70

Warshall's algorithm, 282
Weight, 277
Weight matrix, 284
Weighted graph, 277
Weighted path length, 250
Word processing, 49
Worst case, 28